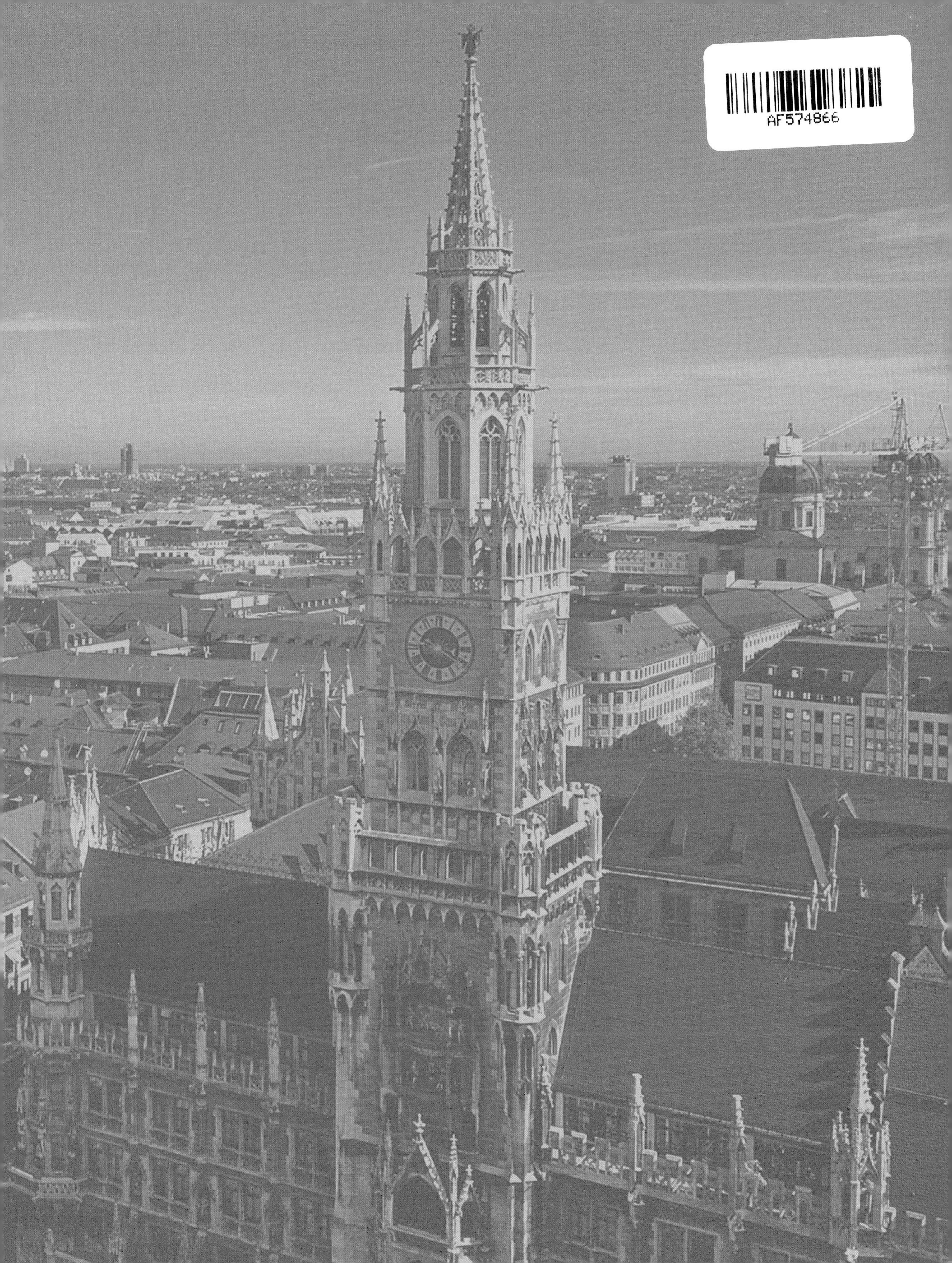

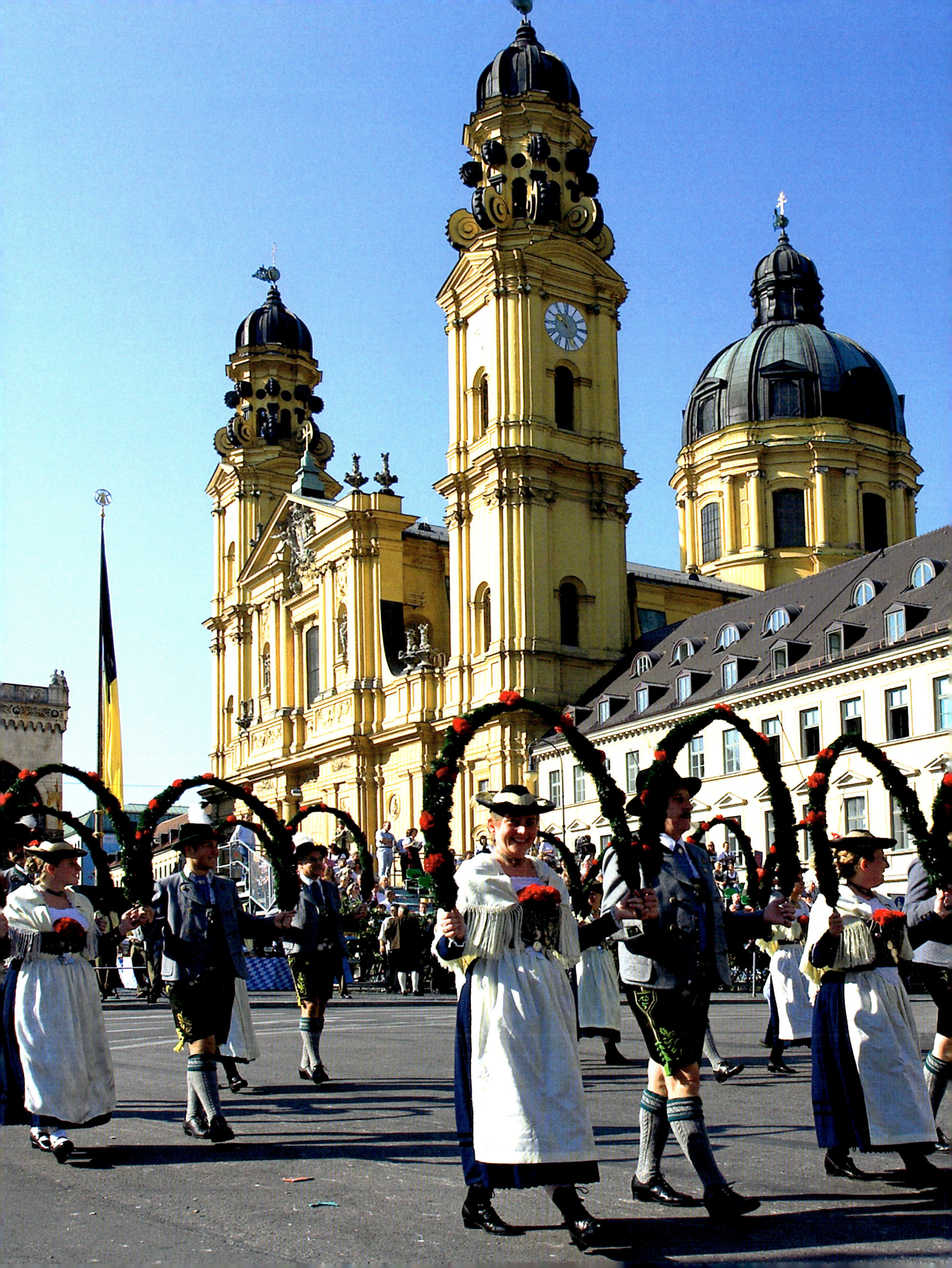

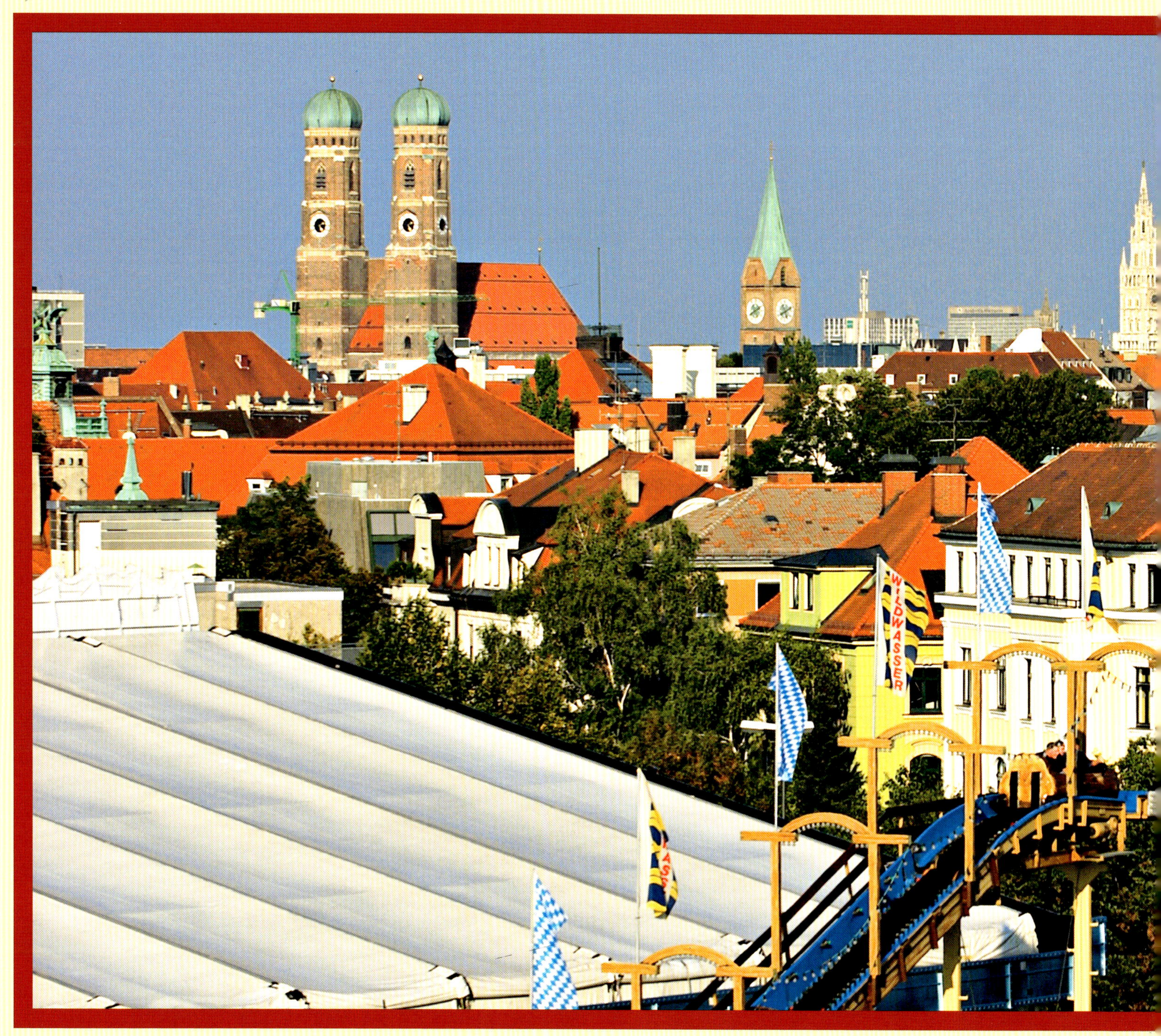

MUNICH

First page:
Procession in local Bavarian dress on Odeonsplatz for the ceremonial opening of the Oktoberfest. The square is dominated by the late baroque Theatine church of St Kajetan.

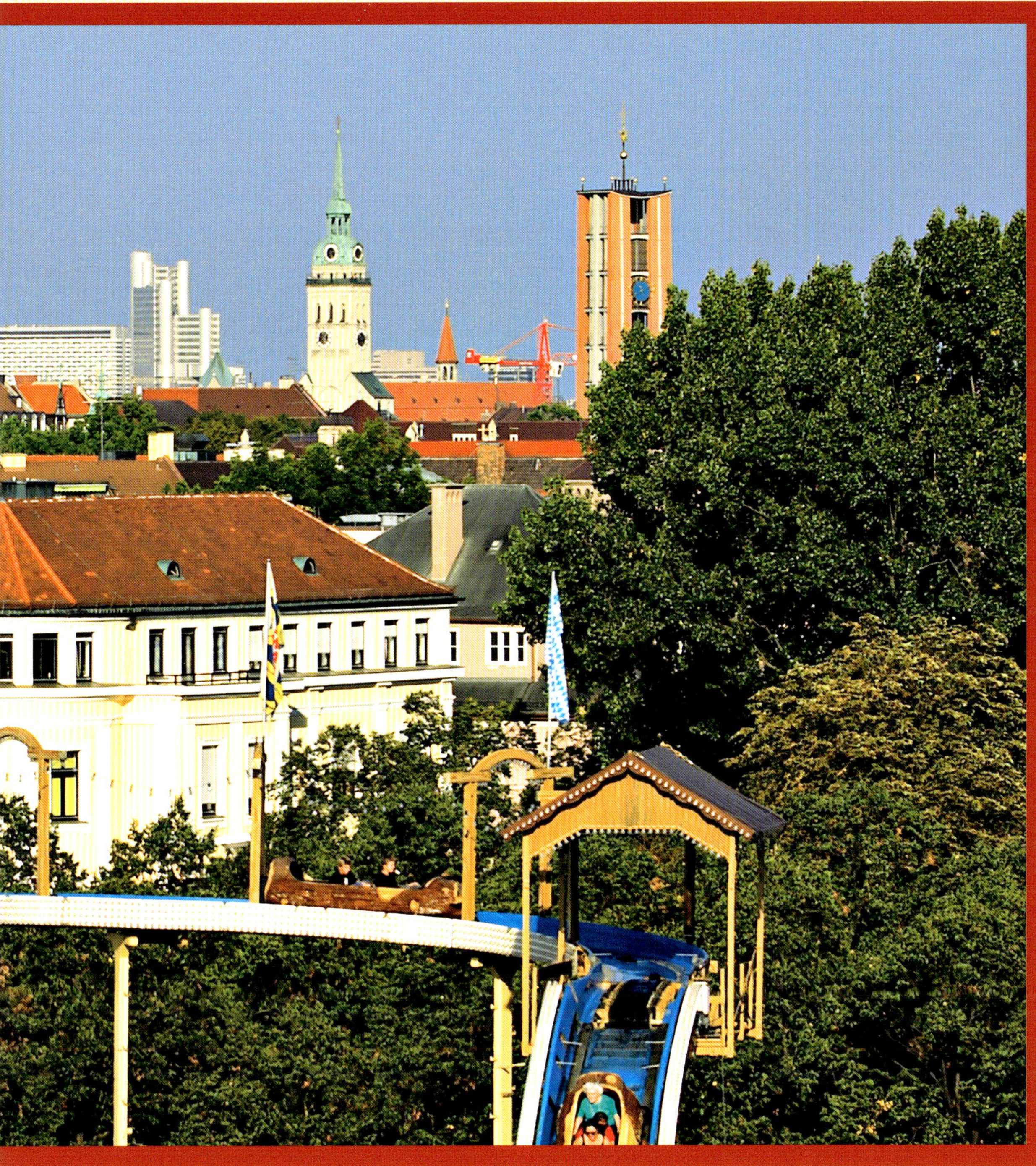

Panorama of the city centre with the Frauenkirche, Rathaus and "Alter Peter" – the nickname the people of Munich have given their parish church of St Peter's.

PHOTOS BY
MARTIN SIEPMANN
TEXT BY
GEORG SCHWIKART

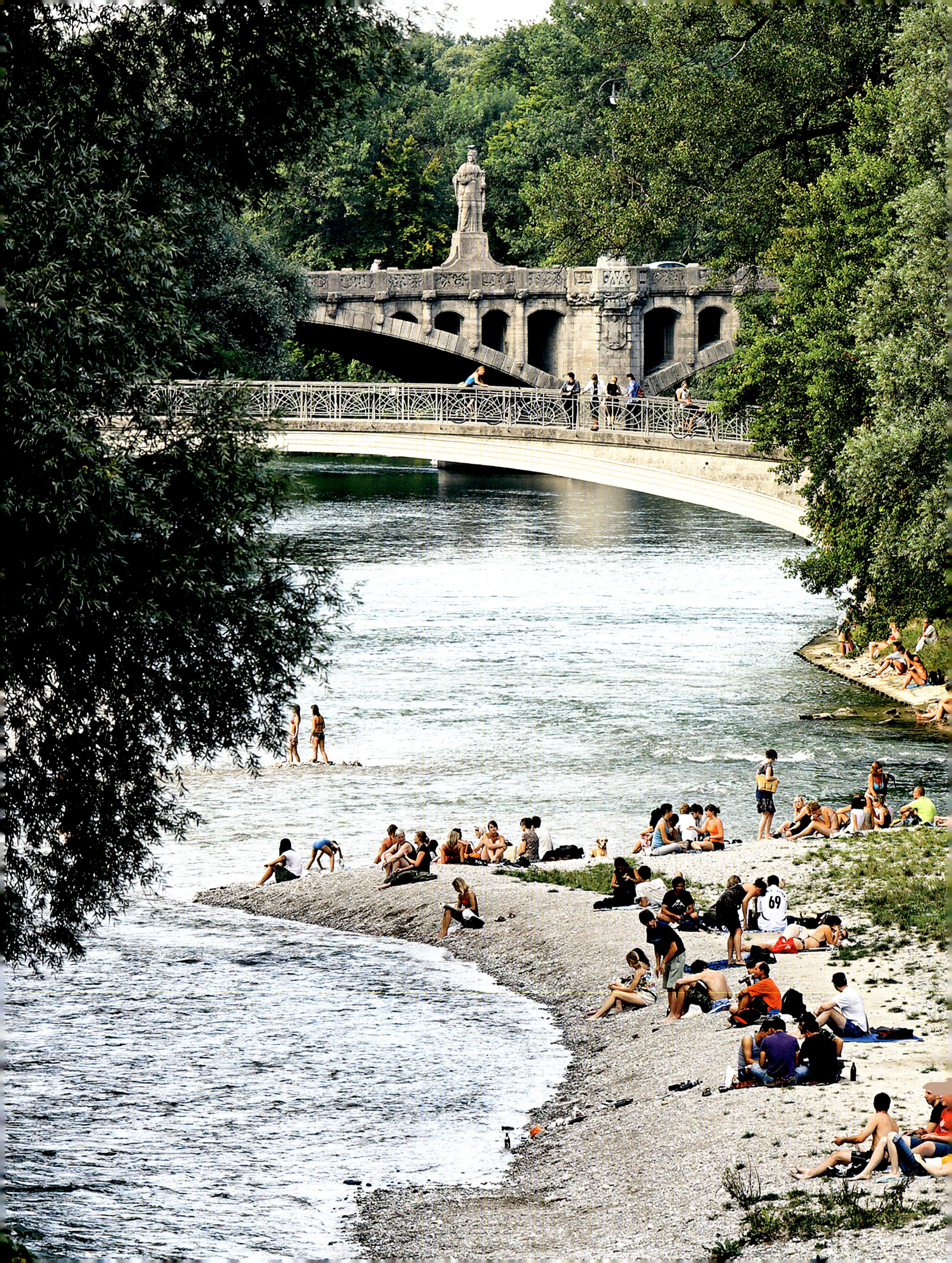

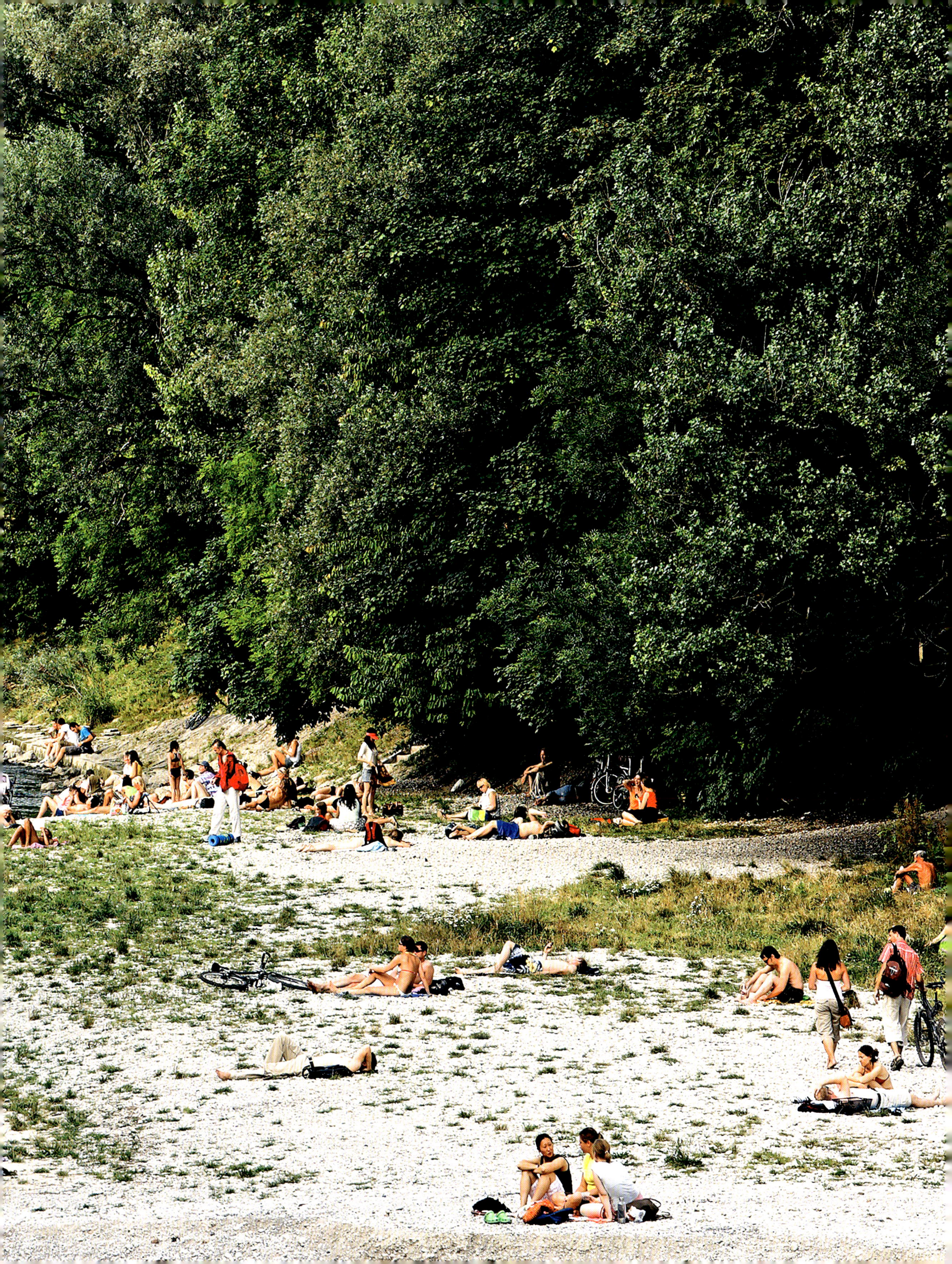

CONTENTS

Page 8/9:
Summer on the River Isar, just a few minutes' walk from the Deutsches Museum. In the background is the Maximiliansbrücke with the elegant Kabelsteg in front of it, a Jugendstil footbridge from 1898.

Page 12/13:
View from the Olympic Tower of the Olympiapark. The unusual roof, an absolute sensation at the time of its construction, is made of Plexiglas and spans the Olympic Stadium, the Olympic Hall and the Olympic Pool.

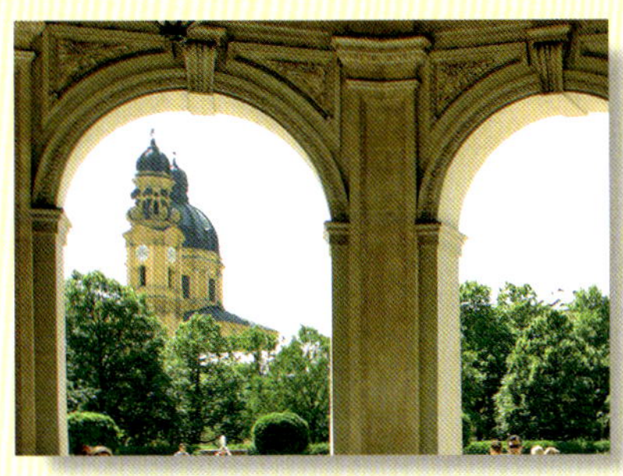

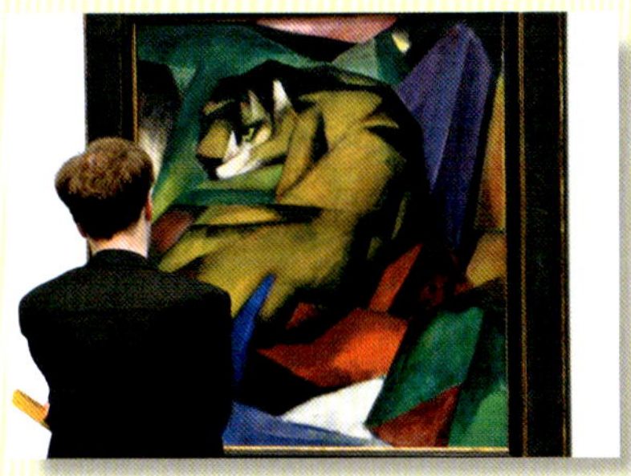

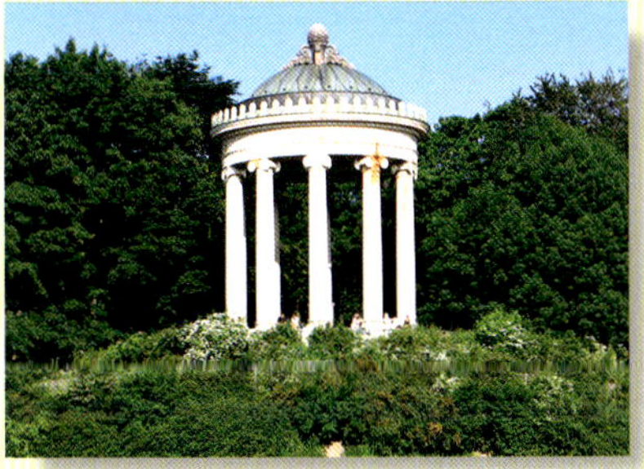

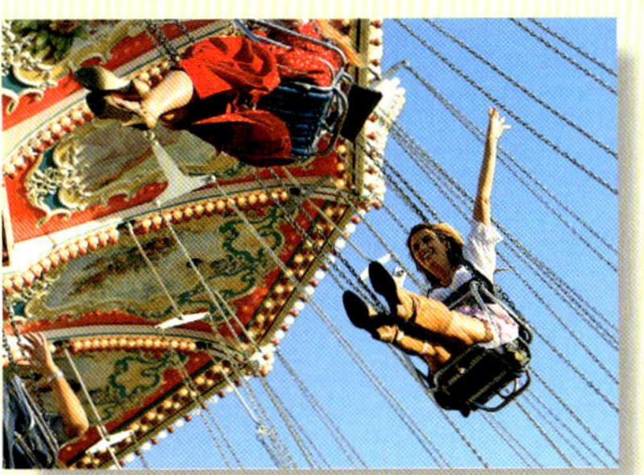

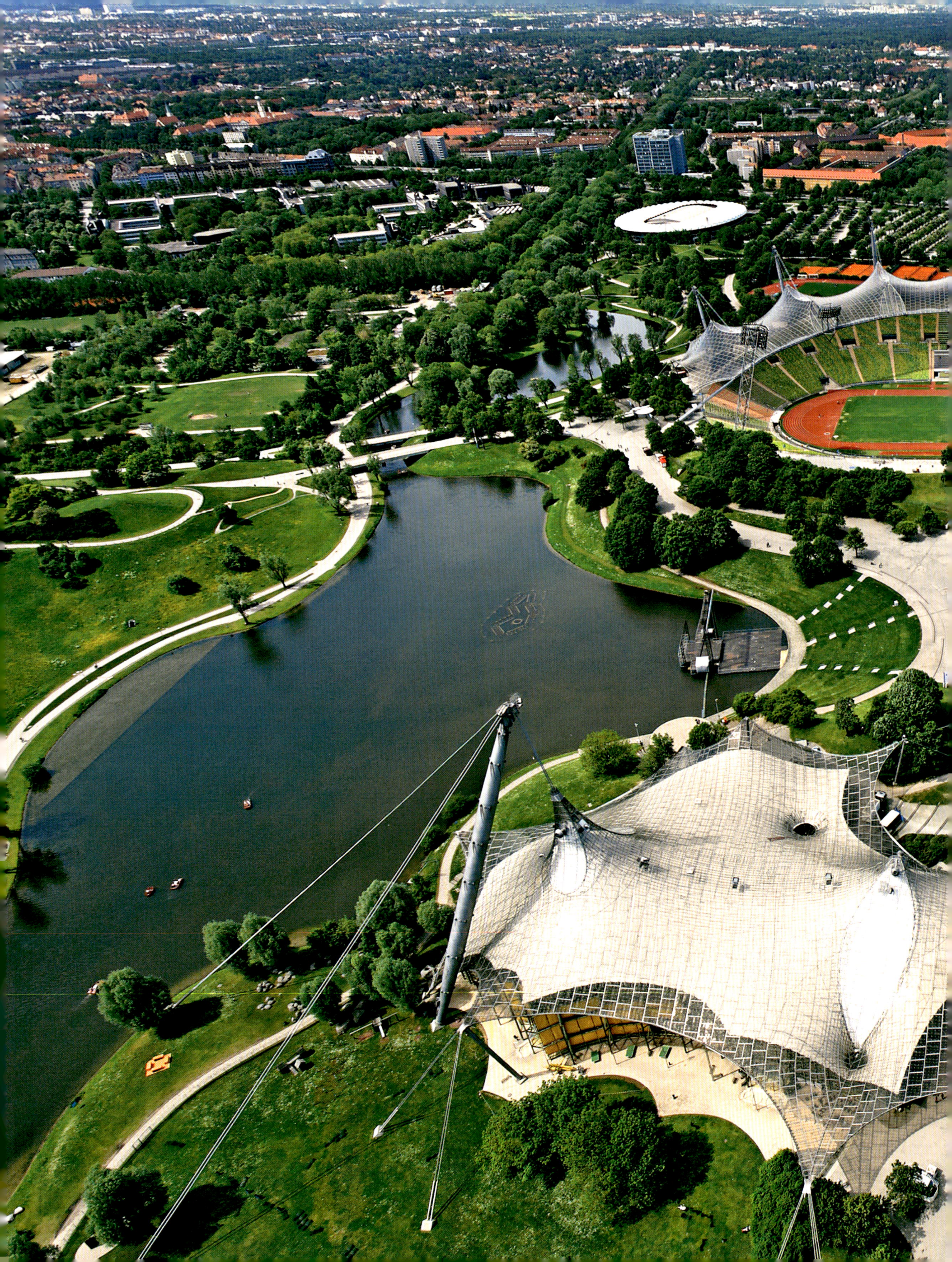

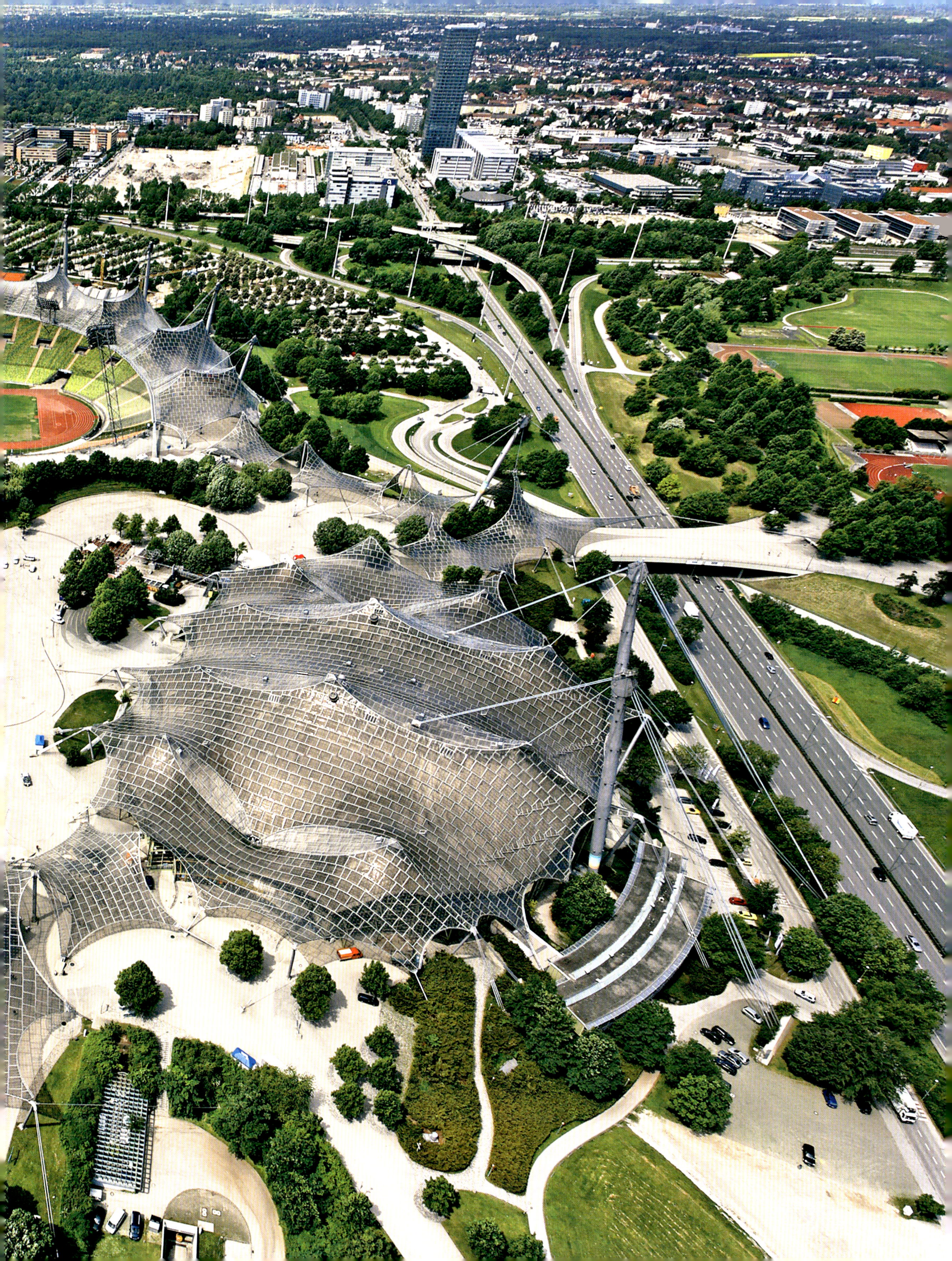

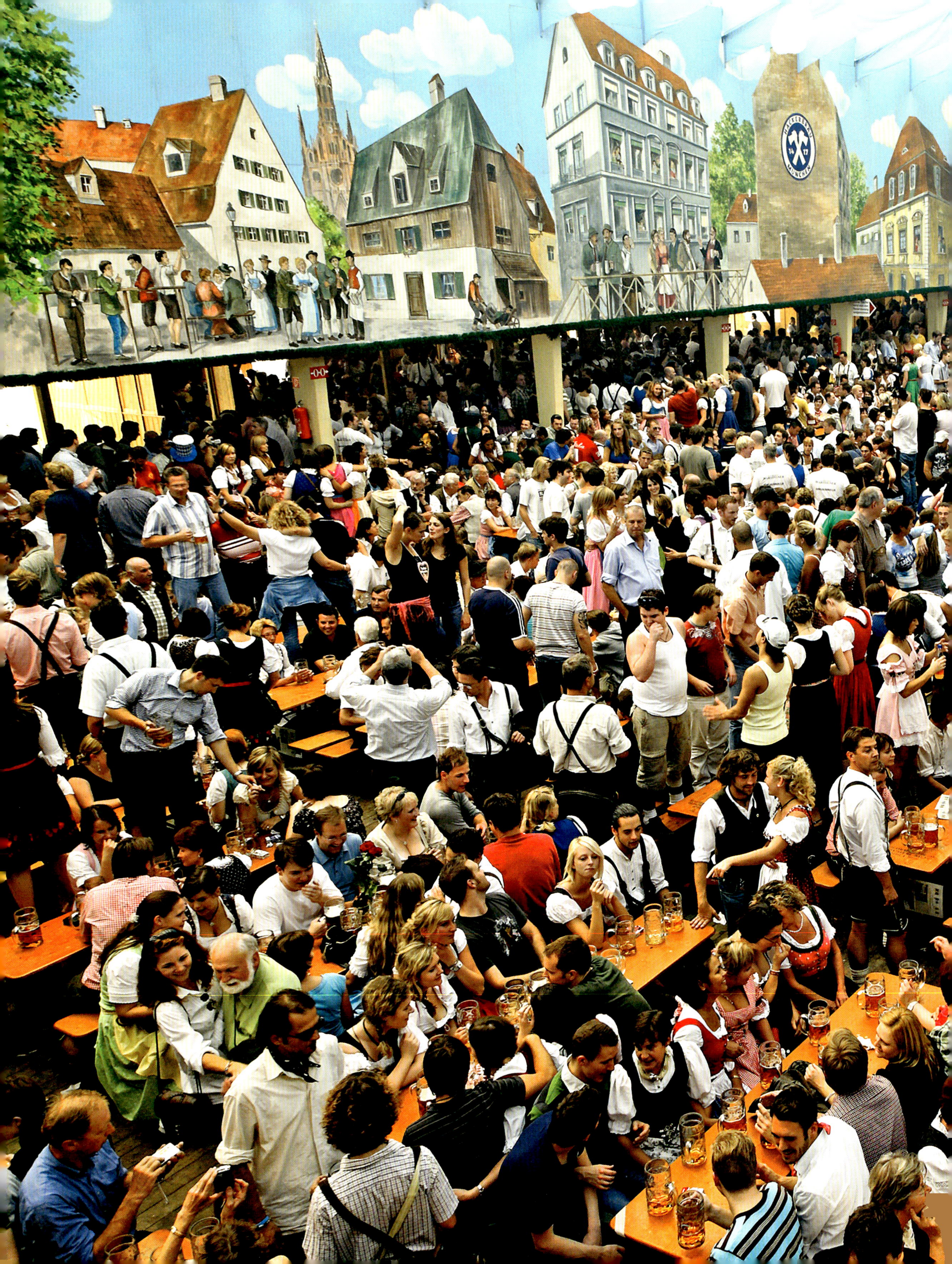
HACKERBRÄU
14 17
MÜNCHEN

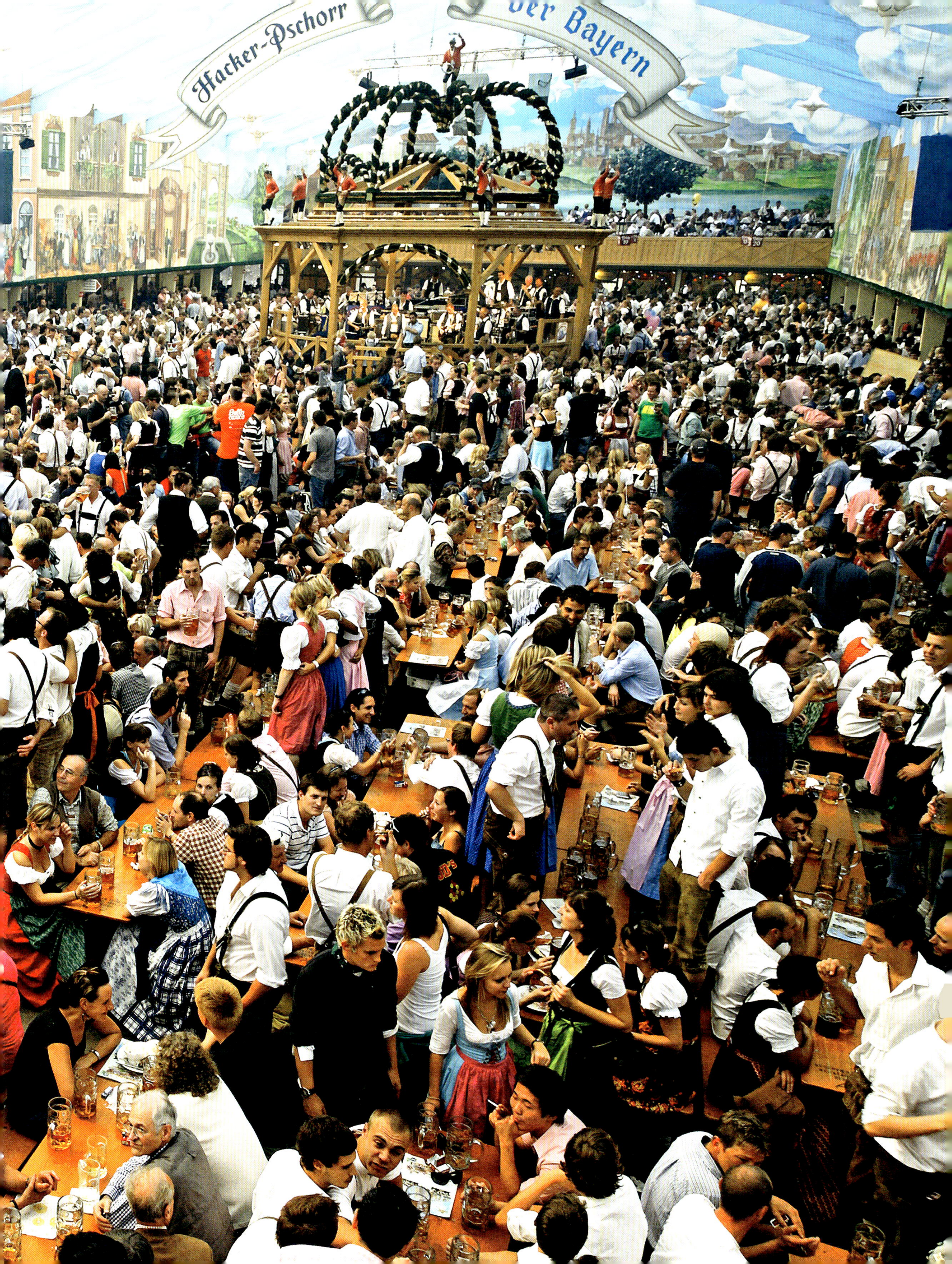
Hacker-Pschorr
Bayern

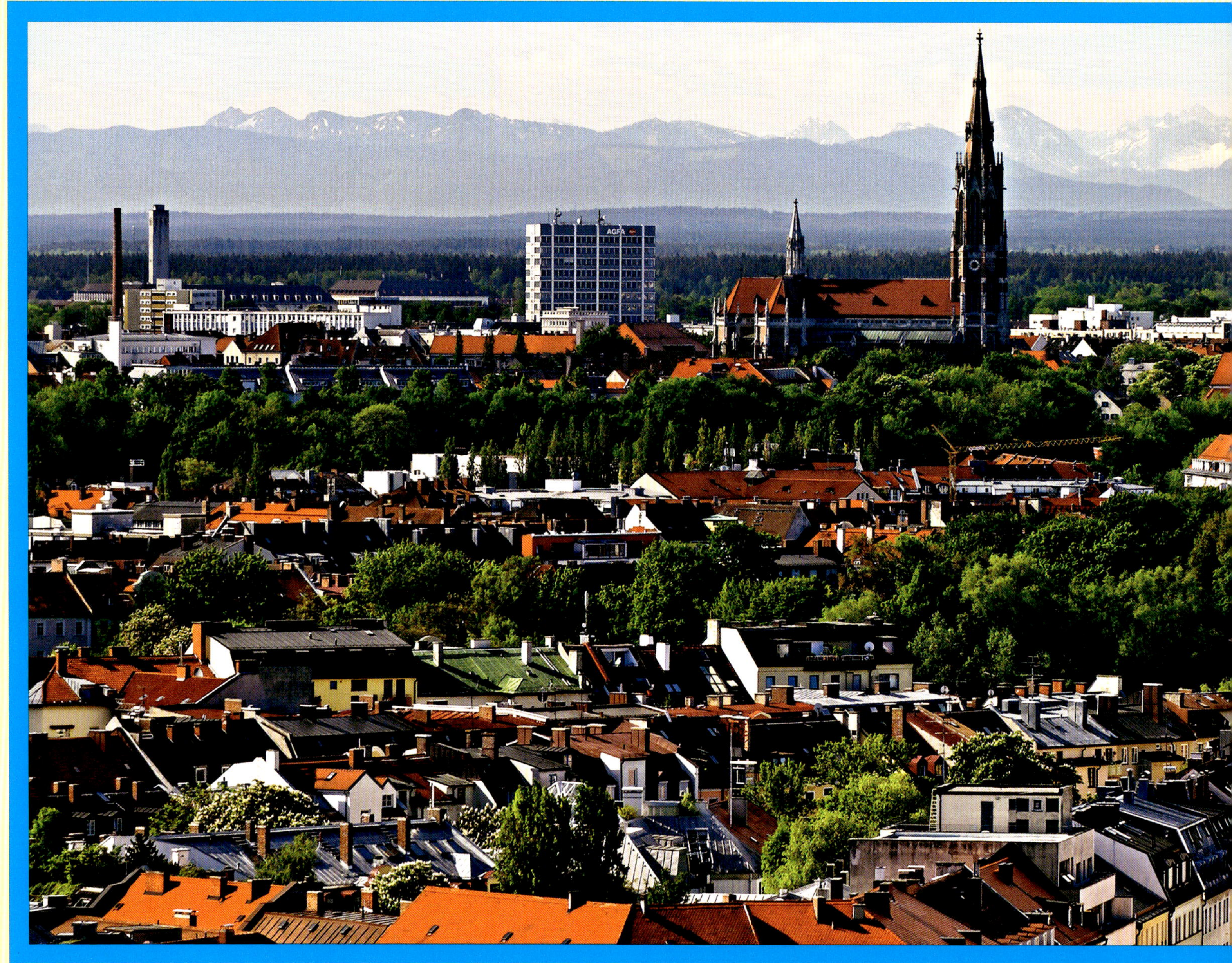

LEDERHOSEN AND LAPTOPS – MUNICH THE METROPOLIS

"Munich was aglow. Above the magnificent squares and white, columned temples, the neo-ancient monuments and baroque churches, the sparkling fountains, palaces and gardens of the Residenz a sky spun of blue silk gleamed, and her expansive and light, green and well-proportioned perspectives lay in the hazy sunshine of a first, beautiful June day. ... And on the squares and along the passageways the unhurried and amusing bustle of this beguiling and leisurely city rolls and hums in waves."

Thus wrote Thomas Mann in his novel Gladius Dei from 1902 – with a twist of irony, it has to be said – of the Munich of the Jugendstil period, the city then a leading metropolis of the arts. Today the capital of the state of Bavaria stands for both

Page 14/15:
The Hacker-Pschorr tent at the Oktoberfest, with its blue and white decor and seating for 7,000 – is supposed to represent heaven – to the Bavarians, at least!

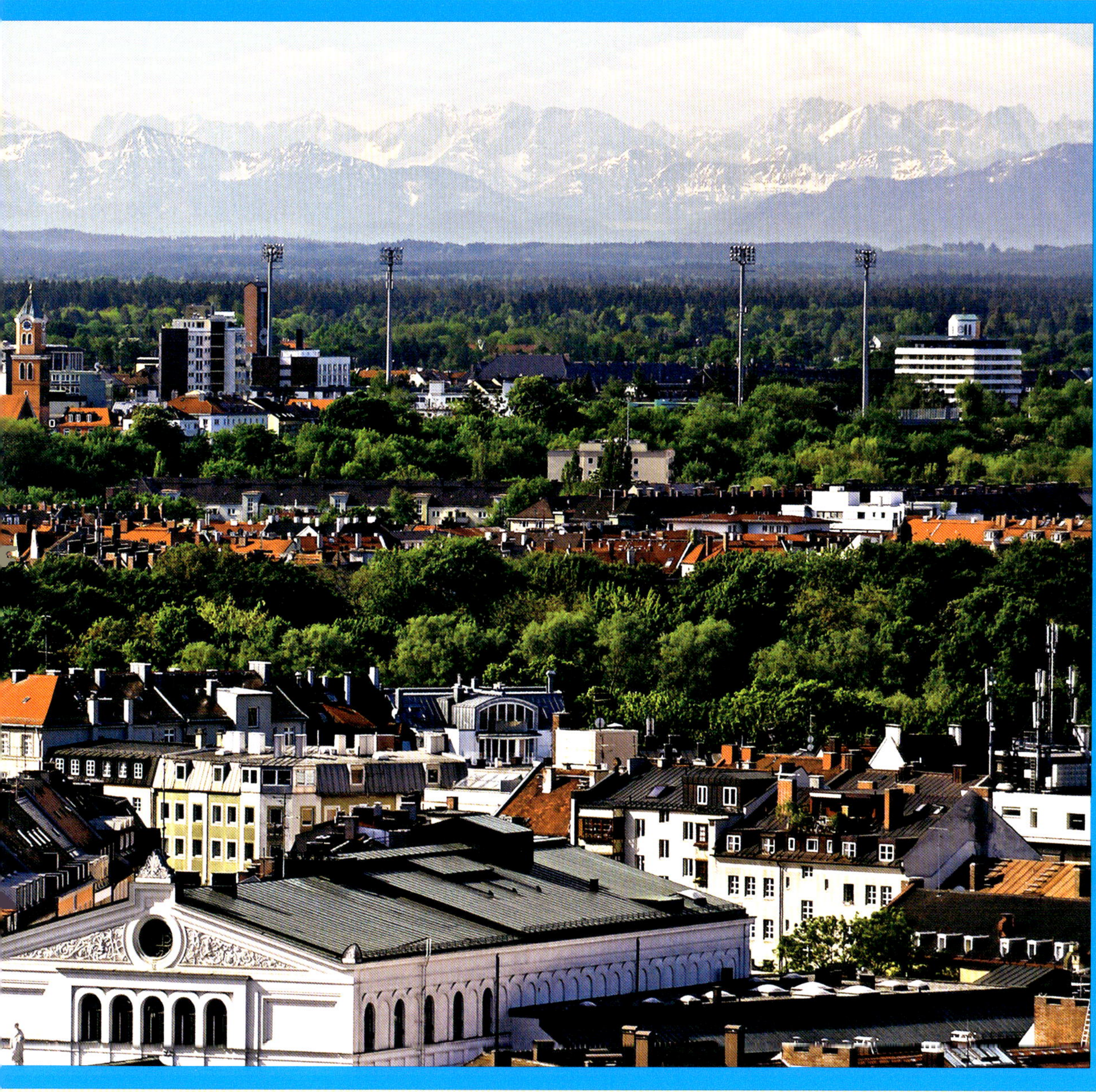

There are marvellous views from the top of St Peter's steeple. The church stands on the Petersbergl, the only hill in the old town of Munich. At the front of the photo is the theatre on Gärtnerplatz, with the neo-Gothic church of Maria Hilf in the background.

culture and natural joie de vivre, sporting success, economical performance and pioneering technology. Former German president Roman Herzog expressed it thus: "In Munich lederhosen and laptops have undergone a symbiosis."

Munich has been given nicknames such as "the secret capital" (of Germany) or "metropolis with a heart". Yet where praise is due, criticism is also rife. Tongues sharpened, detractors mutter that Munich is sinister, all it secretes being arrogance and self-importance, all show and no stuffing. Cabaret artist Oliver Hassencamp (1921–1988) even went as far as to say: "Those who claim Munich is a metropolis with a heart haven't got one." Maybe the pundits only experienced Munich during a föhn. This downslope wind which occurs throughout the countries of the Alps brings warm and dry air down from the mountains to the foothills, causing headaches and cardiovascular complaints. The föhn is blamed for everything that goes wrong, from failed marriages to collapsed soufflés. There is one small compensation, however: during a föhn wind the distant Alps (50 km / 30 miles away) seem close enough to touch.

The 1.3 million inhabitants of the third-largest city in Germany live in an area of 310 square kilometres (120 square miles). At its greatest point Munich stretches ca. 21 kilometres (13 miles) north to south and 27 kilometres (17 miles) east to west. 44 percent of the overall surface area is developed, 17 percent is for road and rail, 20 percent consists of parks and open spaces and 16 percent is used agriculturally. Major industry and research institutions have set up shop in Munich, as have banks, insurance companies and the media. Economically Munich is one of the most successful cities in Germany and has the best perspectives. Statistically speaking, the people of Munich have the highest national spending power but also the biggest debts per head. They also have the highest life expectancies in the country, with 79.2 years quoted for men. Women in Munich also live long and are in third place behind Stuttgart and Dresden.

Below:
The twin spires of the Frauenkirche are everywhere: here, reflected in a goldsmith's shop window.

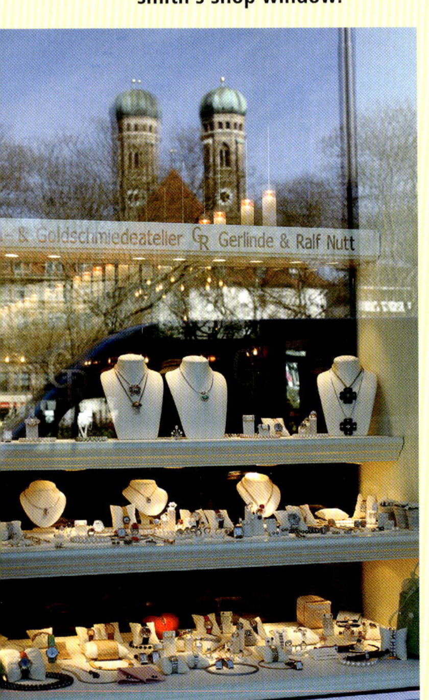

A MÜNCHNER IN HEAVEN

One Munich male whose life was unexpectedly lengthened was porter Alois Hingerl, one of Munich's most famous figures. Upon his demise he enters the gates of heaven where he quickly becomes depressed; the constant merriment and ethereal singing get on his nerves and – to cap it all – there's no beer, just manna. The delightful story of Ein Münchner im Himmel (A Münchner in heaven) was penned by Ludwig Thoma (1867 – 1921) and published in 1911. Many of Bavaria's great folk actors have spoken the role on vinyl, from Adolf Gondrell to Fritz Straßner to Gustl Bayrhammer. God takes pity on the angel Aloisius and decides to give him a job; he is ordered to convey God's advice to the government of Bavaria. This allows him to travel to Munich a couple of times a week. Aloisius immediately seizes his chance and flies straight to the Hofbräuhaus – where he sits to this very day. Maybe that's why the Bavarian government is still waiting for inspiration from on high ...

The multitude of sights, such as palaces, churches, museums and villas, streets, squares and parks, is inexhaustible and worth several journeys, especially if you're culturally and artistically inclined. "Yet to call the entire city New Athens is, between you and me, slightly ridiculous", scorned Heinrich Heine (1797 – 1856). There is indeed one thing Munich can't offer which its Greek counterpart has; thousands of years of history. Munich is much younger than many other Bavarian cities. Regensburg, Passau and Augsburg go back to antiquity; 2,000 years ago they were settled by the Celts and Romans who have left us fascinating proof of their existence. With much ado, in 2008 Munich can just about manage to celebrate its 850th anniversary.

On the Petersbergl in the heart of town, where the parish church of St Peter's now stands, a delegation of monks from the monastery at Schäftlarn put down roots in the 8th century. The first

Right:
The former royal Bavarian confectioner's on Residenzstraße claims: "Ingredients cannot be seen but they can be tasted".

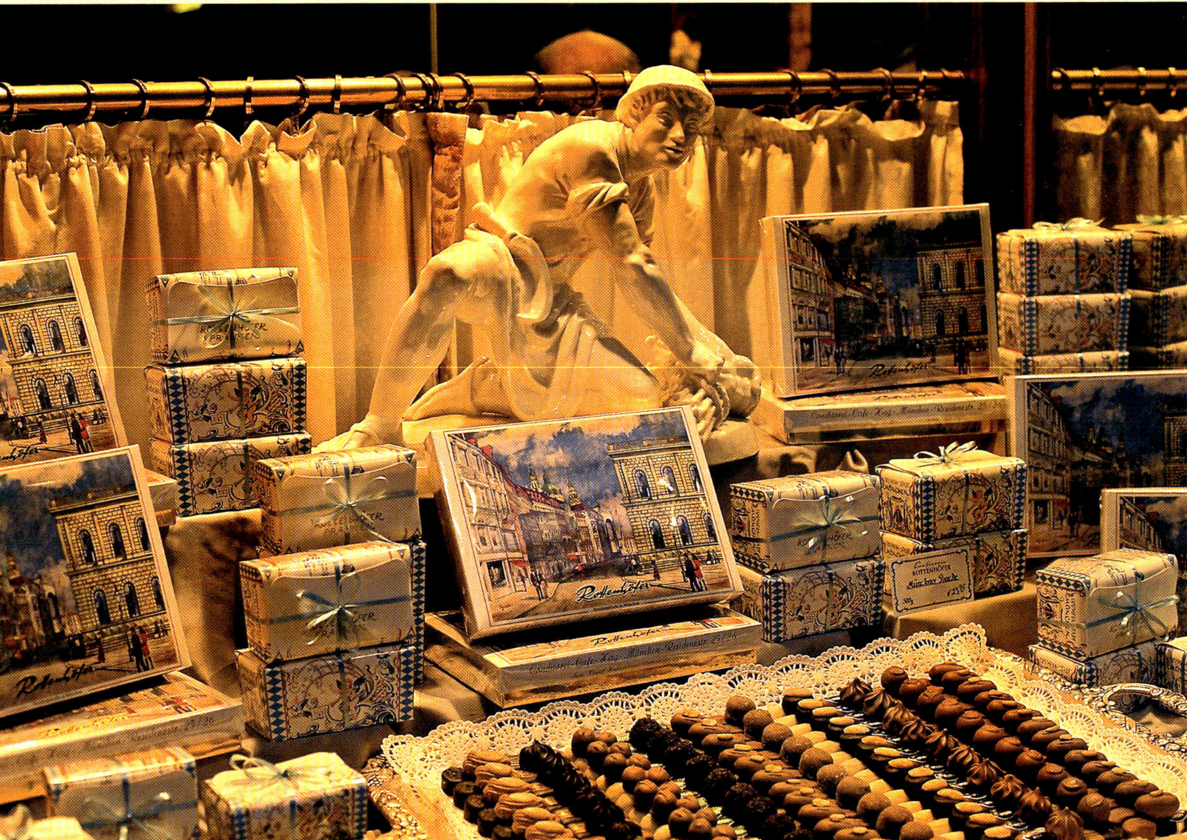

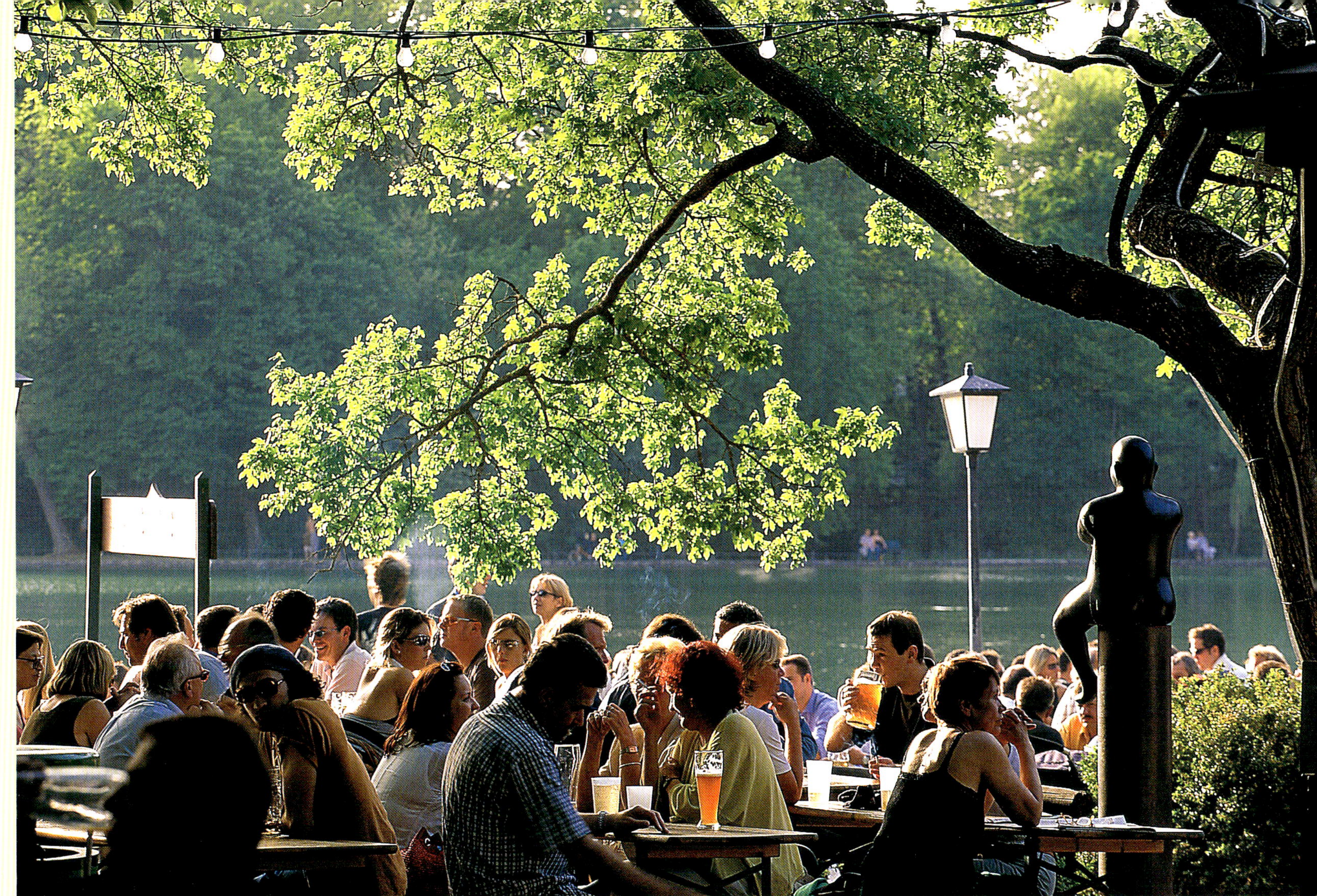

The Kleinhesseloher See is in the middle of the Englischer Garten. One popular watering hole here is the Seehaus beer garden with space for 2,500.

documented mention of Munich is of apud Munichen ("monk's place"). By the early Middle Ages several settlements were sprawled across today's city area, some of which have become the suburbs of Sendling, Schwabing, Pasing and Berg am Laim.

HENRY THE LION FOUNDS A CITY

The city was officially founded on June 14, 1158, by Heinrich den Löwen or Henry the Lion (1129–1195). He was the duke of Bavaria and Saxony and one of the most powerful imperial princes of the 12th century. The story goes that Henry built a bridge over the River Isar not far from the apud after burning down the crossing erected by Bishop Otto of Freising further north. From this point on all wagons of salt loaded with the 'white gold' of the Middle Ages which were destined for Augsburg had to cross the Isar over Henry's bridge and pay the necessary dues. The ensuing feud was settled at the Imperial Diet of Augsburg where Emperor Barbarossa granted Munich the right to hold markets, levy tolls and mint coins – but decreed that a third of the proceeds go to Freising.

In 1240 Munich fell to the house of Wittelsbach and in 1255 was made a ducal residence. The earliest city seal dates back to this period. It depicts a monk in a black habit who later became the Münchner Kindl, the mascot displayed on the city's coat of arms. In 1314 a Wittelsbach, Ludwig IV of Bavaria (1281–1347), was crowned king of Germany and in 1328 emperor of the Holy Roman Empire; Munich was now the seat of an imperial ruler. The first beer brewery on record was also founded in the same year at the Augustinian monastery on Haberfeld, Neuhauser Gasse. This period saw the event of several terrible fires and outbreaks of the plague. The Black Death first decimated the city in 1348, killing 15,000 – almost half of the population. In the following three hundred years the epidemic hit the city time and again, carrying off its last victims in 1649.

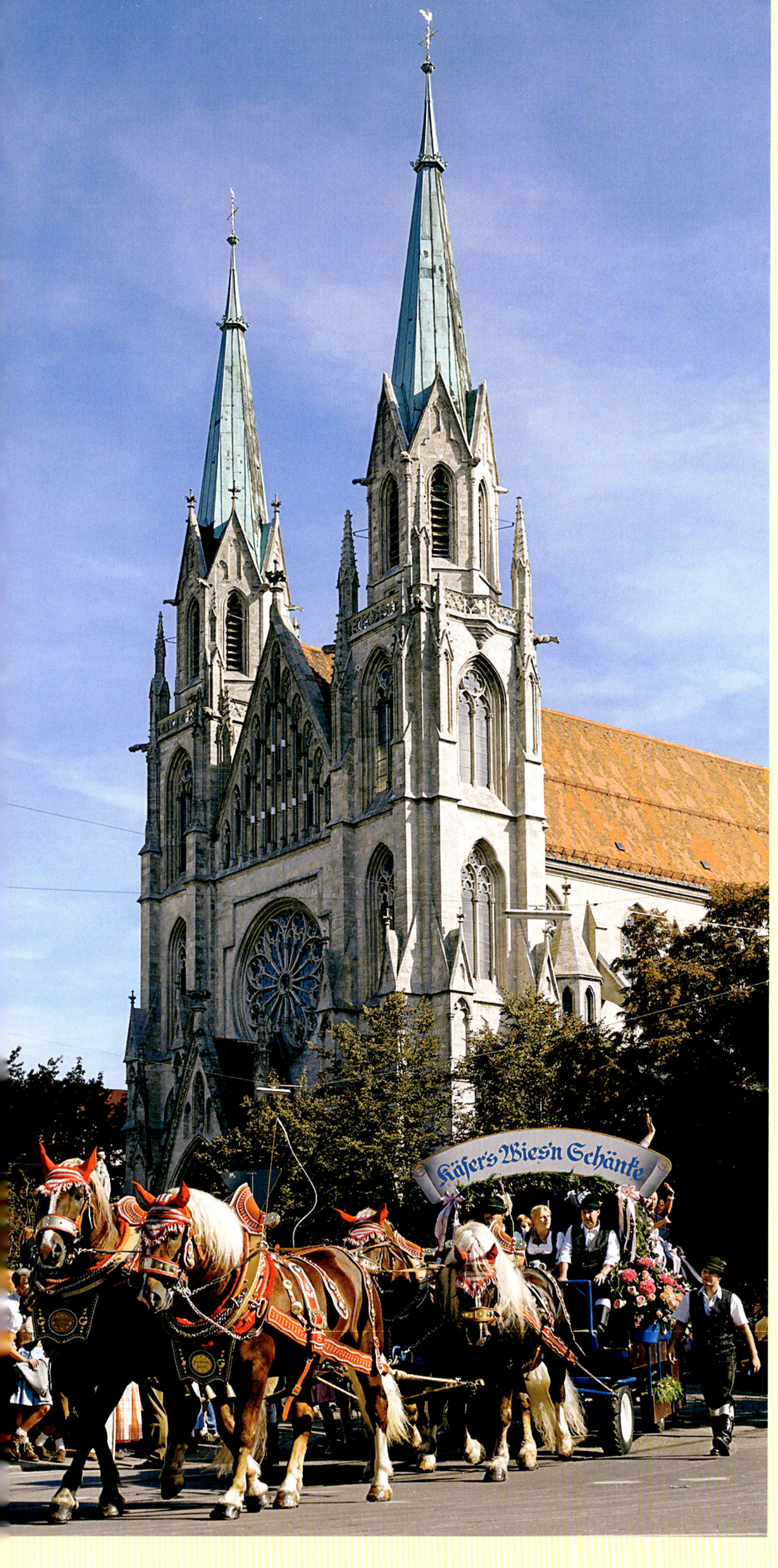

After crushing an uprising of rebellious citizens in 1385 the Wittelsbachs installed a moated castle within the city defences, the Neuveste. Over the centuries this was extended and rebuilt many times and now forms the core of the Residenz. In 1468 the foundations of the new Frauenkirche were laid, with building complete just 20 years later. For reasons of economy the church was built of brick as there was no convenient quarry nearby.

In 1506 Munich was decreed sole capital of the entire country of Bavaria by Emperor Maximilian, the "last knight". One of the oldest regulations governing foodstuffs, the Bavarian purity law, was passed in 1516 which states that beer may only be made from hops, barley malt and water, according to which Munich's ever popular wheat beer shouldn't exist. Various other towns had passed local bylaws at an earlier date (Augsburg in 1156 and Munich in 1363); this one, however, was on a national scale.

AN ECONOMY MEASURE: THE HOFBRÄUHAUS

During the 16th century the city became a stronghold of the Renaissance – but also of the Counter-Reformation. In 1555 Protestantism was forbidden. Wilhelm V the Pious, duke of Bavaria from 1579 to 1597, was an extravagant patron of the arts and the Catholic church. The monumental Jesuit church of St Michael, built from 1583 onwards and consecrated in 1597, almost bankrupt Bavaria. In an attempt to save money Wilhelm set up his own brewery (the Hofbräuhaus) in 1589 so that he no longer had to import beer for the ducal household from elsewhere.

In 1618 the Thirty Years' War broke out. At first Munich was spared the fighting. In the spring of 1632 Swedish troops under King Gustav II burst through the city gates. Munich was occupied yet spared the plundering and destruction by paying an enormous ransom of 300,000 Talers. By way of thanks Elector Maximilian I had the Mariensäule erected – which didn't stop one third of the population being struck down by the plague in the following years.

Once the war was over Munich again blossomed and the Italian baroque flounced into the city. The names of its chief executors sound like makes of expensive Italian confectionery: Zuccalli (1642–1724), Barelli (1627–1687) and Viscardi (1645–1713). In 1662 the elector invited the order of the Theatines to Bavaria and in 1663 the foundations were laid for their own special church, the Theatinerkirche. In 1664 the royal house of Thurn and Taxis set up the first post office in Munich; building commenced on Schloss Nymphenburg and in 1669 the first houses were made available for rent.

THE BIRTH OF THE BIG CITY

Munich began to grow in earnest during the 18th century. In 1701 Elector Max Emanuel began building the Neues Schloss in Schleißheim. The streets were lit up at night by oil lamps in 1733. Gems of the late baroque and Rococo periods were created, among them the church of the Asam brothers on Sendlinger Straße, St Michael's in Berg am Laim by Johann Michael Fischer and the sumptuous theatre in the Residenz by François de Cuvilliés. In 1798, the year of the French Revolution, Elector Karl Theodor ordered that the Englischer Garden be laid out along the banks of the Isar – and had the medieval town walls torn down.

In c. 1800 the city numbered ca. 30,000 inhabitants. By 1850 this had reached 110,000 and by 1871 170,000. The university situated in Ingolstadt between 1472 to 1800 and then in Landshut was moved to Munich by King Ludwig I who reigned from 1825 to 1848. Wishing to make the royal treasures accessible to the public, from 1826 to 1836 the monarch had the Alte Pinakothek constructed on the northern edge of town. In 1850 Munich's academy of the fine arts was one of the greatest art colleges in the world. Ludwig's son Max II was also a great patron of the arts and sciences. His son, Ludwig II, however, showed little interest in the royal capital and shunned public appearance. In 1886 the melancholy fairytale prince was removed from office by governmental decree due to unsoundness of mind; he died five days later in mysterious circumstances in the Starnberger See.

PRINCE REGENT LUITPOLD

His uncle Luitpold (1821–1912) then reigned as prince regent. He loved painting and was taught as a child by royal artist Domenico Quaglio. Luitpold not only admired the Old Masters but was also interested in more progressive styles. The years under his auspicious government were heralded as the golden age of Bavaria. His modesty and efficiency won over the hearts of his subjects who named streets and buildings after him, such as the Prinzregententheater built in the east of the capital from 1900 onwards. In 1896 two periodicals were launched in Munich, both of which have written journal-

Left page:
At the opening of the Oktoberfest thousands of spectators flock to Ludwigsvorstadt and the parish church of St Paul, where from the balustrade of the steeple there are the best views to be had of the Wiesn and the grand parade.

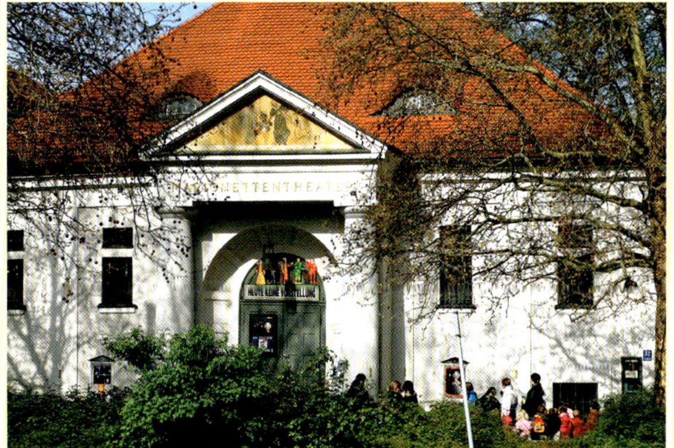

Left:
This neo-classical-looking edifice on Blumenstraße is the first theatre in the world to have been specially built for puppets. Its ambitious performances appeal to both children and adults and include classics such as The Magic Flute and The Little Witch.

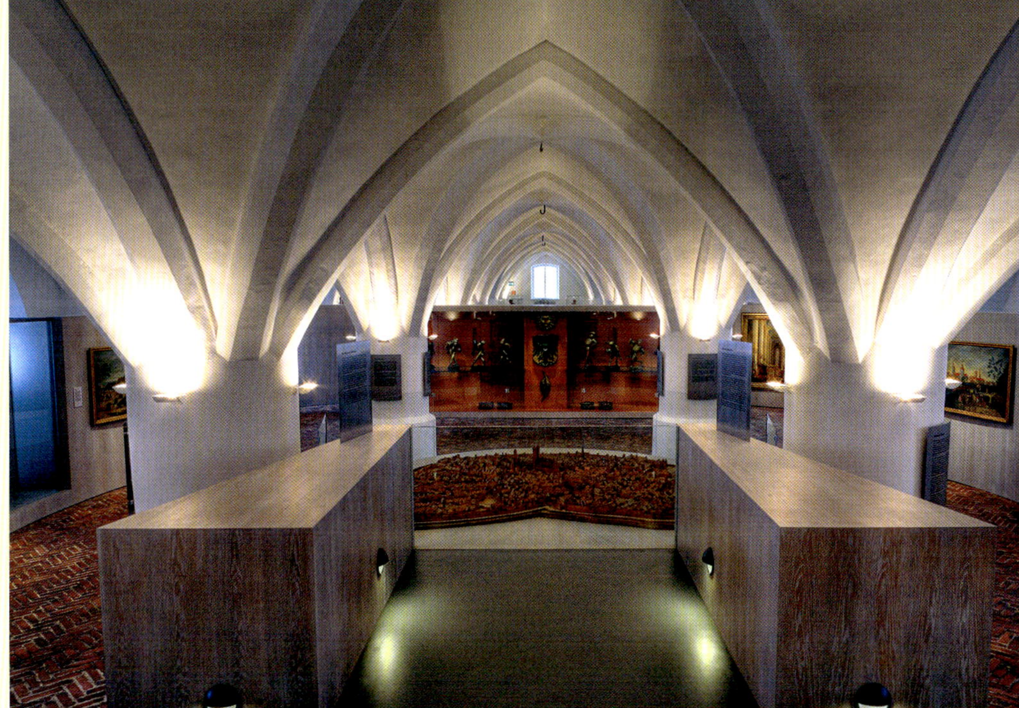

Below:
In celebration of the city's jubilee in 2008 Munich's city museum launched a new permanent exhibition featuring over 400 exhibits entitled Typical Munich.

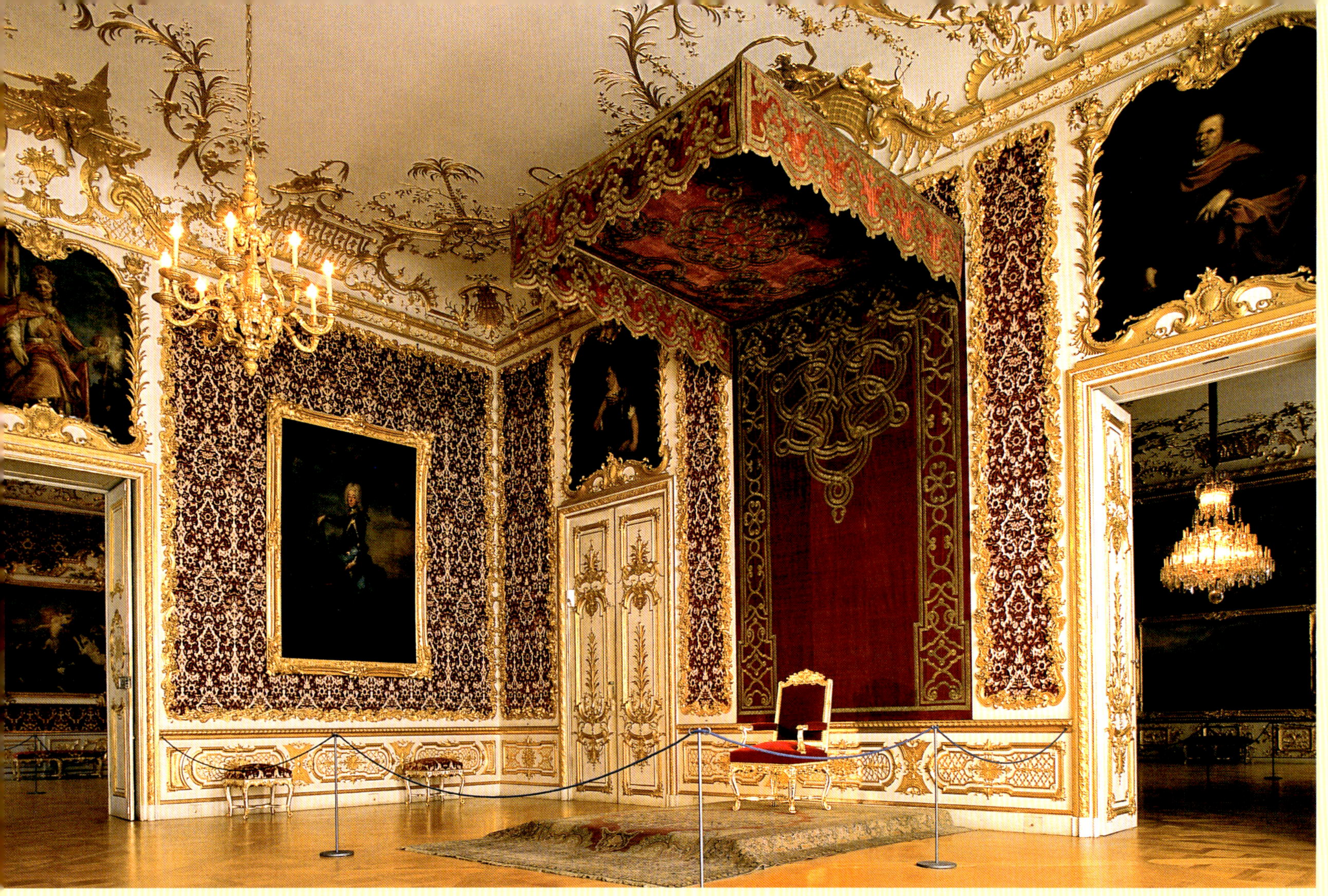

The expansive Residenz has 130 rooms open to the public. The furniture and panelling on the walls and ceilings were stashed safely away during World War II and thus survived. The Reiche Zimmer are among the most sumptuous suites of rooms at the old residential palace.

istic history. The first was the satirical rag Simplicissimus, the second the arts publication Die Jugend which gave rise to an entire artistic movement. Countless artists of various disciplines came from or settled in Munich – mostly in Schwabing – or were inspired by the city. Theodor Fontane (1819–1898) was prompted to remark: "Munich is the only city in Germany where artists can live. The actual stock of the population is so intellectually dead and stubborn as is possible yet the influx of art from all corners of the globe is so immense that a subsidiary populace exists, and in this one can live more freely and with greater freshness than anywhere else."

CENTRE OF THE ARTS

Just a few of Munich's many artistic greats shall be mentioned here. Natives to Munich include architectural painter Domenico Quaglio (1787–1837), sculptor Ludwig von Schwanthaler (1802–1848) and popular artist Carl Spitzweg (1808–1885). Others made Munich their home, such as the Asam brothers, Johann Michael Fischer, Leo von Klenze, "prince of painters" Franz von Lenbach and painter and sculptor Franz von Stuck, whose students at the art academy included Wassily Kandinsky and Paul Klee.

Dozens of writers past and present can also be named who either spent some time in Munich or lived here permanently. The list includes Paul Heyse, Ricarda Huch, Frank Wedekind, Annette Kolb, Rainer Maria Rilke, Thomas Mann, Lion Feuchtwanger, Oskar Maria Graf, Eugen Roth, Bertolt Brecht, Erich Kästner, Luise Rinser, Carl Amery and Herbert Achternbusch. Johannes R Becher, the man behind the GDR hymn Auferstanden aus Ruinen (Resurrected from the ruins), was born in Munich. And Ellis Kaut, creator of the cheeky imp Pumuckl, may have been born in Stuttgart but at the age of 18 played the part of the Münchner Kindl in the opening Oktoberfest procession. By 1901 the number of residents in Munich had risen to 500,000, making it the third-biggest city in the

German Empire after Berlin and Hamburg. In 1914 the assassination in Sarajevo sparked off the First World War. In 1916 three bombs hit Munich but only caused a minimum of damage. The city's civilians were racked by hunger and various epidemics, however, and on November 7, 1918, the Bavarian monarchy was the first to be toppled.

During the Weimar Republic Munich was a breeding ground for National Socialism. In 1920 the NSDAP was founded at the Hofbräuhaus. In 1923 at the Beer Hall Putsch Hitler 'deposed' the imperial government and marched on the Feldherrenhalle with his hangers-on where there was a shoot out with the police. After seizing power the Nazis staged memorial rallies here each year, organising mass marches and swearing in ceremonies. In 1935 Munich was declared the "capital of the Movement". In Dachau, 20 kilometres north of Munich, an old munitions factory was turned into the first concentration camp.

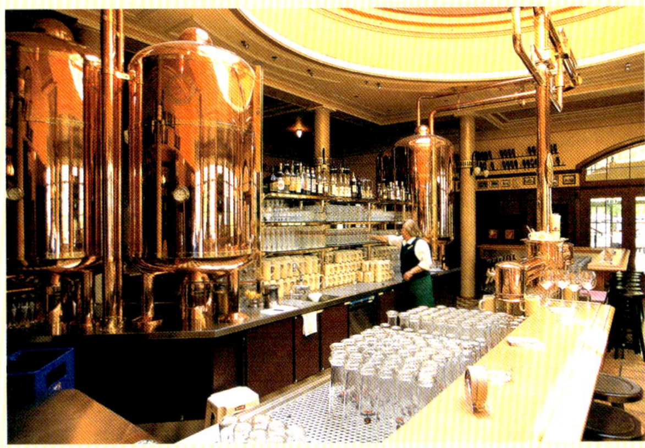

On Prinzregentenstraße at the south end of the Englischer Garten the Nazi regime's first monumental edifice was erected between 1933 and 1937, the Haus der Deutschen Kunst or house of German art. Its purpose was to exhibit and sell National Socialist art. The Führerbau was put up on Königsplatz where in 1938 the Munich Agreement was signed. The building is now the city's music conservatoire.

During World War II Munich was the target of Allied bombing. By the end of the war 90 percent of the historic old town had been annihilated, with just 50 percent of the city as a whole remaining intact. Sections of the vaulting in the Frauenkirche had collapsed, the interior destroyed or plundered. Much of the Alte Pinakothek had been obliterated and nothing remained of the Neue; the Nationaltheater was reduced to its outer walls. Ca. 6,000 people had lost their lives and 15,000 had been injured.

In the rebuilding of Munich great effort was made to preserve the city silhouette, still dominated by the prominent twin steeples of the Frauenkirche. The city administrators now won't allow any buildings taller than 100 metres (3,300 feet) within the Mittlerer Ring. A plebiscite passed in November 2004 also stipulates that no more tall buildings are to be put up within the confines of the city.

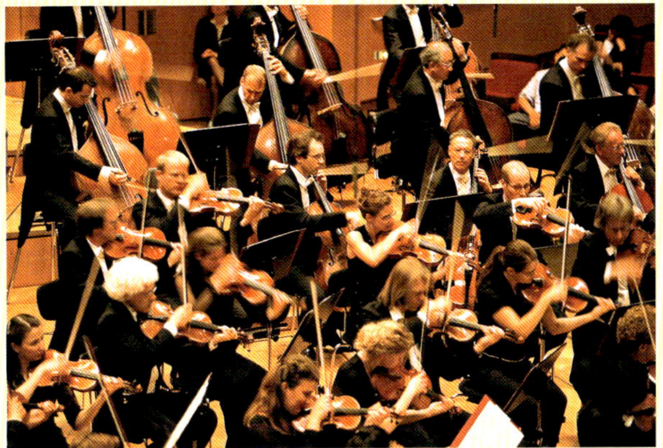

MODERN LANDMARKS

One of Munich's most significant events of the post-war period were the Summer Olympic Games of 1972. The old airport at Oberwiesenfeld was turned into an Olympic village, complete with sports facilities, living quarters and leisure centres and designed by architects Behnisch & Partner and Frei Otto. The Olympic Tower and the huge and rather daring tent roof construction with its 58 steel masts has become Munich's modern city landmark.

The games were supposed to be "happy games". On the morning of September 5, 1972, however, Palestinian terrorists took eleven Israeli athletes hostage. During the kidnapping and failed rescue attempt in Fürstenfeldbrück all hostages,

Below:
In the auditorium of the national theatre or Bavarian State Opera, originally designed by Karl von Fischer and Leo von Klenze. Destroyed in the Second World War it was rebuilt from 1958 to 1963. It can seat 2,100.

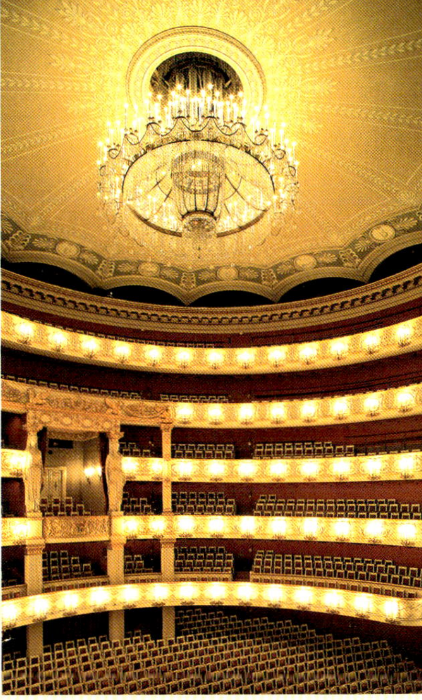

Above left:
The Nockherberg hugs the eastern bank of the Isar between Giesing and Au. Each year a strong beer festival is held here at the Paulaner-Wirtshaus. The grand opening is graced by many local Bavarian politicians and MPs who come for a taste of heady Starkbier.

Above centre:
Concert being given by the Munich Philharmonic at the Philharmonie in the Gasteig. The arts and education centre, built between 1978 and 1984, includes several concert halls, the Richard Strauss Conservatoire and the city library.

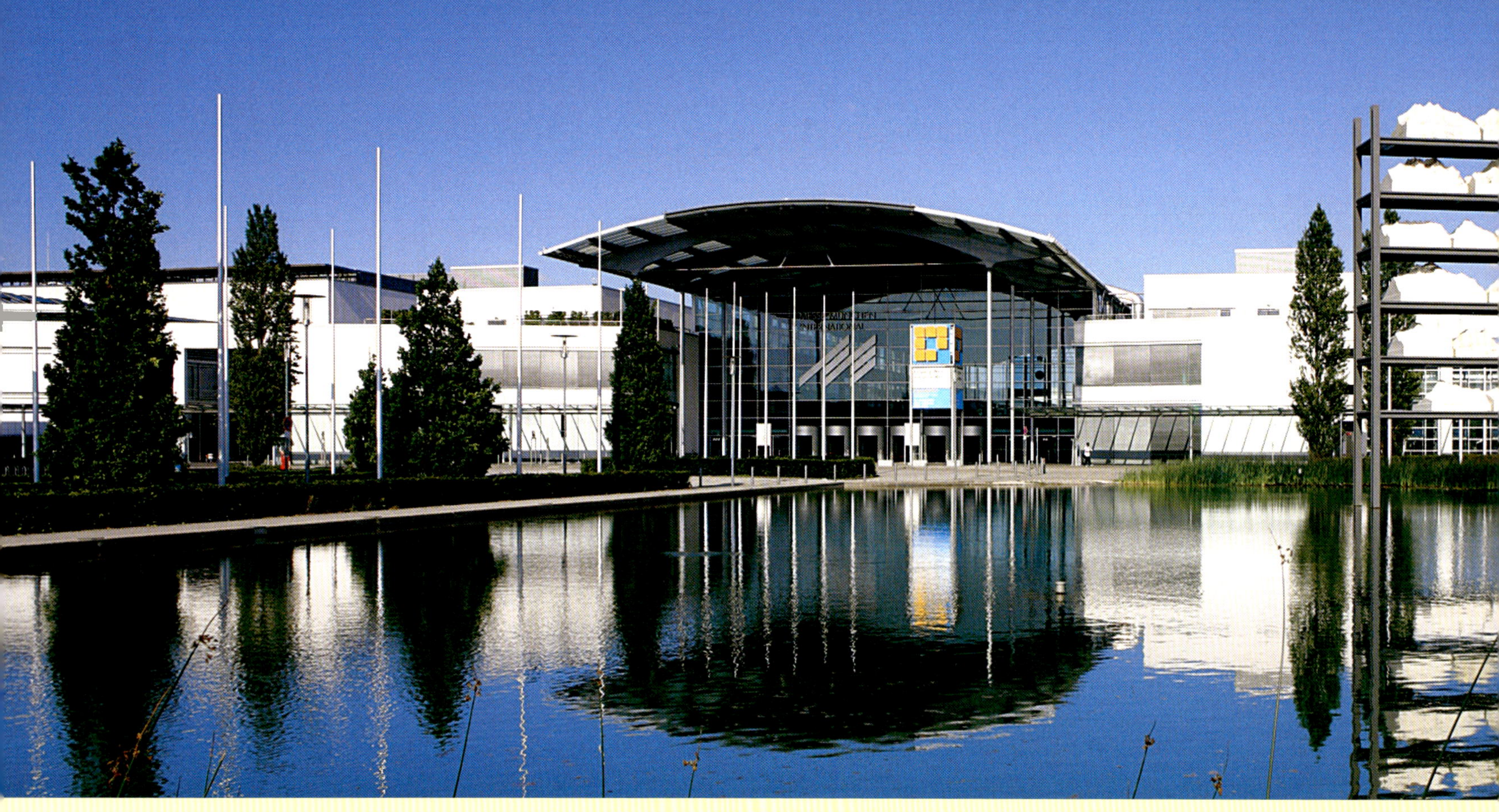

On the closure of Munich-Riem Airport in 1992 the site was redeveloped to house the Munich trade fair. A huge lake twinkles at visitors arriving at the main entrance to the Messe. The Bundesgartenschau, Germany's national garden exhibition, was held here in 2005.

Page 26/27:
Northeast of Marienplatz bang in the middle of town is Platzl, the square which boasts that oh-so-famous brewery the Hofbräuhaus. In the foreground on the right is the Orlando-Haus from 1899, now a stylish restaurant.

five terrorists and a German policeman were killed. The games were stopped for one day and after a service in the Olympic Stadium president of the IOC Avery Brundage continued the event with the words: "The games must go on!"

FOOTBALL IN MUNICH

Sport and Munich are inextricably linked. The two best known clubs are the TSV 1860 (the Blues), whose football team has repeatedly made it to the first division, only to be kicked out again, and FC Bayern München (the Reds), the most successful football club in Germany and with over 140,000 members one of the biggest sport clubs in the world.

In 2005 an architecturally unique stadium was opened for both clubs, the Allianz Arena in the northern suburb of Fröttmaning. It was built in less than three years and from a distance looks like a huge tyre turned on its side. It can be lit in three different colours: red for Bayern München, blue for 1860 München and white for neutral events. Almost 70,000 spectators can be seated here; the stadium was fully booked for the opening of the World Cup in 2006.

TREADING THE BOARDS

Football is by no means the only thing played in Munich. Five state, three municipal and around 50 private theatres stage all kinds of shows catering for all kinds of taste. The major players are the Nationaltheater – Bavaria's state opera – the Neues Residenztheater, the Cuvilliés-Theater, the Prinzregententheater and the Staatstheater am Gärtnerplatz, Munich's second opera house. Good drama is also on offer at the Kammerspiele, the Deutsches Theater, the Kleines Spiel puppet theatre and at various cabaret theatres, such as the Lach- und Schießgesellschaft.

Munich is also of world renown when it comes to music. Richard Wagner was sponsored by King Ludwig II who brought him to Munich; several of his operas were premiered at the national theatre, among them the Mastersingers of Nuremberg in 1868. Richard Strauss was born in Munich in 1864 and Carl Orff in 1895. Several top orchestras are based in Munich: the Bayerisches Staatsorchester, the symphony orchestra of the Bayerischer Rundfunk, the Münchner Rundfunkorchester and the Munich Philharmonic. Munich's Bach Choir is dedicated to performing the works of Johann Sebastian. Most of the boys

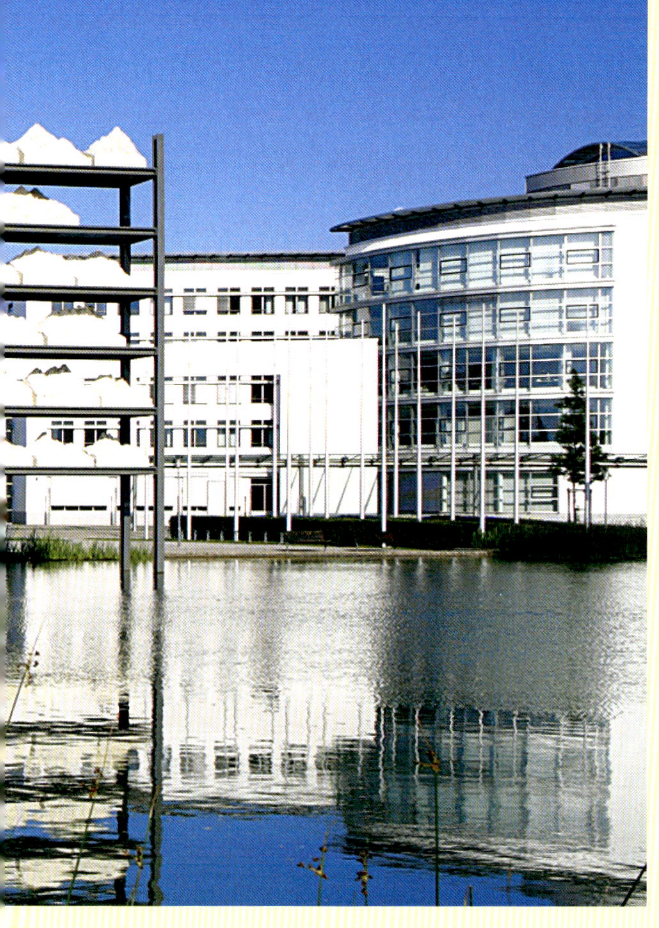

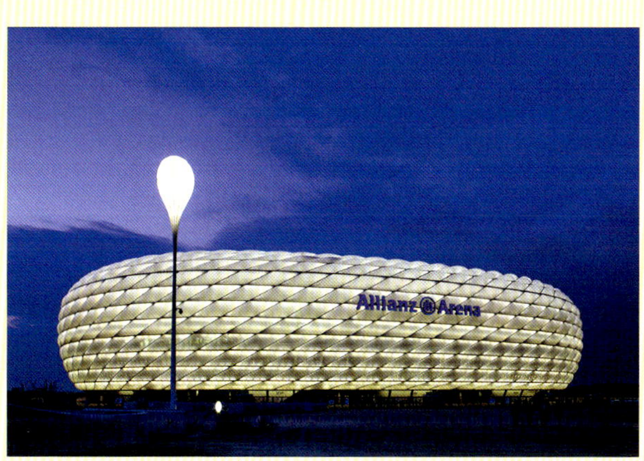

Left:
Between 2002 and 2005 a new stadium was built in the north of Munich for the two sports clubs FC Bayern and TSV. The exterior consists of 2,760 air-filled pockets which can be lit in red, white or blue. Its futurist appearance has earned it the dubious epithets of "rubber ring", " rubber dinghy" – and "imperial toilet".

from the world-famous Tölzer Knabenchor come from Munich. One of the classic names of the singer-songwriter scene is Münchner Konstantin Wecker. The name of the pop group Münchner Freiheit says it all.

Munich is a sophisticated metropolis; even the buskers are hand picked. Ten licences are granted a day. If you want to play the pedestrian zone, you have to prove your worth in front of one of the city administrators early in the morning. After an hour the musicians have to move on so as not to annoy onlookers and shoppers with a litany of the same songs.Buying souvenirs is a less time-consuming business. Besides the common-or-garden, blue-and-white Bavarian kitsch being flogged on every street corner there are items of quality to be had: designer clothes and traditional costume, lederhosen and loden, porcelain from Nymphenburg, verre églomisé pictures and devotional keepsakes. Bavarian specialities also make tasty presents. And if the big names seem a little pricey, simply gazing at the displays of the elegant consumer temples on Marienplatz and Maximilianstraße doesn't cost anything.

Below left:
Munich's Olympic park was laid out in the north of the city for the 20th Summer Olympics in 1972. One of its landmarks is the Olympic Tower, actually a television tower erected between 1965 and 1968.

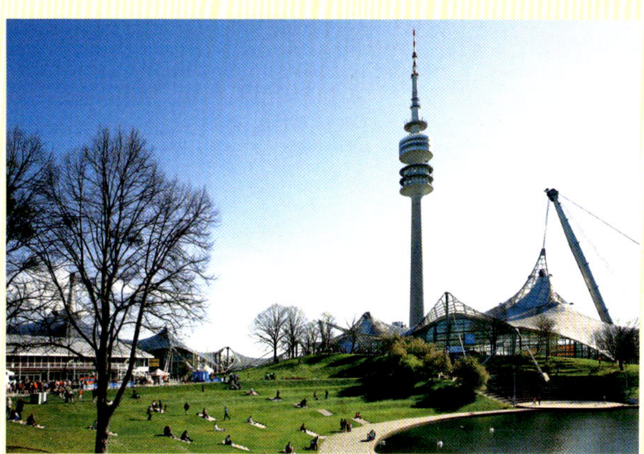

Above:
In May 1992 the planes were redirected from Riem to Erdinger Moos, about 28 kilometres north of the city between Freising and Erding. Munich Airport mark two, named after the former president of Bavaria Franz Josef Strauß, now copes with an influx of about 50 million passengers a year.

Tourists and business travellers alike like Munich because there's plenty to see, do and buy. Almost ten million beds are occupied a year. About half of these are slept in by foreign guests, with Americans, Italians, Britons and Arabs from the Gulf the most frequent. They all want to see the highlights: the Rathaus and Frauenkirche, Königsplatz and the Viktualienmarkt, the Pinakotheks, Deutsches Museum and Englischer Garten – not forgetting the Hofbräuhaus or one of the other traditional beer halls and beer gardens. Over six million flock to the Oktoberfest alone. Some stay here for ever; under 30 percent of the people of Munich were actually born here. But, as Karl Valentin once remarked: "Foreigners are only foreign when they're abroad."

And still Munich is aglow.

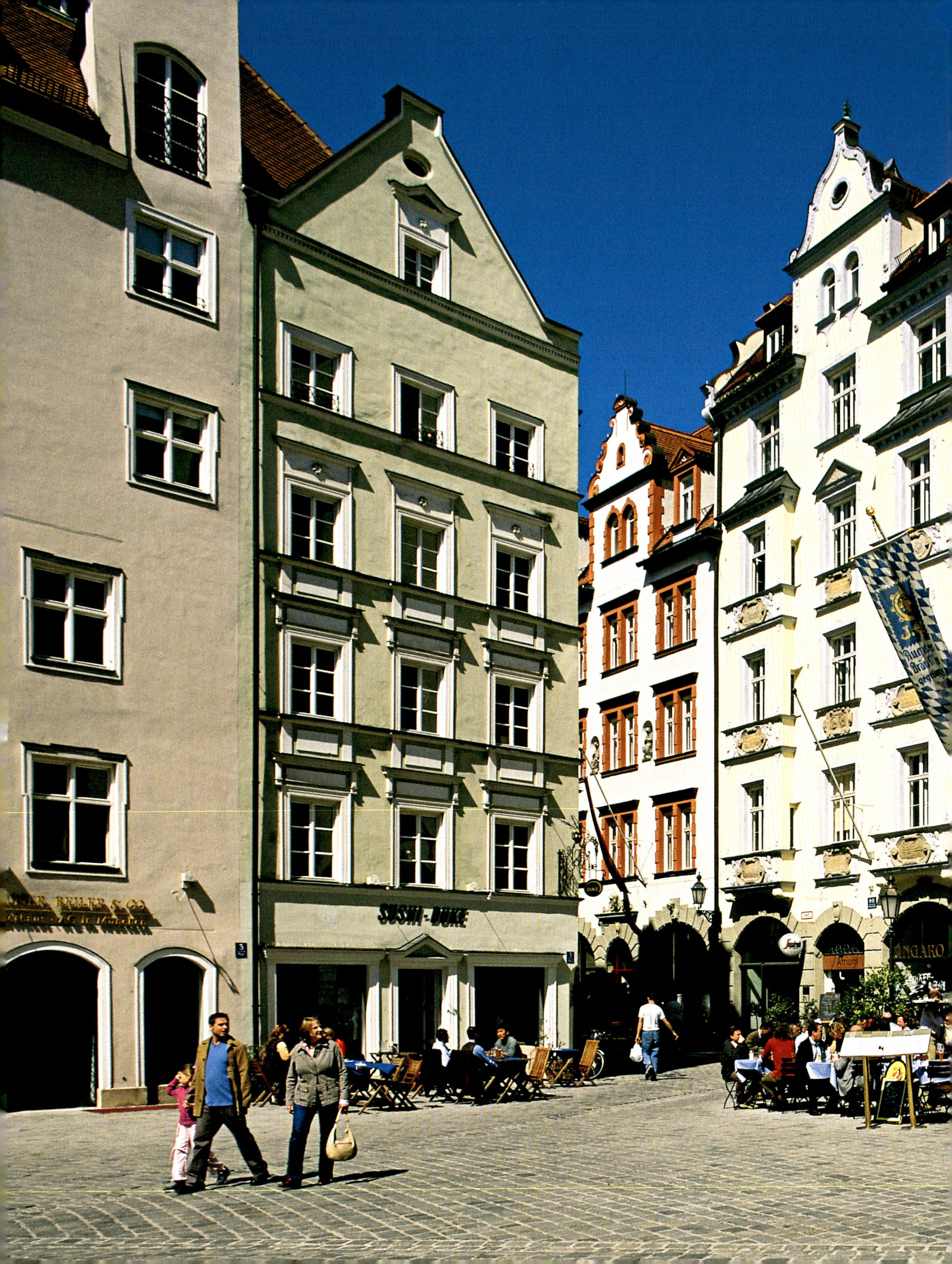
SUSHI-DUKE

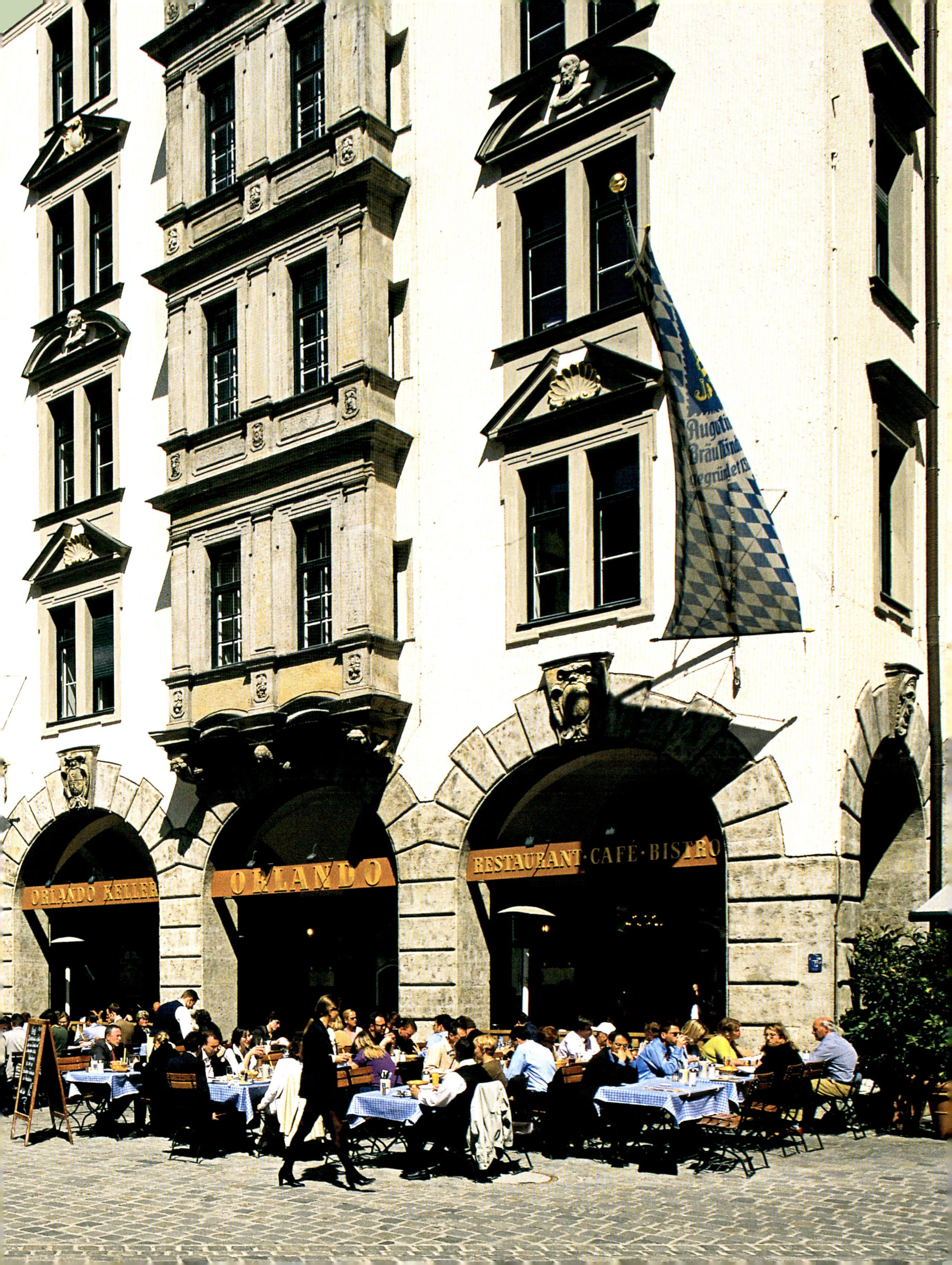
ORLANDO KELLER
ORLANDO
RESTAURANT·CAFÉ·BISTRO

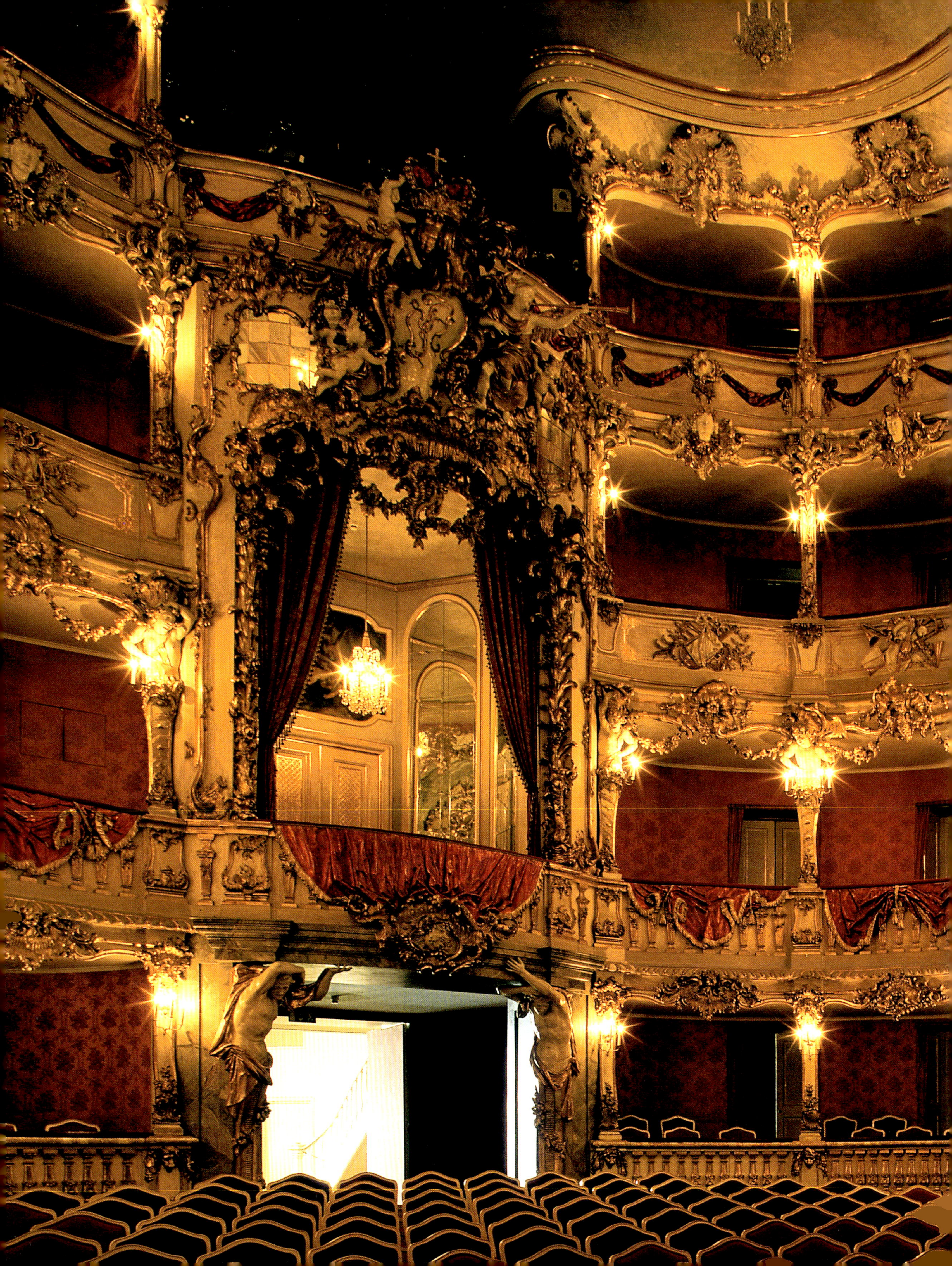

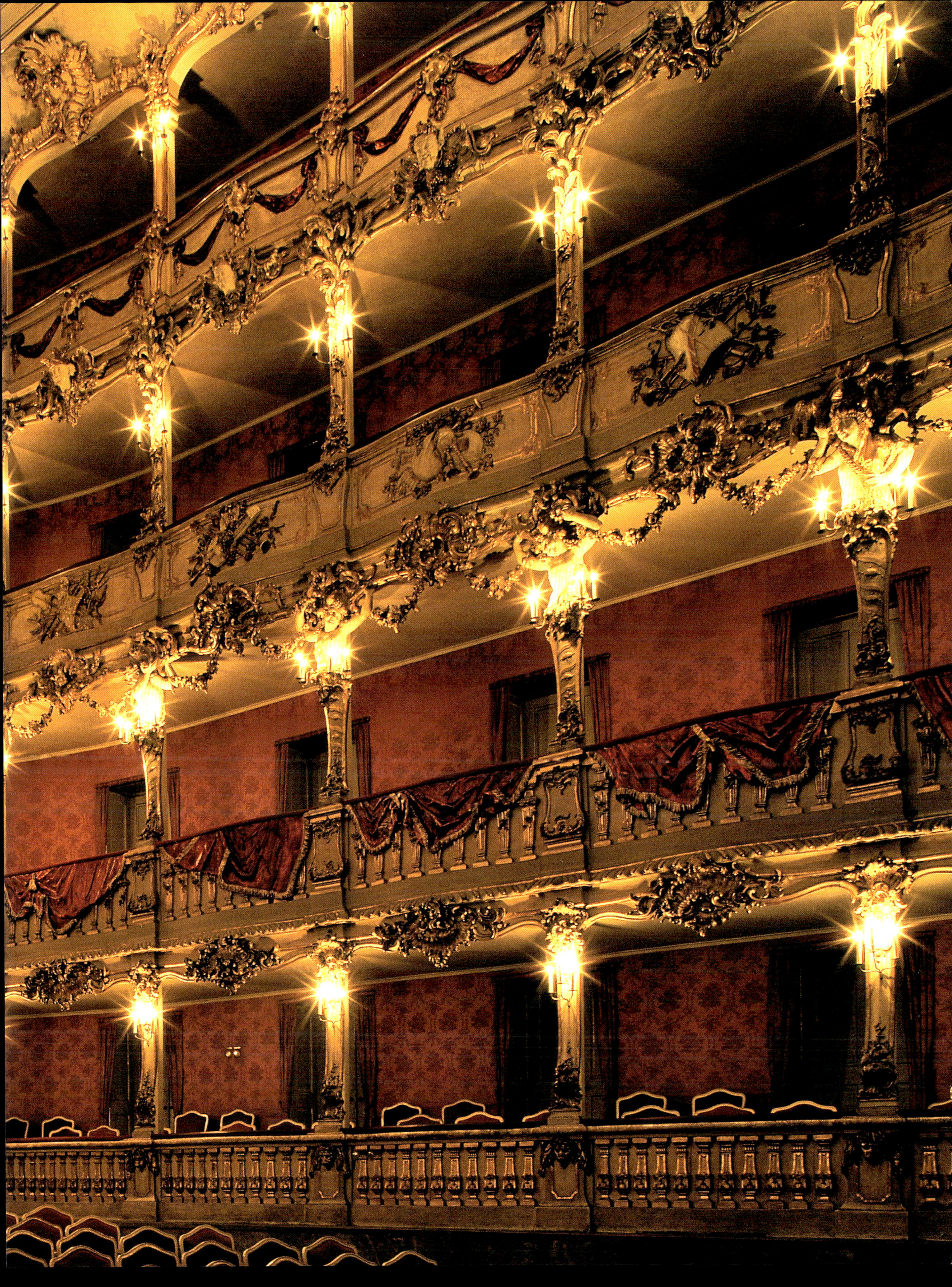

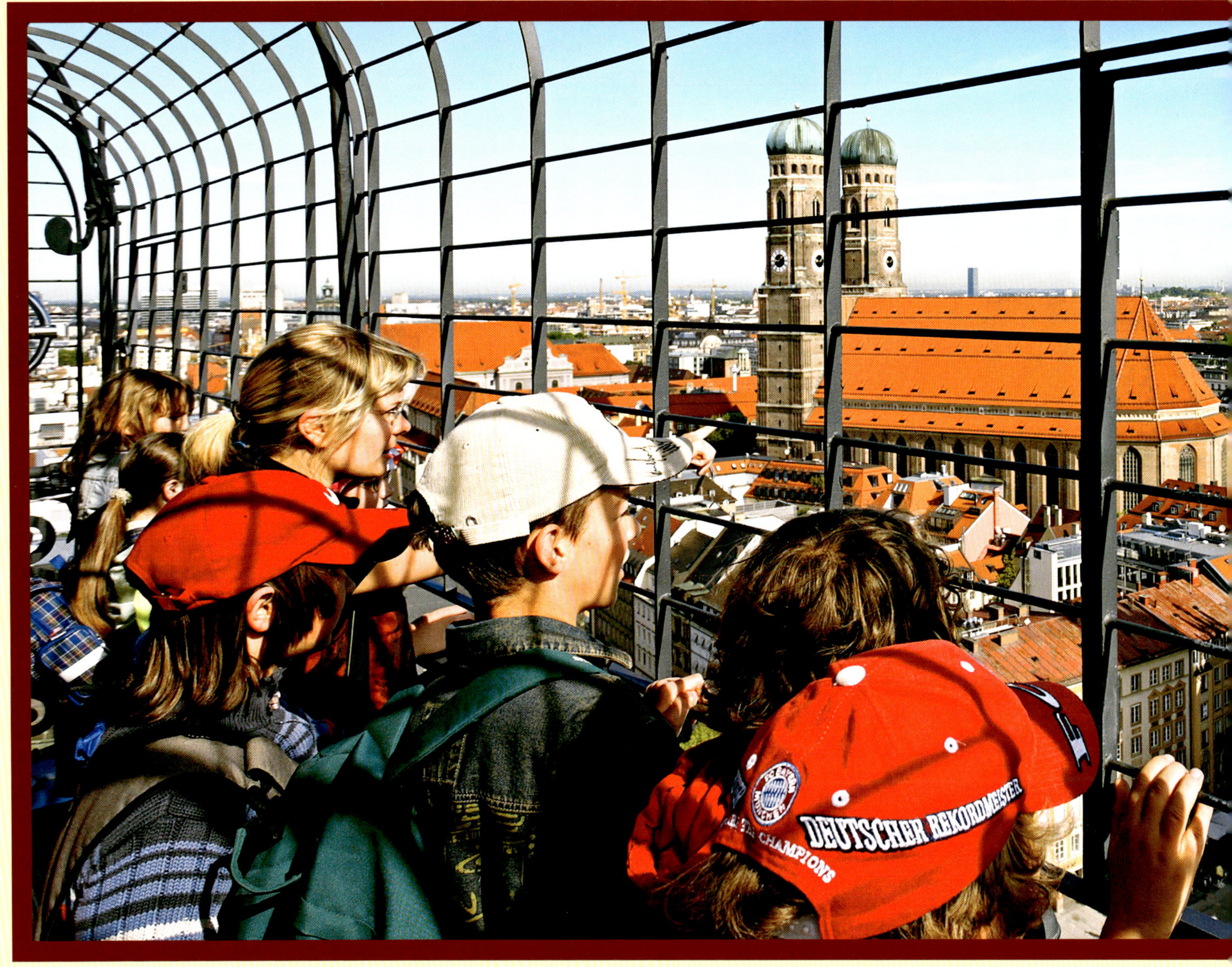

MARIENPLATZ – THE HUMMING HEART OF MUNICH

It's considered to be the geographical nucleus of Munich and is for locals and visitors alike the 'centre' of town: Marienplatz. It has been the humming heart of Munich since the founding of the city in 1158 by Henry the Lion. Initially called Marktplatz or market place after its original use, it later became known as Schrannenplatz, the Southern German word for a corn market. During the Middle Ages this was where tournaments were held and solstice bonfires lit.

In 1638 Elector Maximilian I had a marble pillar installed on the square, crowned by a gilt statue of the Virgin Mary. With it he wished to honour the Madonna as Patrona Bavariae, the

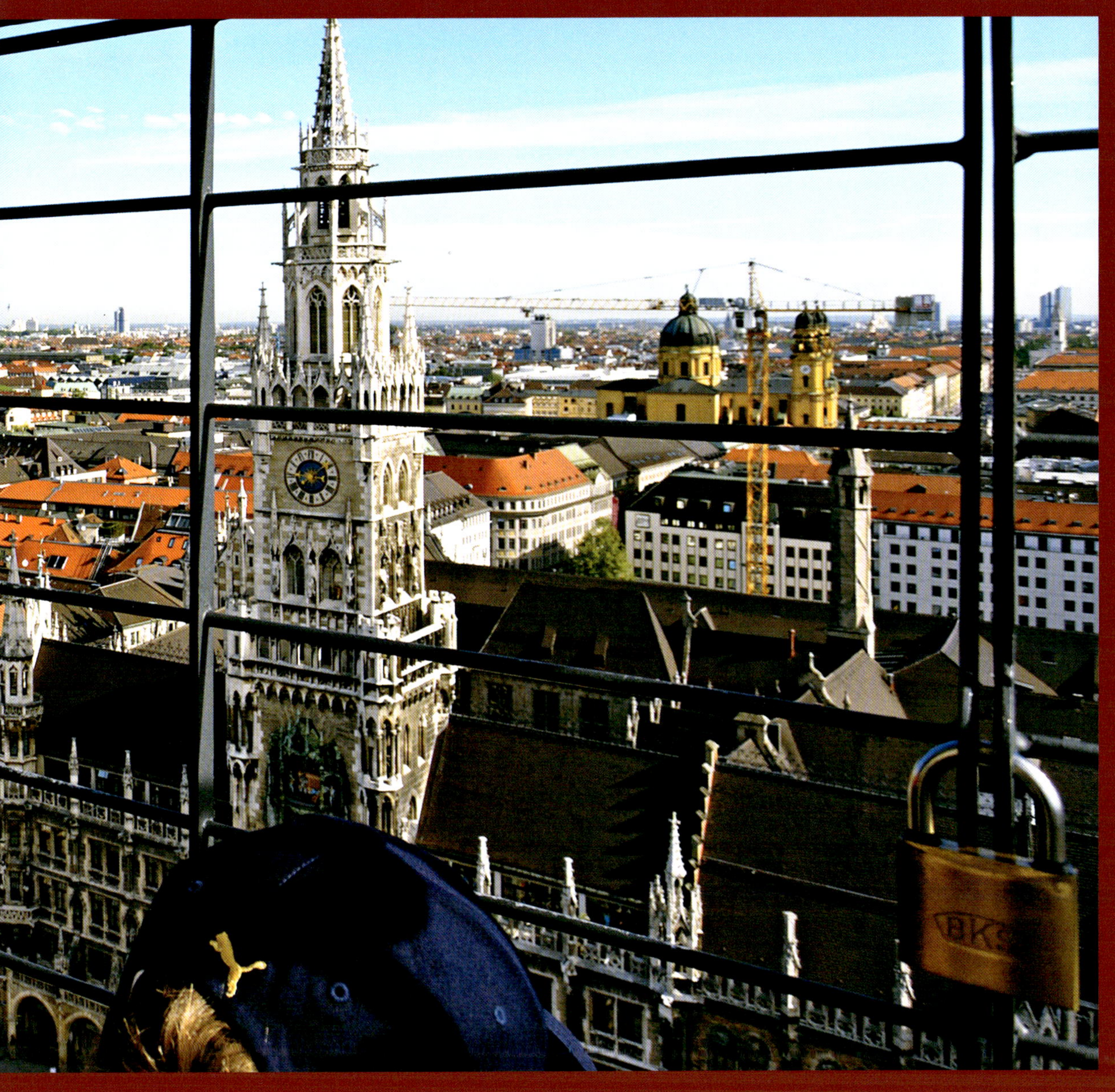

Page 28/29:
The Cuvilliés-Theater, one of the most famous buildings designed by François de Cuvilliés, was once situated on Max-Joseph-Platz where the Neues Residenztheater now stands. The splendid Rococo interior was removed in 1944 shortly before the Residenztheater was destroyed and installed at the residential palace from 1956 to 1958.

From the top of St Peter's you can 'spy' on locals and visitors going about their business on Marienplatz. The cage surrounded the viewing platform is an unsightly but necessary addition – and does little to impair the truly marvellous vistas of Munich and the surrounding area.

patron saint of Bavaria, and to give thanks for the fact that during the Thirty Years' War Munich had remained largely unscathed at the express command of the occupying king of Sweden.

When in 1854 another disaster threatened to strike, namely an outbreak of cholera, the city magistrate renamed Schrannenplatz Marienplatz, placing Munich under the official protection of the Mother of God. Since then the Mariensäule has become something of a place of spiritual refuge in the midst of the worldly madness of the inner city. Every Saturday sees the chanting of the rosary and processions also take place here. New Catholic archbishops are welcomed beneath the Mariensäule. Two of the square's most famous pilgrims were Pope John Paul II (in 1980) and his successor Benedict XVI in 2006.

Marienplatz is a good place from whence to embark on tours of the city. The first stop and a favourite motif is the Neues Rathaus on the long side of the square. Built between 1867 and 1909, the neo-Gothic edifice is the seat of the lord mayor of Munich, the council and the city administration. With its 400 rooms and lofty tower the new town hall was built as a symbol of bourgeois self-confidence – in mild defiance of the monarchy. The carillon on the tower still

Right:
The courtyard of the Residenz features a fountain dedicated to the Wittelsbachs from c. 1610, decorated with figures by Flemish sculptor Hubert Gerhard (~1550 – 1620). Initially conceived for a number of other projects, here they have found a common purpose.

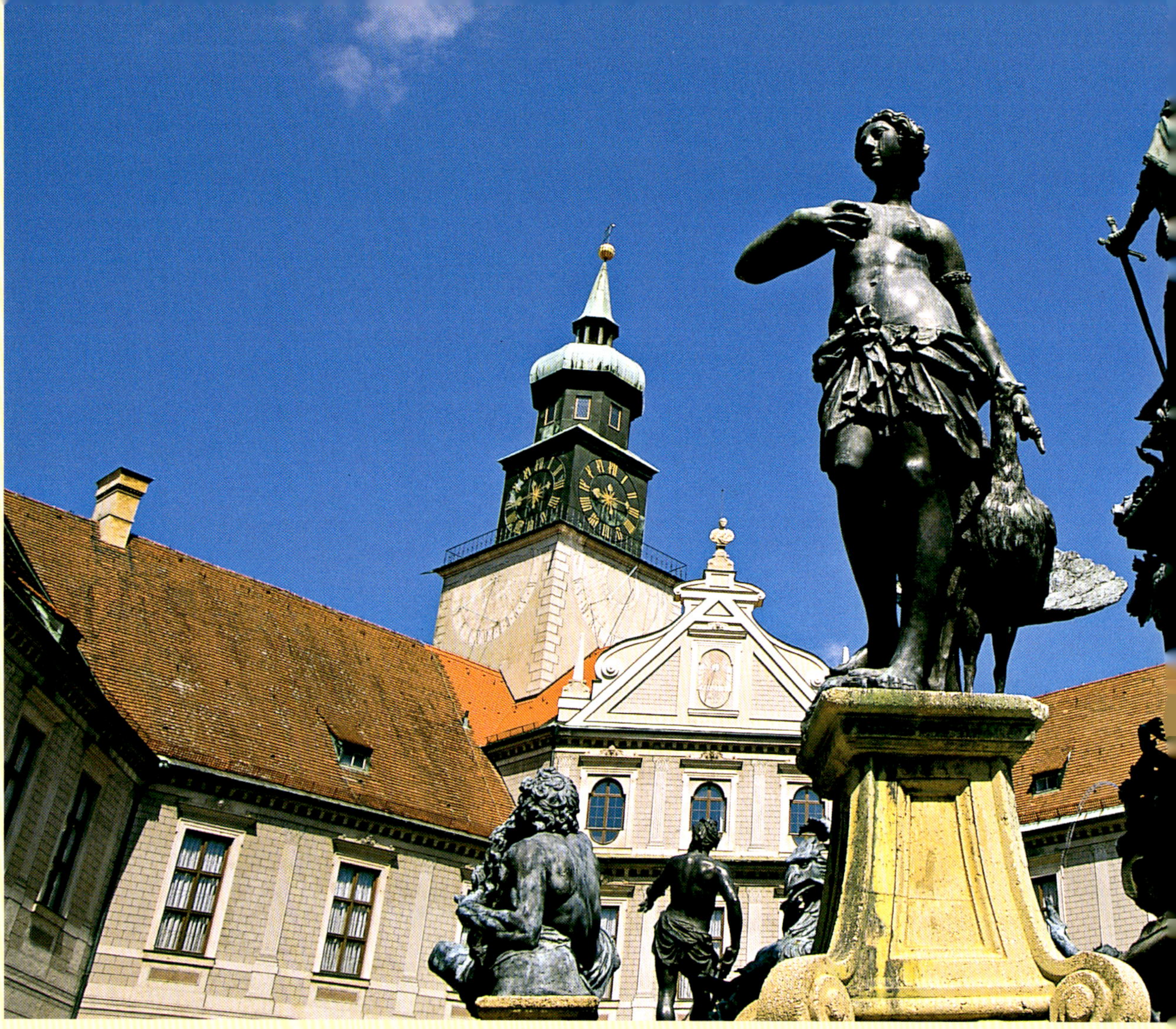

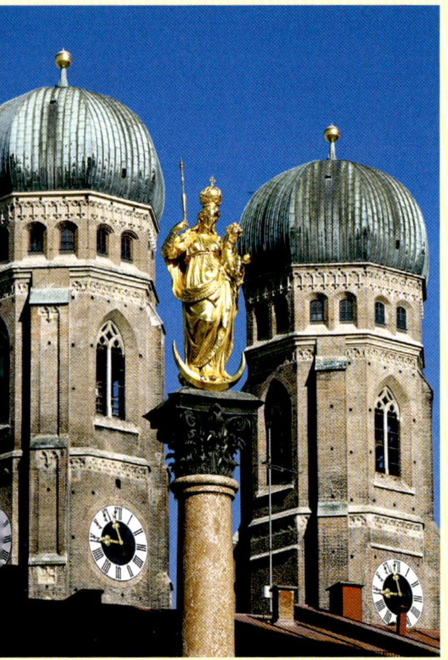

Above:
Patrona Bavariae, the patron saint of Bavaria flanked by the towers of the Frauenkirche. Legend has it that the twin spires differ in height by about a metre; they are in fact almost the same size, with the north tower 98.57 m (323.4 ft) above the ground and the south tower 98.45 m (323 ft) up.

captivates visitors big and small every lunchtime when 32 figures twiddle past those below in an enacted tournament and dance.

THE FRAUENKIRCHE, A MUNICH LANDMARK

Not far from the Rathaus is one of Munich's most famous landmarks, the Dom zu Unserer Lieben Frau or Frauenkirche for short, with its distinctive bulbous onion domes. Erected on the site of a Romanesque chapel dedicated to the Virgin Mary, the foundations of the late Gothic brick cathedral were laid in 1468. Visitors should leave enough time to take in the many works of art contained within this massive structure: its glass windows, paintings, statues and many masterly architectural details.

Munich has many buildings which have survived from the Gothic period. Remnants include the Isartor, Sendlinger Tor, Karlstor and Löwenturm on Rindermarkt, the gates and towers which once constituted part of the city defences. Further Gothic constructions are the Alter Hof, the Altes Rathaus with its ballroom and the arsenal, now part of the city museum.

If churches are your thing, then there's plenty to see in the centre of town. The Jesuit church of St Michael with the largest barrel vault after St Peter's in Rome is a product of the spirit of the Renaissance and is stylistically reminscent of Il Gesù, the mother church of the Society of Jesus in Rome. The Theatine church of St Kajetan with its enormous cupola also emulates a Roman model in that it was the first church north of the Alps to be built in the style of the Italian late baroque.

SOUTHERN GERMAN BAROQUE

Others who set standards in the baroque art of Southern Germany were the brothers Cosmas Damian (1686 –1739) and Egid Quirin Asam (1692 – 1750). Cosmas Damian was a painter and sculptor, Egid Quirin an architect, stucco artist and sculptor. The Asamkirche of St John

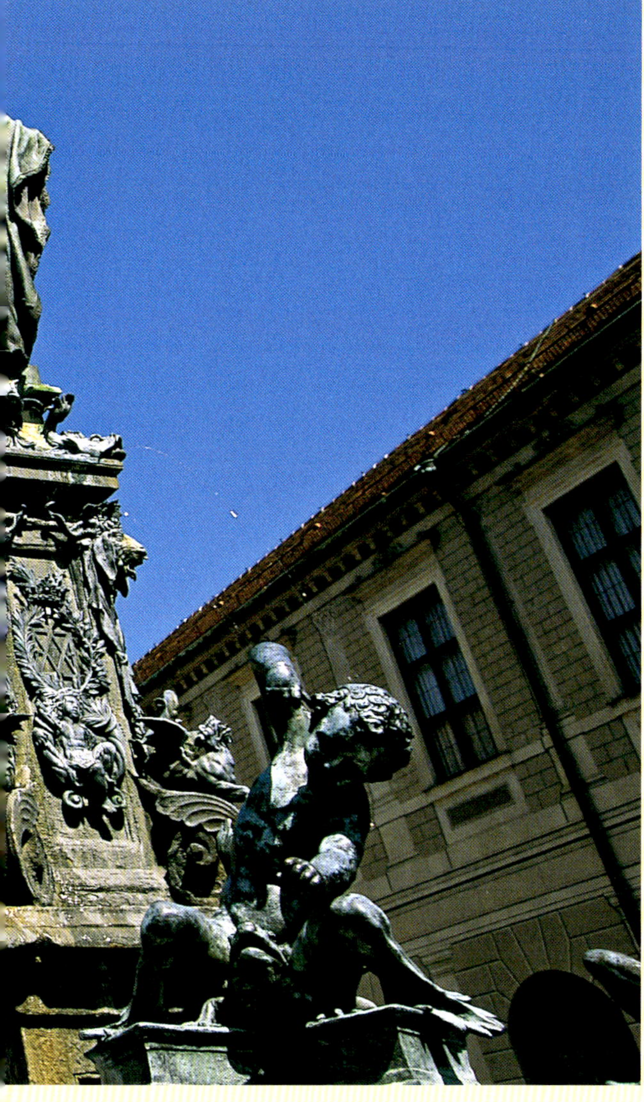

Nepomuk, next to Egid Quirin's house on Sendlinger Straße, represents the absolute pinnacle of their careers. This gem was squeezed into a tiny space measuring just 22 by eight metres (72 by 25 feet), erected in 1734 as their private place of worship. Another religious site well worth seeing is the Jüdisches Zentrum on Jakobsplatz with its synagogue, museum and kosher restaurant.

One of the cultural highlights of the city is the Residenz. The largest city palace in Germany was the residential and administrative headquarters of Bavaria's dukes, electors and kings from 1508 to 1918. A Gothic moated castle (the Neuveste or new fortress) existed here as early as 1385. This was gradually extended down the centuries to produce the prestigious abode you now see before you, surrounded by courtyards and gardens spreading out across the city.

State rooms and art collections from the Renaissance, baroque, Rococo and neoclassical periods bear witness to the artistic sympathies and political aspirations of the house of Wittelsbach. Together with the sites run by the Bayerische Schlösserverwaltung (the Residenz museum, treasury, Cuvilliés Theatre and Hofkirche) and various other cultural institutions the Residenz is one of the largest museum complexes in Bavaria. If you're tired out after all your sightseeing, walking and shopping in Munich, respite is on hand in the Hofgarten and many other public parks dotted around the city, in traditional pubs and idyllic beer gardens. British writer Katherine Mansfield (1888–1923) once urged a friend: "You must travel to Munich. You have not seen Germany if you have not been to Munich." And she was right.

Below:
The church of St John Nepomuk, fashioned by brothers Cosmas Damian and Egid Quirin Asam between 1733 and 1746, is one of the most significant products of the Southern German late baroque. The facade is tucked almost apologetically into a row of houses on Sendlinger Straße.

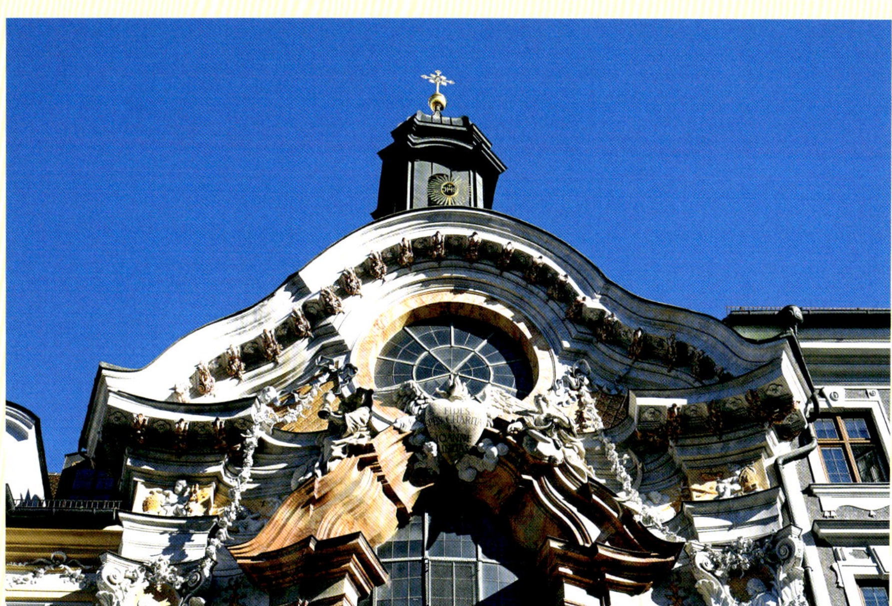

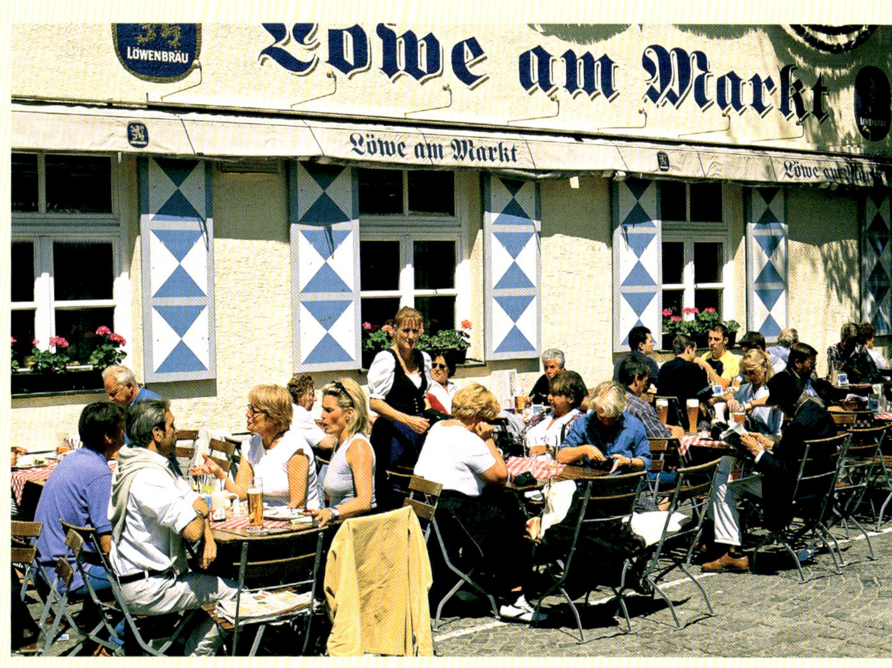

Above:
This traditional pub is on the Viktualienmarkt on Dreifaltigkeitsplatz. Here you can enjoy a hearty meal while watching the world go by on the colourful market, its main business still the sale of food as the name "victuals market" clearly indicates.

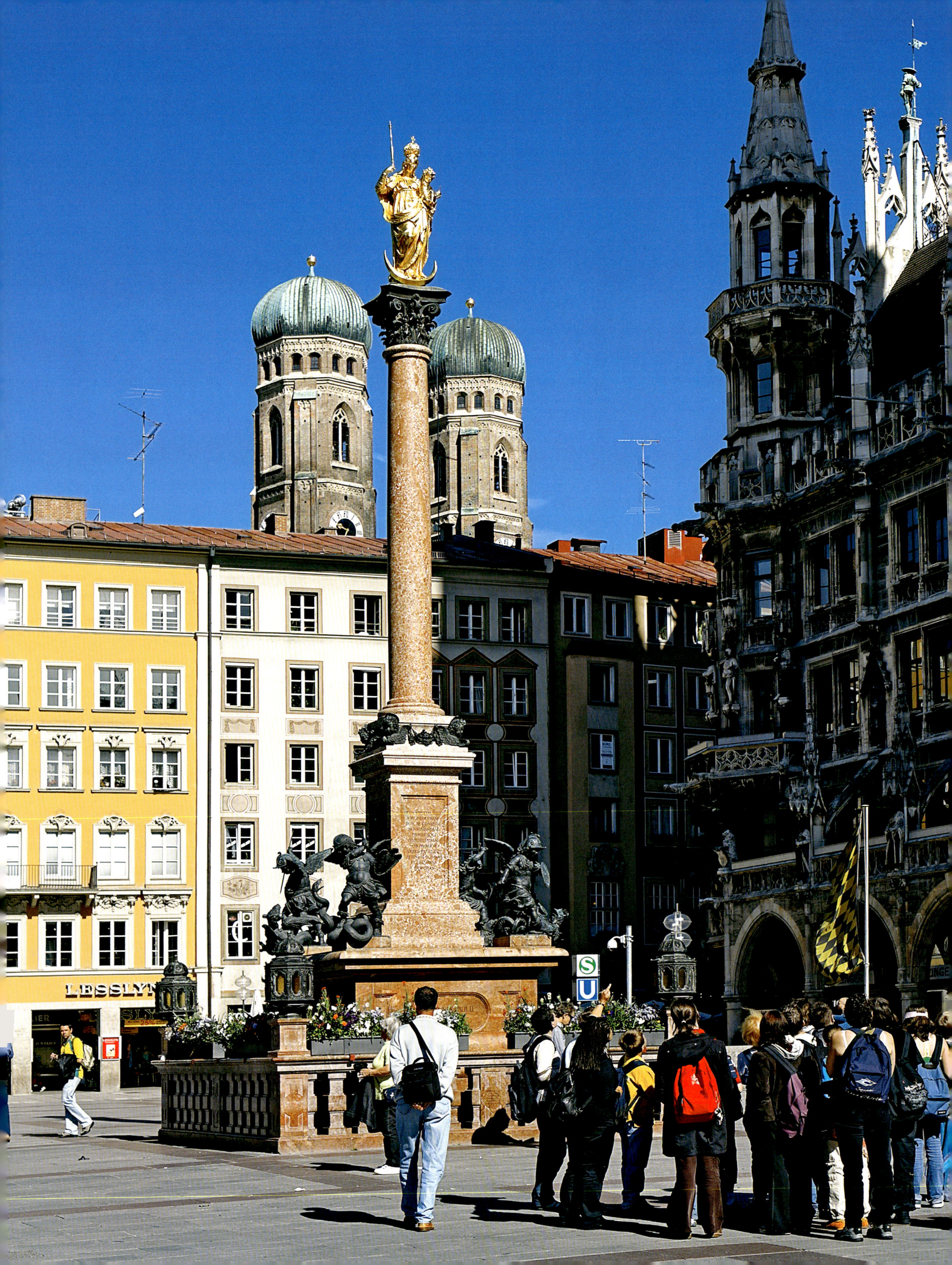

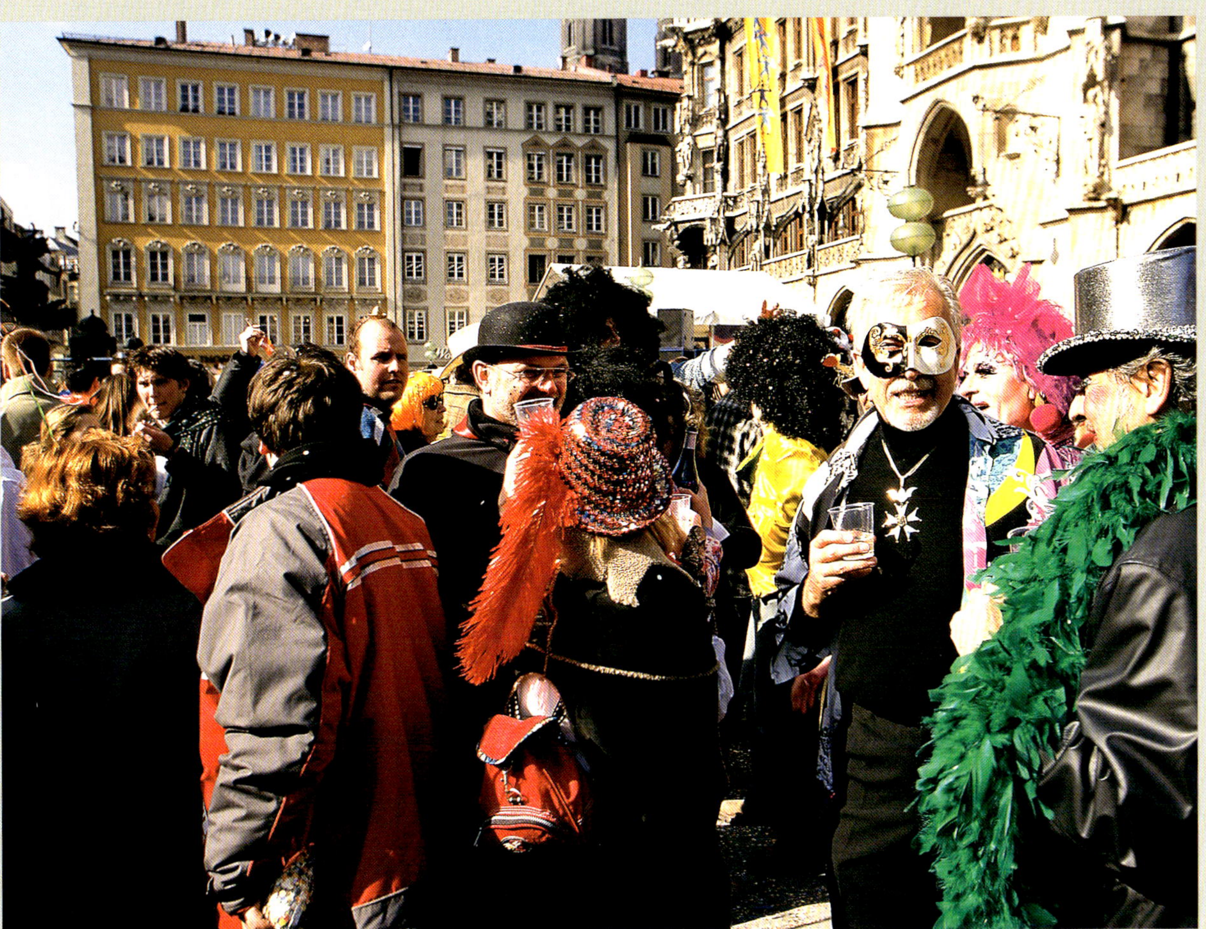

Left page:
The pillar of the Madonna on Marienplatz was donated and unveiled in 1638 by Elector Maximilian I. The column is made of red marble; the bronze and gilt statue of the Mother of God is probably by Hubert Gerhard.

Carnival in Munich. Like on the Rhine the 'silly season' is tantamount to one huge party in Munich with 700 or so events on the calender – from posh gala balls to the rustic dance of the market sellers on the Viktualienmarkt on Shrove Tuesday.

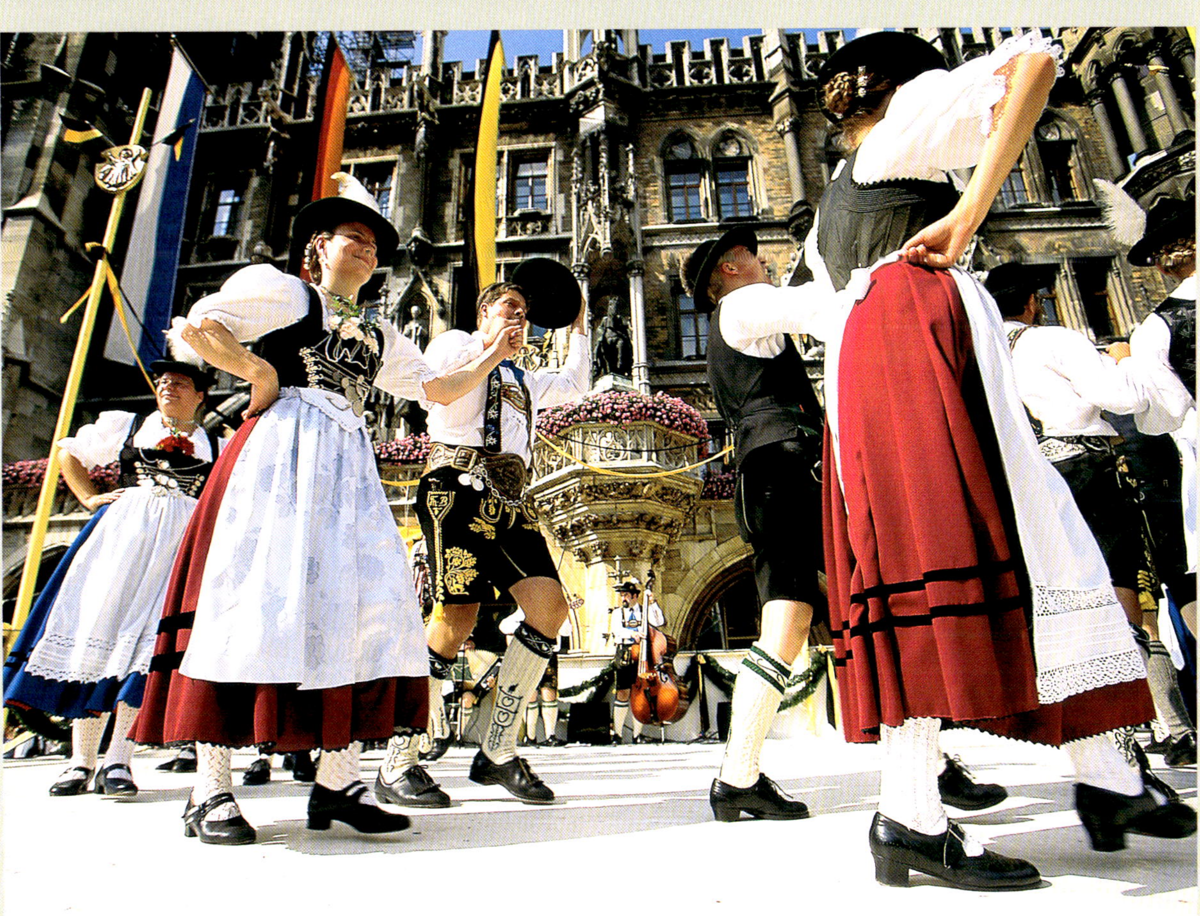

Each year in the middle of June the founding of the city of Munich is suitably celebrated by a mixed programme of events staged on the streets between Marienplatz and Odeonsplatz. Folk groups, cabaret artists, opera, rock and pop, an artisan's village and intrepid fire eaters all contribute to the general sense of occasion.

Right page:
The tower of the Altes Rathaus from 1493 was bulldozed in 1940 to enable tanks to pass. It was rebuilt true to its original design in 1971–1974.

Right:
The Altes Rathaus marks the east end of Marienplatz. In c. 1480 sculptor Erasmus Grasser (1450–1518) made these famous wooden figurines for its ballroom. His Morisco or Moorish Dancers allude to a dance which was very popular in Southern Germany in c. 1500.

Far right:
Outside the Altes Rathaus stands a present from Munich's twin town of Verona: a statue of Shakespeare's Juliet, a rose threaded through her elbow by a romantic admirer.

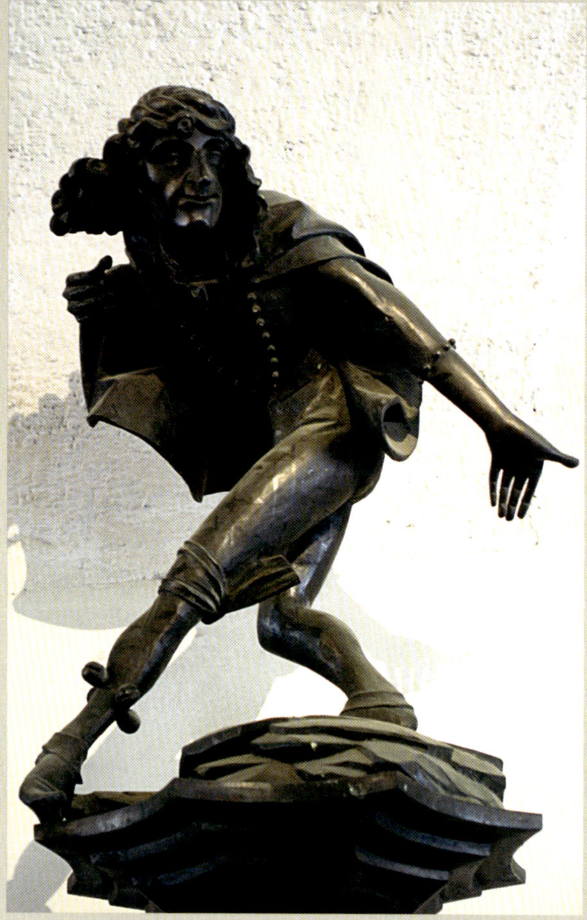

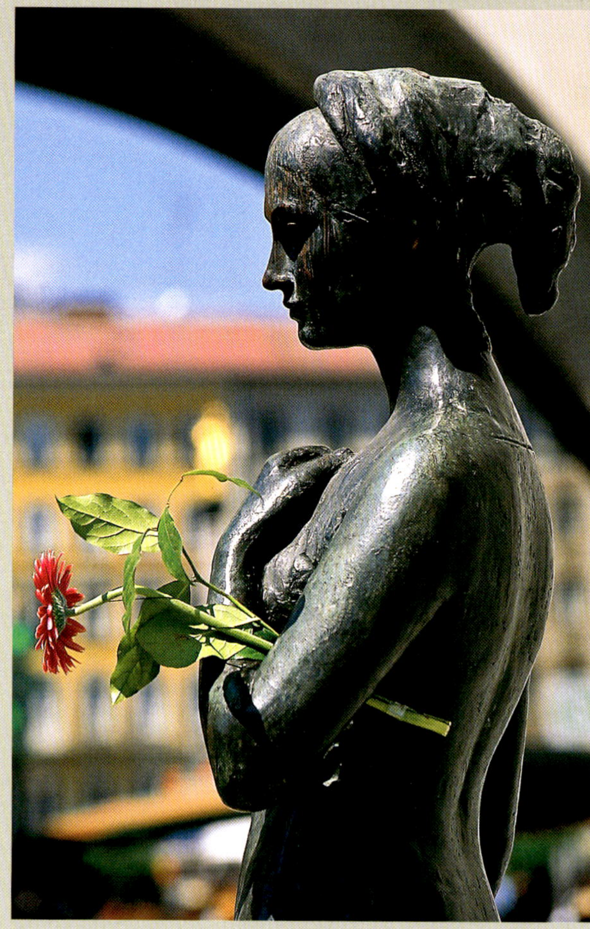

The tower of the old town hall houses a toy museum opened by Czech writer and illustrator Ivan Steiger. Exhibits from Europe and America are spread over four storeys.

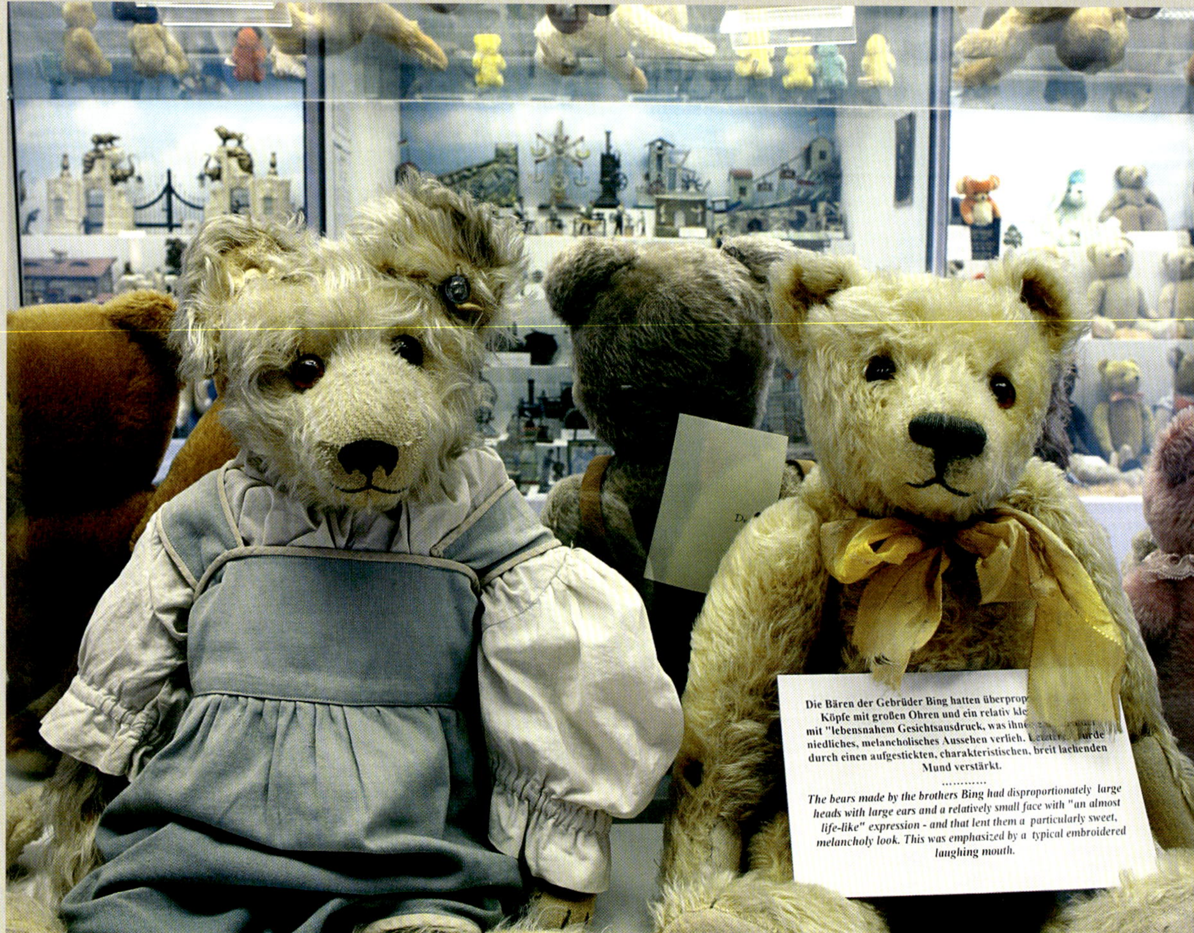

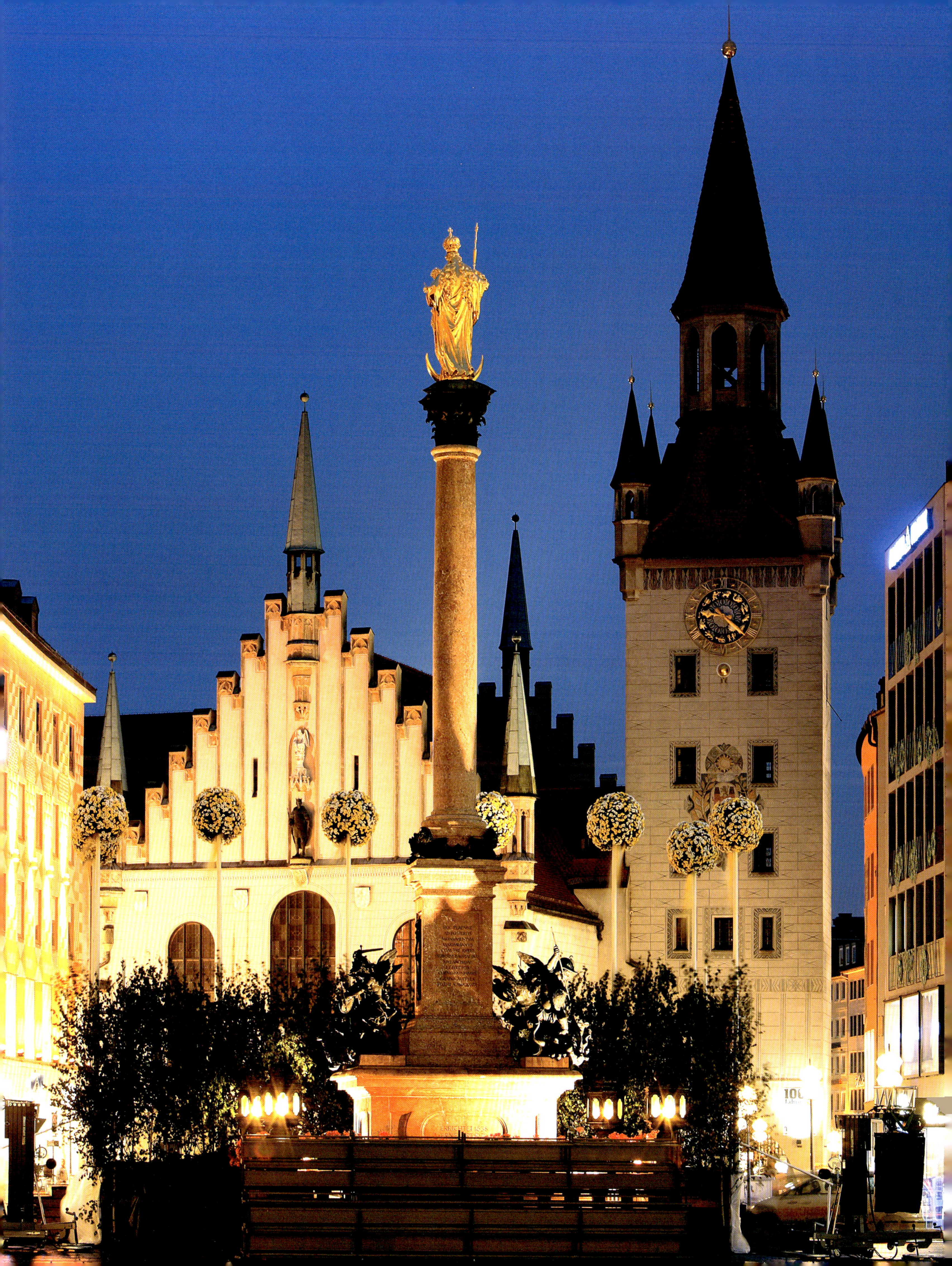

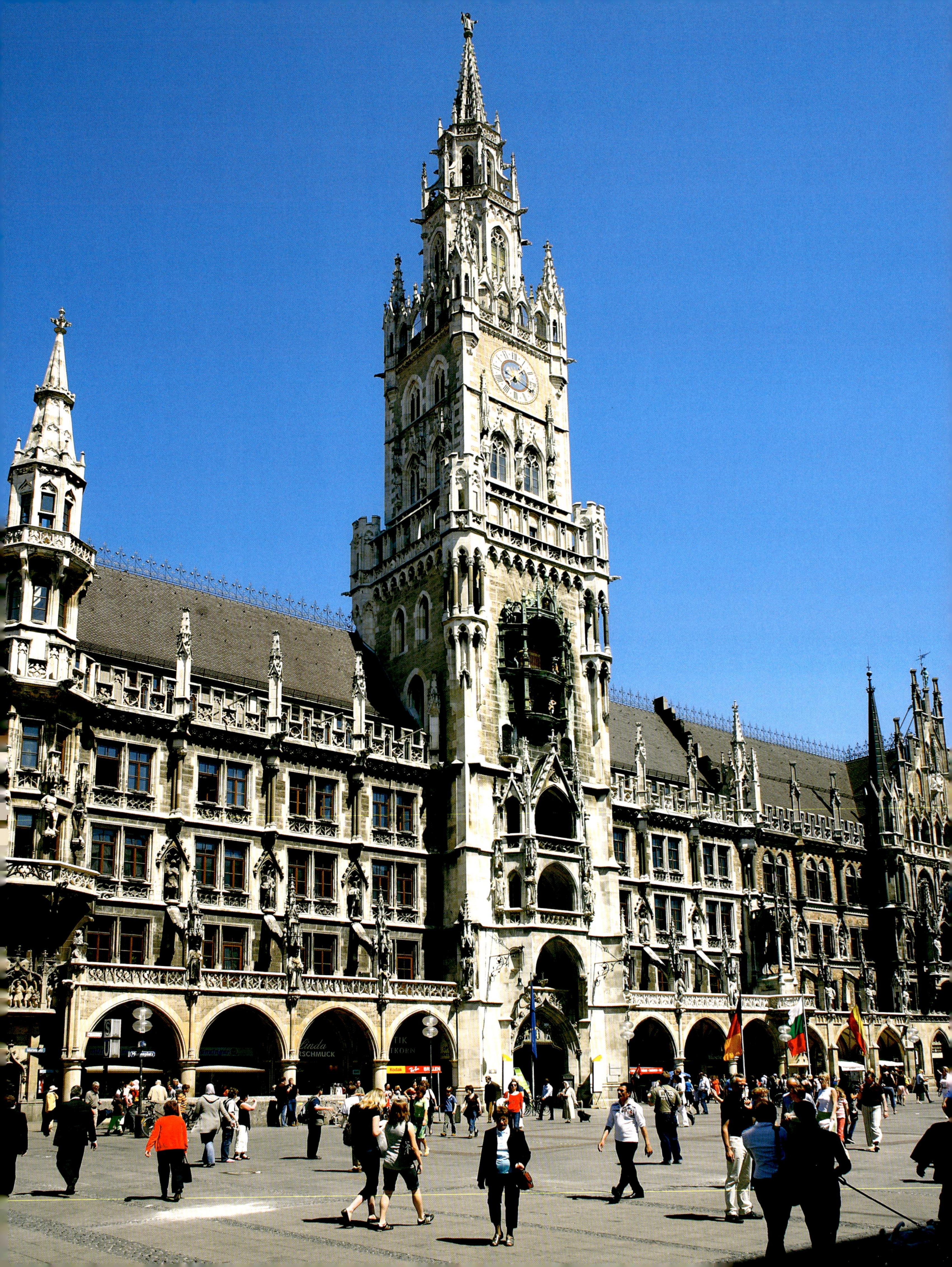

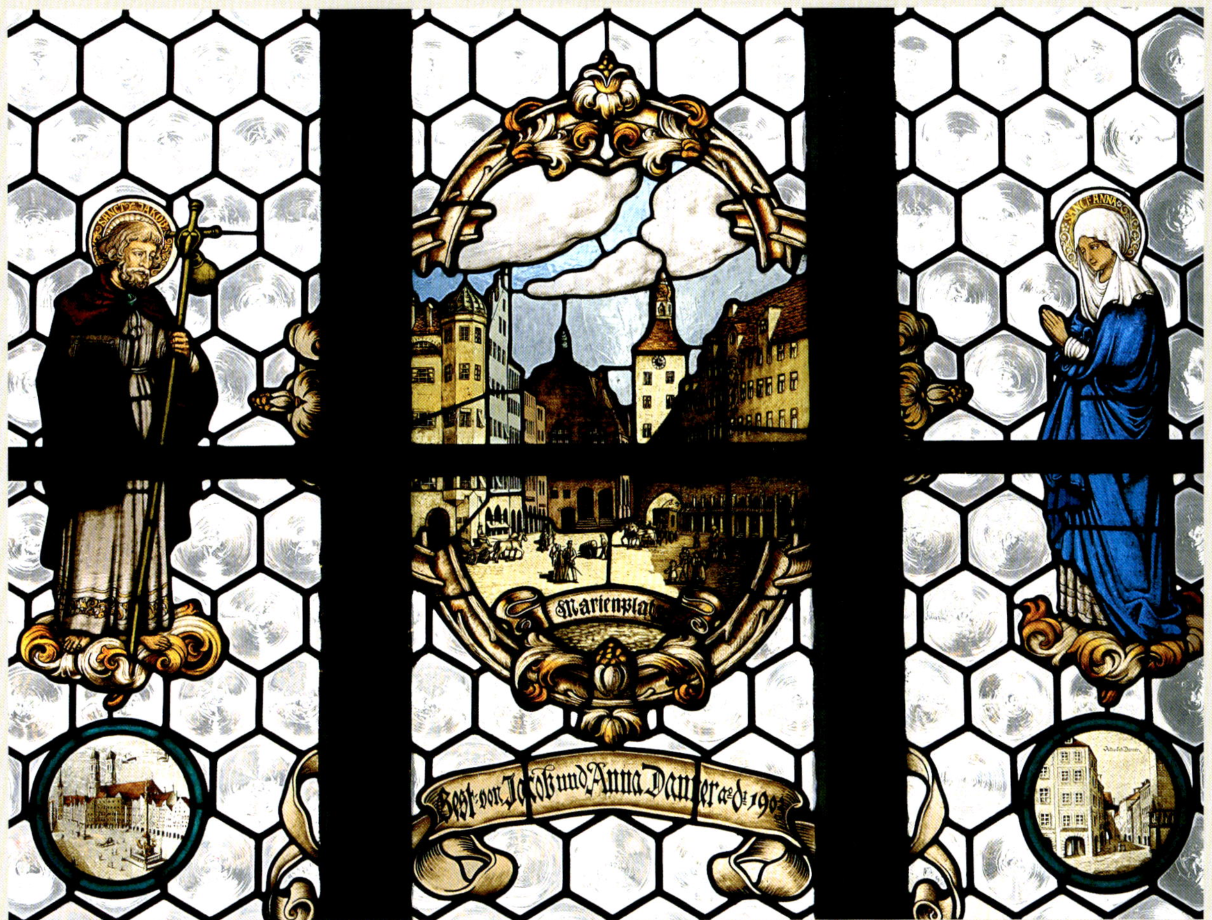

Left page:
The neo-Gothic Neues Rathaus was erected between 1867 and 1909 by German-Austrian architect Georg von Hauberrisser. He modelled his creation on the town halls in Brussels and Vienna.

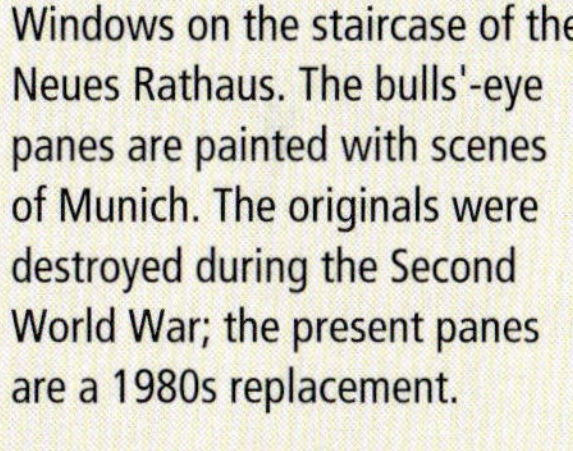

Windows on the staircase of the Neues Rathaus. The bulls'-eye panes are painted with scenes of Munich. The originals were destroyed during the Second World War; the present panes are a 1980s replacement.

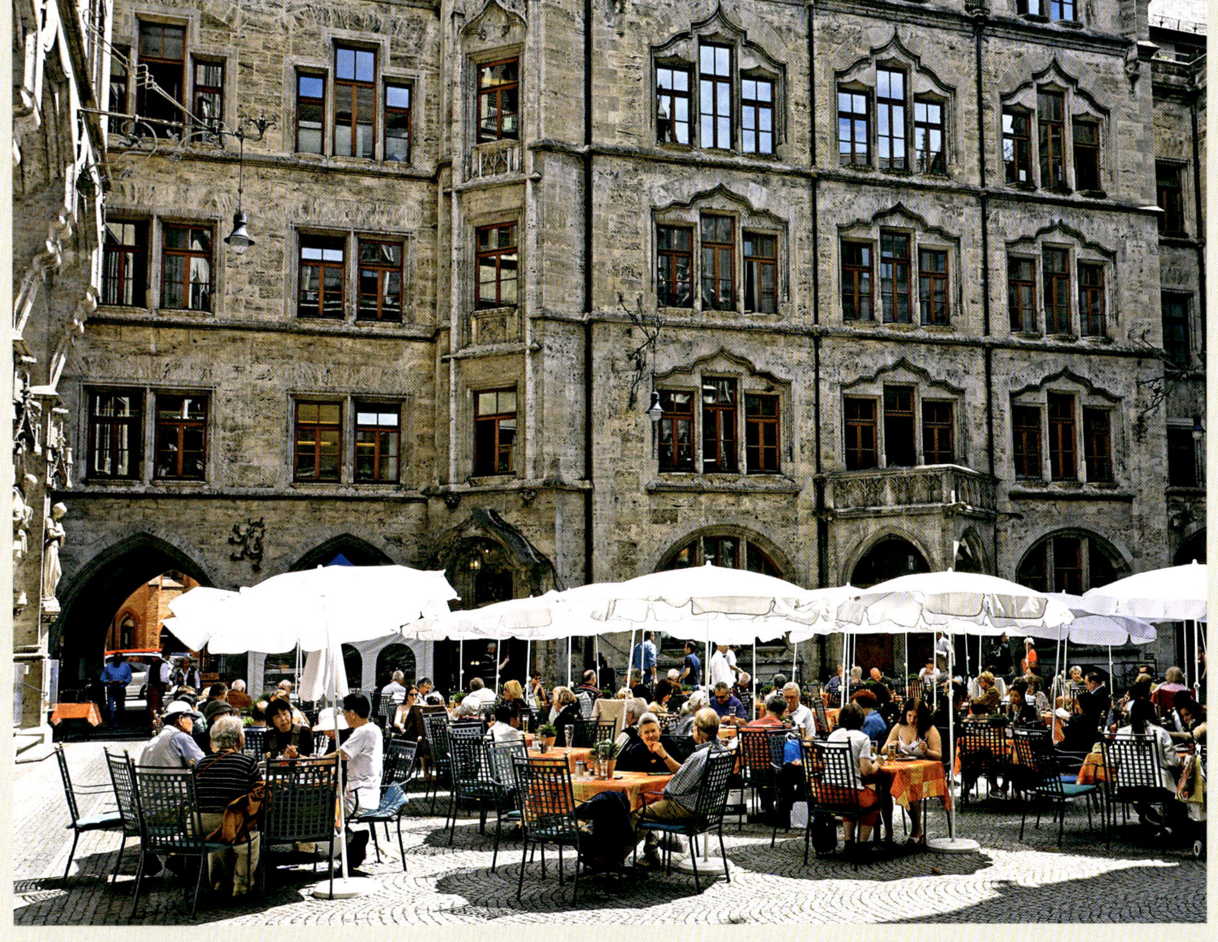

The huge complex has no less than six courtyards. In summer the Ratskeller operates a pavement café here on the Prunkhof.

Right:
This colossal canvas entitled Allegorie Monachia or Allegory to Munich was painted for the great chamber by Carl Theodor von Piloty (1826–1886) and completed in 1879. 15.3 x 4.6 m (50.2 x 15.09 ft) in size, it's the biggest painting in Bavaria and was painstakingly restored just a few years ago.

Below:
View of the second floor and staircase of the Neues Rathaus. This is now the headquarters of the city mayor, currently genuine Münchner Christian Ude who has been in office since 1993.

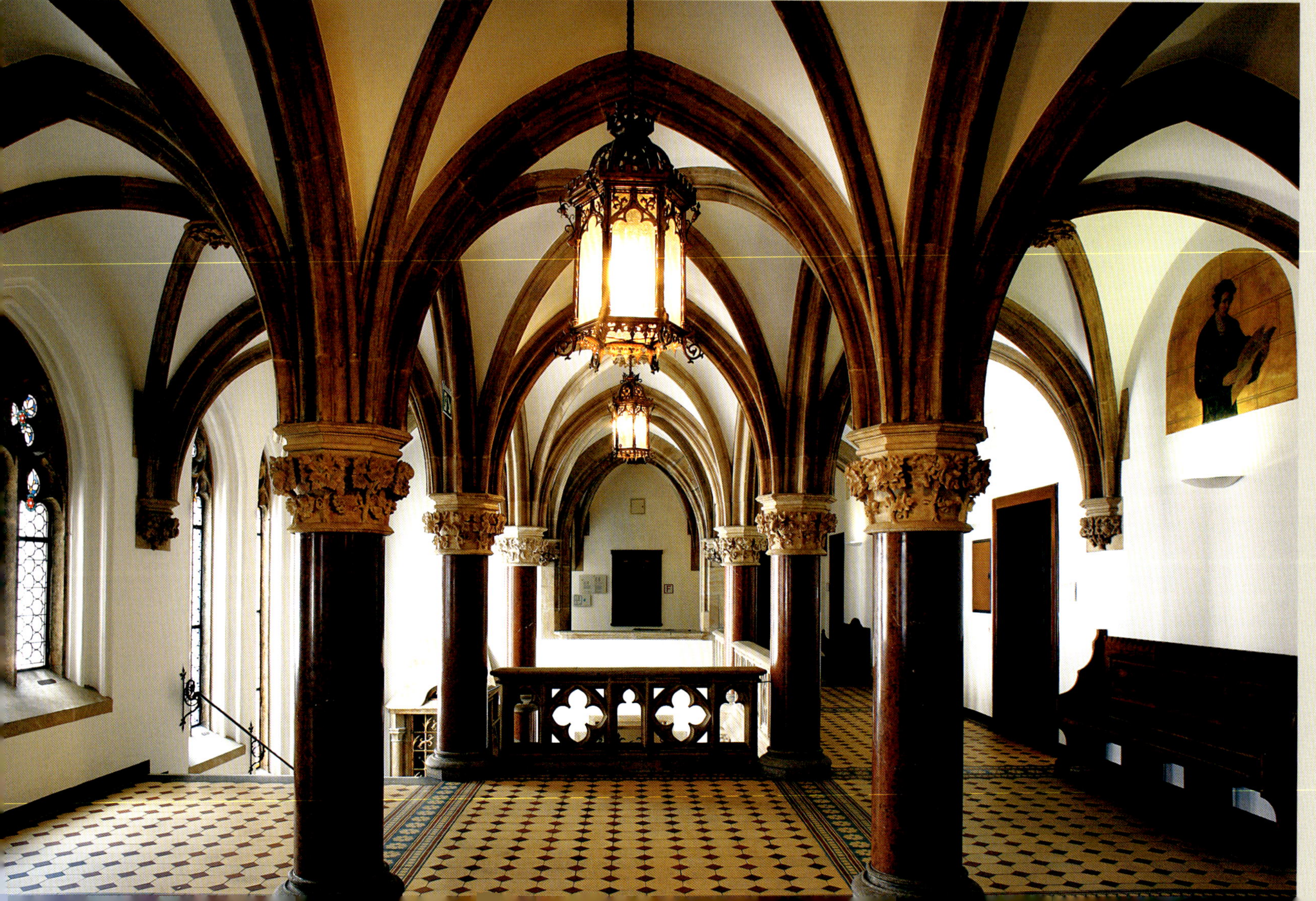

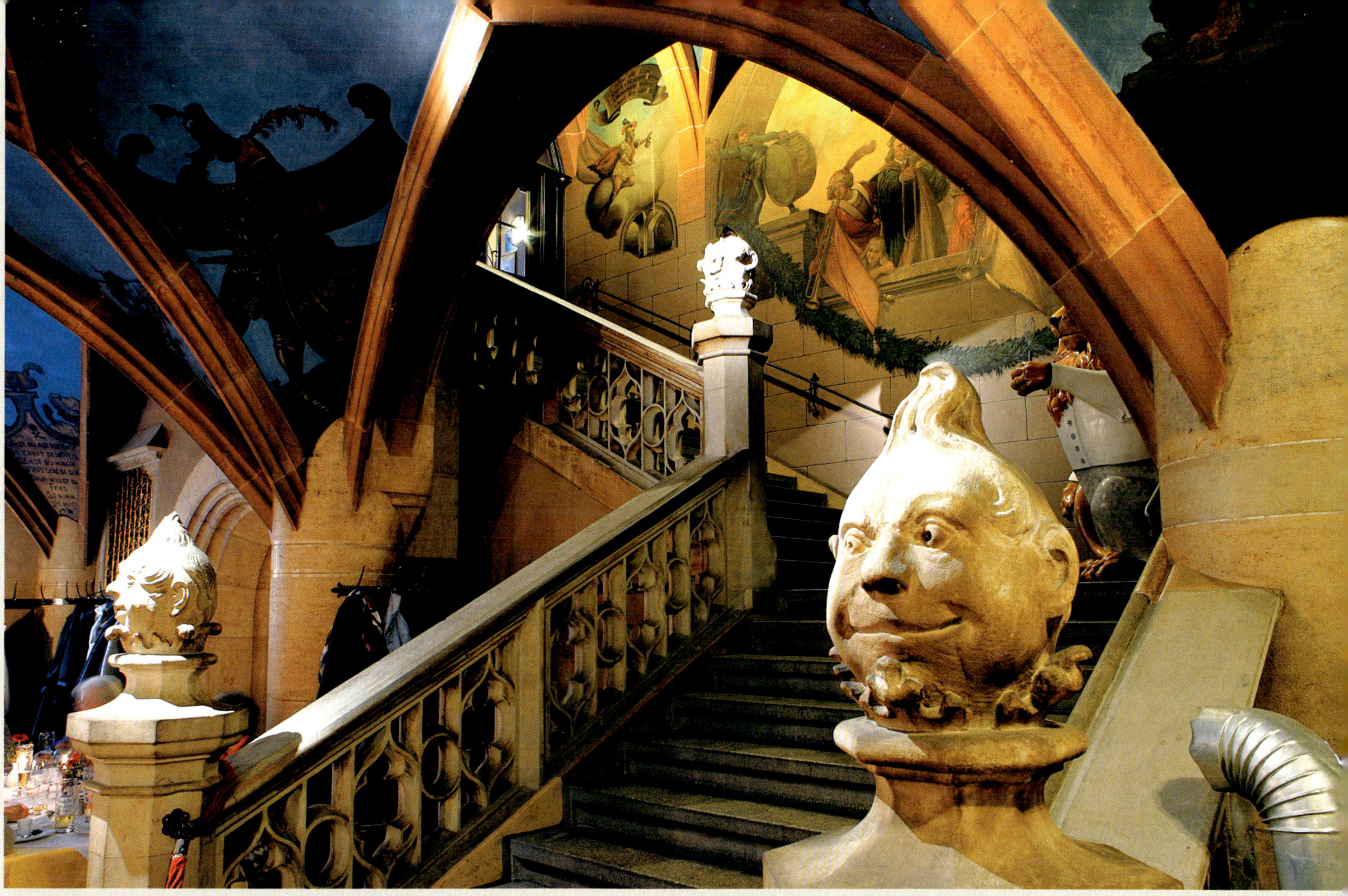

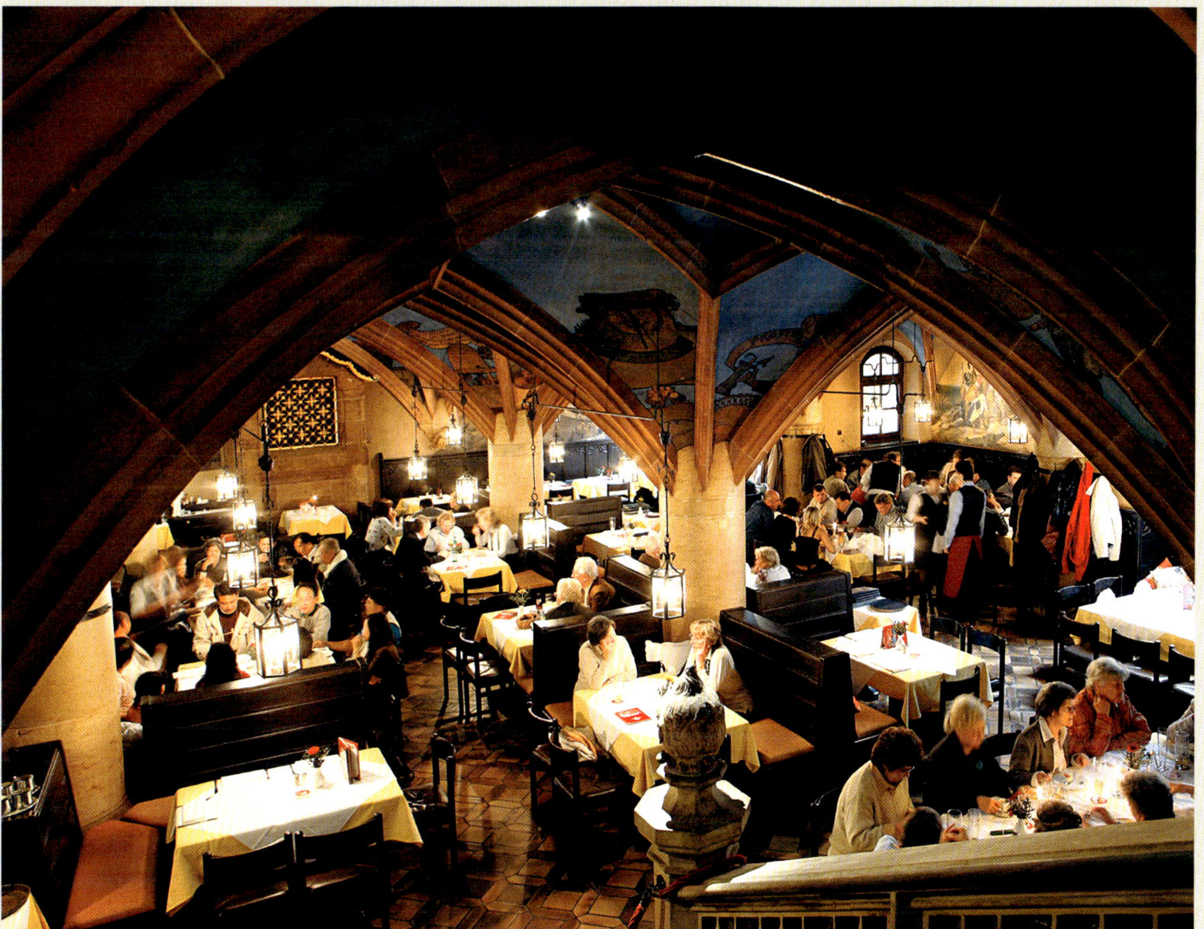

Above:
The Ratskeller restaurant in the Neues Rathaus serves specialities from throughout the region. In keeping with the fads of the day architect Hauberrisser designed the interior in the style of 16th-century Gothic. Opened on August 1, 1874, the establishment itself is now also historic.

Left:
The vaults of the Ratskeller are adorned with humorous paintings executed by historical painters from Bavaria which tell of the history of Munich and of the consumption of alcoholic beverages ...

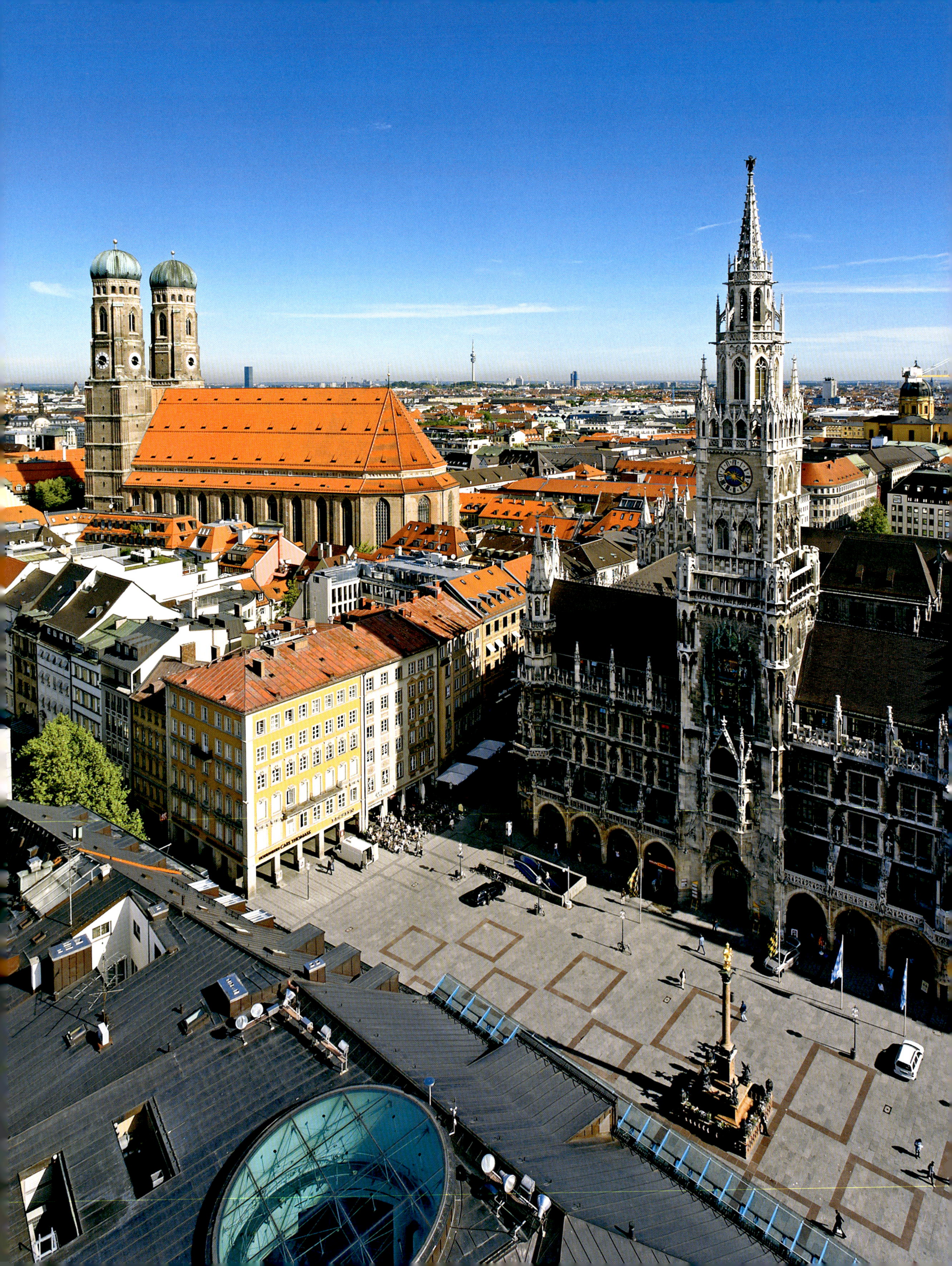

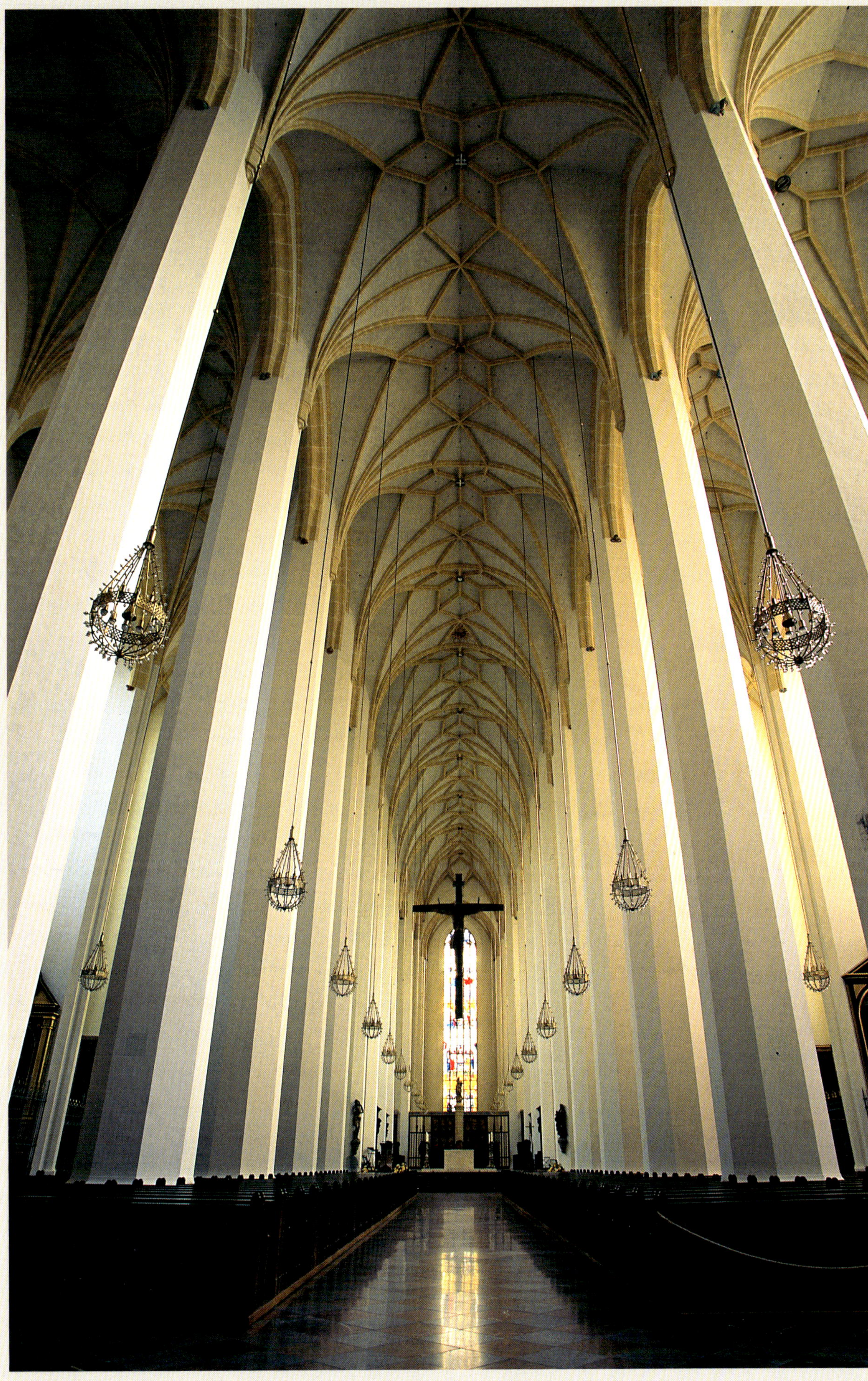

Left page:
Since the founding of Munich by Henry the Lion Marienplatz has formed the centre of town. Pedestrianised in 1972, its cheerful hustle and bustle is echoed deep beneath the surface on Marienplatz underground station, one of the busiest junctions in the city.

Left:
View of the nave of the Frauenkirche. Twenty-two octagonal pillars create transparent walls of light between the nave and aisles.

Right page:
Next to his house on Sendlinger Straße Egid Quirin Asam built a private church together with his brother Cosmas Damian and dedicated it to St John Nepomuk. This jewel of the late baroque is squeezed into a tiny space measuring just 8 by 22 m (26 by 72 ft).

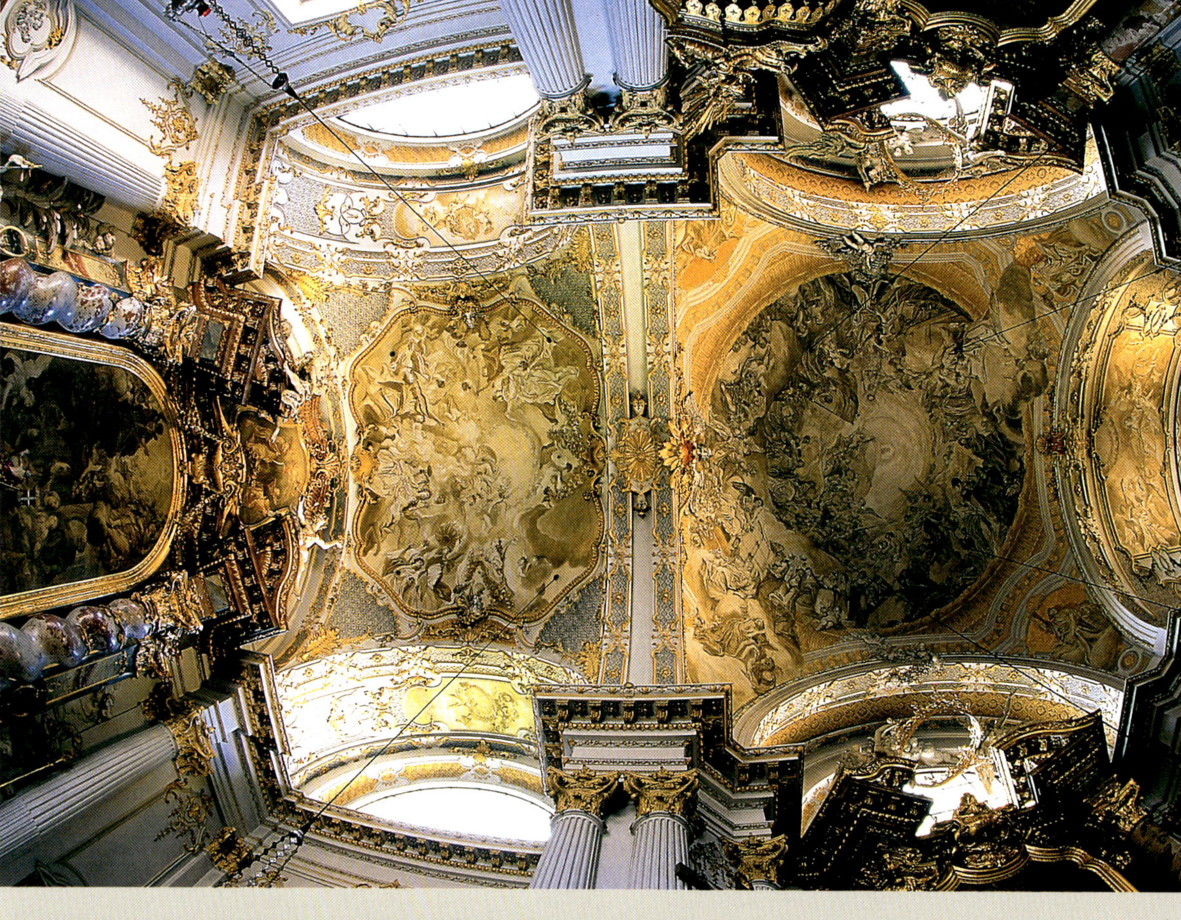

The collegiate church of St Anna on Altheimer Eck was built between 1733 and 1735. After the air raids of the last war only the outer walls were left standing. All that remained of the frescoes on the roof were a few black and white photographs, prompting restorers to avoid the use of colour in their 1980s reconstruction of the ceiling.

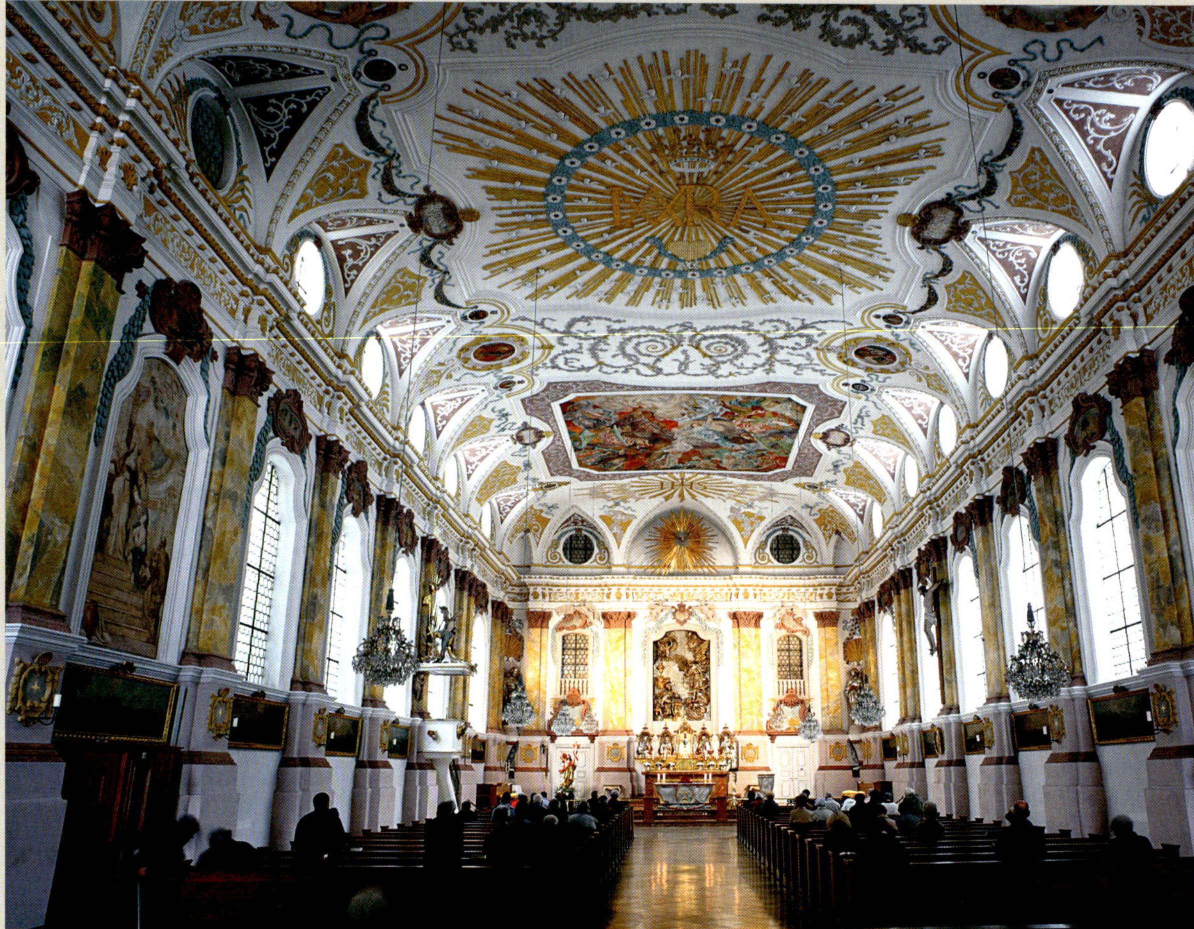

The Bürgersaal on Neuhauser Straße 14, unofficially known as the Bürgersaalkirche church, was built from plans by Giovanni Antonio Viscardi in 1709/10. Resistance fighter Father Rupert Mayer was buried here.

Page 46/47:
The Jesuit church of St Michael's on Neuhauser Straße 6 is dedicated to Archangel Michael. This, the first Renaissance church north of the Alps, was built between 1583 and 1597 in emulation of Il Gesù, the mother church of the Society of Jesus in Rome.

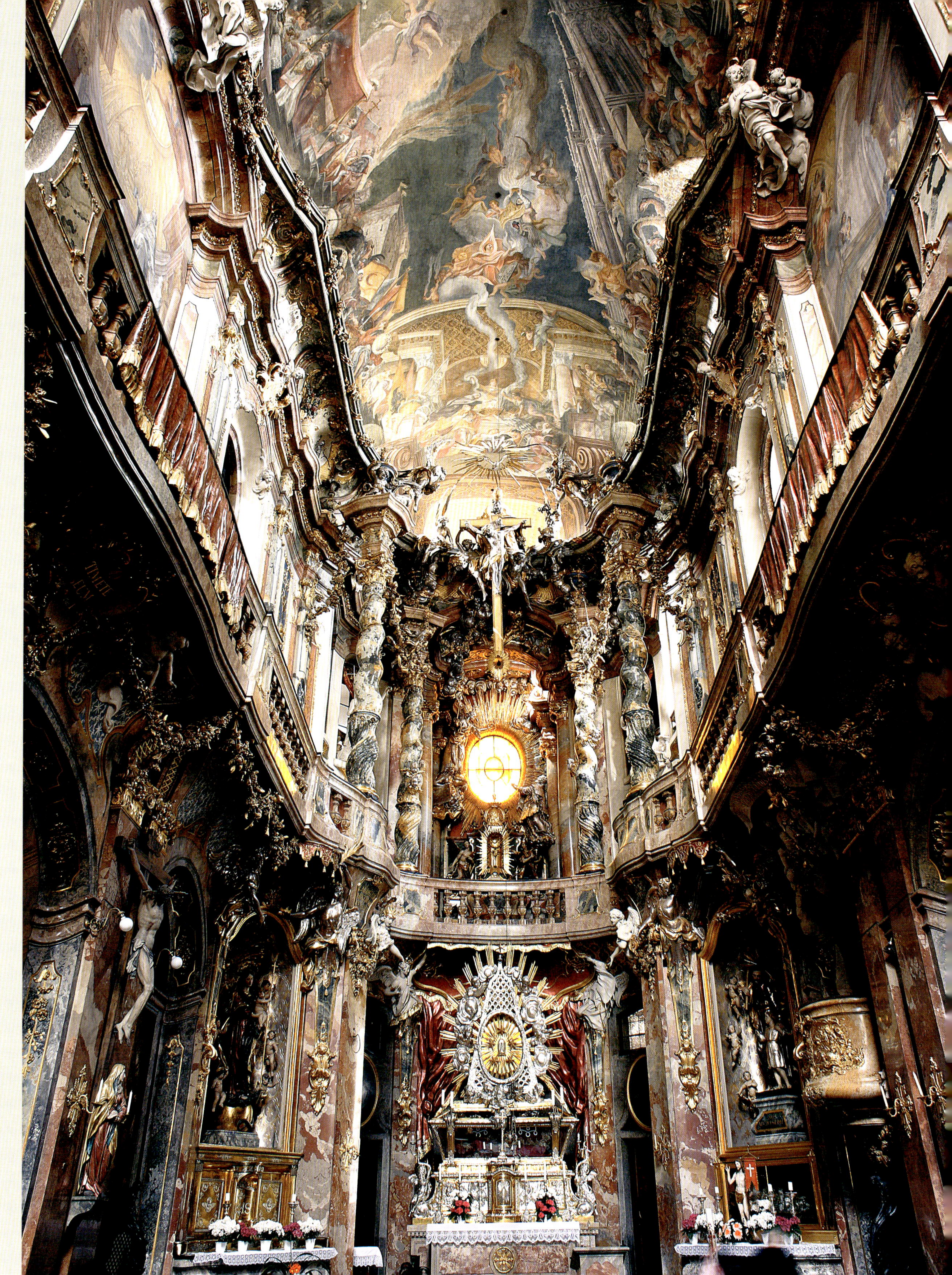

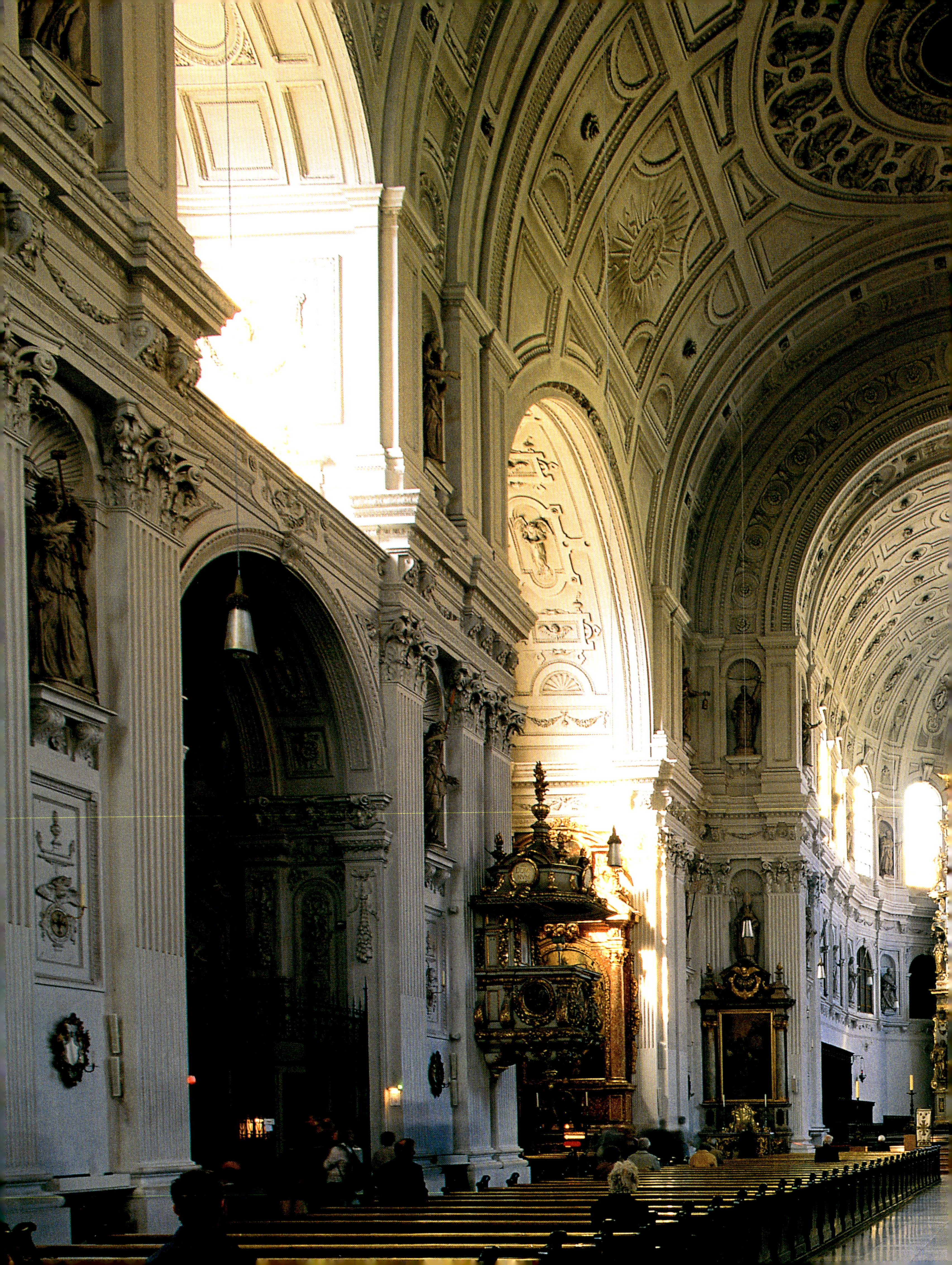

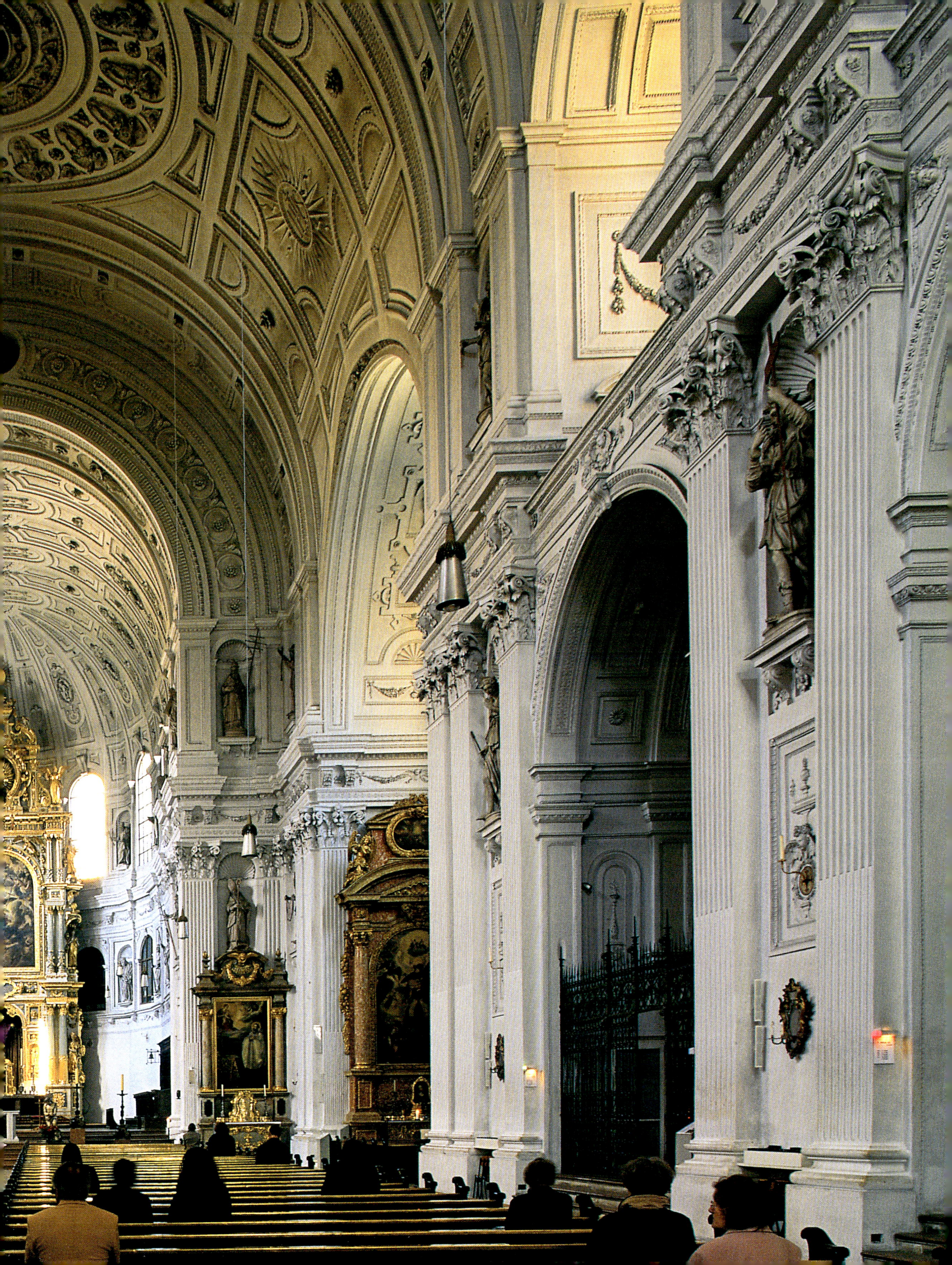

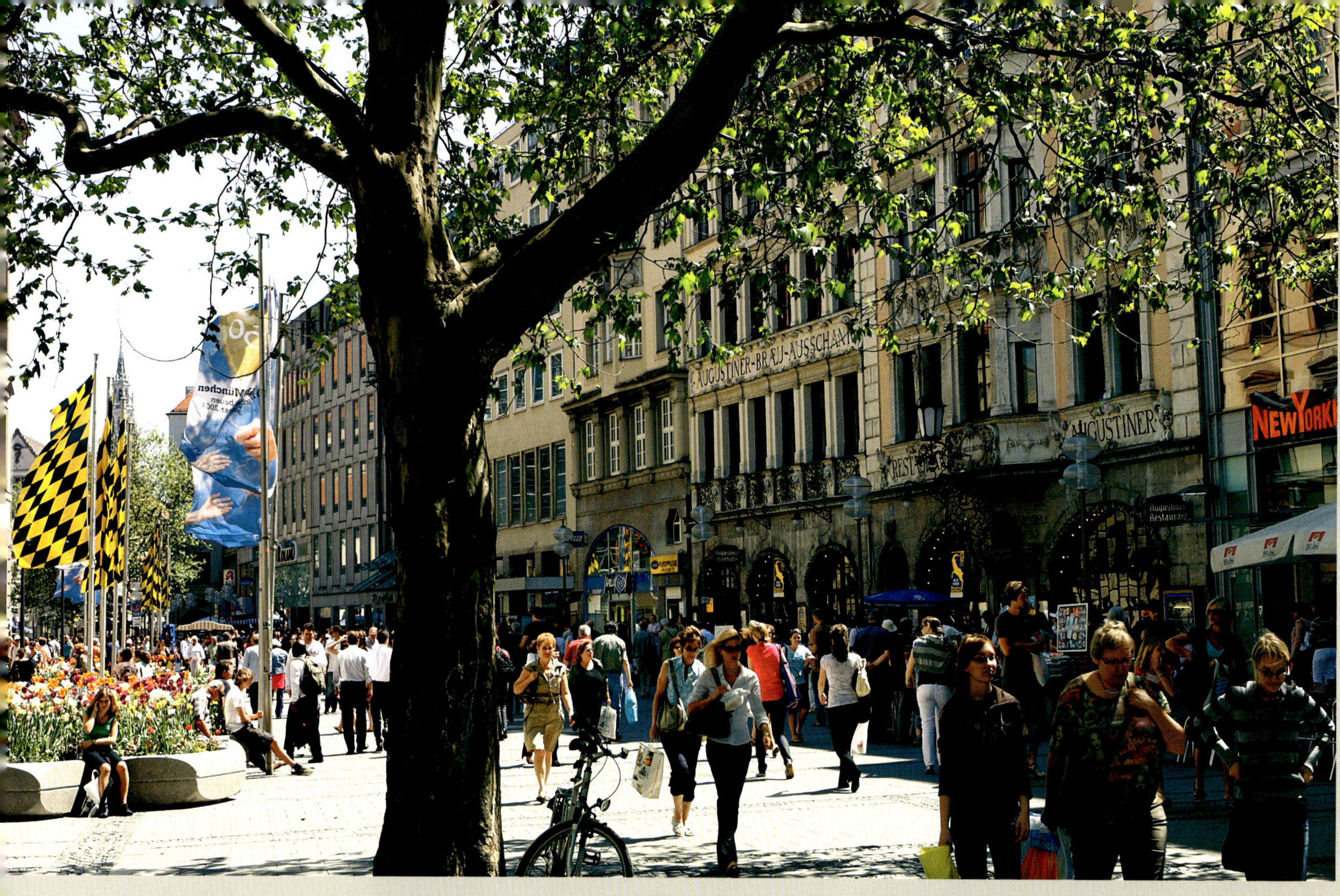

Above:
The busy pedestrianised Kaufingerstraße/Neuhauser Straße, Munich's main street of shops running from Marienplatz to the Karlstor.

Right:
At the Karlstor you come across the Brunnenbuberl, the naked cherub sculpted by Matthias Gasteiger of Munich (1871–1934) in 1895. None other than Prince Regent Luitpold himself is said to have demanded that the boy's modesty be covered by a fig leaf – a plea the artist ignored.

Far right:
The Richard-Strauss-Brunnen on Neuhauser Straße 8 is by sculptor Hans Wimmer (1907–1992) and features motifs from the opera Salome by Richard Strauss who was born in Munich in 1964.

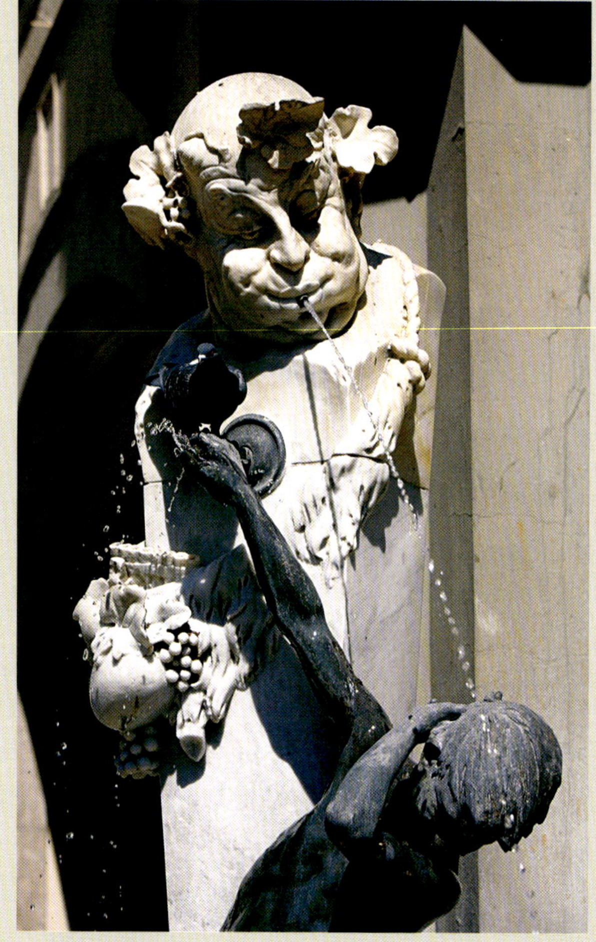

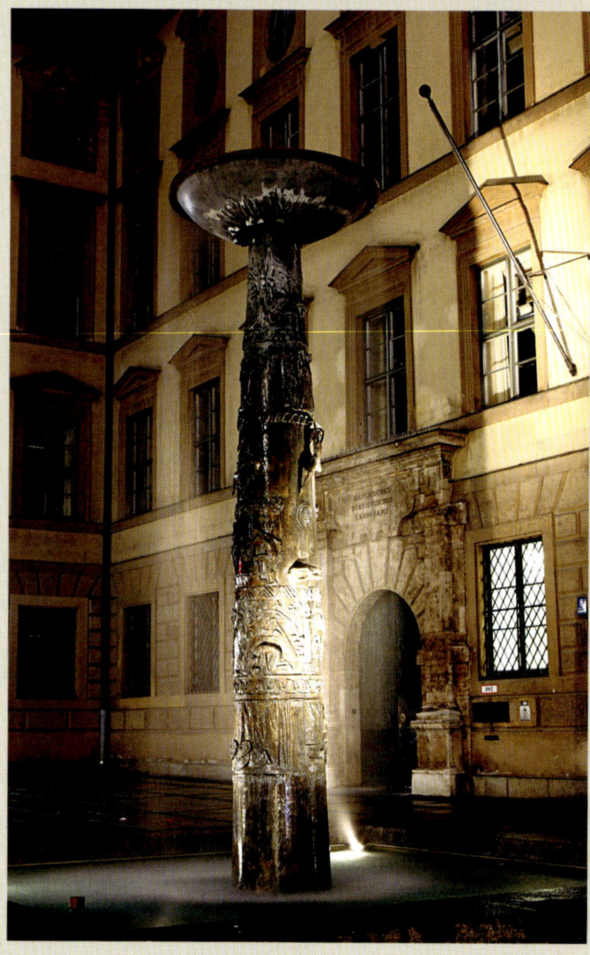

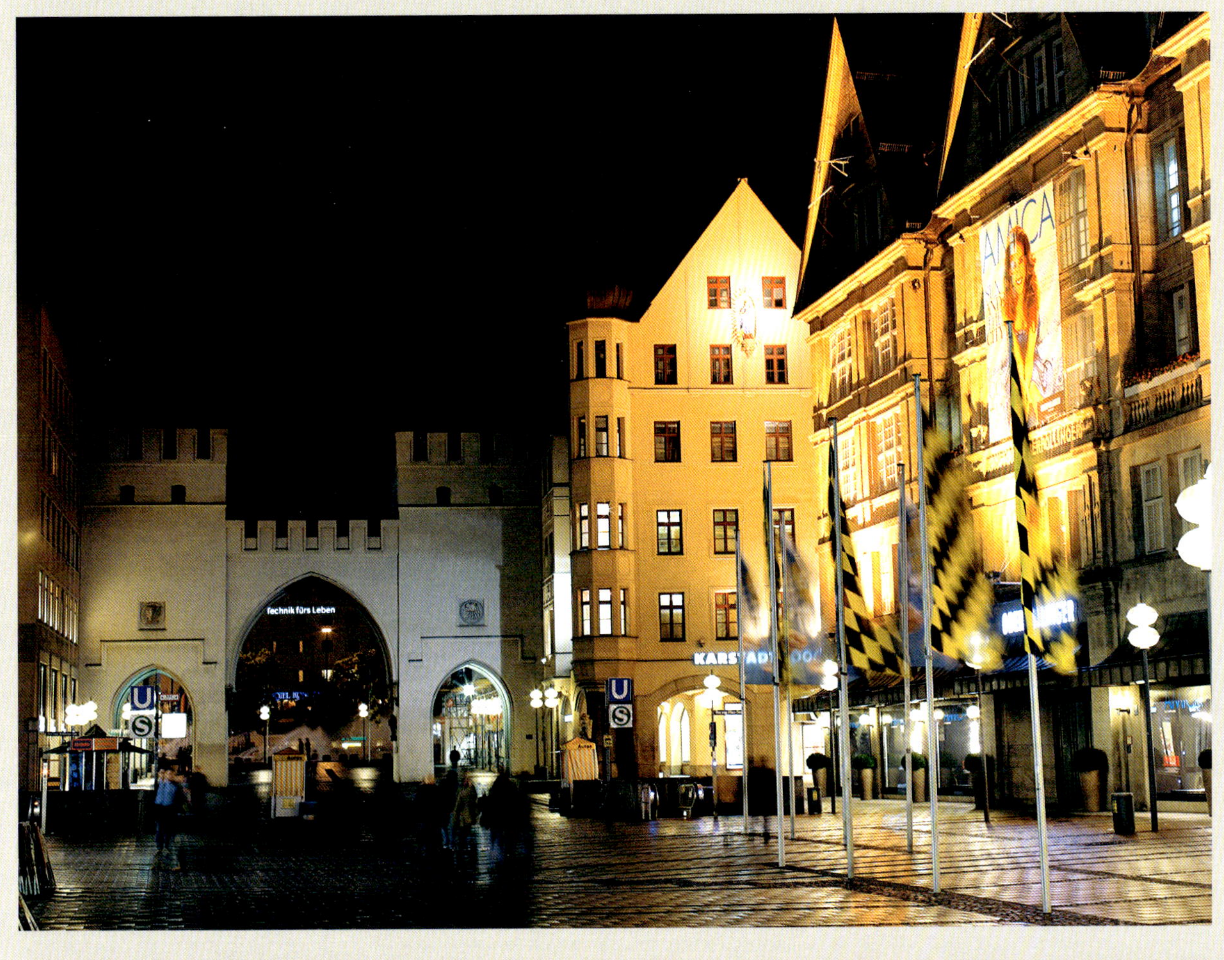

Left:
The Karlstor was the west gate of the historic old city of Munich. It was given its neo-Gothic visage in 1861/62. Next door is the famous Oberpollinger department store, established in 1905.

Below:
Up until 1885 beer was brewed here at the Augustinerbräu on Neuhauser Straße. Today you can savour regional cuisine in its hallowed halls and also try a frothy glass or two of Augustiner beer, otherwise known as Gustl.

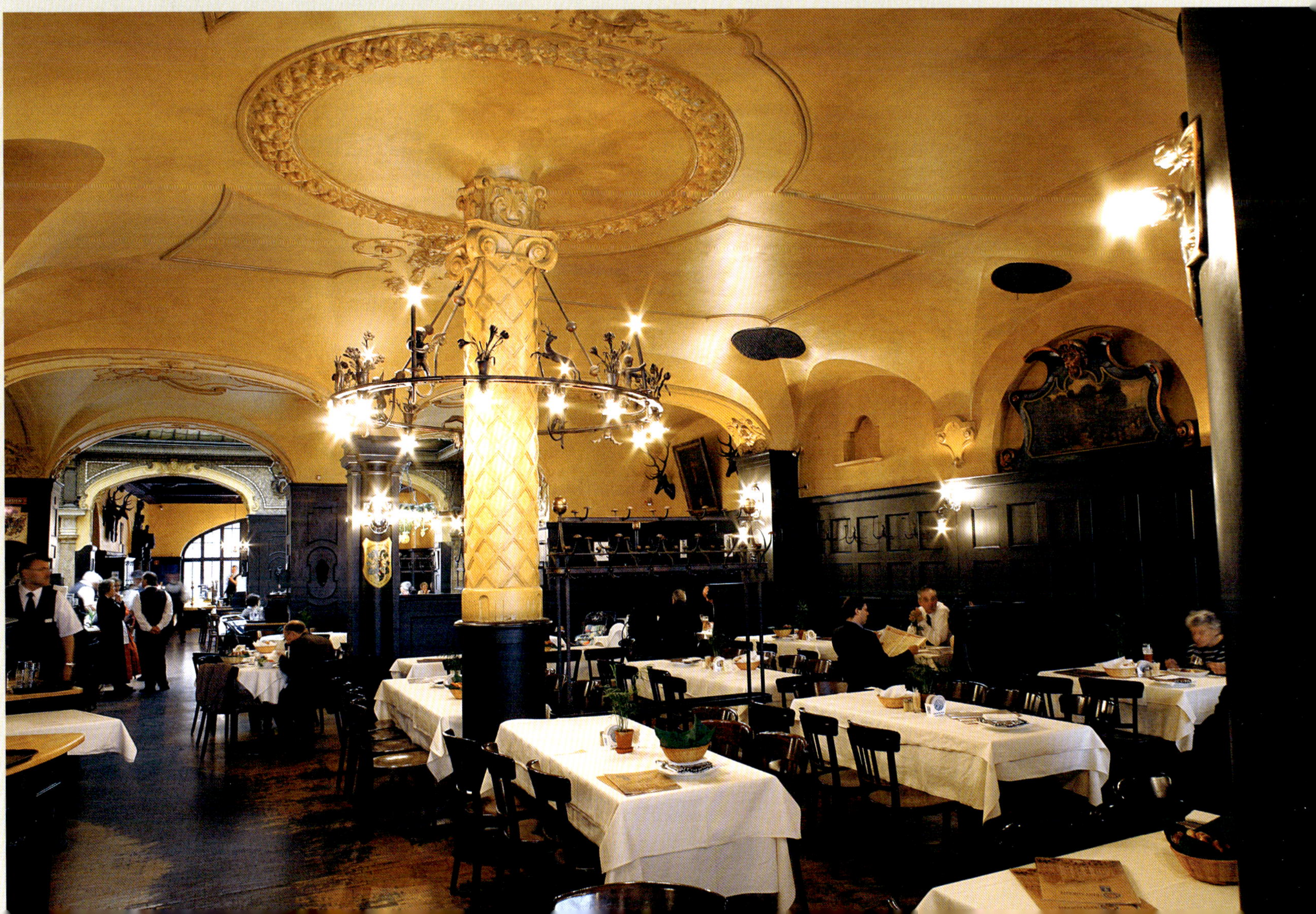

PRETZELS, BEER AND OBATZTER –

CULINARY MU

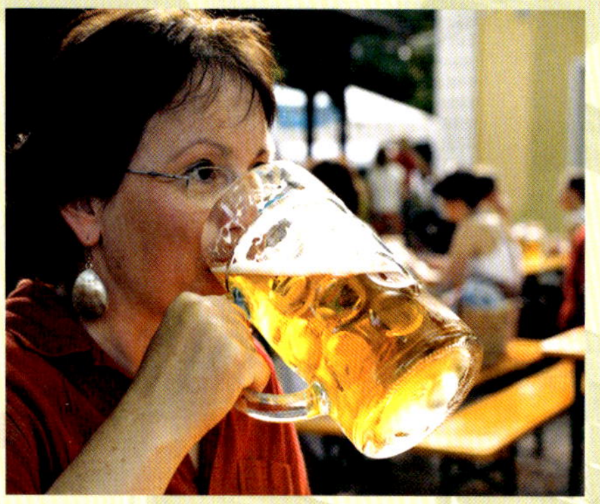

Above:
Beer doesn't come small here. Asking for "ein Bier" in Bavaria will get you a Maß – a full litre of pale, fizzy Pilsner, here being enjoyed at Zum Flaucher in Thalkirchen.

Centre:
This must be the most famous pub in the world: the Hofbräuhaus on Platzl.

Suckling pig with dumplings. Young pigs, often roasted or grilled whole on a spit, are said to have a particularly mild taste.

Munich has a multitude of top restaurants which specialise in international cuisine, served in establishments boasting a wide range of unique and stylish settings. You can dine like a Roman, reclining on a chaise longue, or eat with your fingers at a medieval banquet; you can be seated amongst fine works of art or try to find your victuals in total darkness at a trendy "unlit" meal. There's kosher and there's vegetarian, in short whatever your heart – or stomach – desires.

You can't talk about Munich and food in the same breath without that infamous ditty springing to mind, however: In München steht ein Hofbräuhaus (yes, the one about THAT brewery). And it's not only the people of Munich who consider it to be the most famous pub in the world; whether you're from Twickenham, Texas or Tokyo, everyone's heard of the Hofbräuhaus. And you can forget nouvelle cuisine here; this is the domain of the sausage and huge, crispy knuckles of pork. The top item on the menu is Weißwurst, a rather dubious looking squat white sausage. This has to consist of at least 51% veal, minced to the finest degree. To this is added back bacon and boiled pork rind. The meat mixture is seasoned with parsley, lemon, nutmeg, onion and various other spices, depending on the recipe.

Weißwürste are not salted, hence their pale whitish grey colour. They are eaten warm with the skin removed, the innards either being sucked out or carefully dissected from the casing. The unwritten law that no Weißwurst should hear the clock strike midday dates back to the days before fridges when the freshly prepared sausages quickly spoiled. Modern technology now allows us to tuck into a plate of them whatever the time of day. Weißwurst is eaten with a mild, sweet mustard, a Brezn, a salt pretzel which is crisp on the outside and nice and soft inside, and a glass of light, fizzy Weißbier.

There is, of course, much more to classic Bavarian fare than the Weißwurst. With the pig looming incredibly large, there is also roast pork, sucking pig, knuckle of pork, Leberkäs (meatloaf), Fleischpflanzerl (rissoles) and spicy Klosterseufzer sausages. There are also dumplings galore, made with breadcrumbs (Semmelknödel), liver (Leberknödel) and potatoes (Kartoffelknödel). The Hofbräuhaus, for example, notches up a

NICH

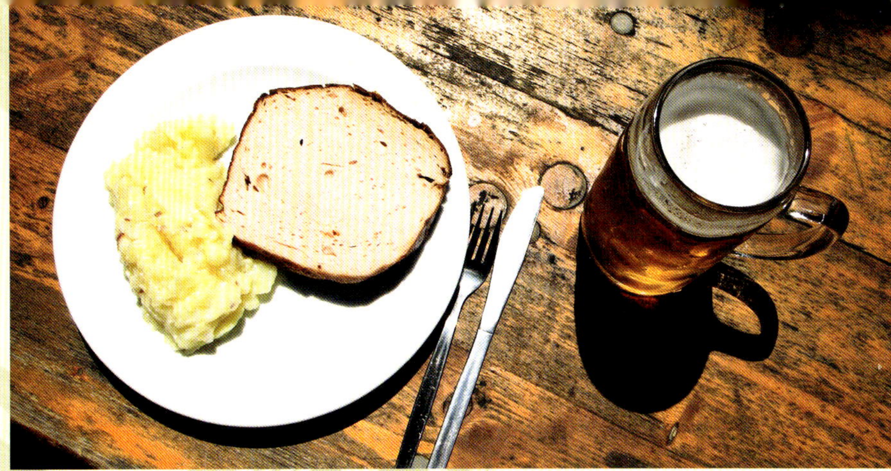

Above:
In 1776 it was allegedly in Munich that the meatloaf with the confusing name of Leberkäs was invented – which may contain traces of liver (Leber) but certainly not cheese (Käse).

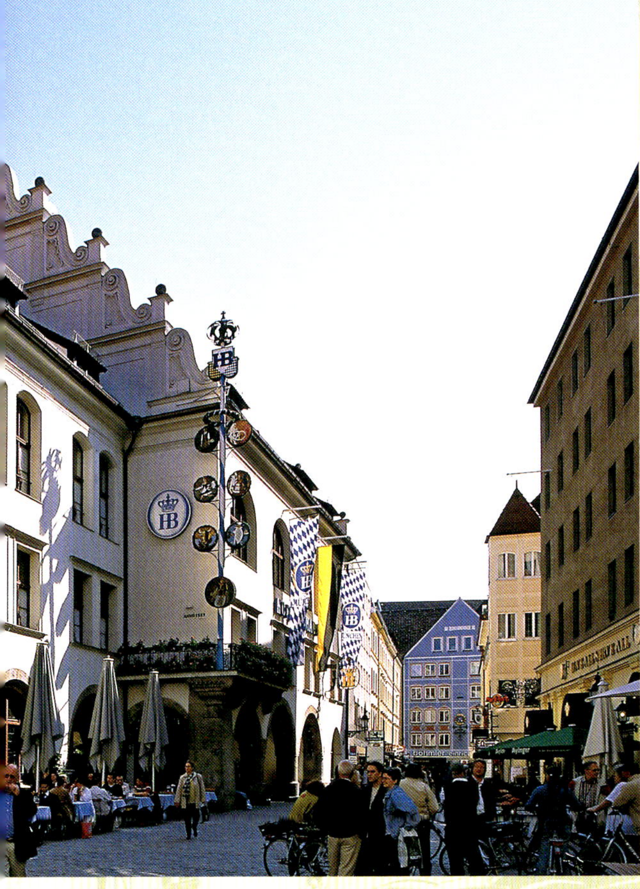

yearly dumpling turnover of 160,000, each one carefully made by hand. Amongst the orgy of meat on local menus there are also dishes suitable for vegetarians. Obatzter, to name but one, is a tasty mixture of soft cheese, onions and paprika. Desserts include sweet dumplings (Dampfnudeln) and Bayerische Creme, a pudding made from egg yoke, sugar, milk and cream and served with fruits and berries. Another delicacy for the more robust constitution is Kuttelfleck, made from root vegetables, streaky bacon, potatoes – and offal. As Munich writer Eugen Roth (1895–1976) once remarked, it's not to everyone's taste: *"Ein Mensch isst gerne Kuttelfleck. / Ein andrer graust sich – vor dem Dreck" ("Kuttelfleck some like to suck / Others think it tastes like muck")*...

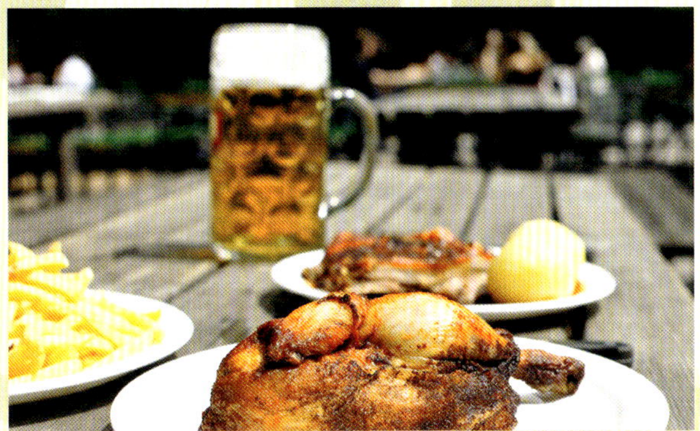

Left:
Grilled chicken became a popular poultry dish during the 19th century – and is still consumed in vast quantities in the beer gardens in and around Munich.

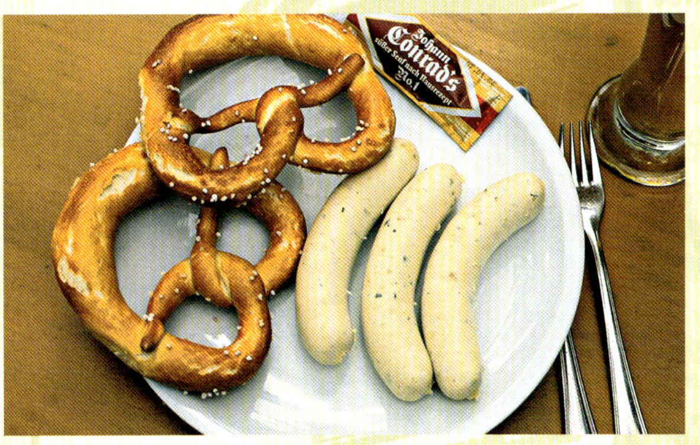

Left:
Weißwürste, Munich's anaemic-looking but tasty sausages, are best served straight from the pot with a generous dollop of sweet mustard and a Brezn.

Opinion is less divided when it comes to Munich's beer. A purity law was passed in the 15th century which decreed that beer may only consist of water, malt and hops. This is still zealously adhered to, with yeast being added to some brands. There are over a dozen different types of beer in Munich, from mild to strong, among them Helles, Export (light or dark), pilsner, weissbier, Kristallweizen and Hefeweizen (wheat beers, the latter light or dark), Märzen, Bockbier, Doppelbock, Schwarzbier – and of course the one and only Oktoberfestbier.

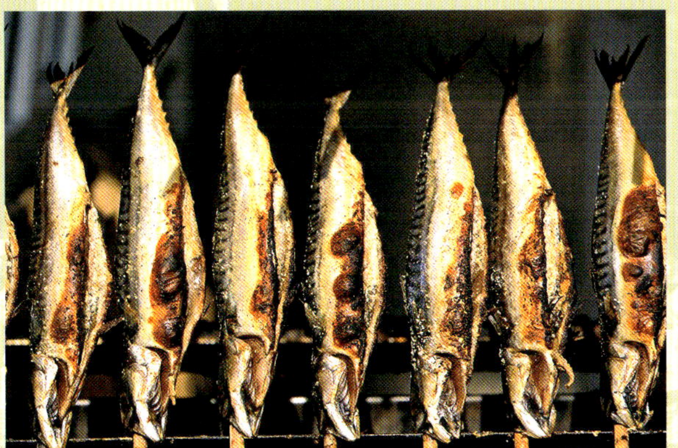

The Auer Dult is a traditional fair held in the suburb of Au. Here you are intoxicated by the smell of Steckerlfisch, fish fried on a stick and eaten straight out of the paper it's wrapped in.

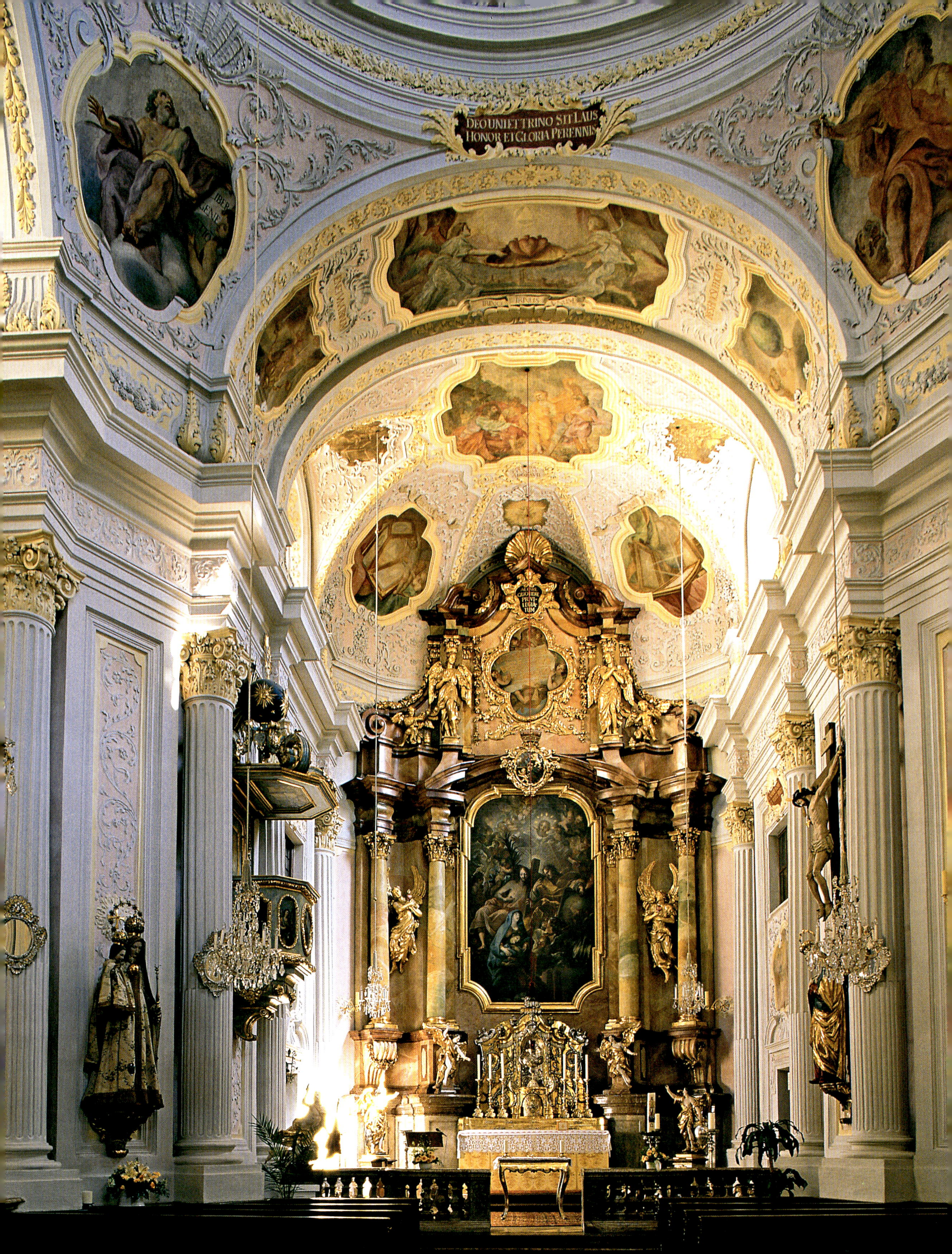
DEO UNI ET TRINO SIT LAUS
HONOR ET GLORIA PERENNIS

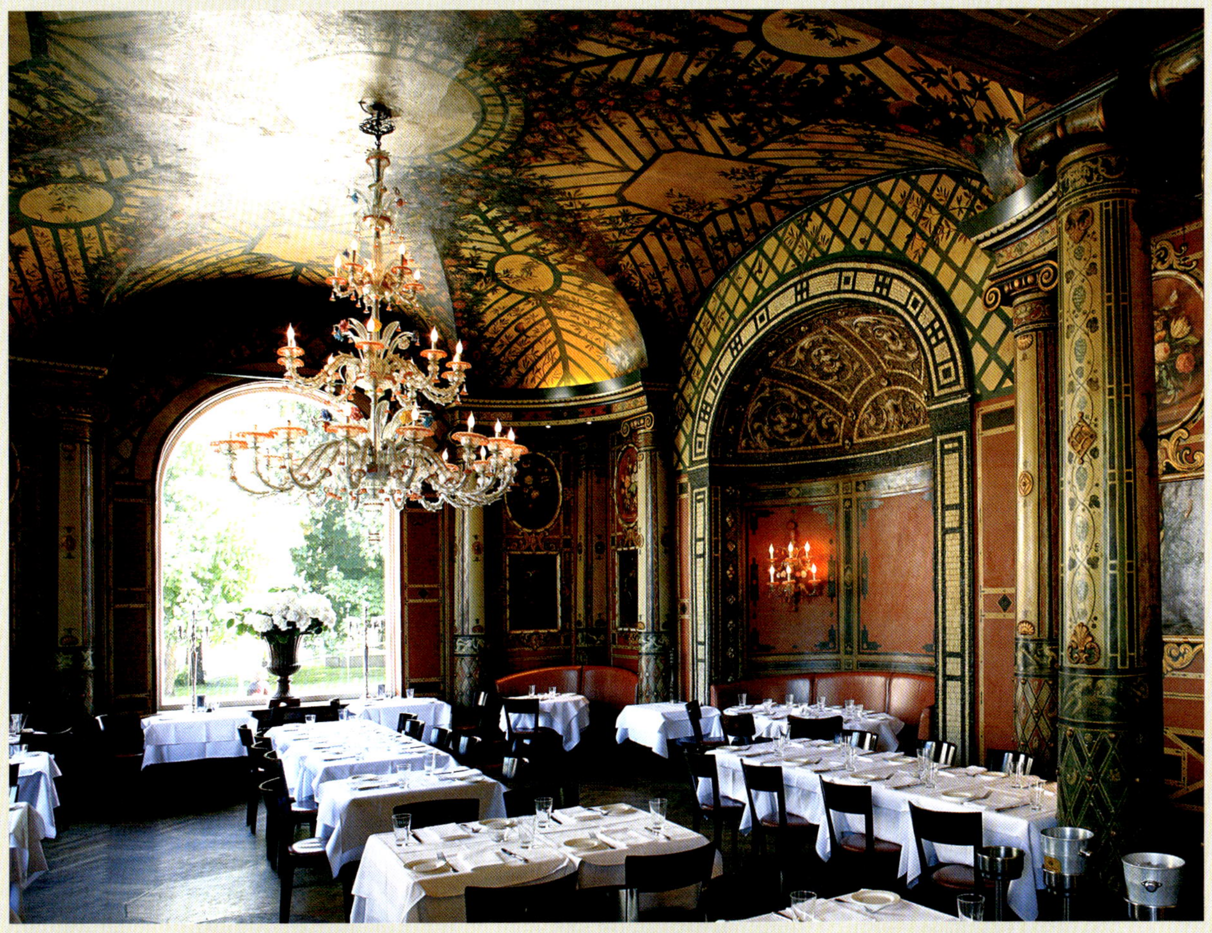

Left page:
The Dreifaltigkeitskirche on Pacellistraße was fashioned in Rococo by Giovanni Antonio Viscardi from 1711 to 1718. In 1714/15 Cosmas Damian Asam added the first baroque cupola fresco in Munich. The church of the Holy Trinity was the only one in Munich to come through the bombings of the Second World War unscathed.

The Künstlerhaus on Lenbachplatz, opened in 1900, was to act as a meeting place for the artist world and the upper classes of Munich. Its interior was renovated in 1998 and once again provides a stylish setting in which to wine and dine à la fin de siècle.

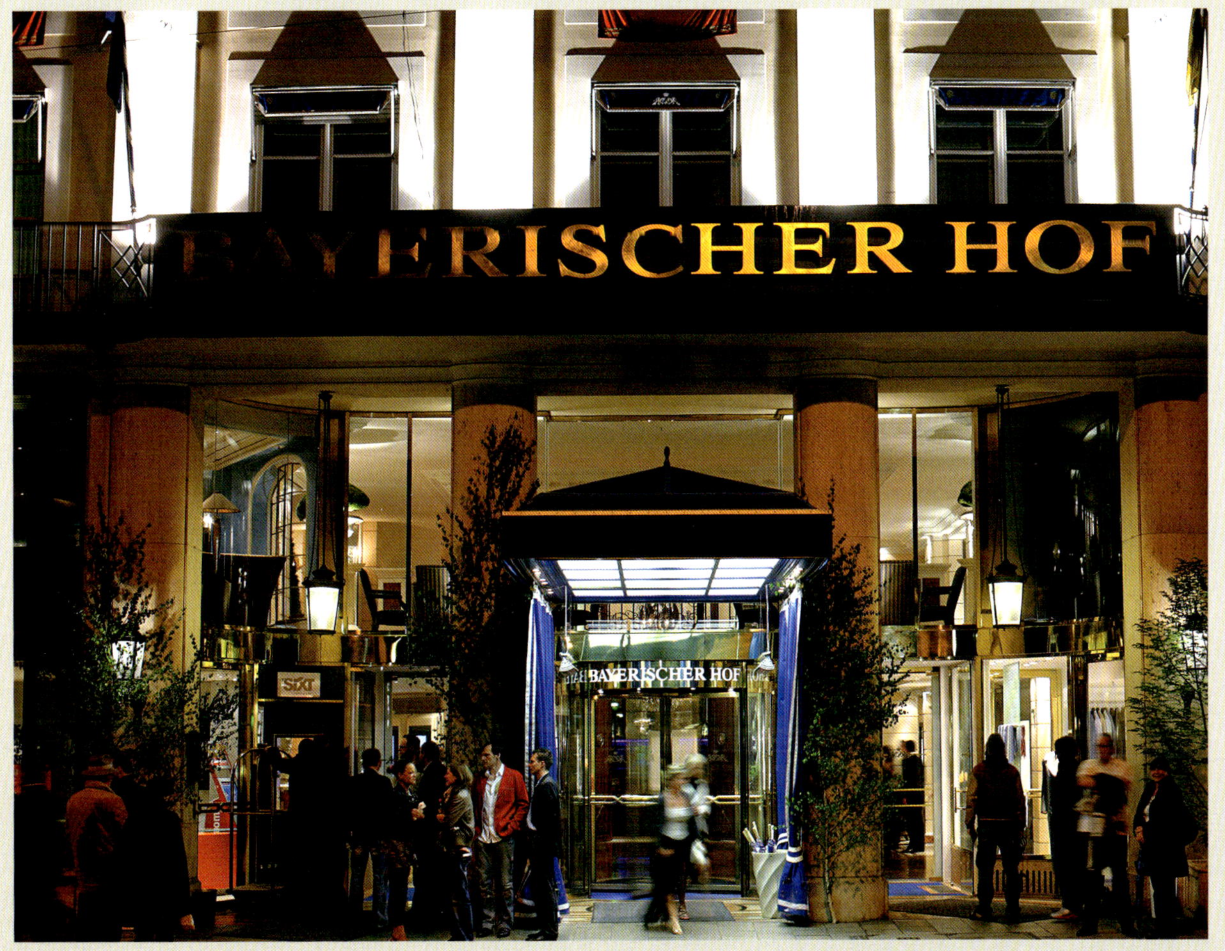

The Hotel Bayerischer Hof on Promenadeplatz is one of Munich's top establishments. It was constructed at the behest of King Ludwig I who required a comfortable hostelry for his guests. VIPs from kings to pop stars have resided here – albeit only temporarily – since 1841.

Right:
Even today the twin towers of the Frauenkirche can be seen from just about any point in the Munich Altstadt (here on Kardinal-Faulhaber-Straße). Their distinctive onion domes smack of the Italian Renaissance. They date back to 1525 and were the first of their kind north of the Alps.

Below:
Palais Holnstein was built by François de Cuvilliés the Elder between 1733 and 1737 and was more or less untouched by the bombs of World War II. It has served as the seat of the archbishop of Munich and Freising since 1818.

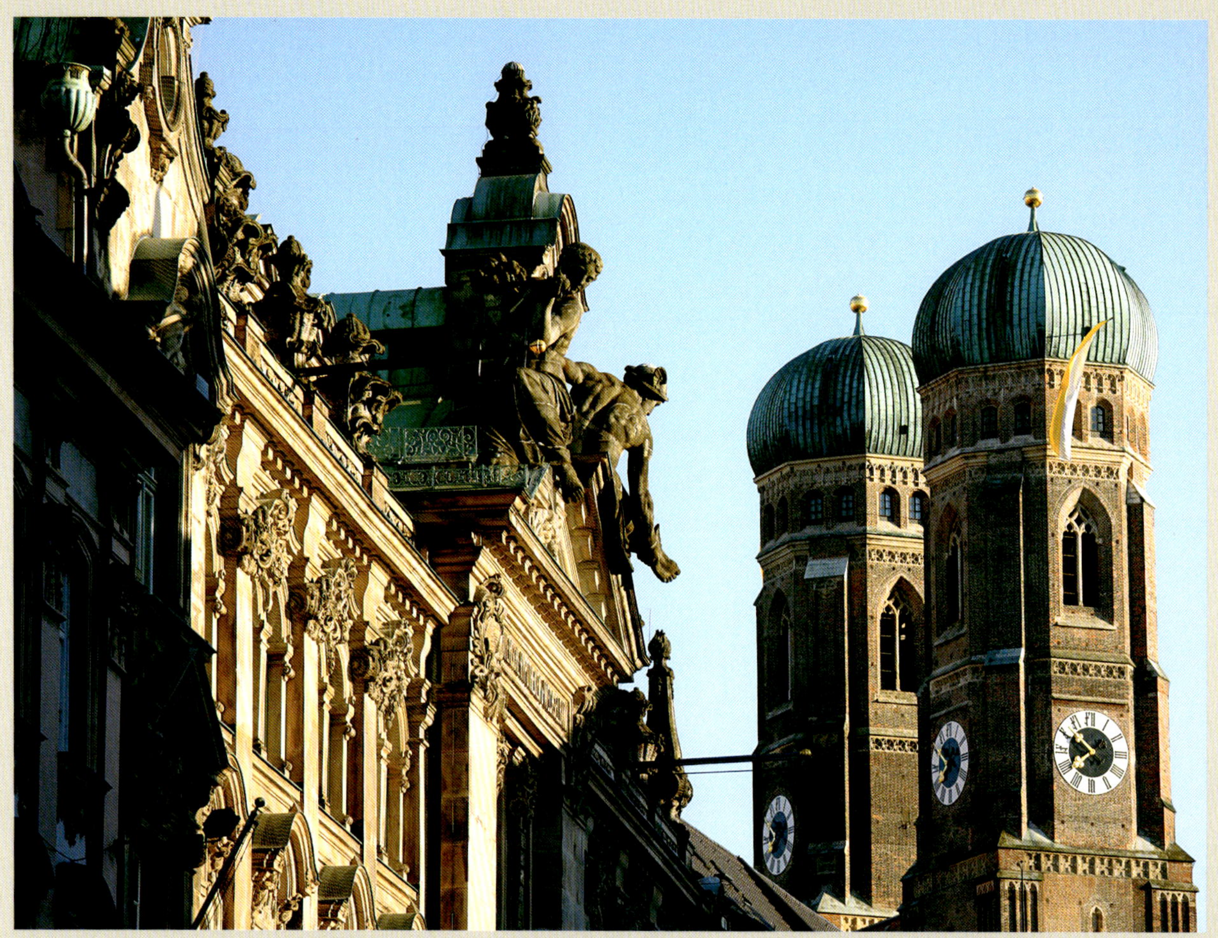

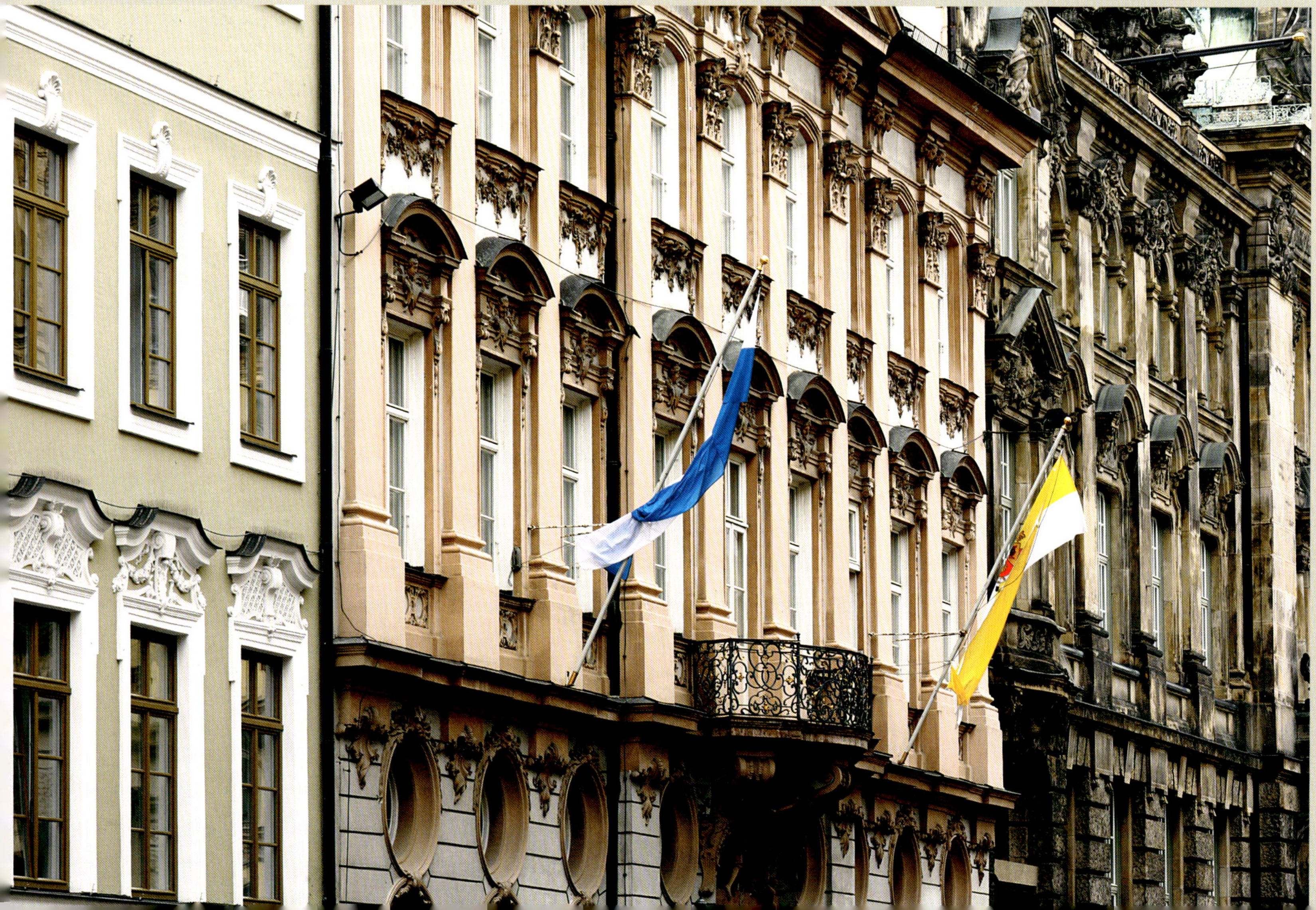

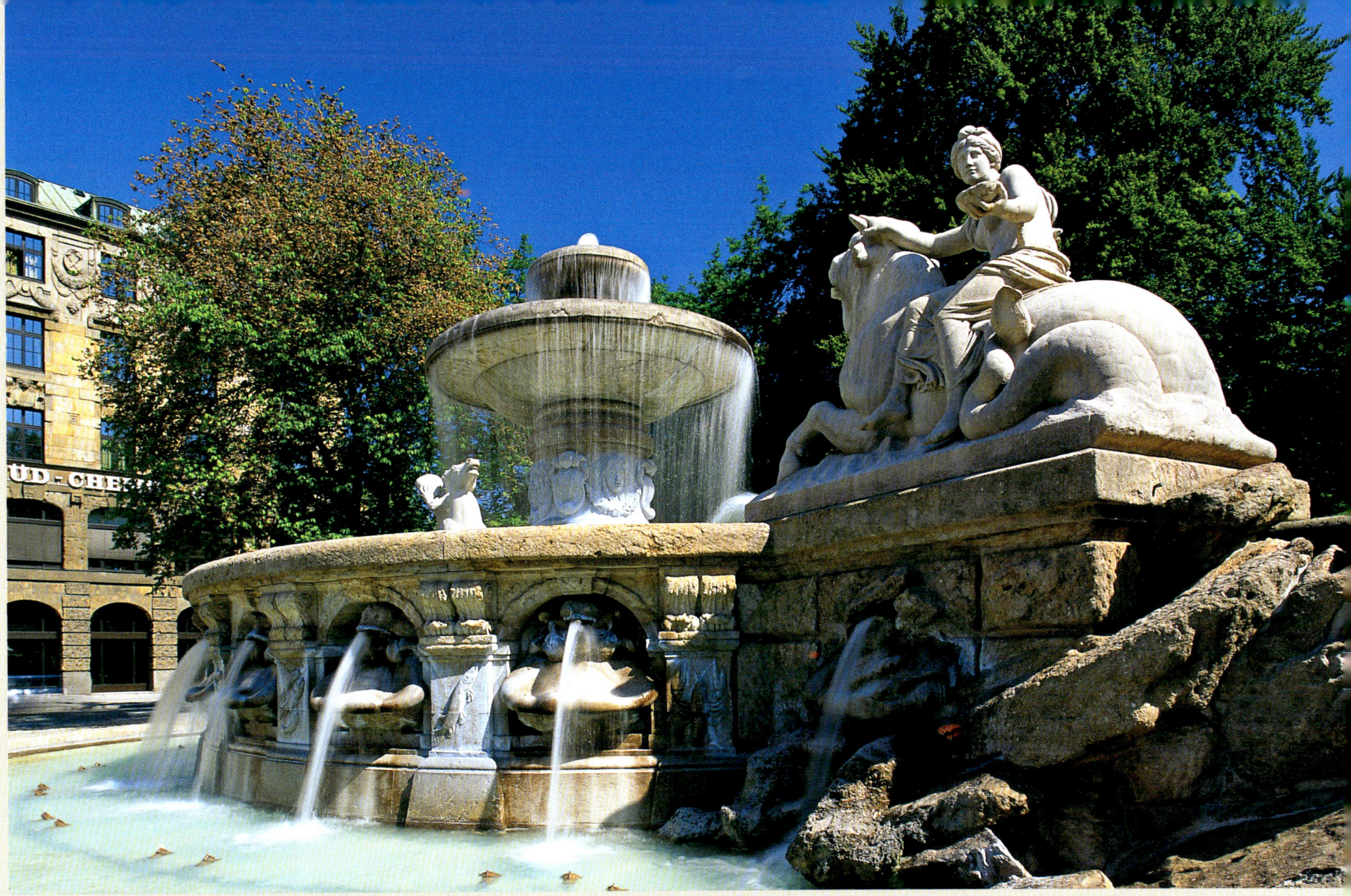

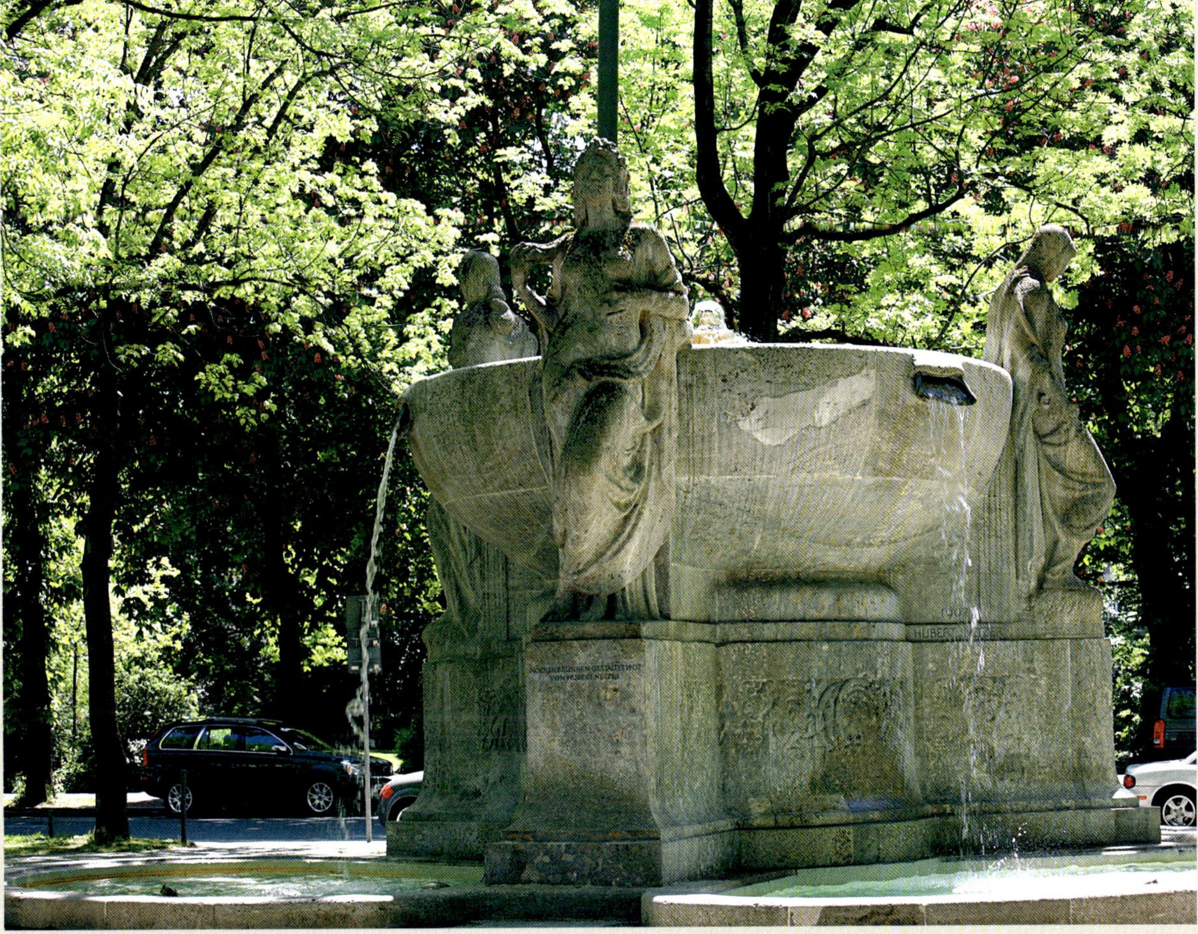

Above:
The Wittelsbacherbrunnen, one of Munich's more impressive fountains, is tucked in between Lenbachplatz and Maximiliansplatz. It was erected between 1893 and 1895 to mark the completion of the water supply system which still pipes fresh drinking water from the springs of the Mangfall into Munich.

Left:
In 1907 sculptor Hubert Netzer from the Allgäu (1865–1939) made the Nornenbrunnen which depicts the three Norse fates of Urd, Verdandi and Skuld. It originally stood on Stachus and was moved to its present location on Maximiliansplatz in 1965.

Right:
Royal gardens freshen up the heart of town, laid out by Elector Maximilian I from 1613 to 1617. The Hofgarten gate leading to the Theatine church from 1816 is the first building in Munich by Leo von Klenze.

Far right:
The house of literature next to the Salvatorian church is an eldorado for writers, publishers, booksellers and journalists.

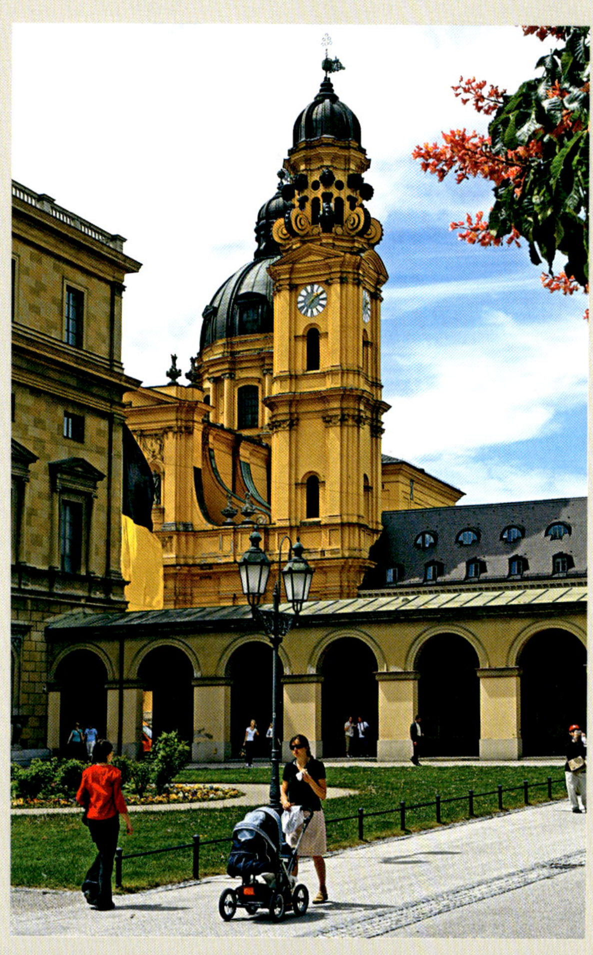

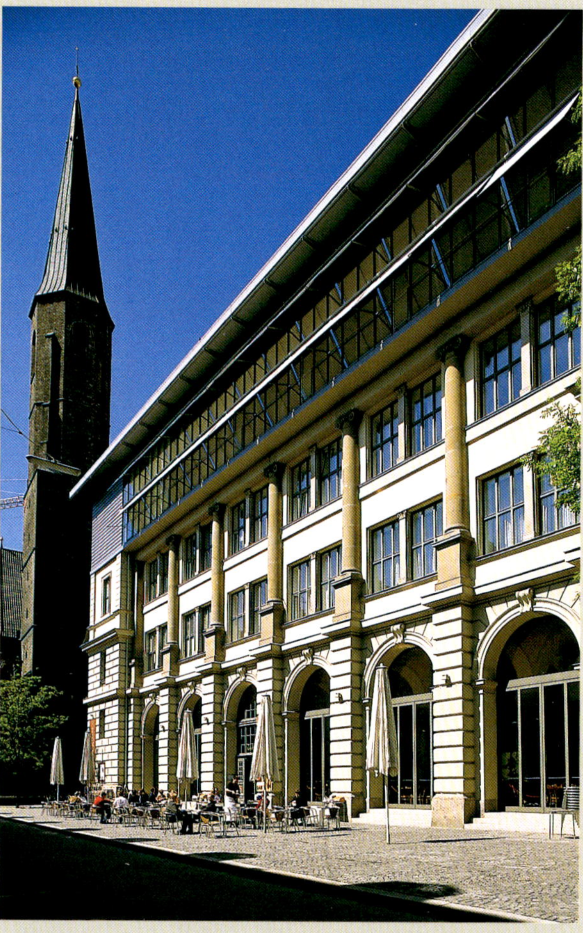

Below:
The Temple of Diana marks the centre of the Hofgarten in Munich. This is where concerts are staged, where buskers entertain passers by and where you can shake a leg on a warm summer's night to the glorious sound of music played under the stars.

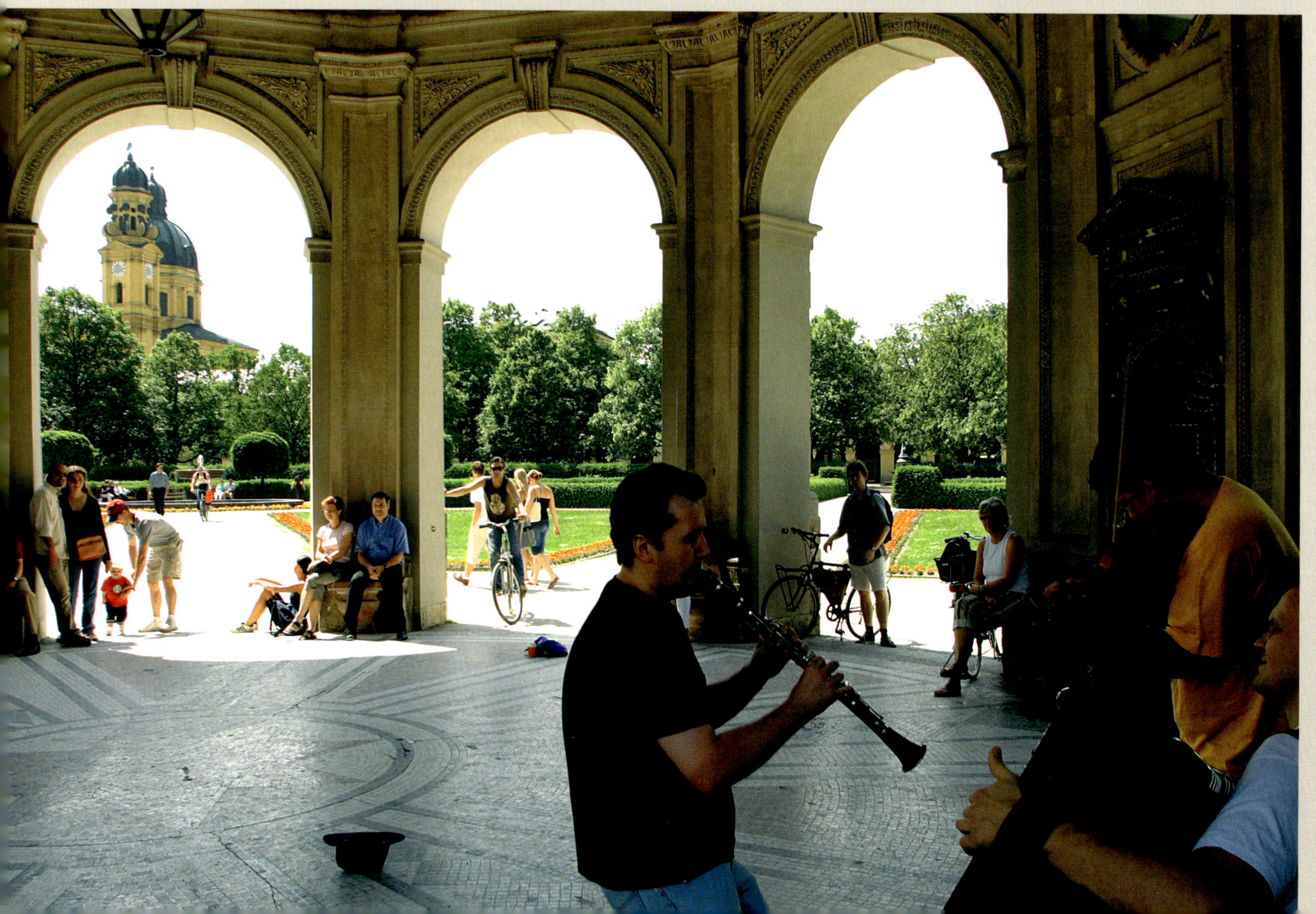

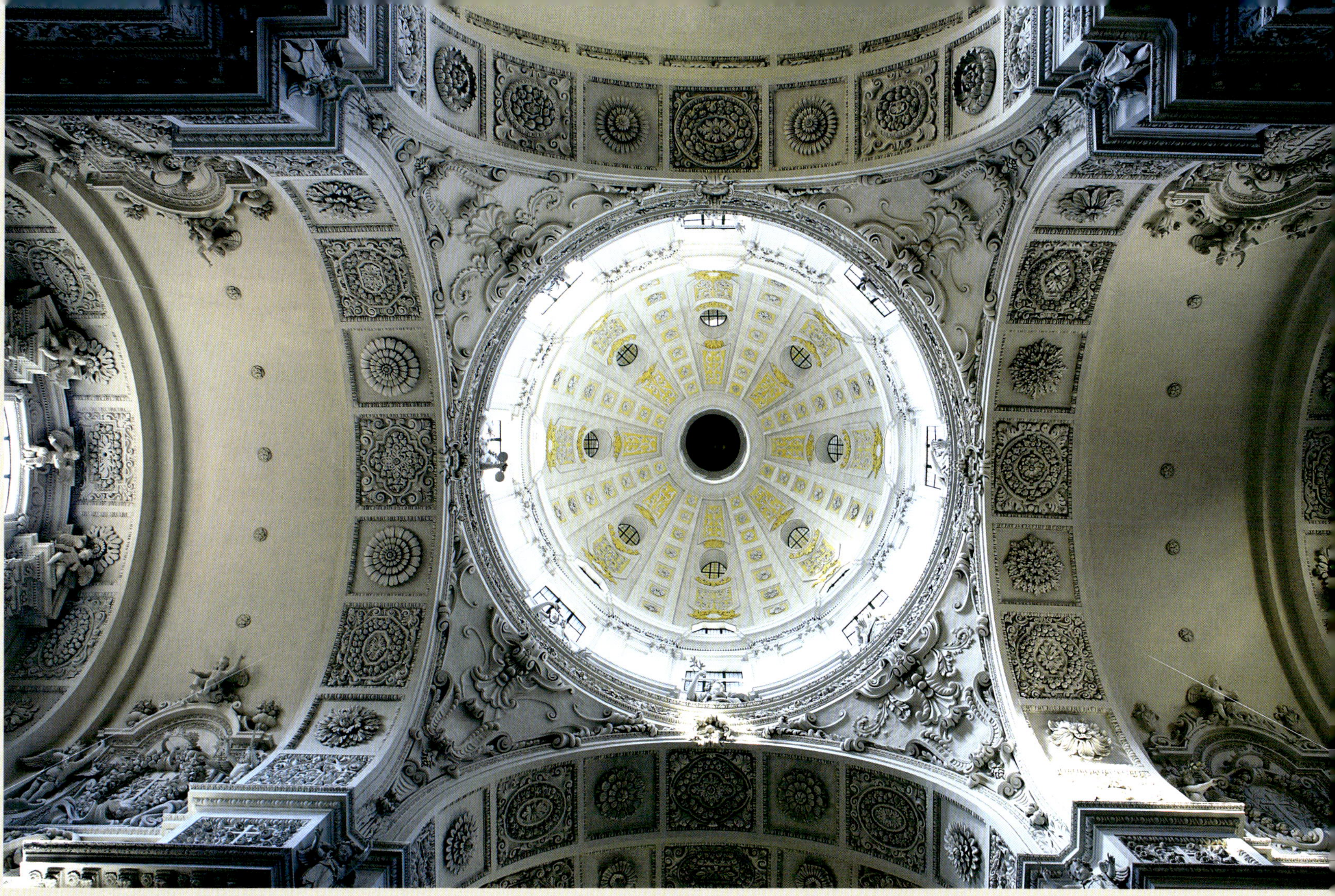

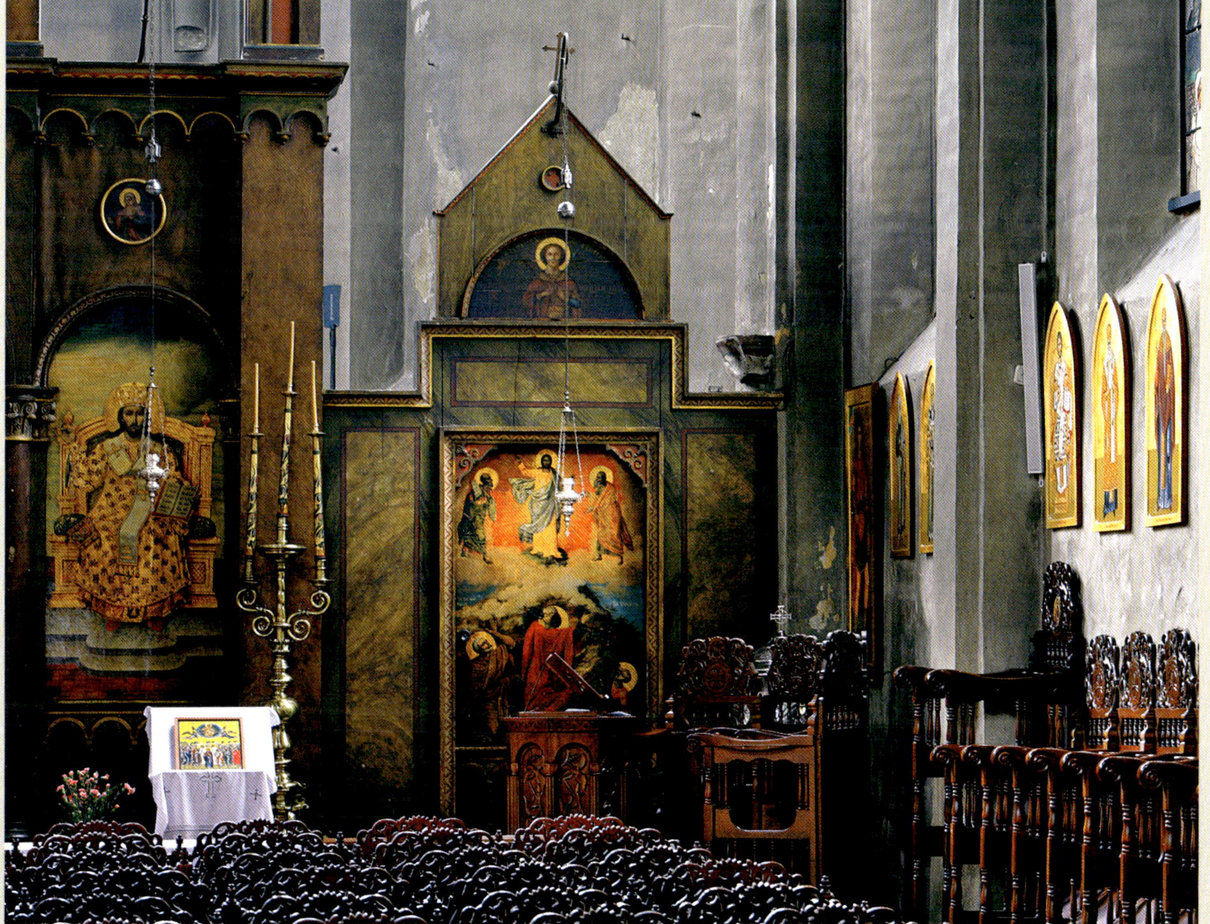

Above:
Looking up into the dome of the Theatinerkirche. The interior of the church is a positive orgy of stucco. 49 members of the house of Wittelsbach lie buried in its crypt.

Left:
The church of St Salvator was once the cemetery church belonging to the Frauenkirche, used by Munich's Greek Orthodox community since 1829. It's now the seat of the Metropolitan of Germany and Exarch of Central Europe.

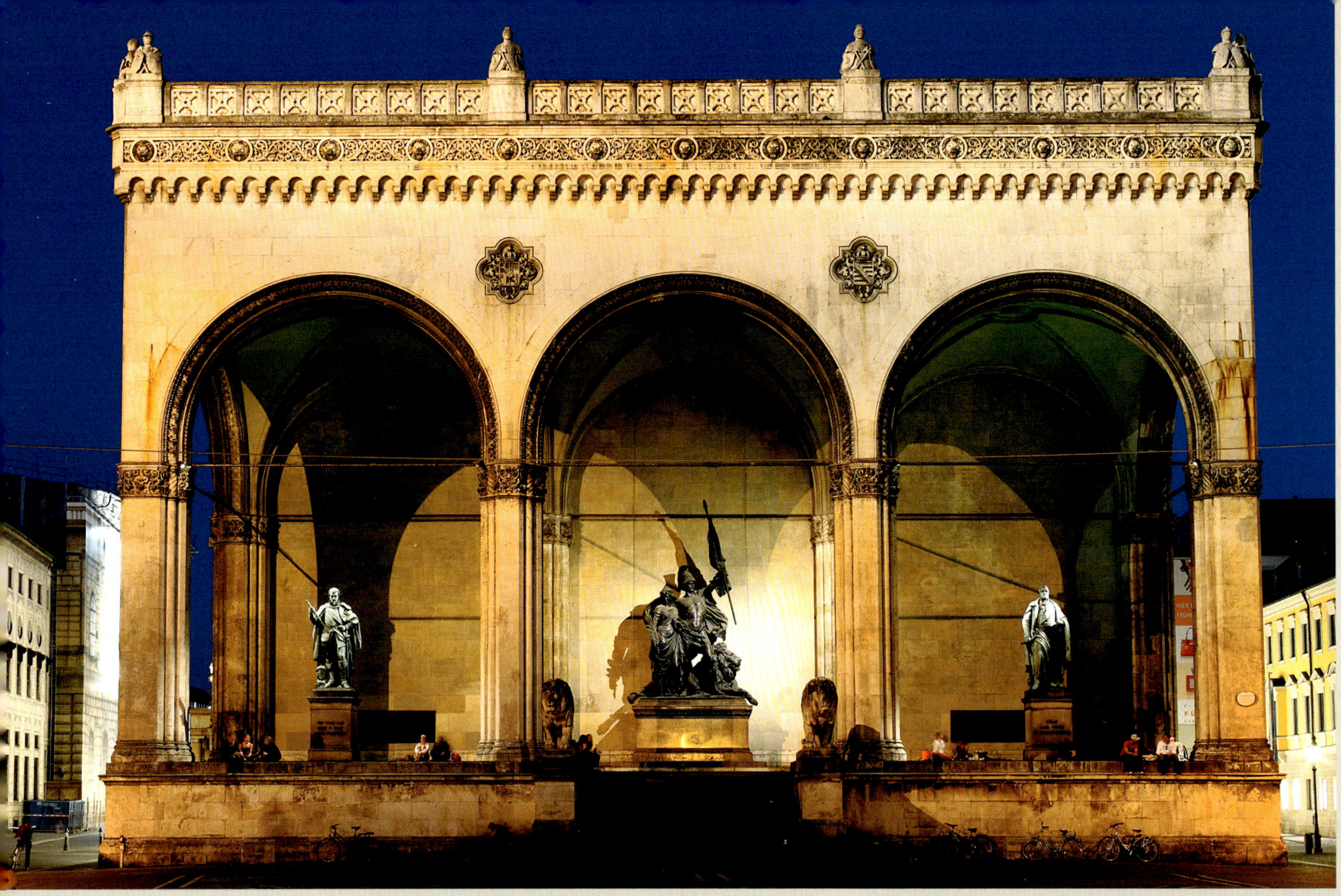

Above:
Based on the Loggia dei Lanzi in Florence, the Feldherrnhalle was built by Friedrich von Gärtner from 1841 to 1844. In 1923 it witnessed the famous shootout between Hitler and his lackeys and the police.

Right:
The bronze statues of Count Tilly (photo) and Prince Wrede were made by brass founder Ferdinand von Miller (1813–1887) from designs by Ludwig von Schwanthaler. The name Bayerische Feldherrnhalle (hall of the Bavarian commanders) causes some amusement amongst the people of Munich who claim: "One wasn't a Bavarian and the other wasn't a commander".

Far right:
The statue of King Ludwig I on horseback on Odeonsplatz was made by a pupil of Schwanthaler's, Max von Widnmann (1812–1895).

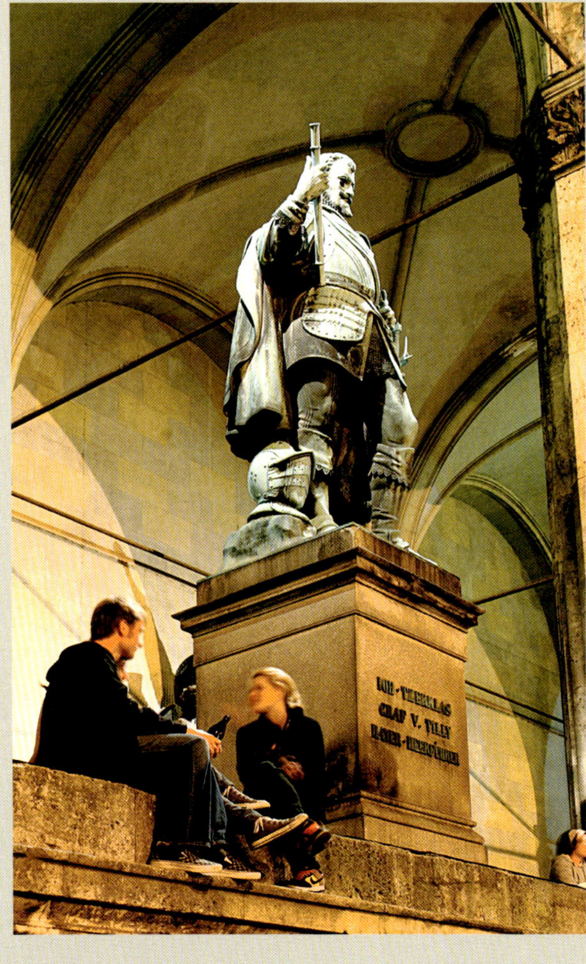

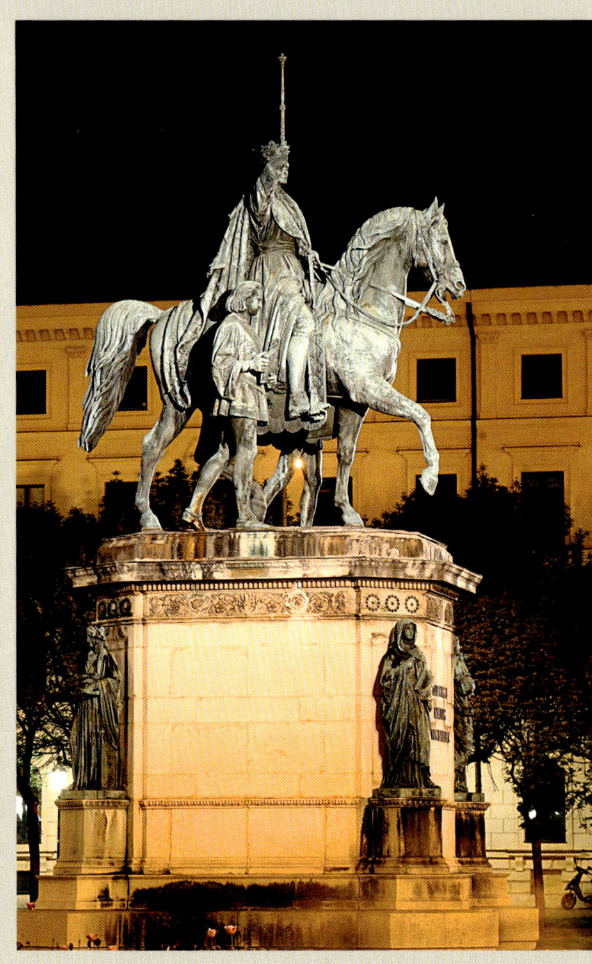

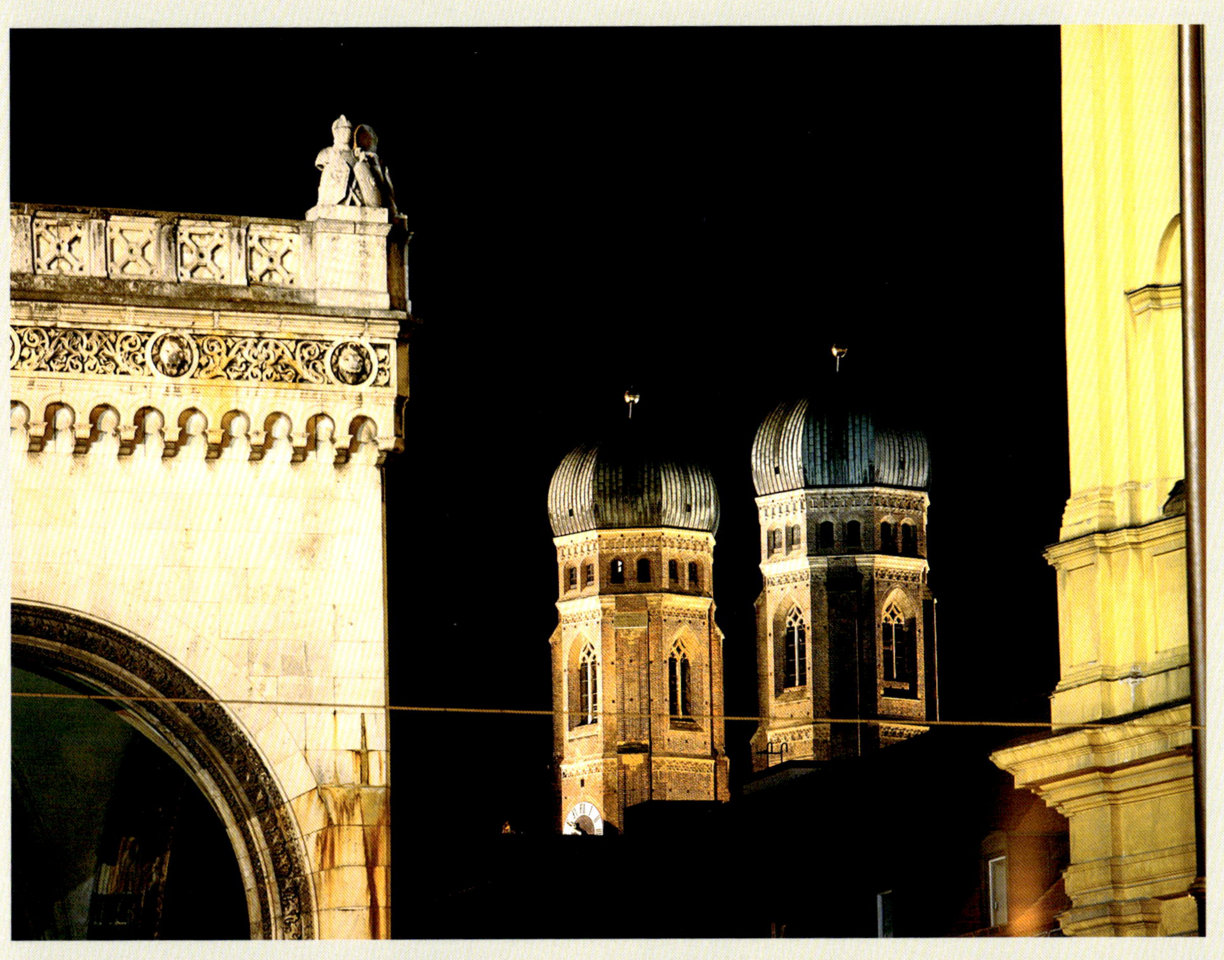

Left:
"In the Frauenkirche in Munich there is more than one landmark and more than one legend surrounding it. It is a wonderful, stately building, for which the mortar for its foundations and walls was mixed with Bavarian wine", claims an enthusiastic Ludwig Bechstein.

Below:
When on a warm summer's night the smell of espresso gently wafts across the square, it's almost as if you were in Italy. The Café am Hofgarten (shown here) is the oldest coffee house in Munich. It has been run by the descendants of one Giuseppe Tambosi, King Ludwig I's royal cellarer, for several generations.

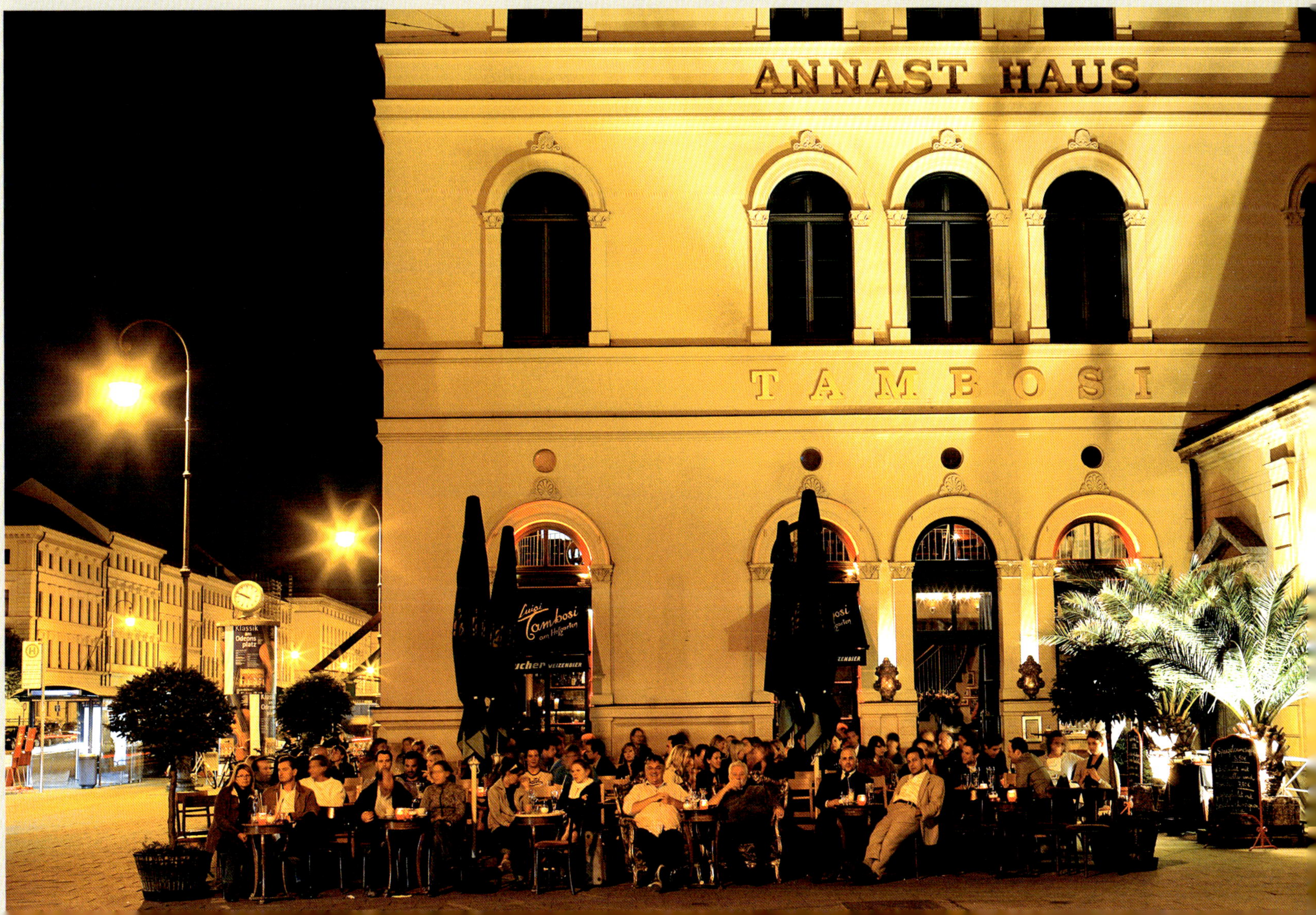

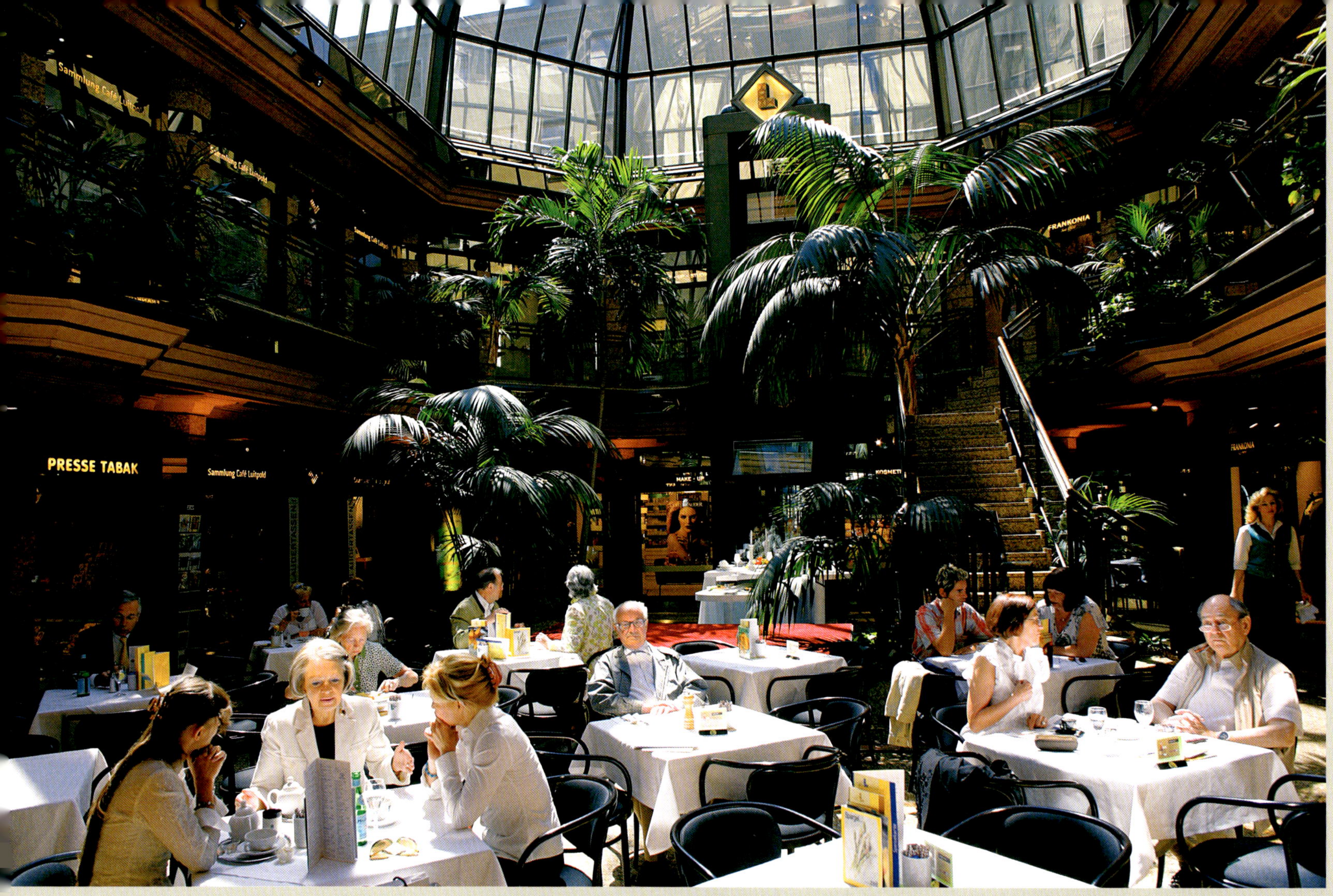

Above:
Palm court takes on a new dimension under the huge glass dome of the Luitpoldblock on Brienner Straße, a luxury shopping arcade. In the 1890s this is where the high society of Munich came for afternoon coffee and slices of cream cake.

Right:
This café on Kaufingerstraße is named after the Gugelhupf (Café Guglhupf), a ring sponge cake once baked in Roman clay ovens.

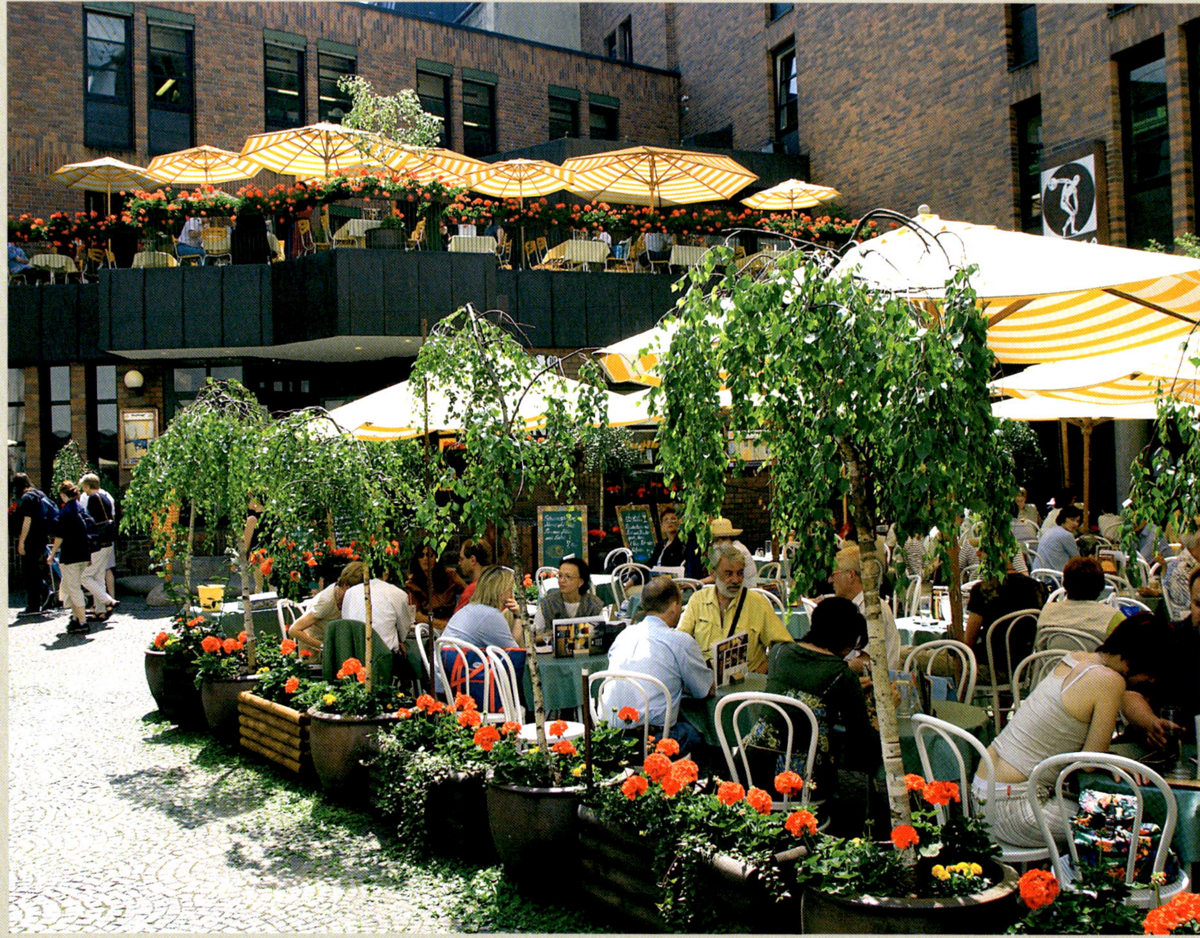

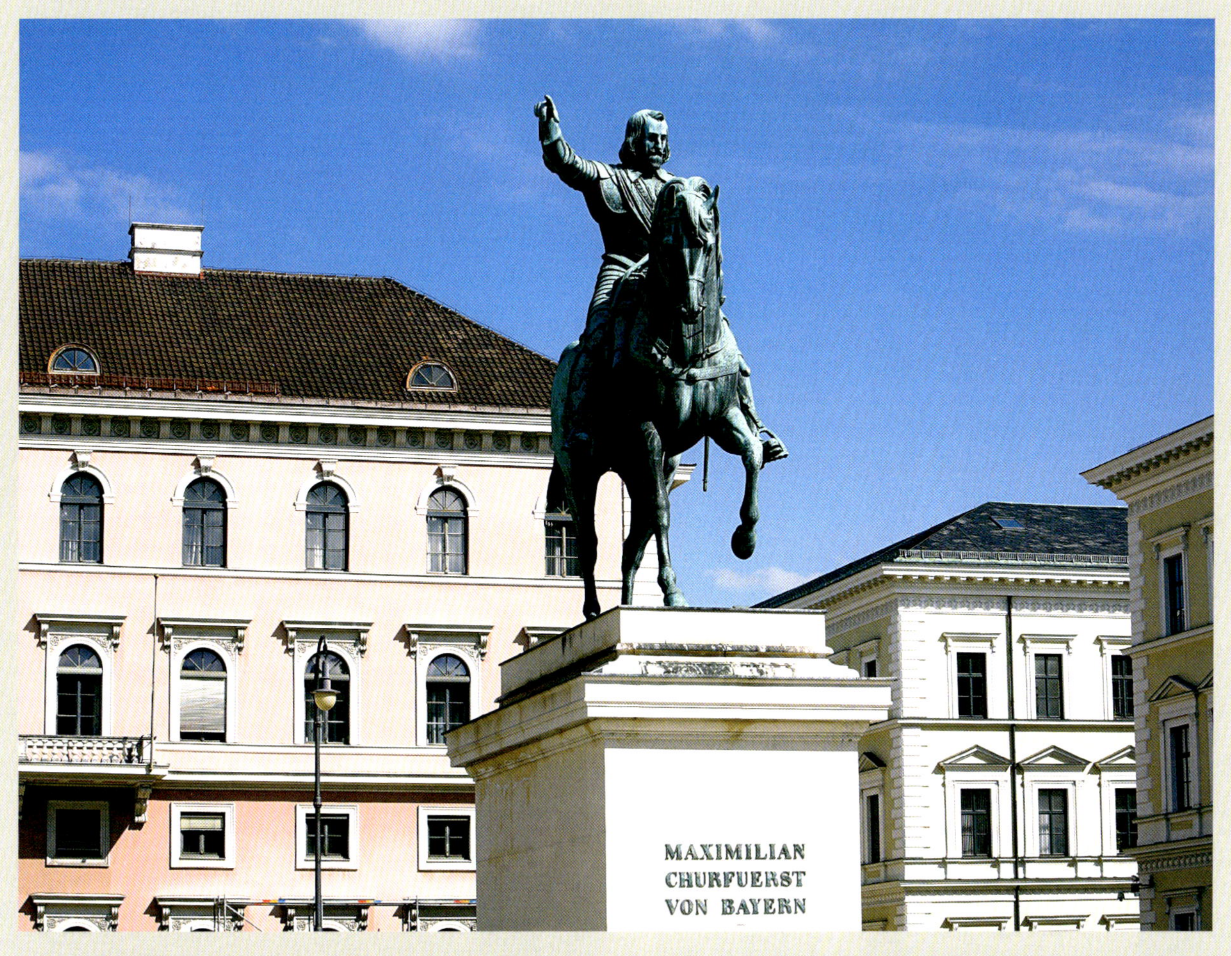

Left:
Outside the Palais Ludwig Ferdinand on Wittelsbacherplatz, built by Leo von Klenze, stands a statue of Elector Maximilian I from a model by Danish sculptor Bertel Thorvaldsen (1770–1844).

Below:
The Bavarian State Chancellery supports the president and government of the Free State of Bavaria on constitutional matters. The state's top administrative body has its headquarters in a new building on Hofgarten which has had the cupola of the old Bavarian army museum incorporated into it. Here the facade.

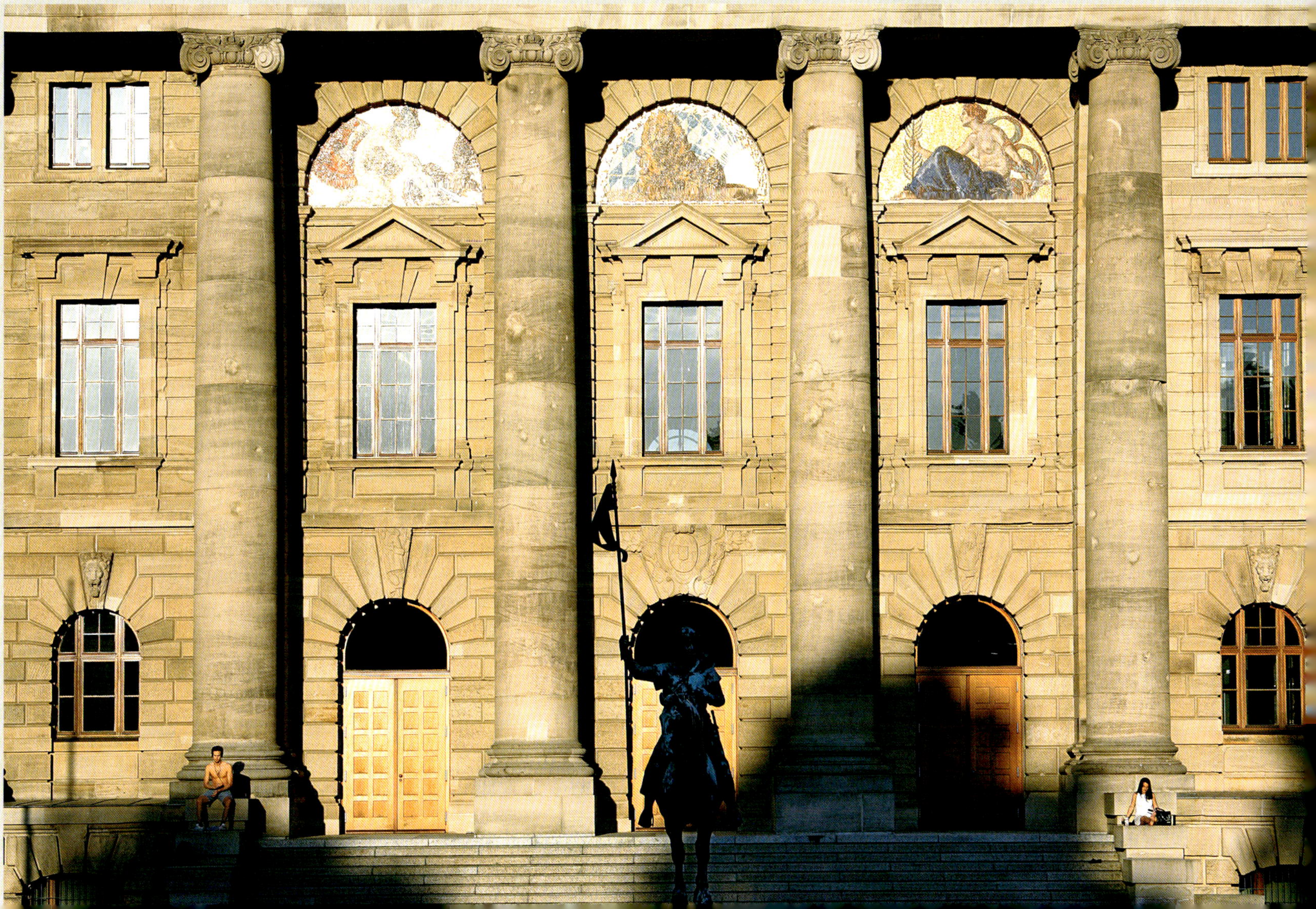

CULTURE, KITSCH AND CURIOSITIES – MUNICH'S MUSEUMS

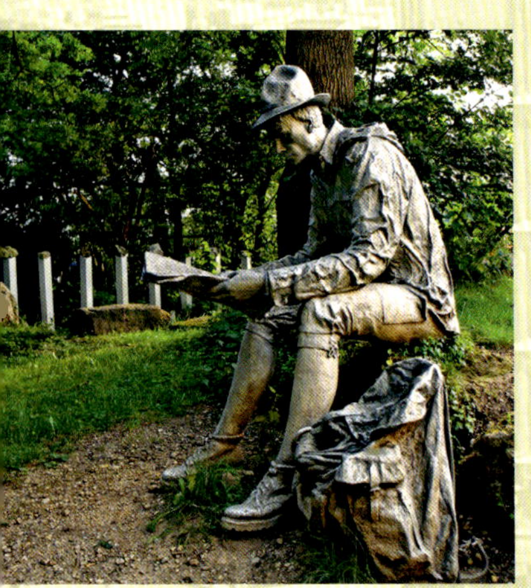

Above:
The Alpine Museum on Praterinsel was founded in 1907 and charts the history of Alpinism.

Centre:
One of the most important galleries of painting in the world is the Alte Pinakothek, with pictures from the Middle Ages to the mid 18th century on display. View of the Rubens room which contains such major works as The Hippopotamus Hunt and The Rape of the Daughters of Leucippus.

Right:
The Mensch and Natur Museum in the north wing of Schloss Nymphenburg has one very unusual inhabitant: Bruno, the bear shot in 2006 and stuffed in no less than 1,400 man hours. He is not alone; the museum also features the last brown bear in Bavaria (to date) who was dispatched by hunters over 170 years ago in Ruhpolding.

One of the most significant art galleries in the world is in Munich: the Alte Pinakothek. It has works from the 14th to 18th centuries on display, among them paintings by Rembrandt and Rubens, and Munich's hot favourite, The Battle of Alexander at Issus by Albrecht Altdorfer. The Neue Pinakothek shows pictures from the late 18th and 19th centuries, from Goya to Caspar David Friedrich and Carl Spitzweg to van Gogh and Rodin. The stylish Pinakothek der Moderne is dedicated to art and design of the 20th and 21st centuries and was opened in 2002. There are also Munich galleries which focus on contemporary art, design and photography. The Glyptothek has ancient sculptures, the museum of porcelain in Schloss Nymphenburg over 1,000 exhibits from the porcelain manufacturer's launched here in 1761.

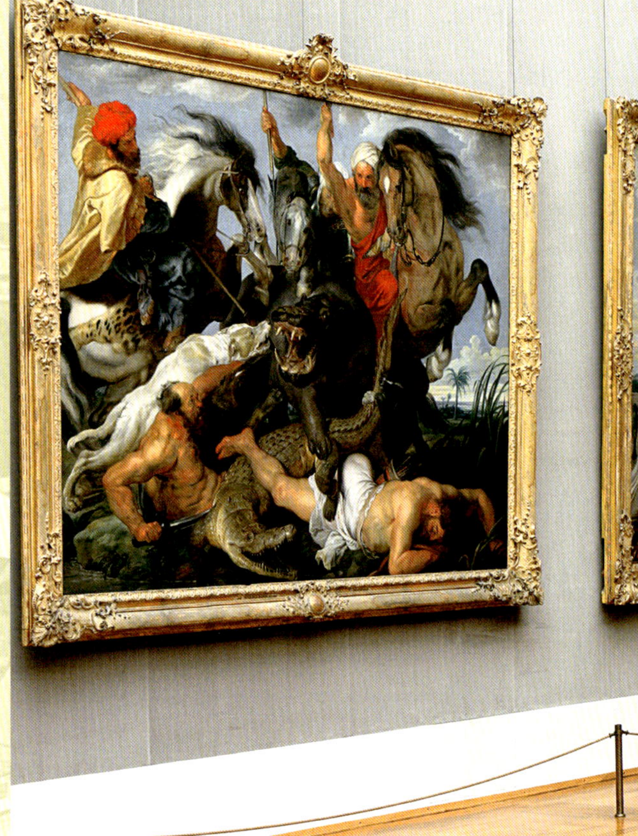

Technology buffs can't fail to be enthused by the Deutsches Museum. The biggest museum of science and technology in the world attracts 1.5 million visitors a year. Several different venues demonstrate just what science and engineering are capable of achieving, from the first motorised Benz to the printing press. Other museums in a similar vein are the BMW Museum, collections of electricity meters and shaving apparatus, a museum of work and safety and the Mensch and Natur Museum whose artefacts include the escaped bear of recent renown, Bruno (now stuffed).

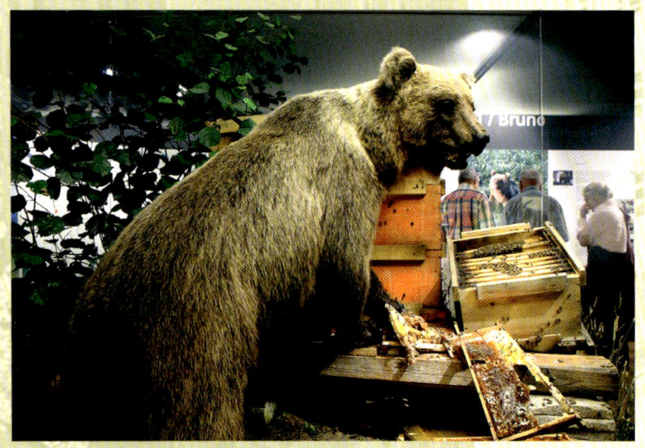

THE WONDERS OF NATURE

You can be transported into a sparkling world of crystals in the section of the Mineralogische Staatssammlung or state collection of minerals open to the public. The Paläontologisches Museum has fossils from various prehistoric periods and the largest and smallest dinosaurs in Bavaria to be marvelled at. The history of Bavaria from the Stone Age onwards can be studied at the Archäologische Staatssammlung or state museum of archaeology. The museums of anthropology and botany are also among Munich's institutions devoted to natural history, as is the zoo with its live exhibits at the Tierpark Hellabrunn.

The Bayerisches Nationalmuseum with its unique array of items tells you all you ever wanted to know about the art and cultural history of

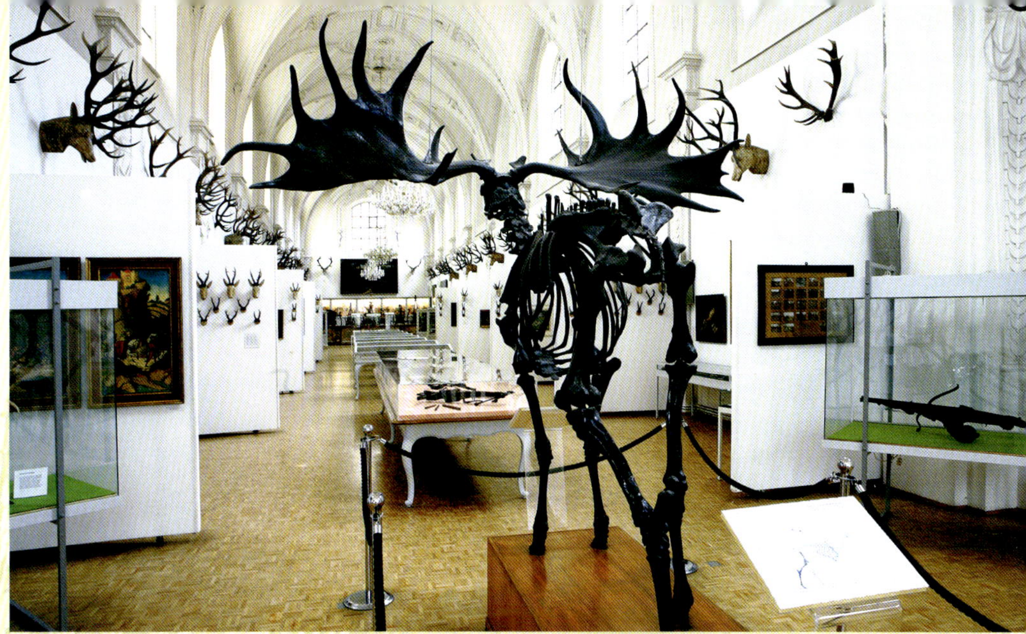

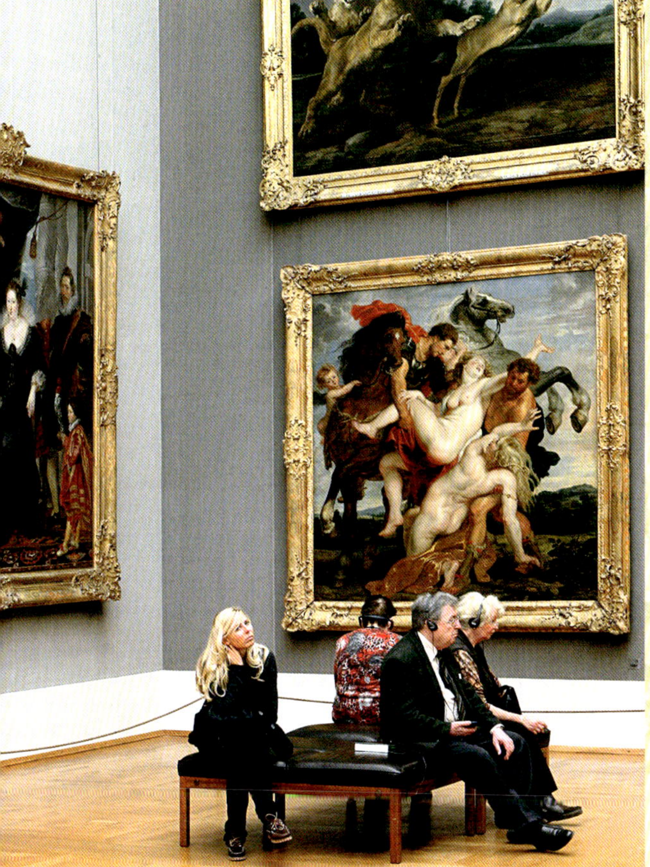

Bavaria, with one of the highlights its collection of Christmas cribs from all over Europe. The city of Munich itself is the main feature of the newly renovated Stadtmuseum and of the (inevitable) museum of beer and the Oktoberfest.

Munich is also home to one of the oldest and most extensive museums of ethnology in the world, which has no less than 150,00 exhibits. The Ägyptisches Museum saves you the expense of a trip along the Nile; it's all here! The new Jewish Museum is especially impressive and provides a fascinating insight into the lives and culture of the Jewish community resident in the provincial capital of Bavaria. There are museums of the theatre, of hunting and fishing, the

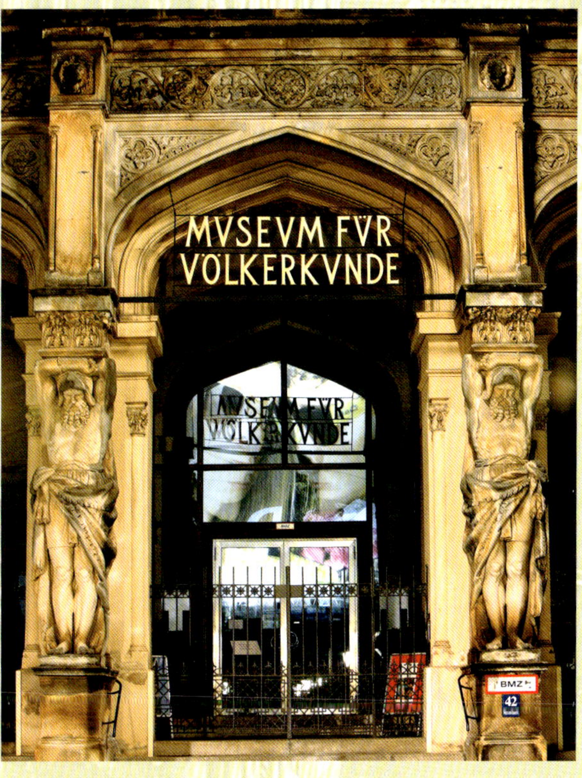

potato, rock and pop, dolls and toys. A mint and collection of bank notes embellish the spectrum, as does the Alpine Museum run by none other than the Deutscher Alpenverein or German Alpine Association. Kids will enjoy the museum for children and young adults.

There are edifices dedicated to famous individuals, such as Karl Valentin and Liesl Karlstadt, Erich Kästner, James Krüss and Michael Ende, all of which have a special connection with Munich. Perhaps the most poignant of them all is DenkStätte, the museum which honours the courageous and very young members of the Weiße Rose, the student movement which opposed – and was quashed by – the Nazi regime.

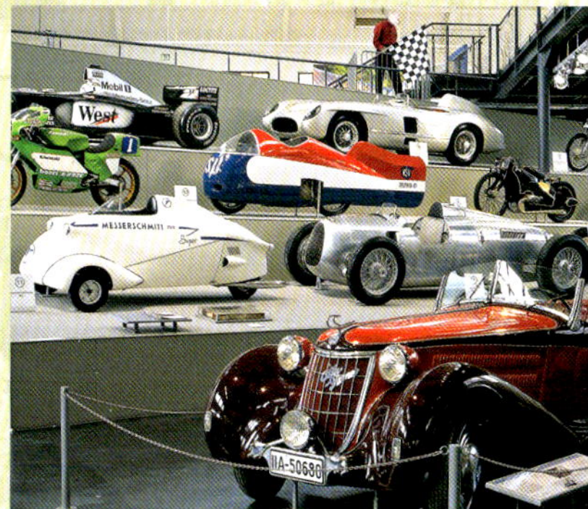

Far above:
The German museum of hunting and fishing on Neuhauser Straße was the church of the Augustinians until its secularisation in 1803. One of its highlights – life-size, stuffed and very rare – is the fabled Wolpertinger, a rabbit with antlers and wings said to inhabit the Alps ...

Above:
The Theresienhöhe branch of the Deutsches Museum, set up in 1903, focuses on mobility and technology, with carriages, bicycles, trains, cars and motorbikes amongst the exhibits.

Above right:
Entrance to the state museum of ethnology on Maximilianstraße. It's the second largest museum of its kind in Germany, with around 150,000 exhibits from all countries outside Europe.

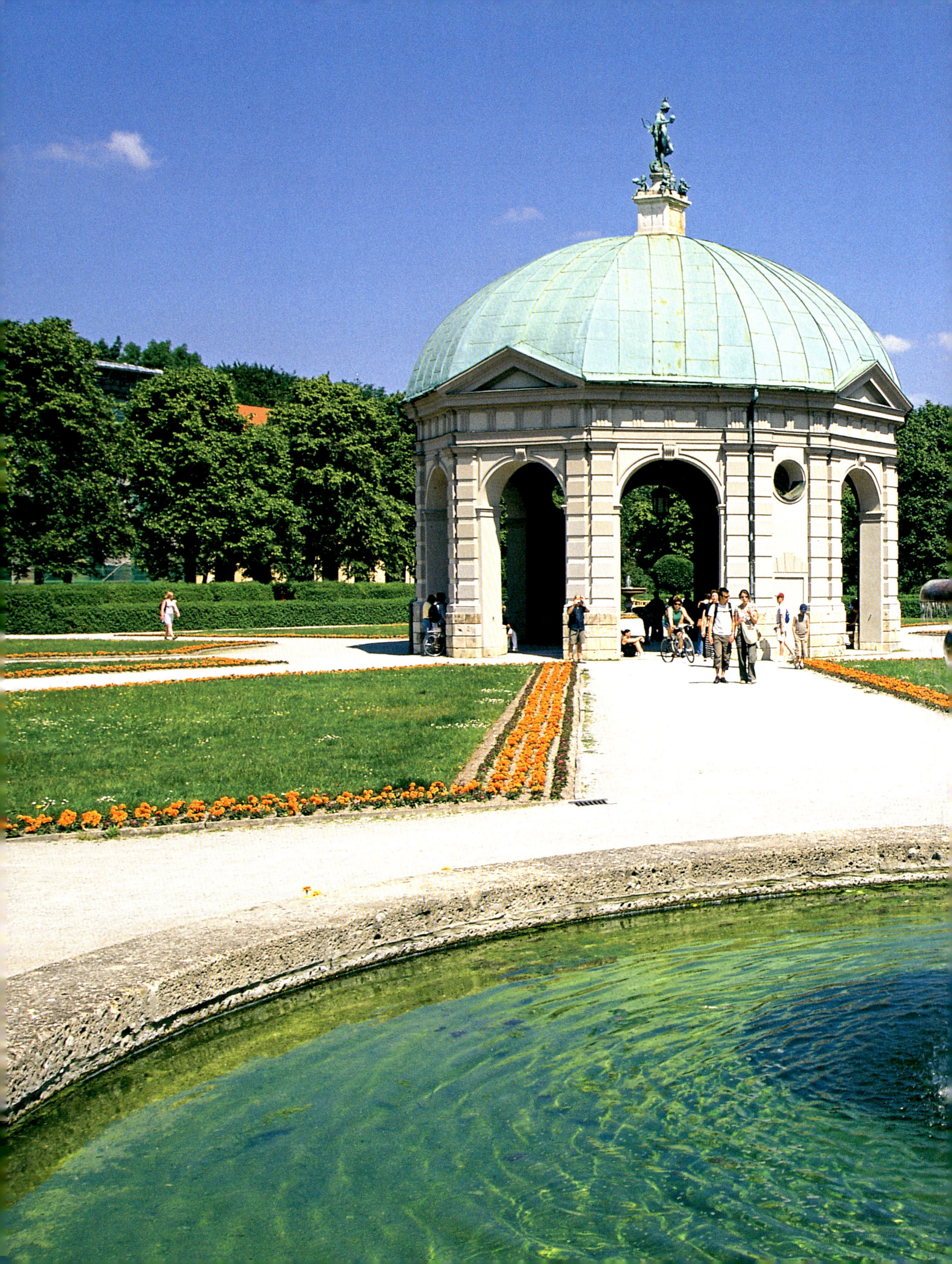

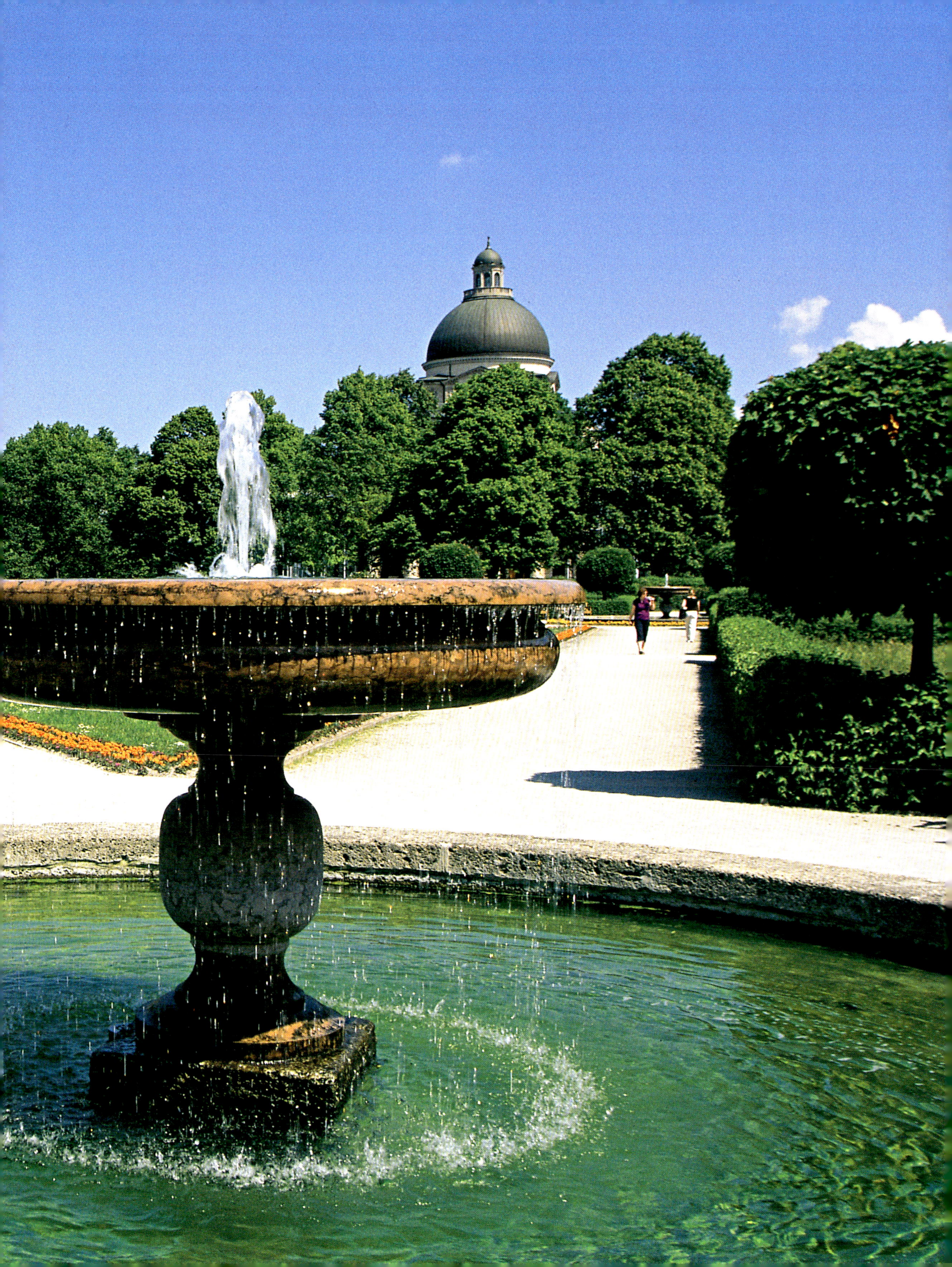

Page 64/65:
The Temple of Diana in the middle of the Hofgarten was probably erected by Heinrich Schön the Elder in c. 1615.
On the dome is a copy of Tellus Bavarica by Hubert Gerhard, a bronze personification of the riches of Bavaria (grain, game, water and salt).

Right:
Before the Brunnenhof in the Residenz was enclosed on all sides tournaments were held here. The courtyard is now a tasteful venue for summer concerts and all kinds of theatrical offerings.

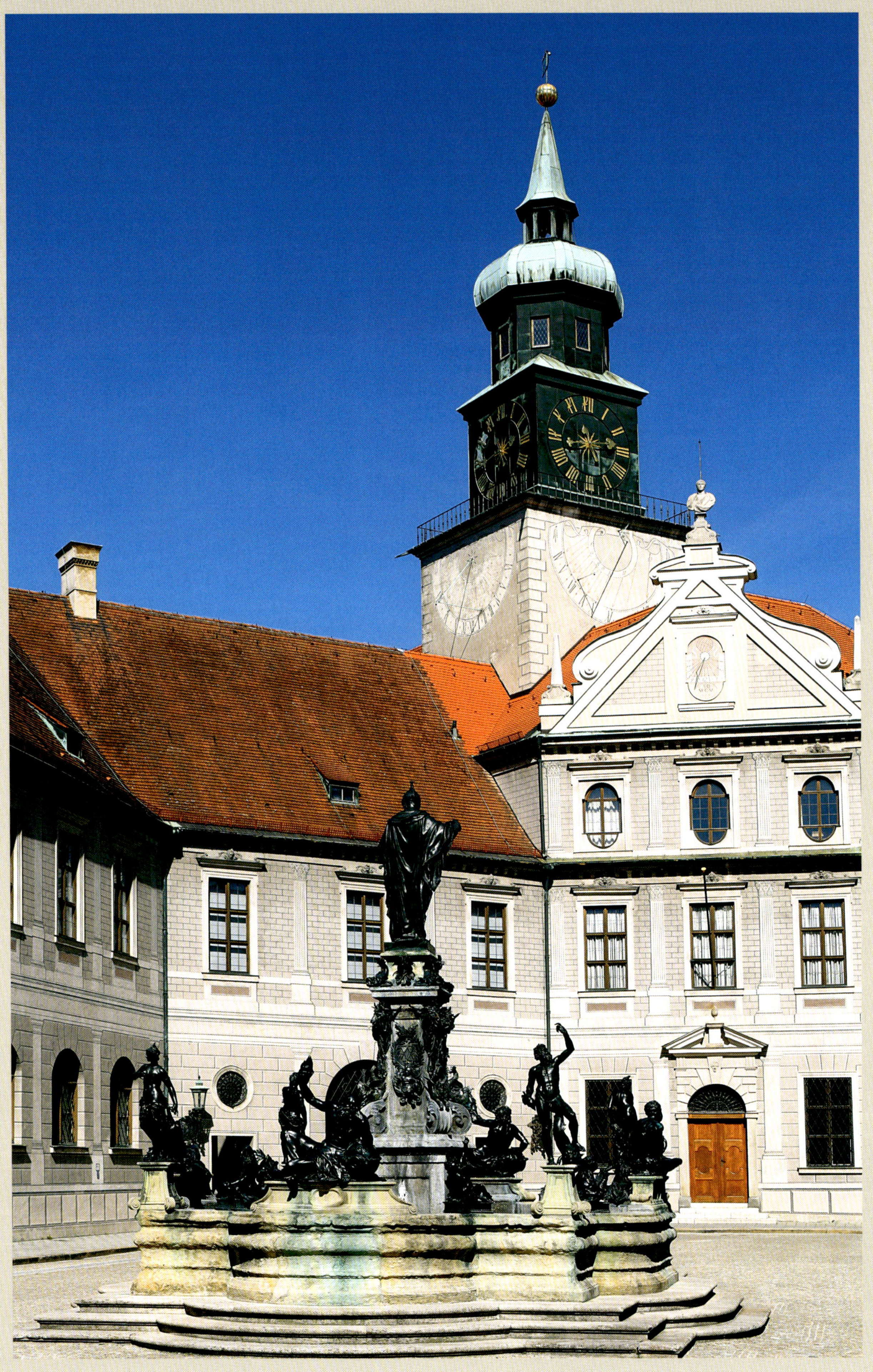

The Hofkirche, the palace church of All Souls, was built by Leo von Klenze in 1826–1837. Practically obliterated during the Second World War, by 2003 it had been fully restored and is now a magnificent backdrop for concerts of classical music and various other ceremonial occasions.

The Festsaalbau at the residential palace, seen from the gardens. Following its reconstruction after the war the ballroom complex now contains the Herkulessaal whose excellent acoustics make it the perfect place for concerts.

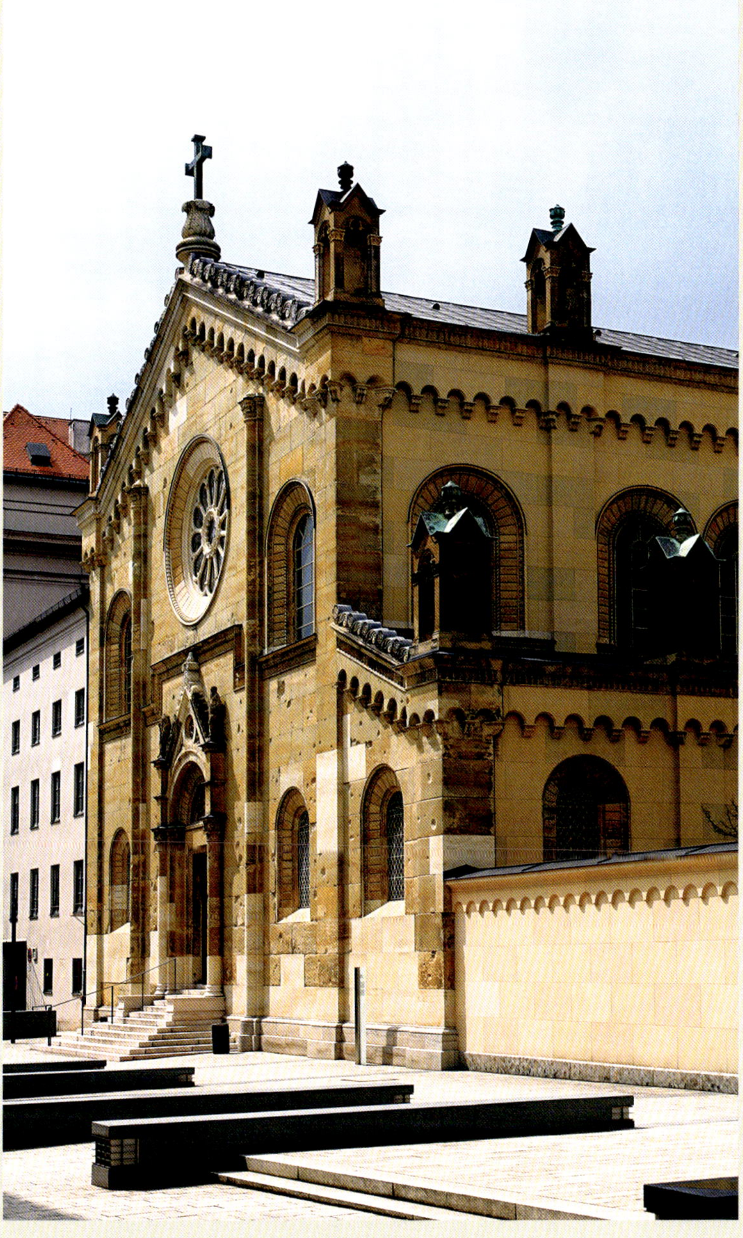

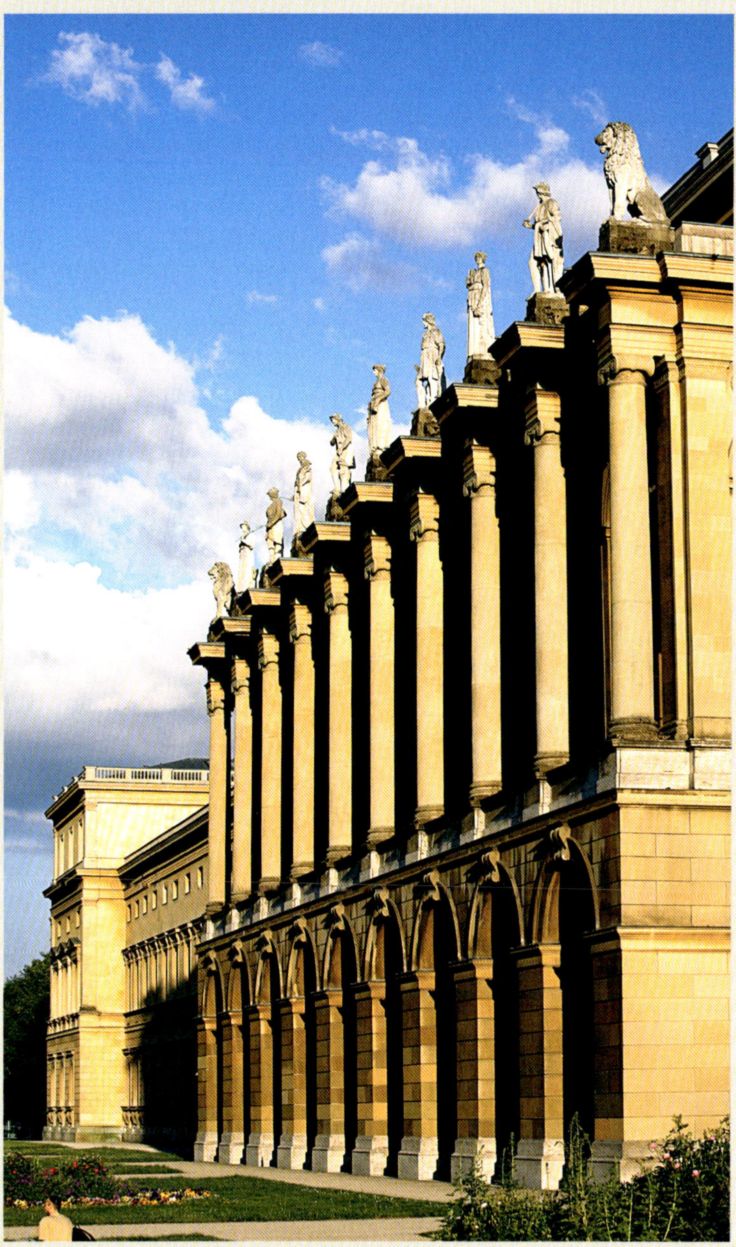

Right page:
At 69 m (226 ft) in length the Antiquarium in the Residenz is the largest Renaissance hall north of the Alps. It was built between 1568 and 1571 as a showcase for Duke Albrecht V's collection of antique sculptures.

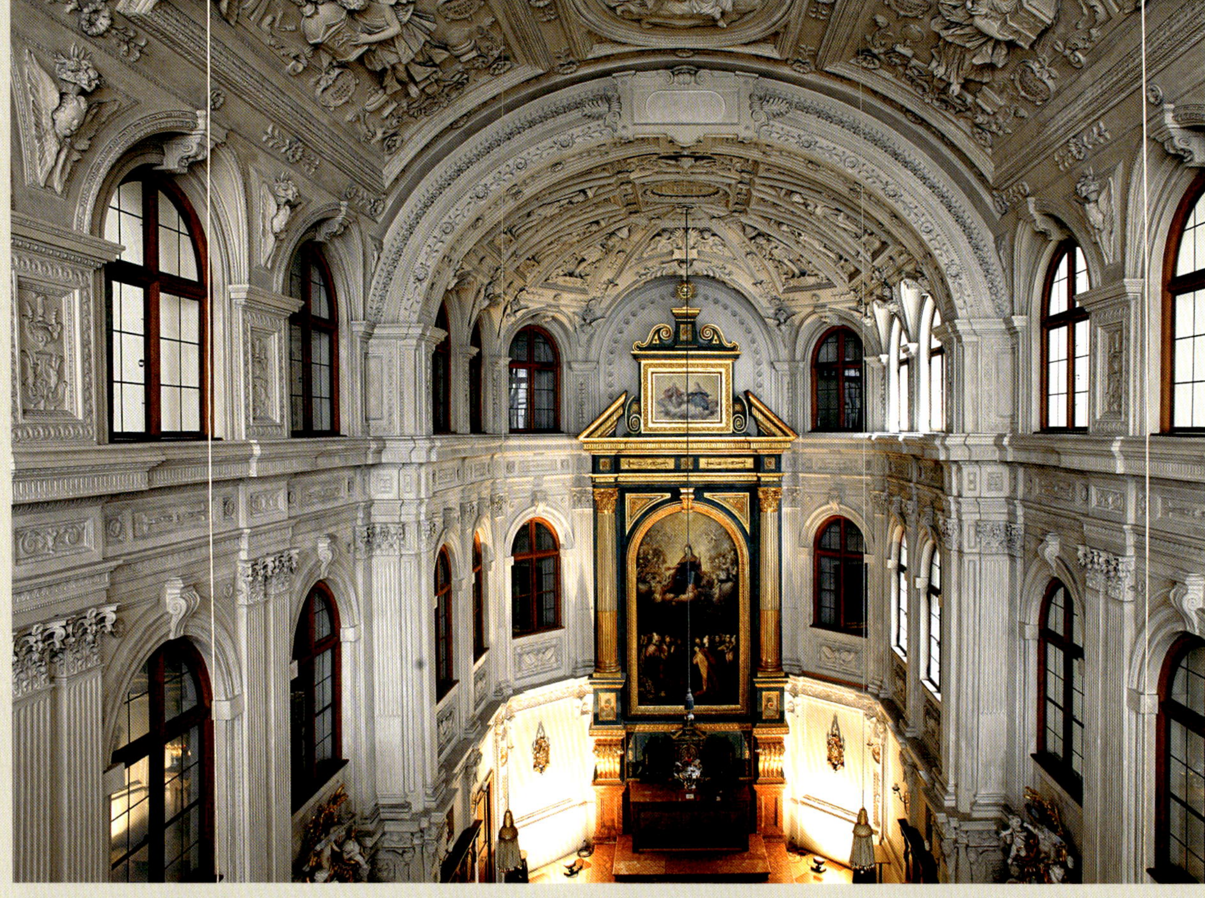

The Hofkapelle or royal chapel at the Residenz was begun under Duke Maximilian I at the beginning of the 17th century, with the chancel added in 1630. The high altar is assumed to be the work of Hans Krumpper (~1570–1634).

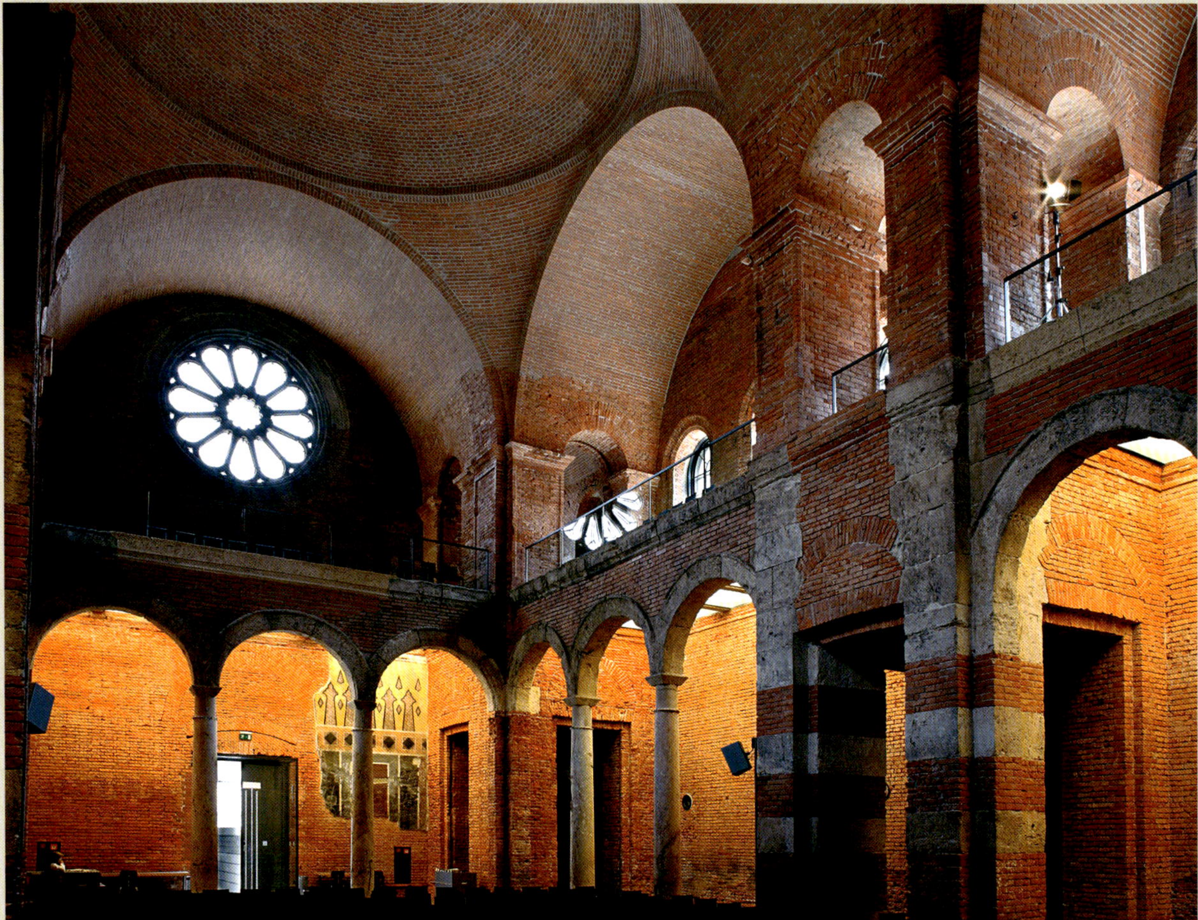

The Hofkirche imitates the styles of the Byzantine and Romanesque periods. It was the first church to be built in Bavaria after secularisation in 1803 and is thus dedicated to "all souls".

Page 70/71:
There are over one hundred portraits of the members of the house of Wittelsbach set into the carved, gilt wall panelling of the ancestral gallery at the royal residence. The elaborate stucco work is by Johann Baptist Zimmermann (1680–1758), he of the famous Wessobrunn School.

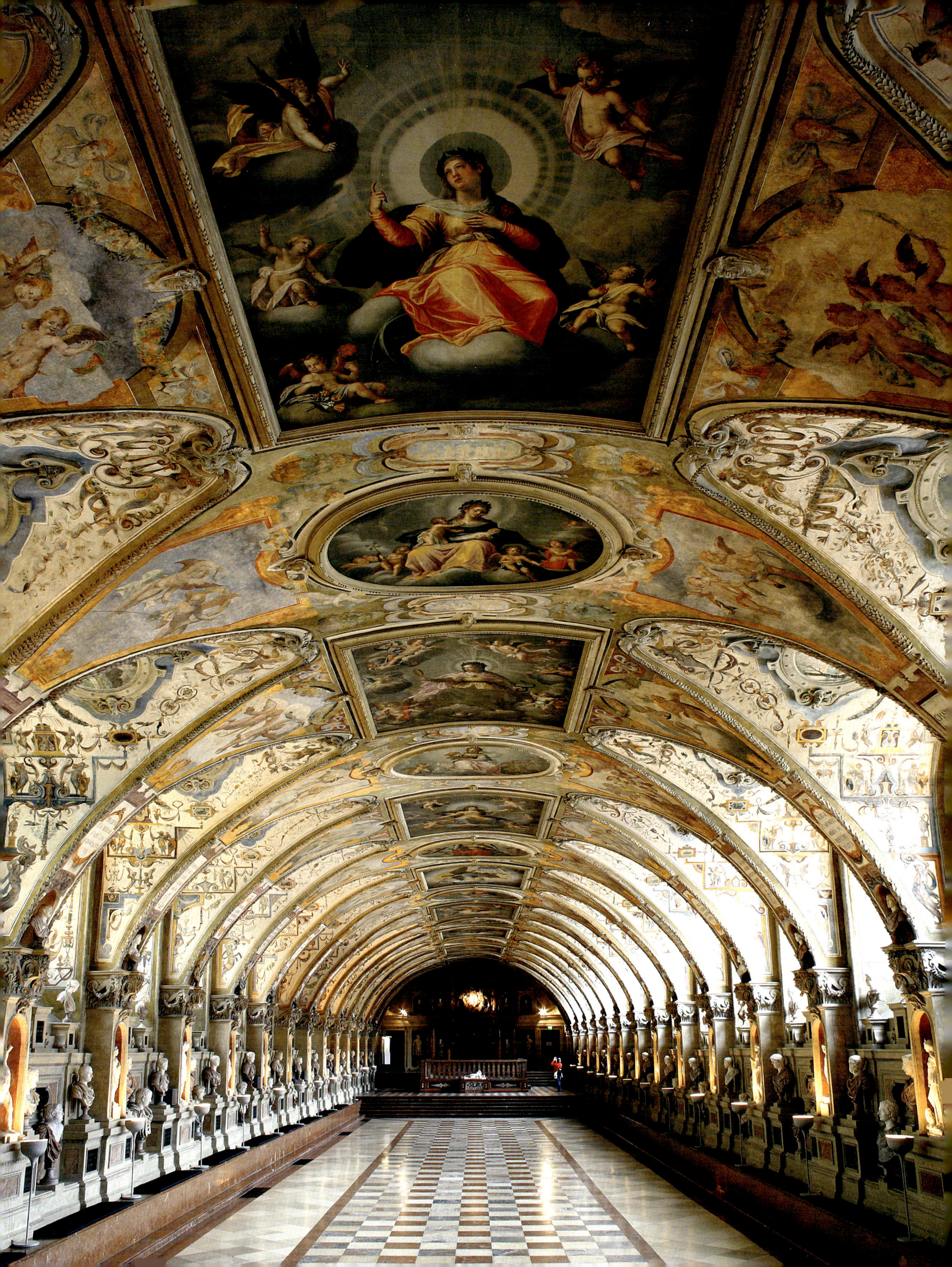

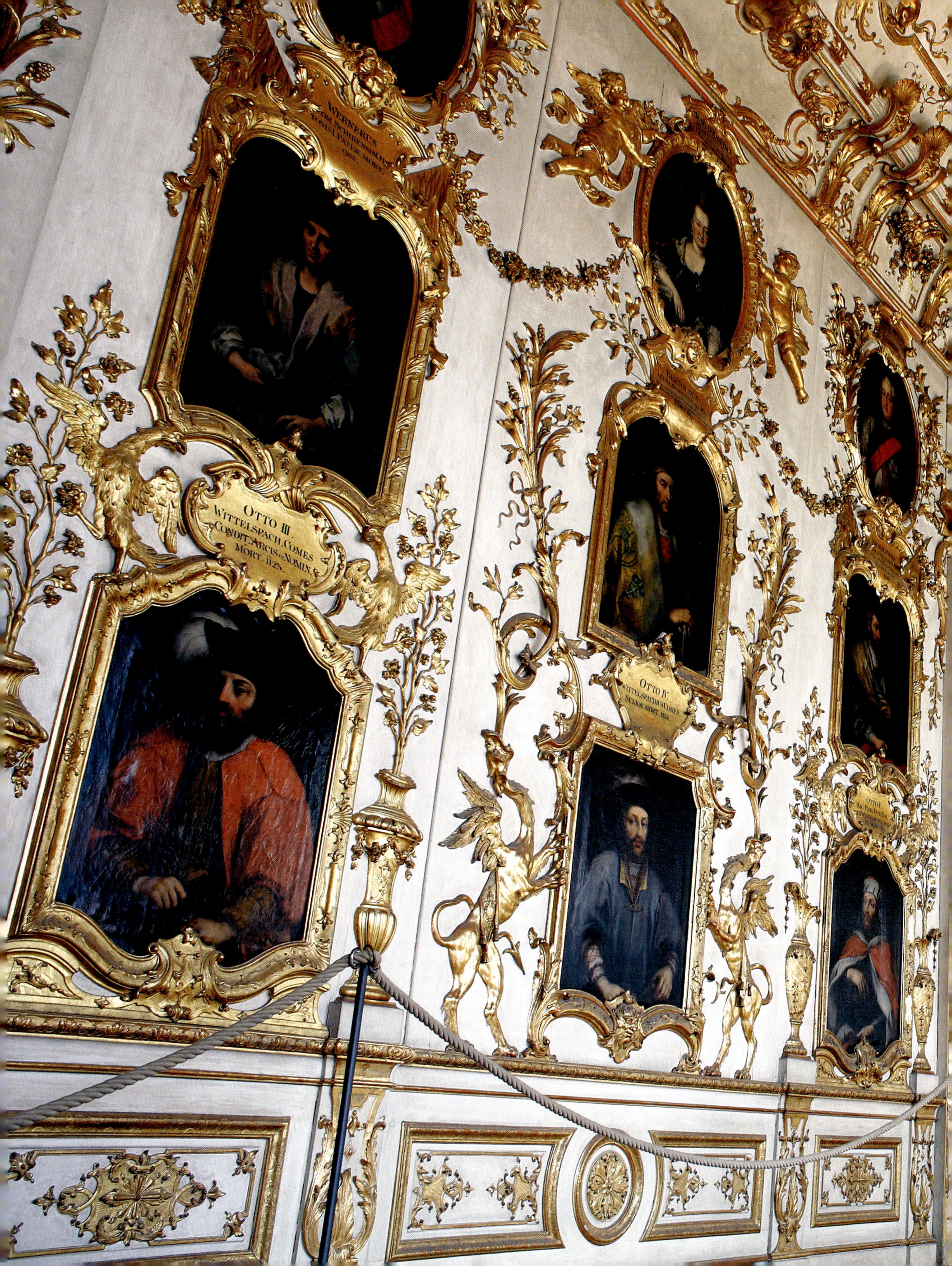
WERNERUS
OTTO III.
WITTELSPACH.COMES
CONDIT.ARCIS ET NOMIN.
MORT. 1125.
OTTO IV.
WITTELSPACHIUS COMES
SENIOR MORT. 1155.

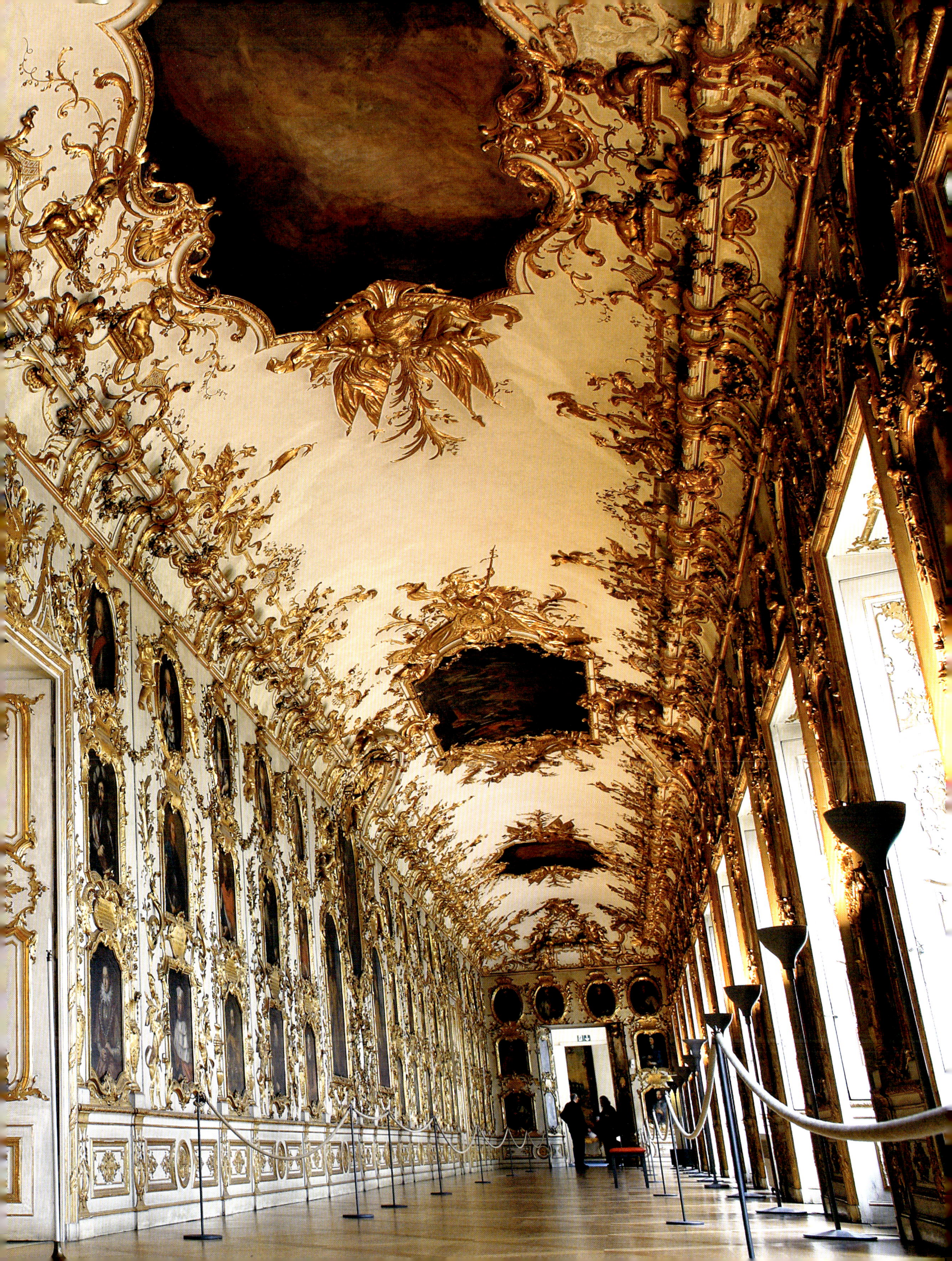

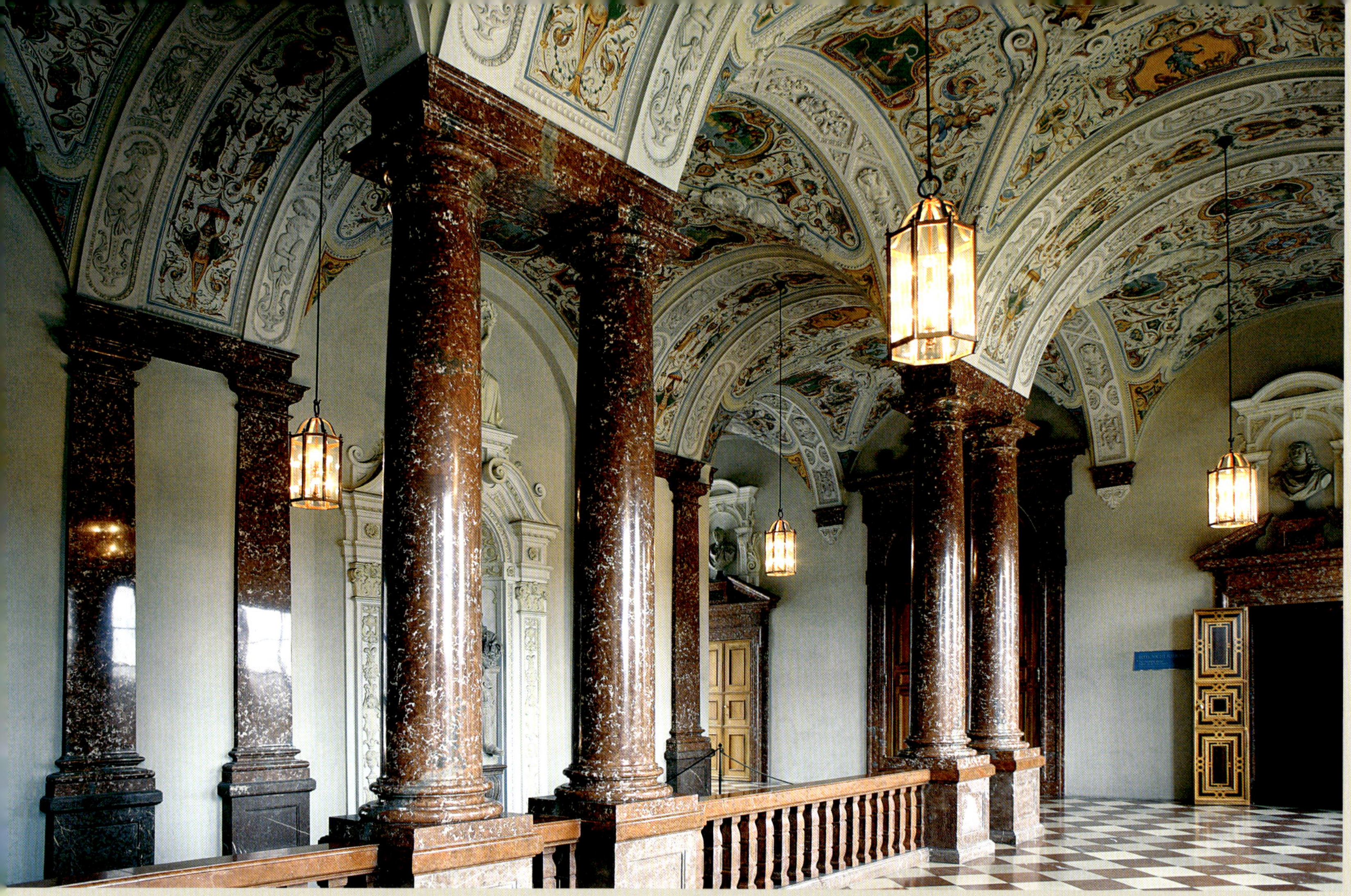

Above:
Between 1612 and 1618 Duke Maximilian I had this wing added to the Kaiserhof. A magnificent staircase leads up to the first floor and the equally sumptuous Kaisersaal or imperial hall.

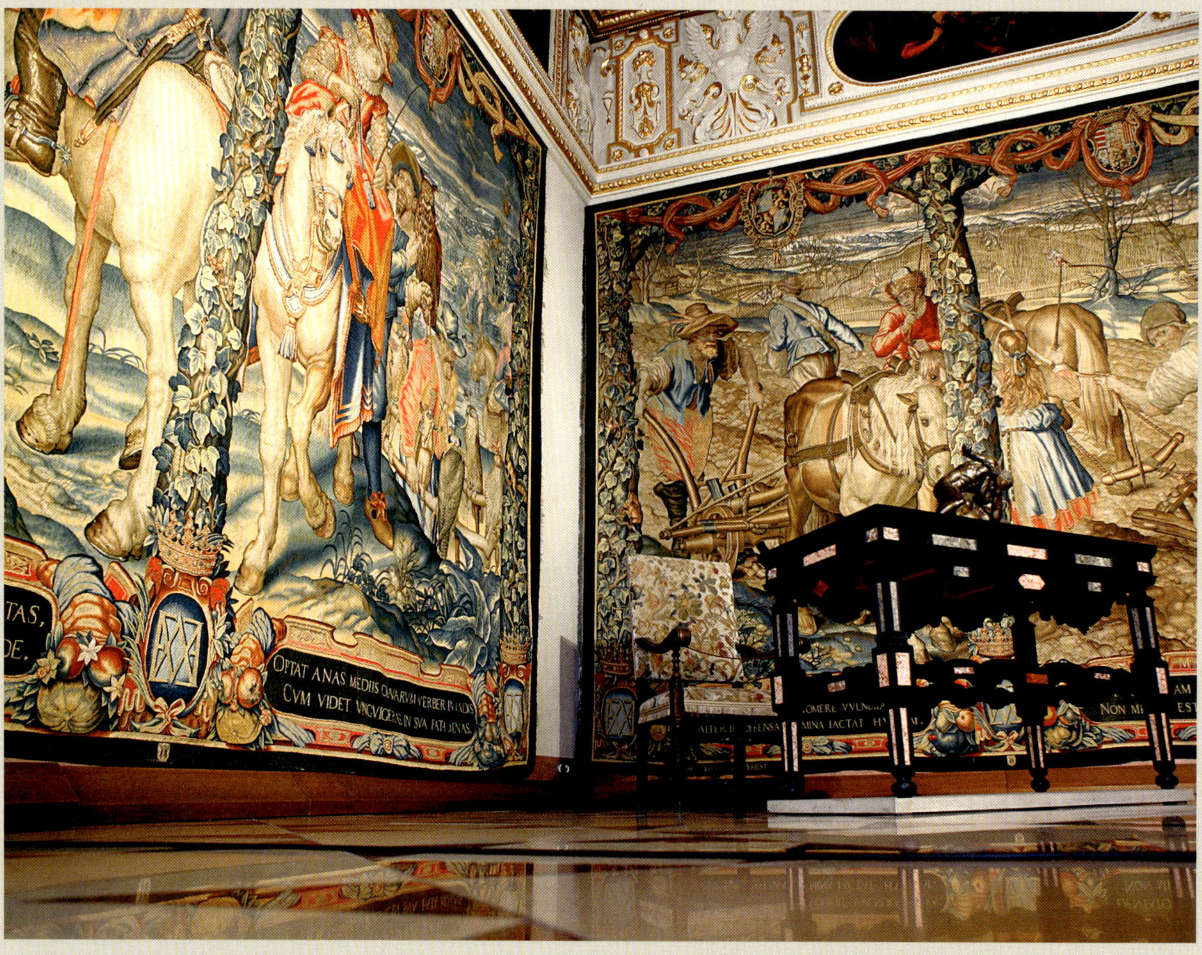

Right:
The Trierzimmer in the east wing of the Residenz are named after Klemens Wenzeslaus of Saxony, elector and archbishop of Trier, who spent much of his time here during the 18th century. The rooms are from the early 17th century.

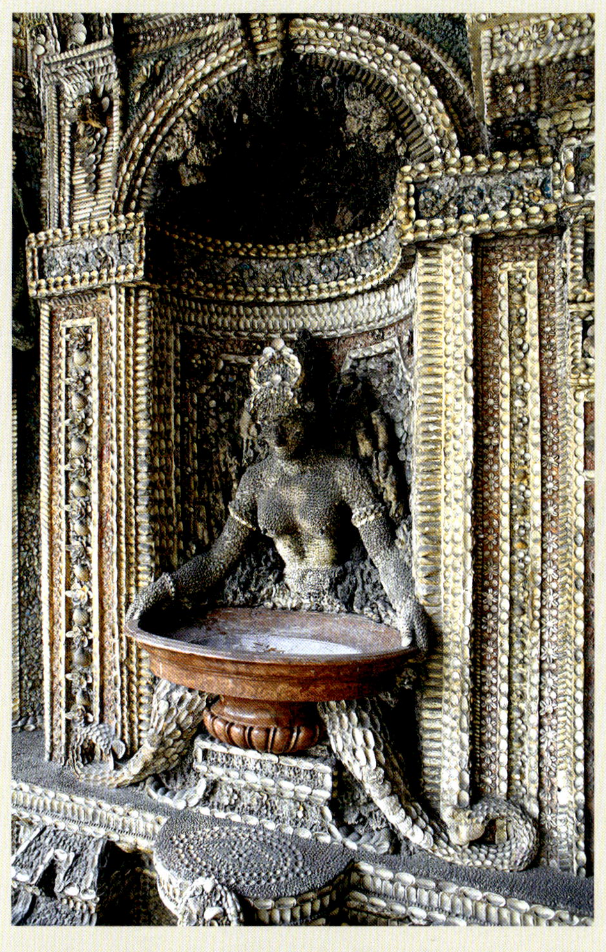

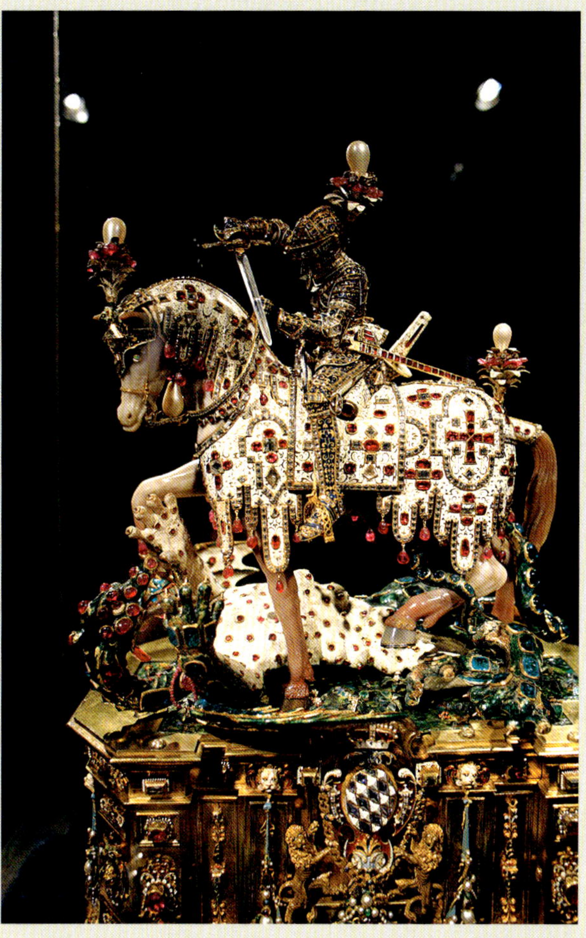

Far left:
Prince Regent Luitpold allowed his subjects to visit the rooms of the Residenz which were not used by the royal family. The present museum has over 130 rooms open to the public.

Left:
The treasury at the residential palace is full to bursting with precious artefacts collected by the various rulers of Bavaria over hundreds of years. This priceless statuette of St George was made in Munich between 1586 and 1597.

Below:
In its day the Kaisersaal added to the Residenz by Duke Maximilian I at the start of the 17th century was the largest and most important ballroom in the palace. The ceiling frescoes by Flemish painter Peter Candid (1548–1628) glorify the virtues of royal leadership.

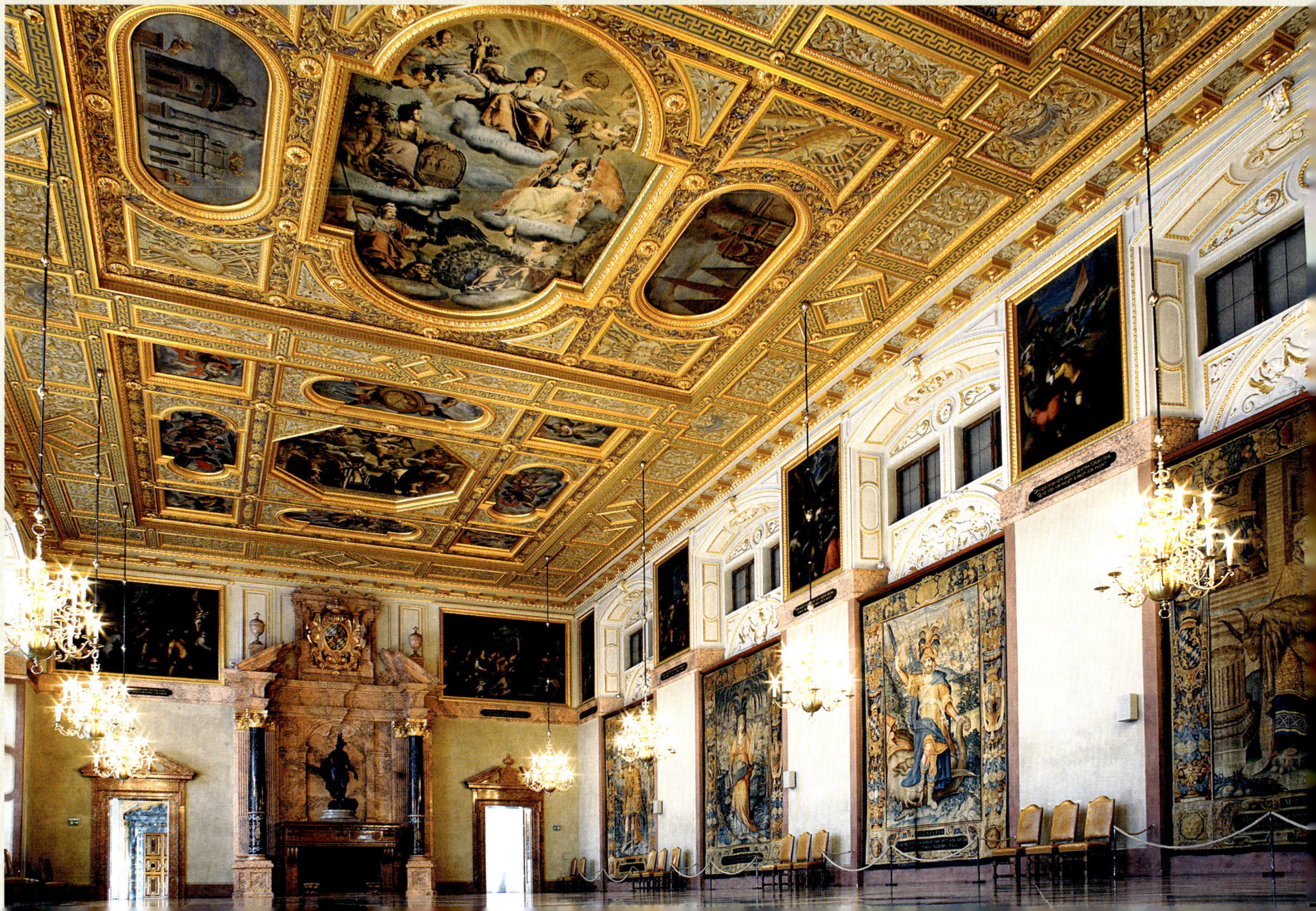

Right:
The Nationaltheater on Max-Joseph-Platz is home to the Bayerische Staatsoper and the Bayerisches Staatsballett. During the reign of King Ludwig II this is where Wagner's operas Tristan and Isolde, The Mastersingers of Nuremberg, The Rheingold and The Valkyrie were performed.

Below:
Shortly after he ascended to the throne nineteen-year-old King Ludwig II invited Wagner to Munich. The splendid royal box at the national theatre is in the middle of the auditorium.

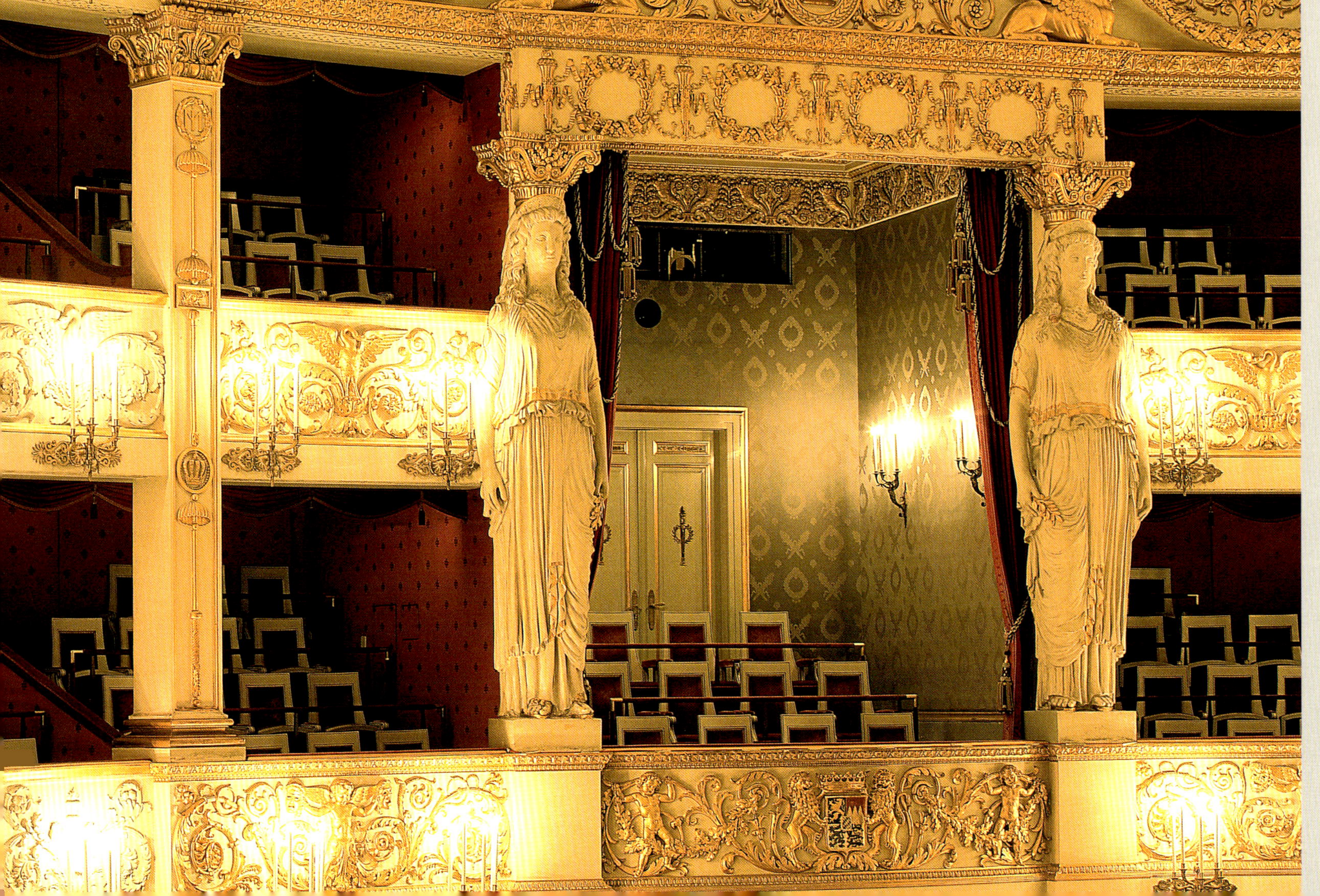

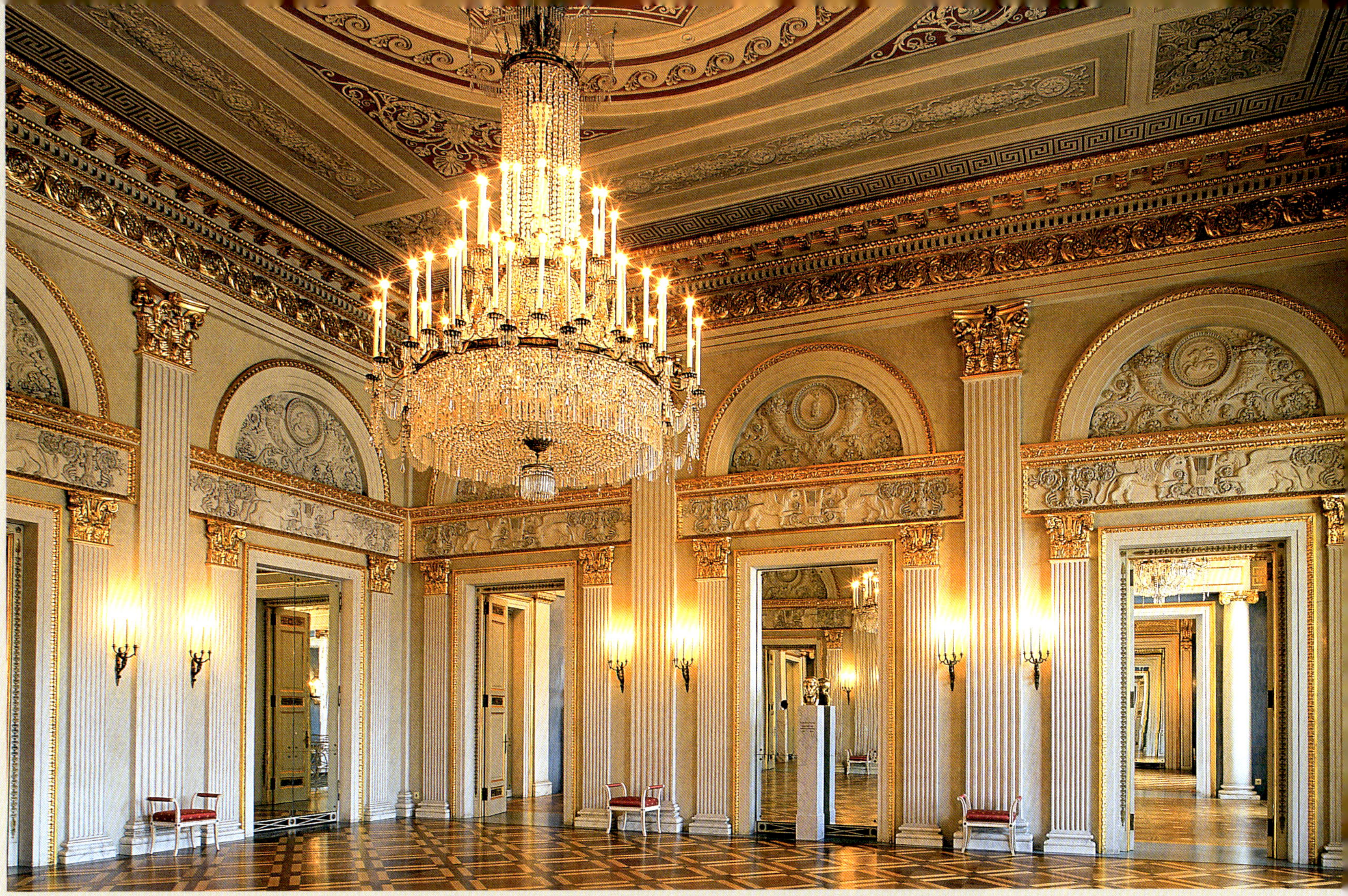

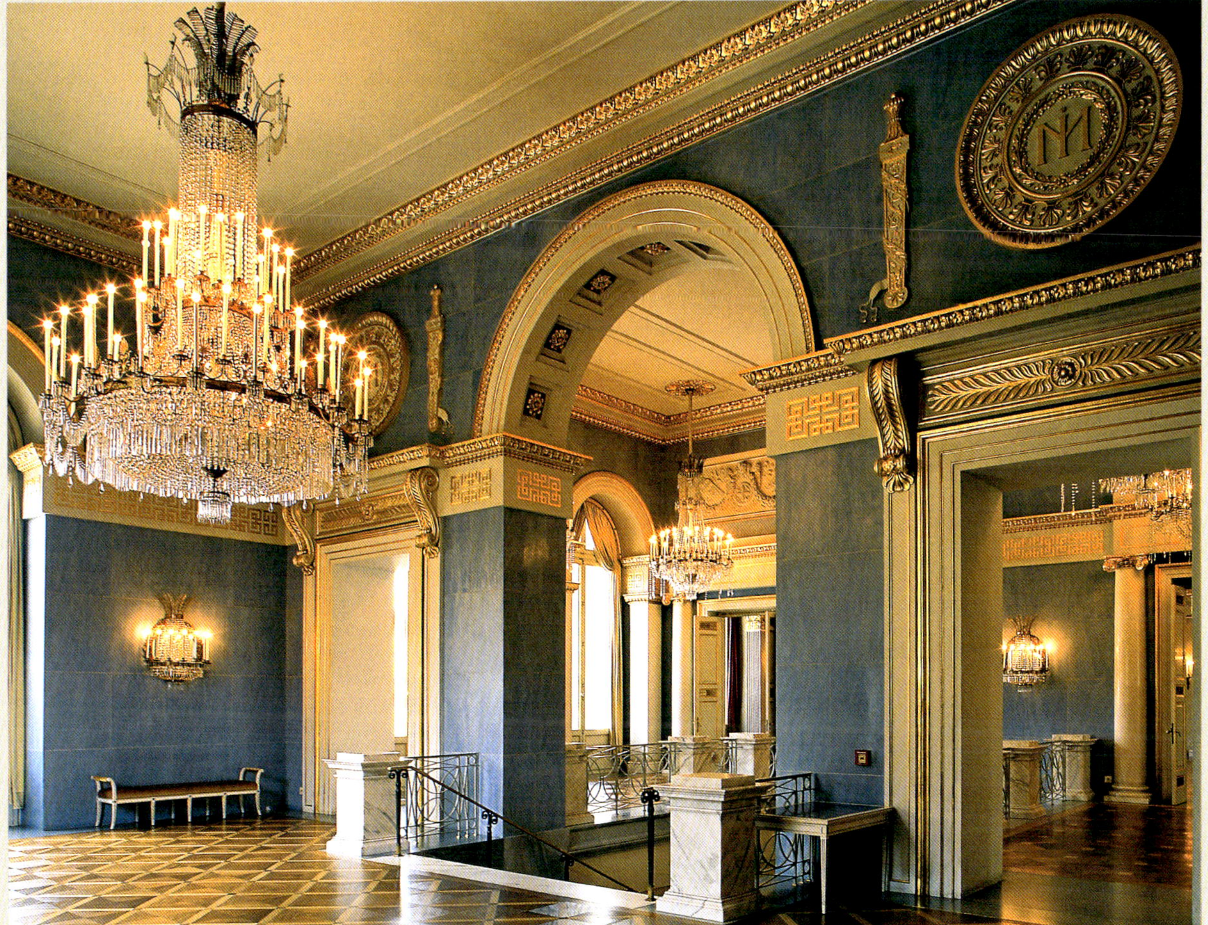

Above:
The Königssaal or royal hall at the Nationaltheater provides a fine setting for exhibitions, chamber music, receptions and discussions.

Left:
The Mosaiksaal is decorated in blue, white and gold. Munich's national theatre was destroyed in an air raid on October 3, 1943. It took five years to rebuild (from 1958 to 1963). The theatre now has one of the biggest stages for opera productions in the world.

Right page:
Looking south from the top of Alter Peter you can see the spires of St Maximilian set against an Alpine backdrop, "where greetings by white peaks open the heart so wide," to quote Richard Strauß' opera Feuersnot.

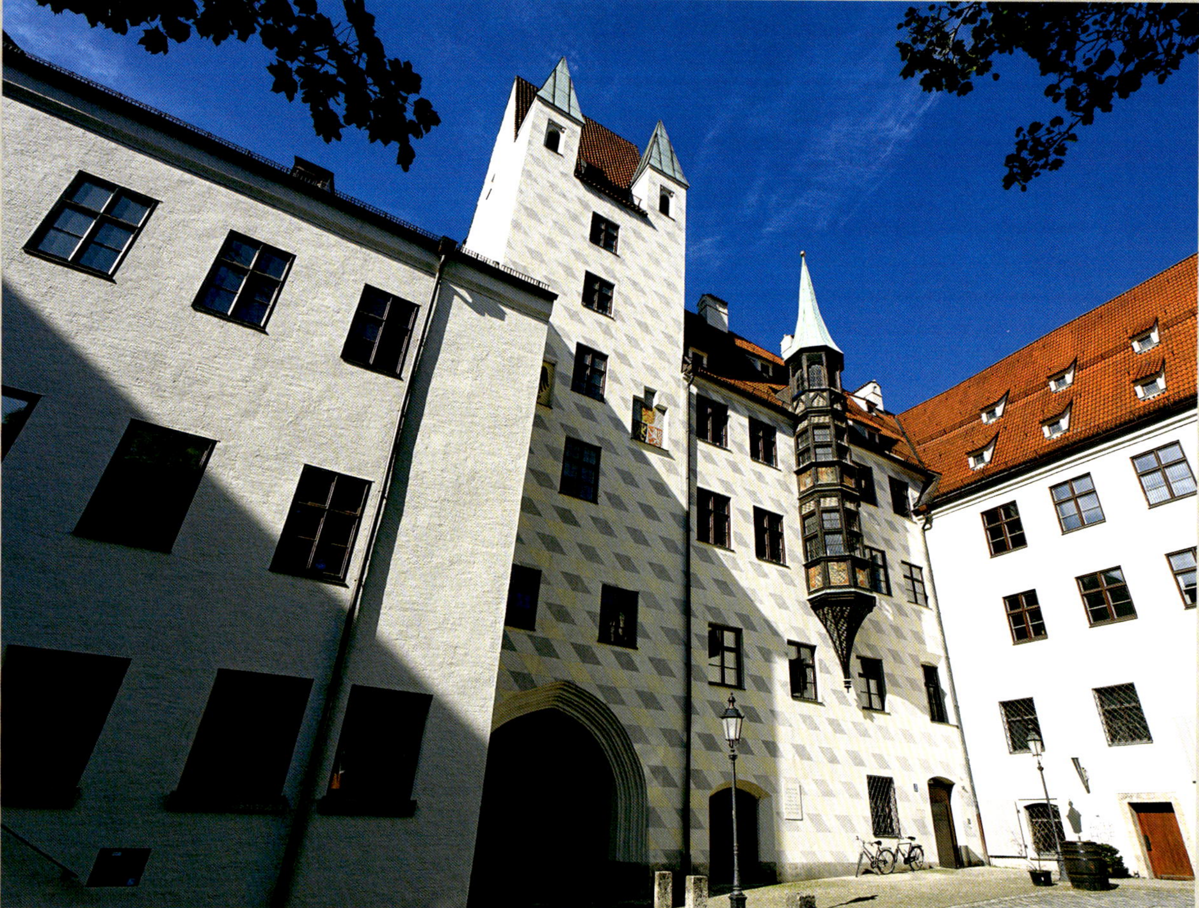

The Alter Hof is the old imperial residence of Ludwig the Bavarian in the heart of town. It was the seat of the Wittelsbachs from the 13th to the 15th century, rebuilt after much of it was destroyed during World War II.

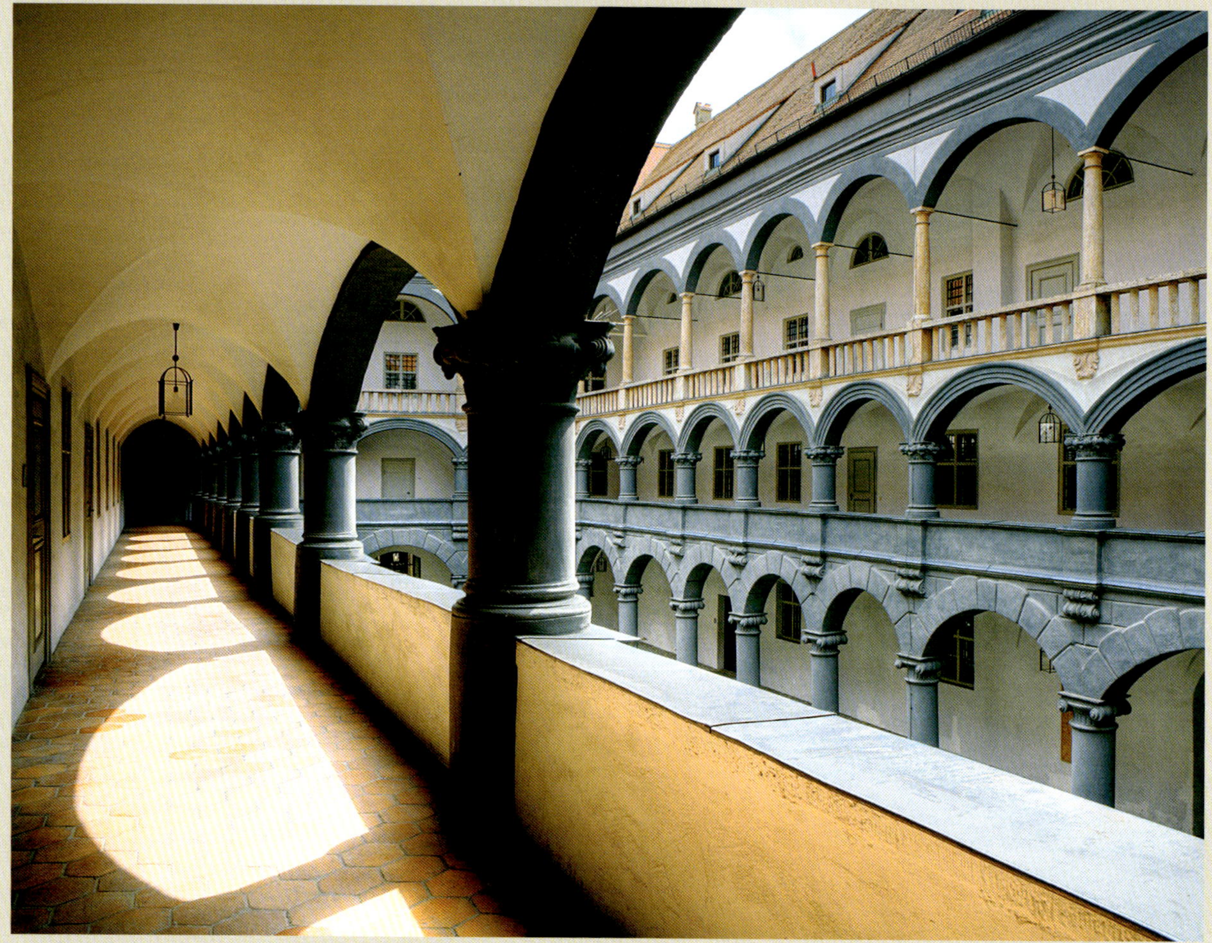

The Renaissance courtyard of the old royal mint. The former stable buildings on Hofgraben, built in 1563–1567 by Duke Albrecht V and refurbished by Andreas Gärtner in 1809, were used by the mint from 1809 to 1983. The building now houses Bavaria's ministry of works, the Bayerisches Landesamt für Denkmalpflege.

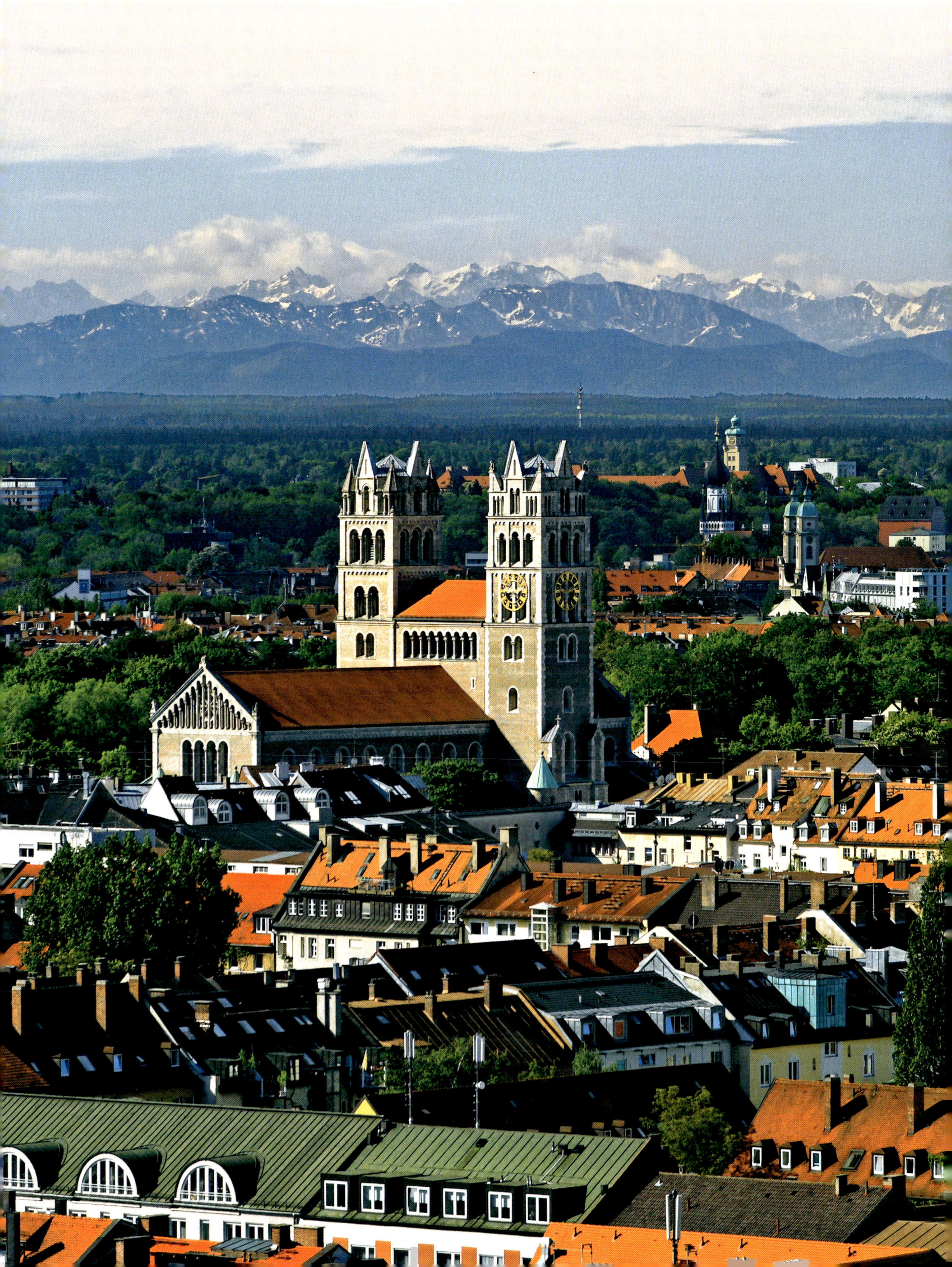

Top right page:
Another culinary attraction on Platzl is star chef Alfons Schuhbeck's restaurant. Top Bavarian cuisine is served at the Südtiroler Stuben, with the Bistro-Café Orlando the perfect place to round off a pleasant evening and observe Munich by night.

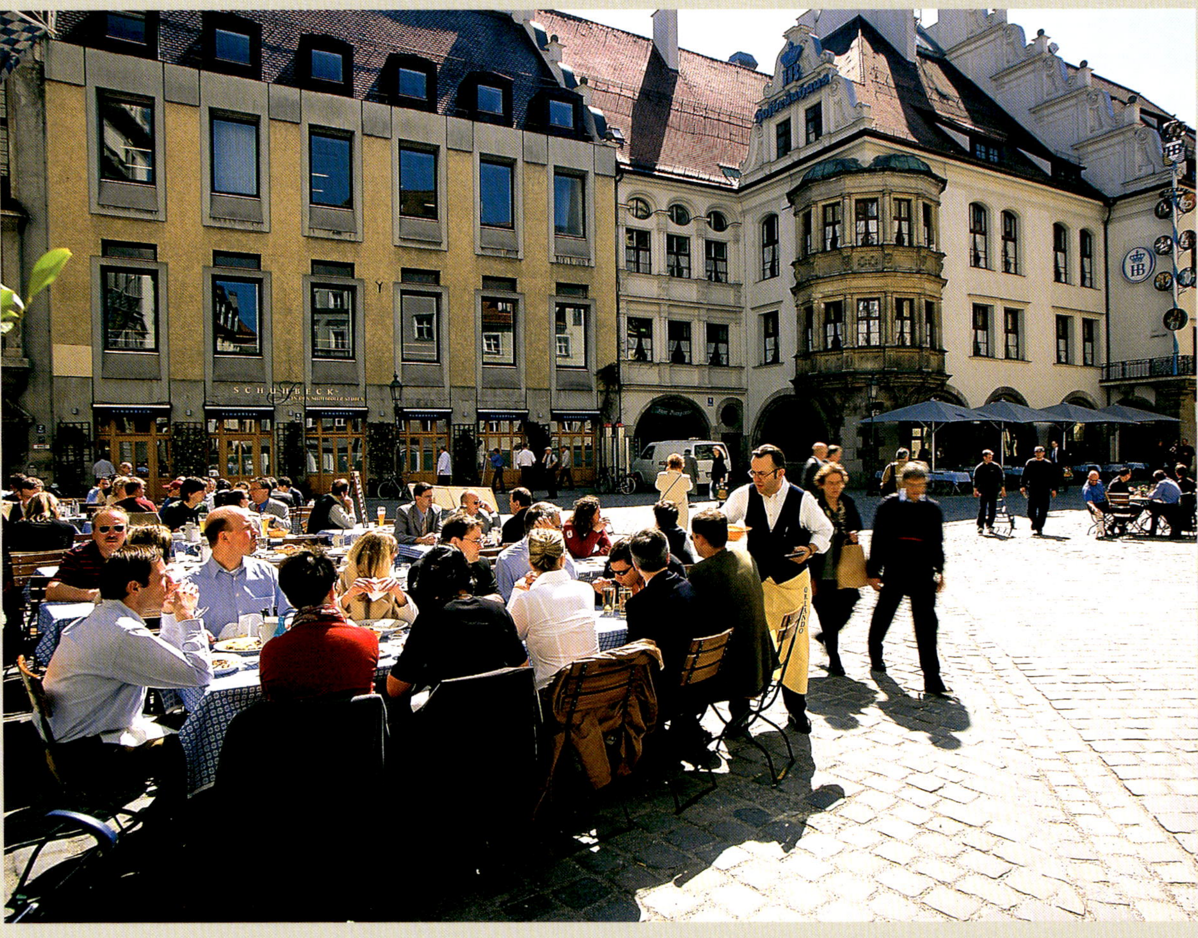

The Hofbräuhaus isn't the only famous locality on Platzl. The Orlandoblock is named after the Munich Hofkapellmeister Orlando di Lasso (1530–1594) who used to live in one of the old buildings here.

According to historian Cornelia Oelwein, Platzl is "joie de vivre in a square". There's certainly plenty of it to be had in the shady beer garden of the Hofbräuhaus, depicted here.

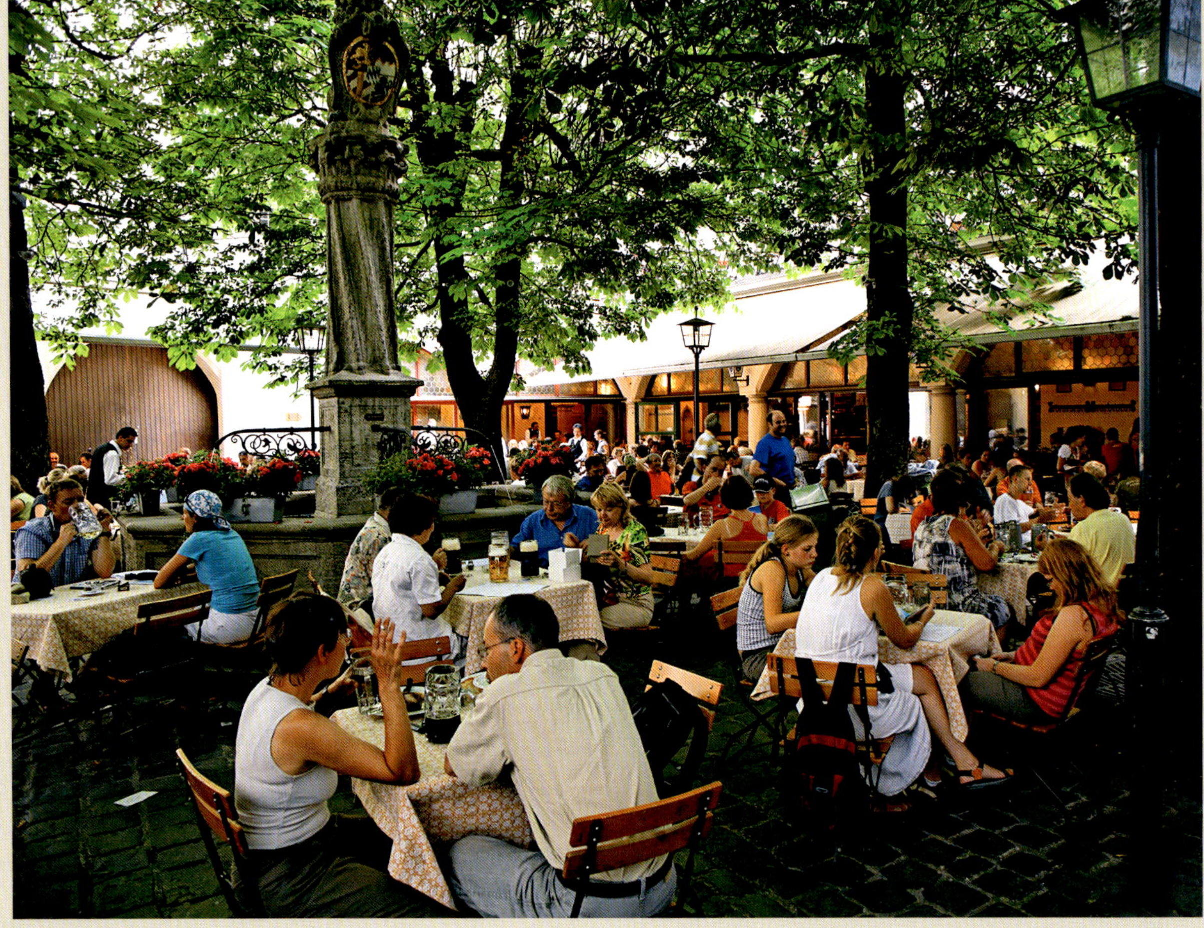

Bottom right page:
The traditional Hofbräuhaus not only serves that infamous beer but also Weißwürste, Munich's white sausages, made by the brewery's own butcher. Famous guests have included Mozart, Empress Sisi of Austria, Lenin and Josephine Baker.

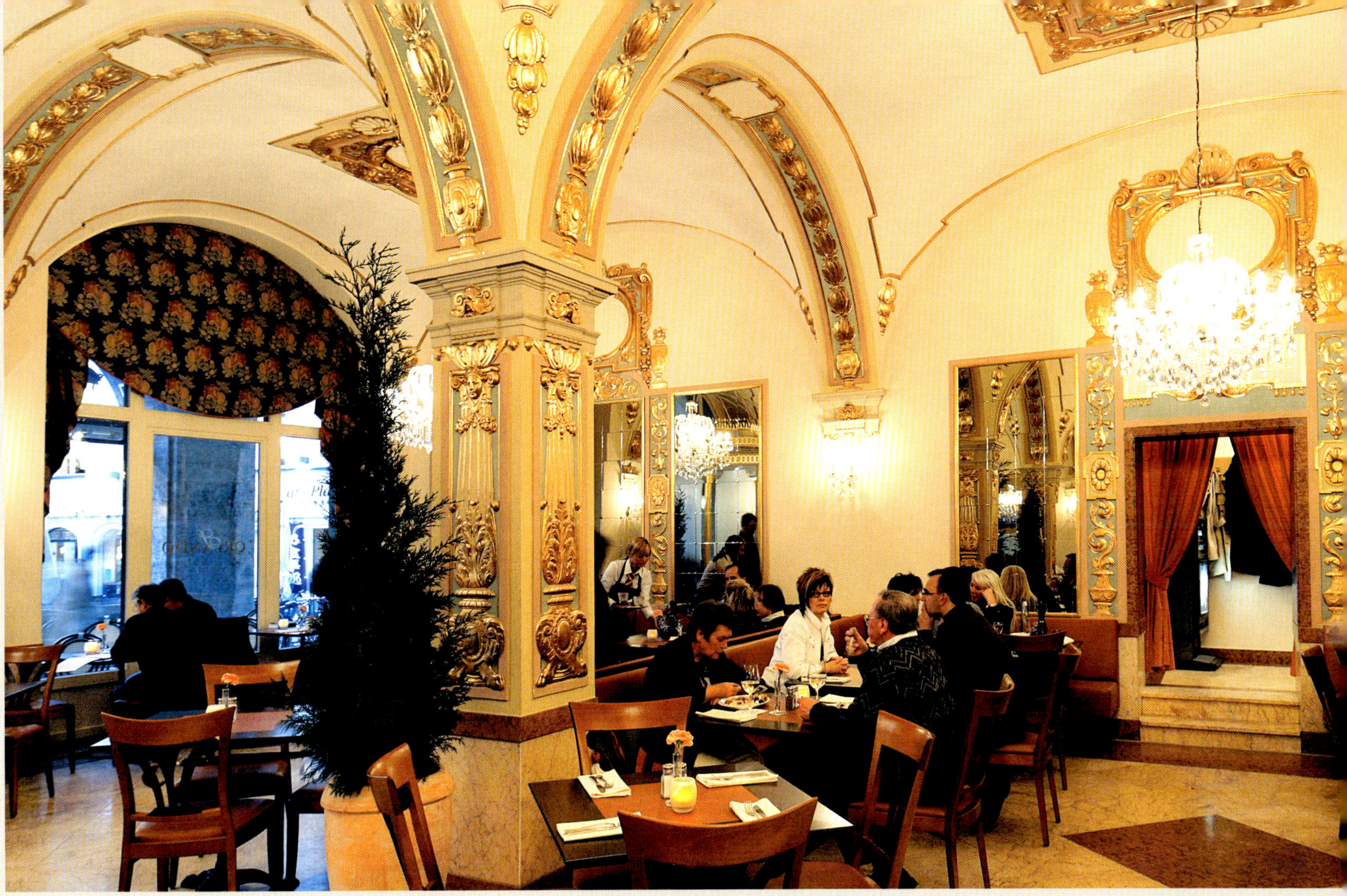

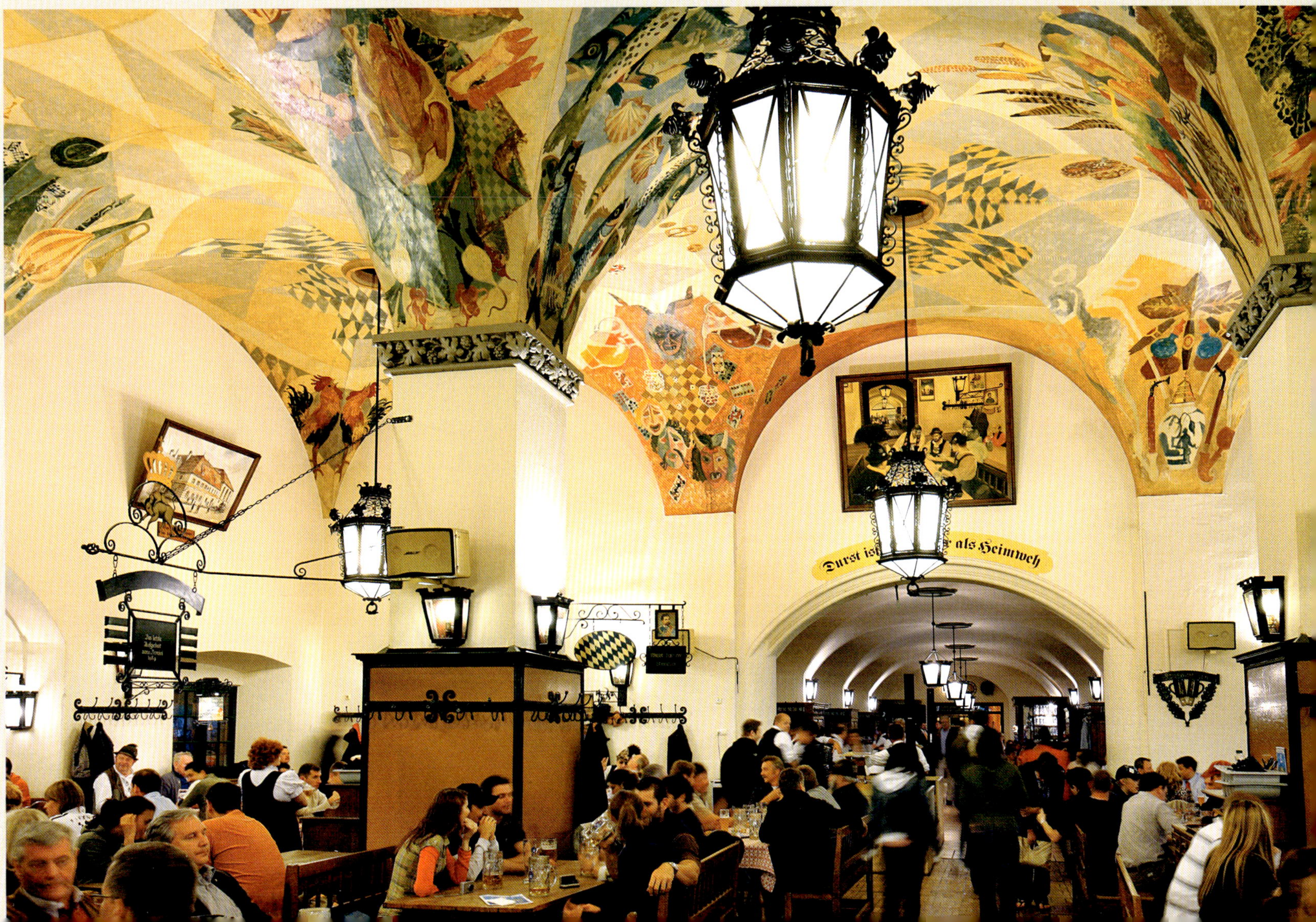

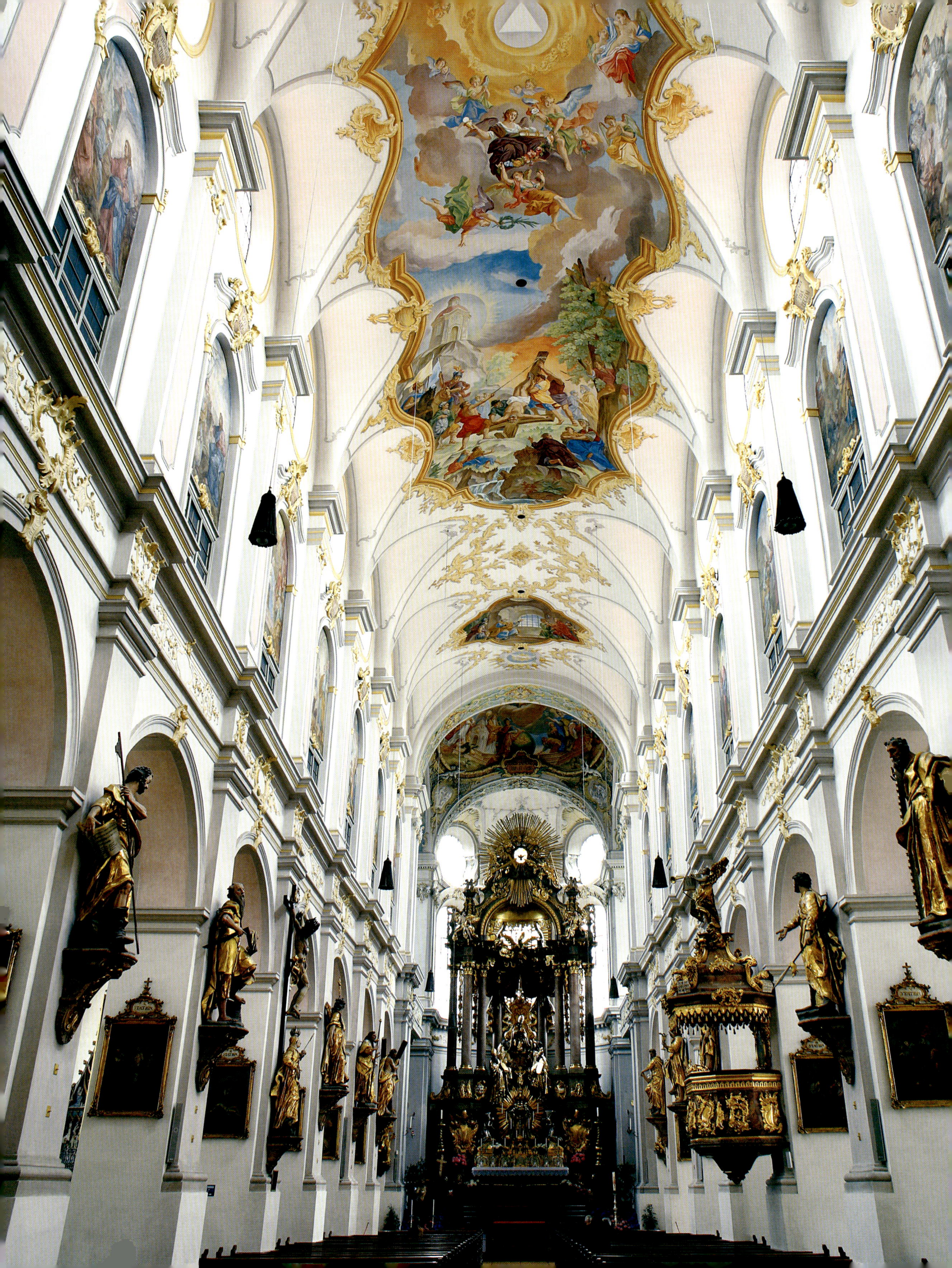

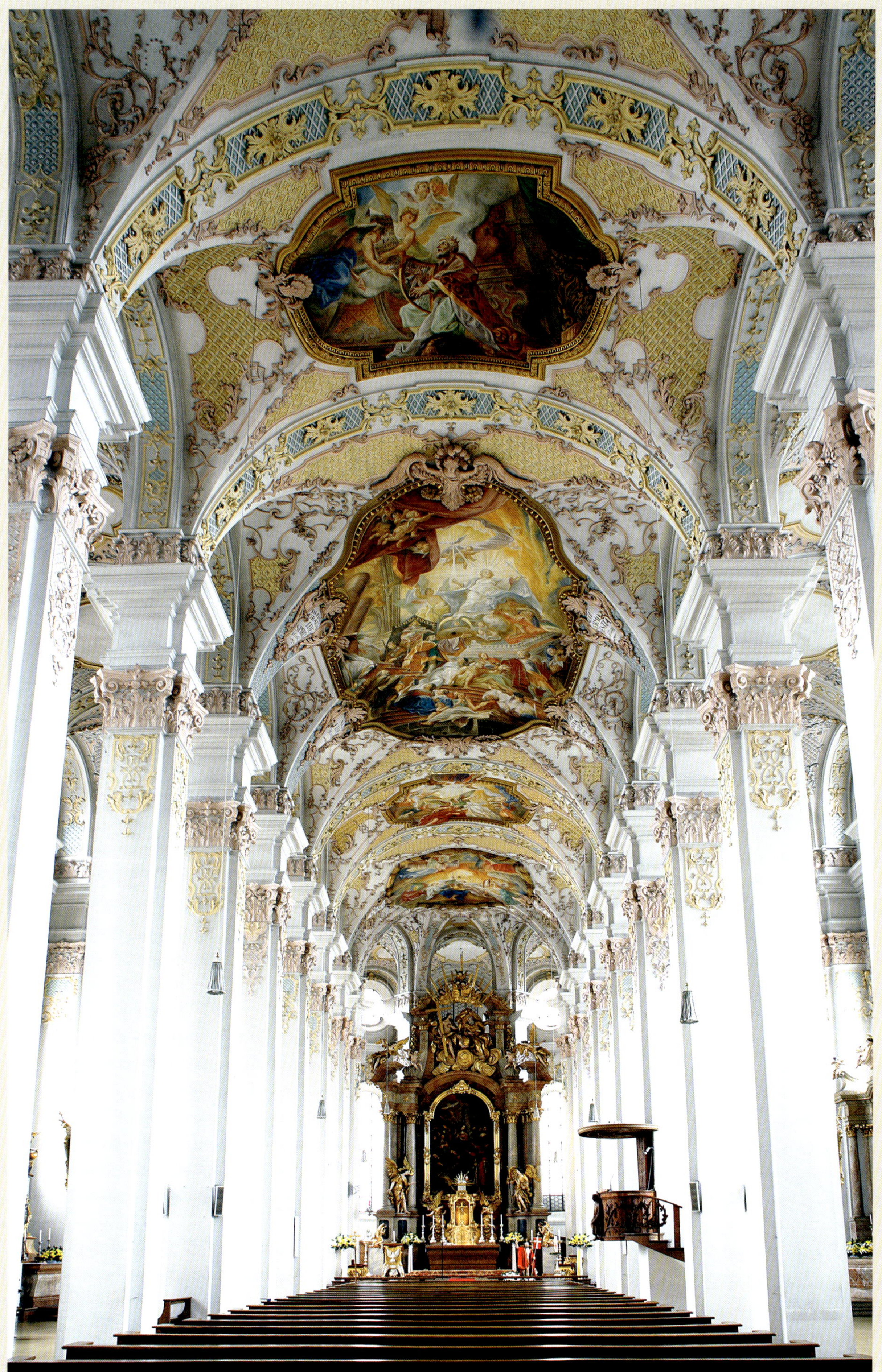

Left page:
The Rococo interior of the parish church of St Peter's was almost totally destroyed during the Second World War. It took until the year 2000 until everything was back in place. The ceiling frescoes depict scenes from the life of the apostle Peter.
The originals were by Johann Baptist Zimmermann.

The Heilig-Geist-Kirche near the Viktualienmarkt is one of the oldest churches in Munich. It was baroqueified by the Asam brothers in 1724–1730 and bombed to smithereens in 1944/45. Work on the interior is still going on.

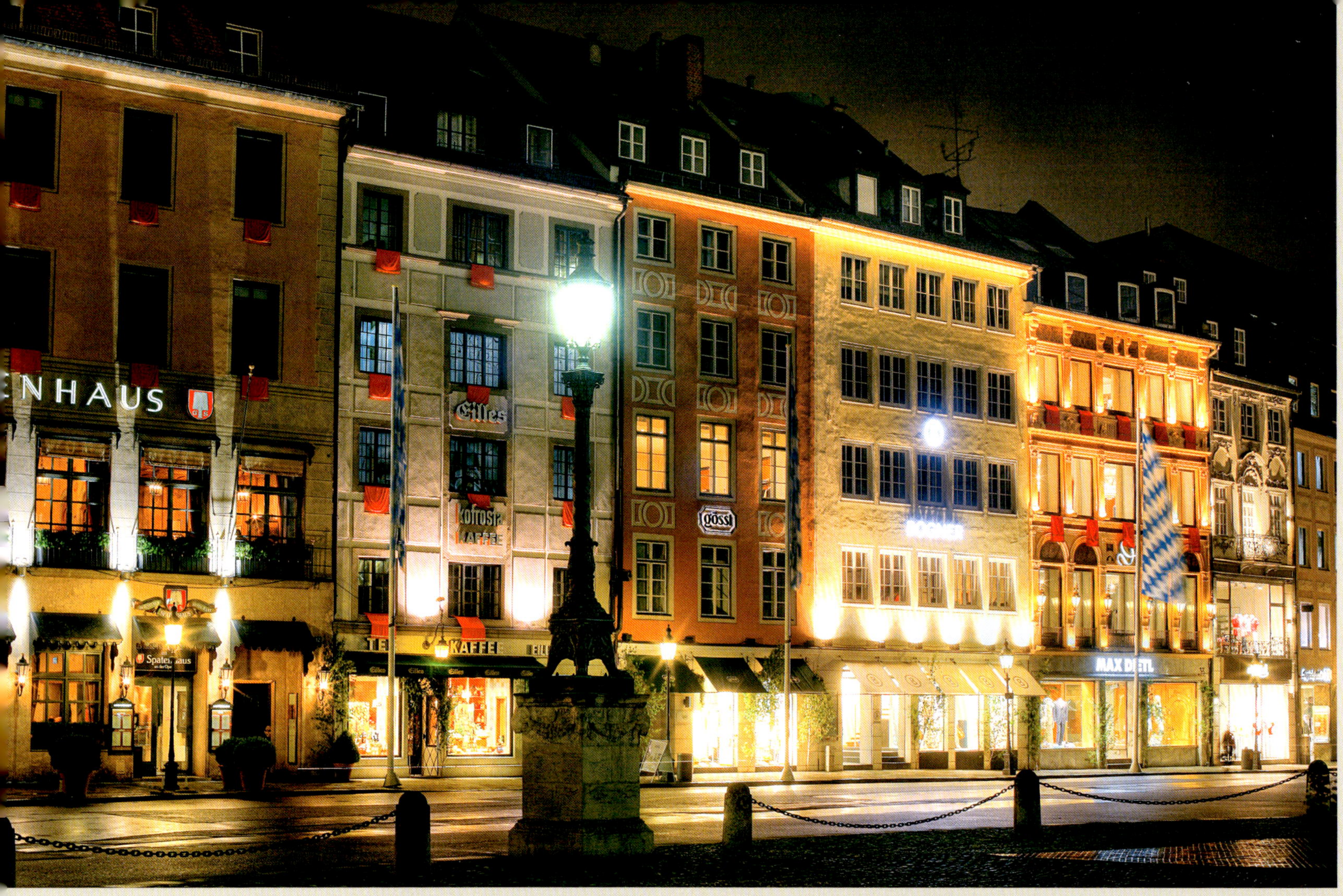

Above:
Residenzstraße provides shoppers with plenty of opportunities to get rid of their money: designer clothes, status symbols, Bavarian delicacies ...

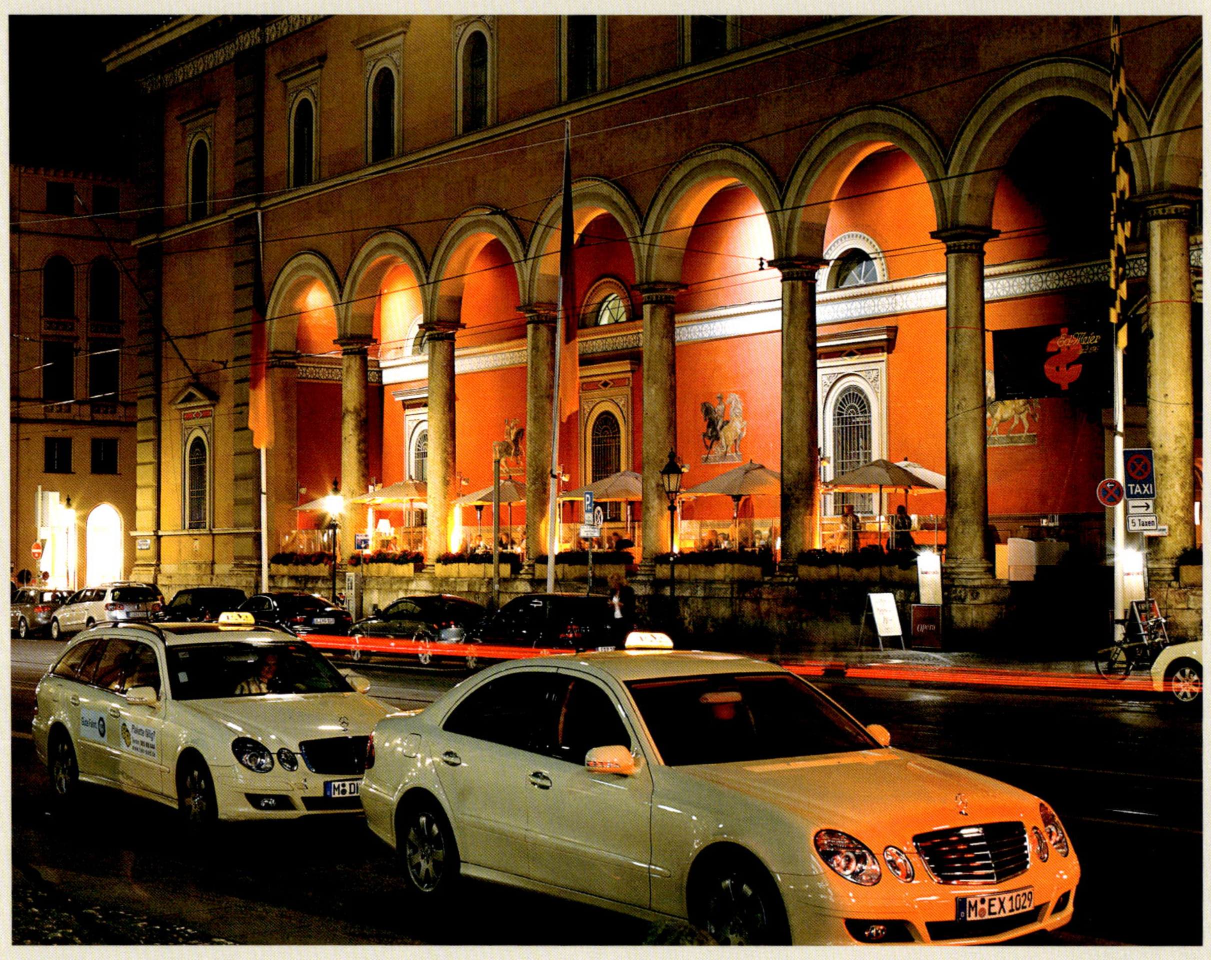

Right:
Palais Toerring-Jettenbach on Maximilianstraße 2 was turned into Munich's main post office by Leo von Klenze between 1827 and 1838. Its hall of pillars and arcading were based on buildings in Florence and now house the Café Opera, among other prestigious venues.

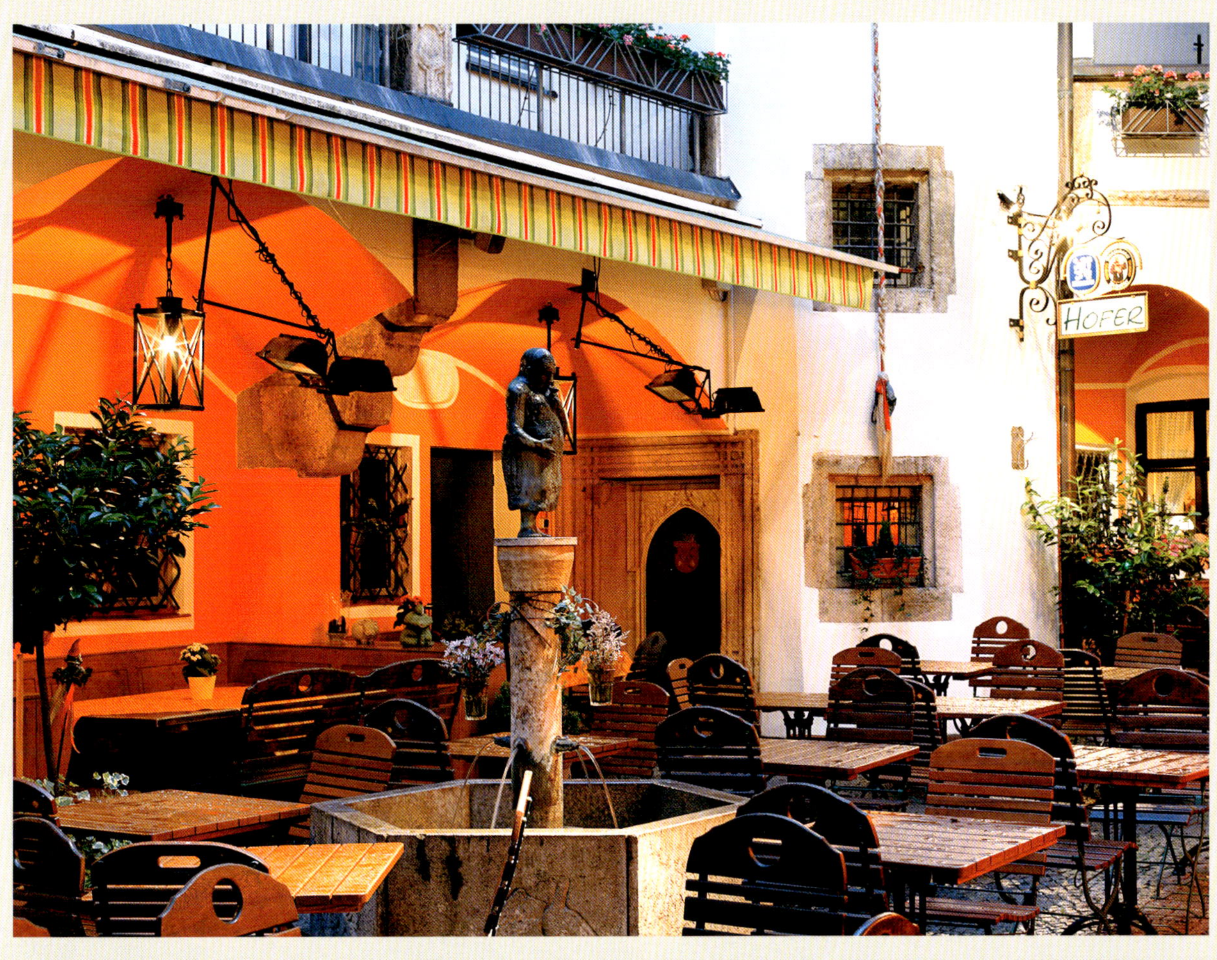

Left:
The oldest town house in Munich, built in 1551/52, is now the Hofer inn. On a fine day you can sit outside in the courtyard and enjoy some good Bavarian and Austrian cuisine.

Below:
The second line of city defences, which included the Isartor, was built under Emperor Ludwig the Bavarian (1282 – 1347). The gate's flanking towers have been home to the Valentin-Karlstadt-Musäum since 1959.

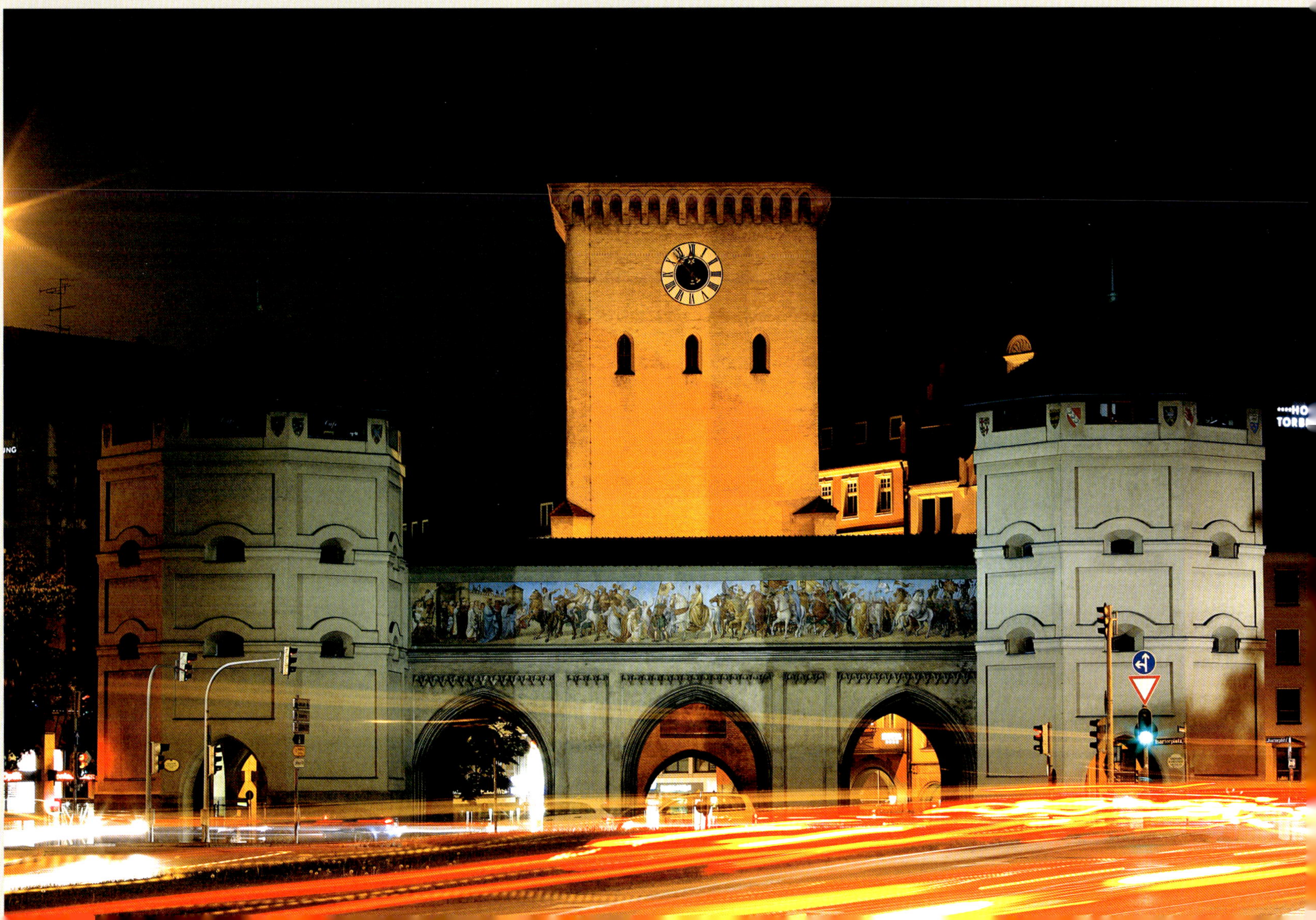

NOT A PERSON BUT A BAVARIAN –

KARL VALENTIN

"The future was better in the good old days" or *"It's all been said – but not yet by everybody"* are just two of the famous idiosyncratic utterings of someone Munich is proud to call its own: Karl Valentin, the comedian-cum-writer-cum-figure of fun, famous for his witty remarks, Pinocchio nose and gaunt, bent figure.

Centre:
Die Orchesterprobe (The orchestral rehearsal) from 1933 is one of the funniest films by Karl Valentin, in which he plays a rebellious musician and Lisl Karlstadt the pompous conductor.

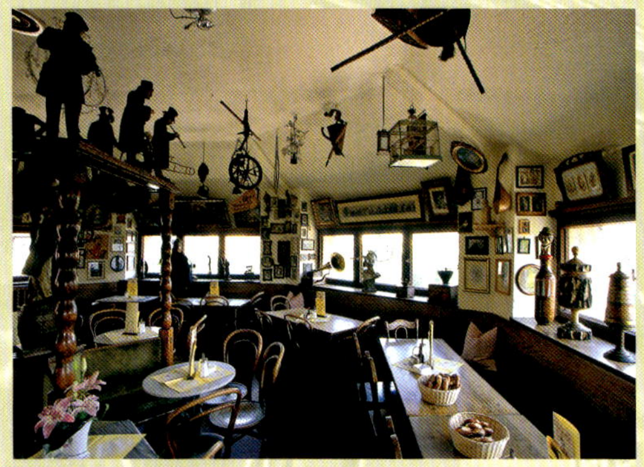

Above:
At the Turmstüberl pub in the Valentin-Karlstadt-Musäum smoking is banned. The reason given is pure Valentin: the curtains could turn yellow from the smoke – if there were any, that is.

He was born on June 4, 1882, as Valentin Ludwig Fey in the Munich suburb of Au. *"When I saw the midwife who delivered me, I was speechless. I had never seen this woman before in my entire life."* His time at school was later described as a "sentence in a house of correction". Following this he trained as a carpenter. This was a form of education from which he was to profit his whole life, enabling him to build the sets for his plays himself.

His first appearance on stage was in Nuremberg in 1902. The death of his father rapidly put a stop to Karl's life as an artiste, however; he was promptly called back to Munich to run his father's transport agency with his mother – which he bankrupt in 1906.

His breakthrough was in 1908 with his monologue entitled The Aquarium. Karl Valentin, the multitalented author-actor-musician, mutated into a linguistic acrobat. He worked hard ("Art is great but is hard work") and often reaped great success in his various roles as a cabaret artist, writer and film producer. He set up his own film studio in Munich and starred in about 40 silent movies from 1912 onwards, many of which were based on his sketches.

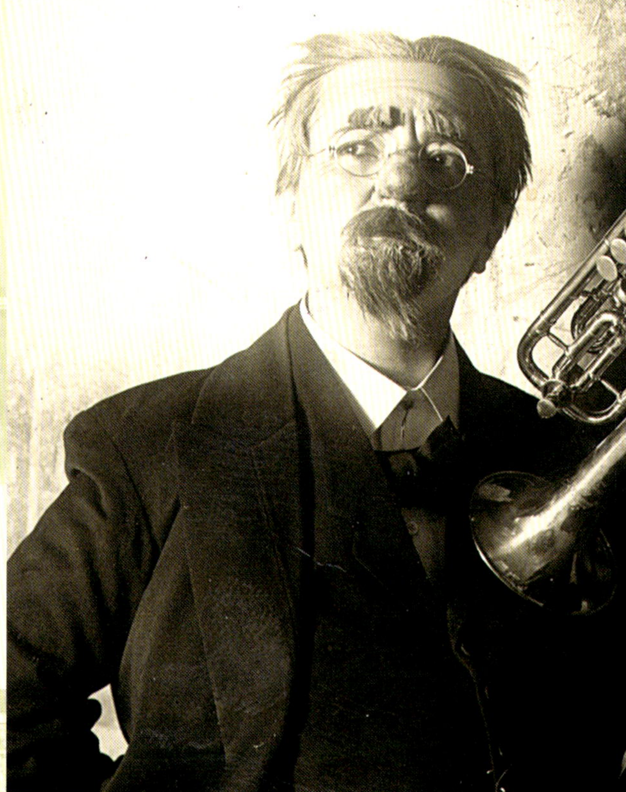

In 1911 he married Gisela Royes, the maid employed at his parents' home, with whom he had two daughters, Gisela (*1905) and Bertha (*1910). The fact that he suffered from asthma luckily exempt him from serving in the First World War.

LIESL KARLSTADT

Karl rose to fame locally in Munich with the help of his stage partner, Elisabeth Wellano alias Liesl Karlstadt (1892 – 1960), whom he met in 1911. During the 1920s the couple toured Zürich, Vienna and Berlin where they positively triumphed. In the 25 years in which they worked together almost 400 sketches and comedies were produced. During the Nazi period the pair fell quiet. Several projects failed, among them a curiosity shop (his Panoptikum), a theatre and a pub-cum-cabaret. These enterprises swallowed up the combined private fortune of the duo; Liesl Karlstadt had a nervous breakdown and was forced to rest for quite a time.

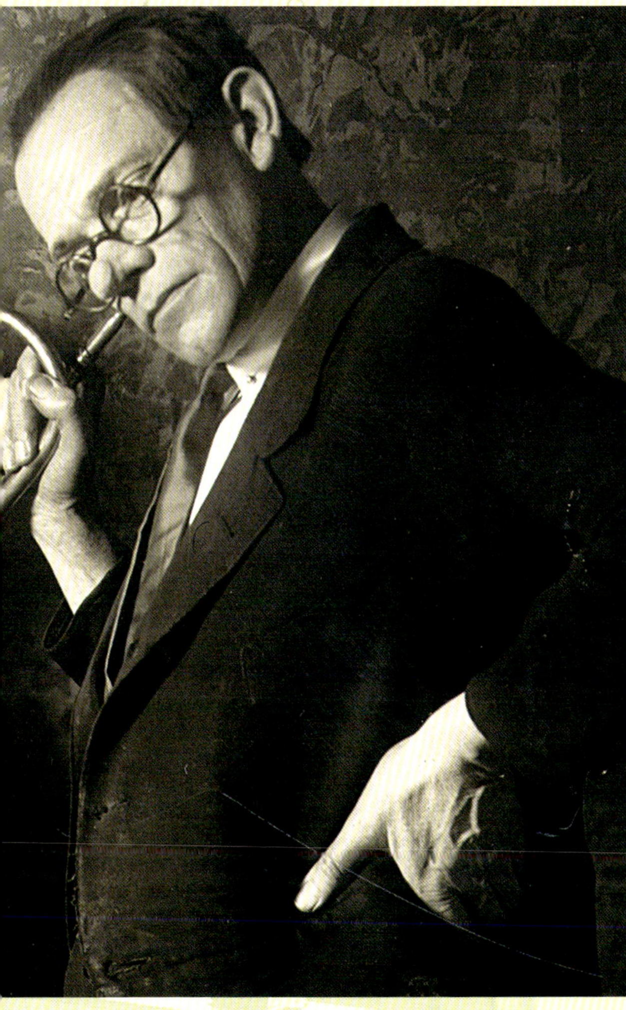

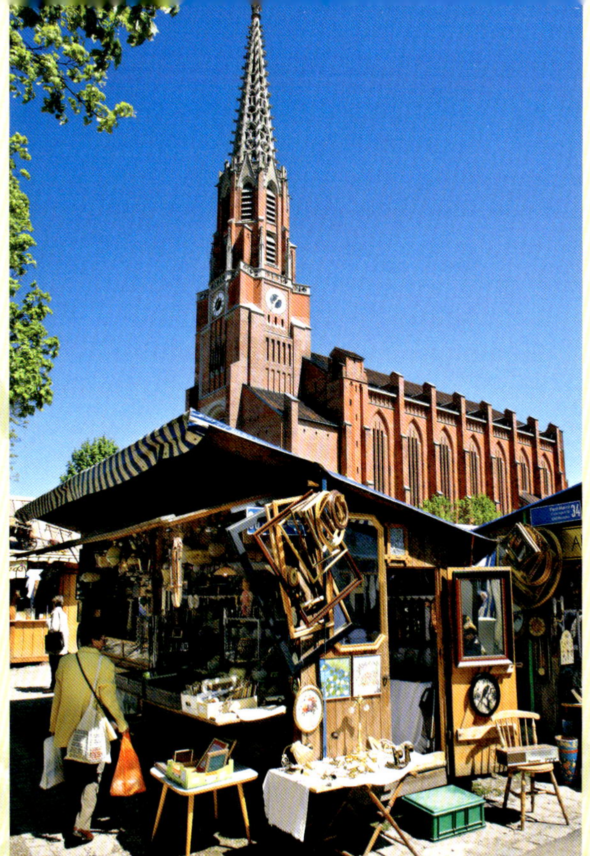

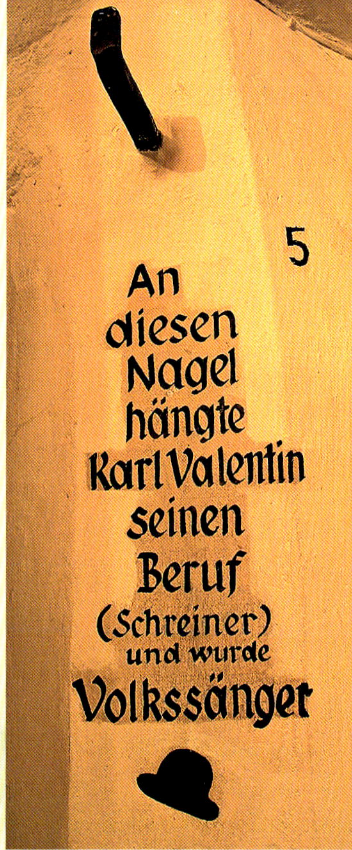

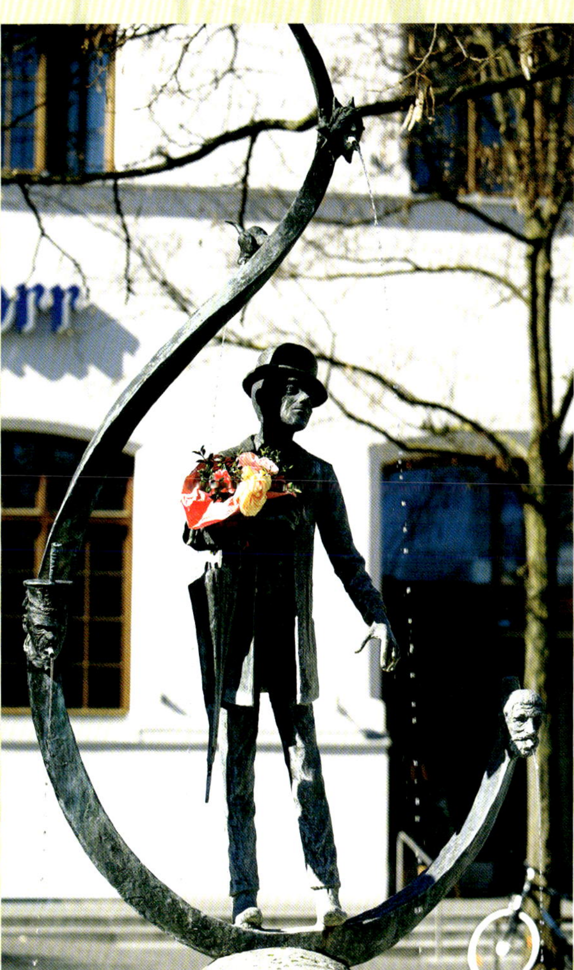

Above left:
Munich original Karl Valentin has a street named after him at the Auer Dult market close to the neo-Gothic church of Maria Hilf. Valentin was an avid collector of pictures of Old Munich; maybe he found a piece or two here.

Above:
Among the many curiosities on display at the museum are the nail symbolising Valentin's failed career as a carpenter, the legendary winter tooth pick covered in fur and a flat standing collar.

Left:
Five years after Valentin's death on October 18, 1953, a fountain was unveiled in his honour on the Viktualienmarkt. Liesl Karlstadt was present. The bronze was taken from a Bavarian lion on the Siegestor which was 'shot' during the Second World War.

From 1941 to 1947 Valentin gave no public performances. After years of separation he again acted with Liesl Karlstadt in 1947/48; the undertaking was a flop. His sketches were too pessimistic for his audience. On February 9, 1948, badly undernourished, he died of a common cold – on Germany's biggest day of merriment in the year, Rosenmontag or Carnival Monday.
In 1959 a museum was opened in his honour in the Isartor gate on private initiative. It features much of his estate and informs visitors that the museum "Can be visited day and night, even during rainshine, only on the outside and free of charge." Perhaps we should let Valentin have the last word. He once described himself thus: *"My weight is unimportant, my height lengthy, my walk agile, my character characteristic, my posture ludicrous and my shirt coloured."* Or, to put it more succinctly: *"I'm not a person; I'm a Bavarian."*

Right:
Since 1962 Viktualienmarkt has had its very own Maypole, painted blue and white for Bavaria and adorned with traditional wooden signs depicting local events, professions and customs.

Far right:
A total of six fountains on Viktualienmarkt pay homage to the famous folk actors and singers of Munich, including Roider Jackl. After the war Jakob Roider (1906–1975) became famous for his Gstanzln, short satirical songs or verse in Bavarian.

Right:
Liesl Karlstadt is commemorated by a fountain by Hans Osel on Viktualienmarkt, Munich's main food market, unveiled in 1961.

Far right:
Watching the world go by on Viktualienmarkt over a Maß of beer. What better way to spend an hour or two?

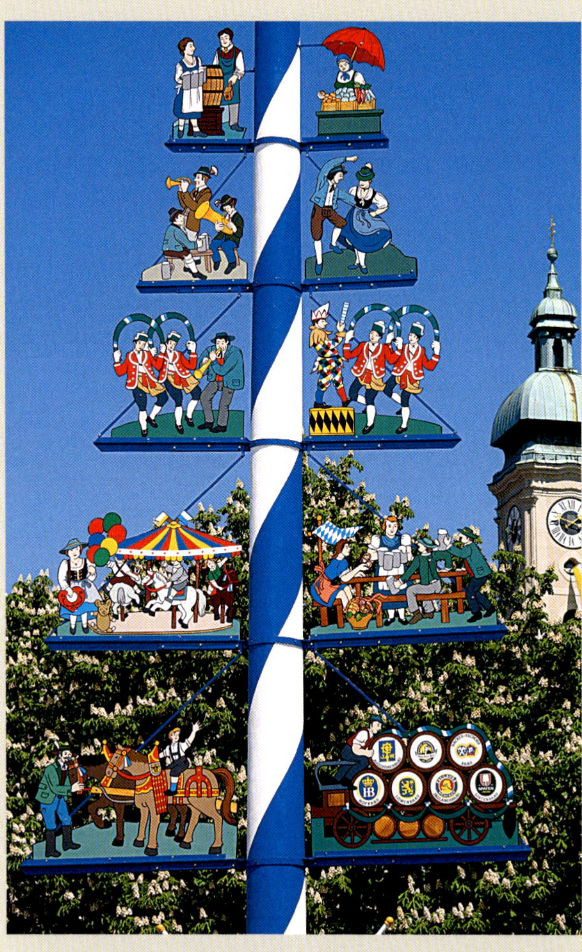

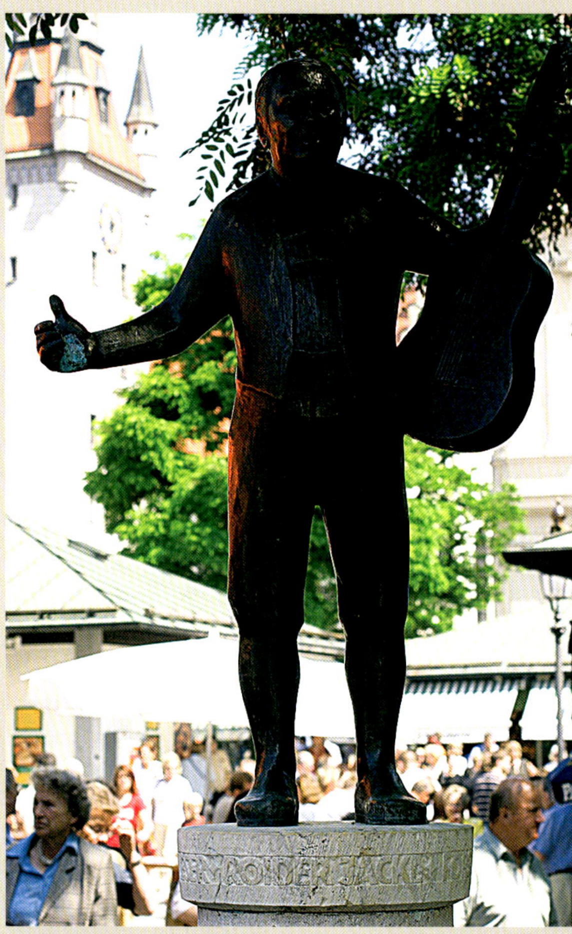

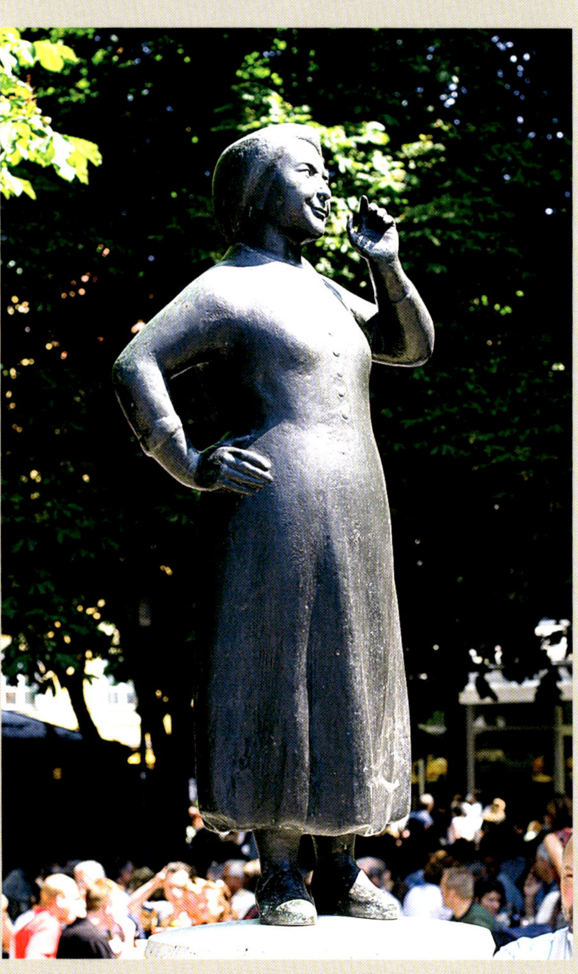

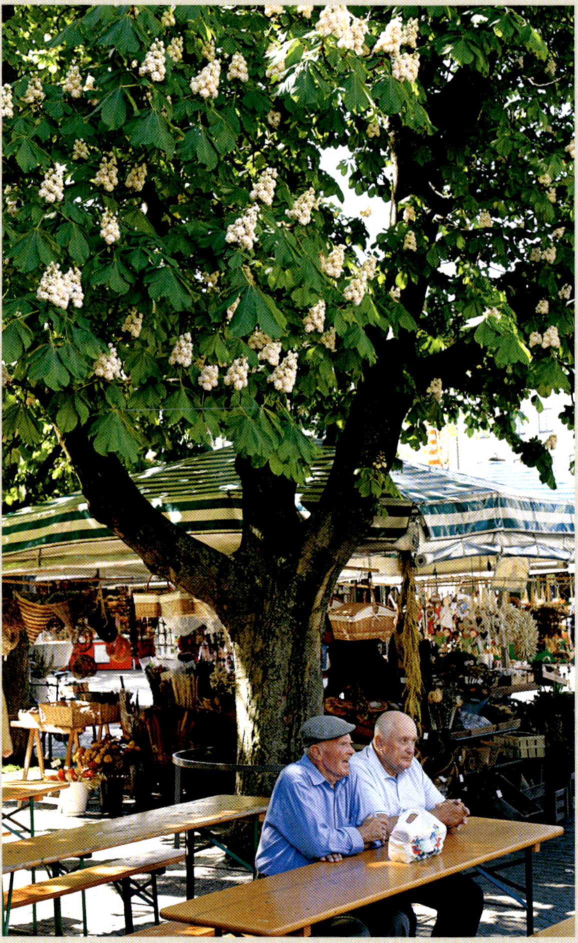

Viktualienmarkt has long been much more than just a farmer's market.

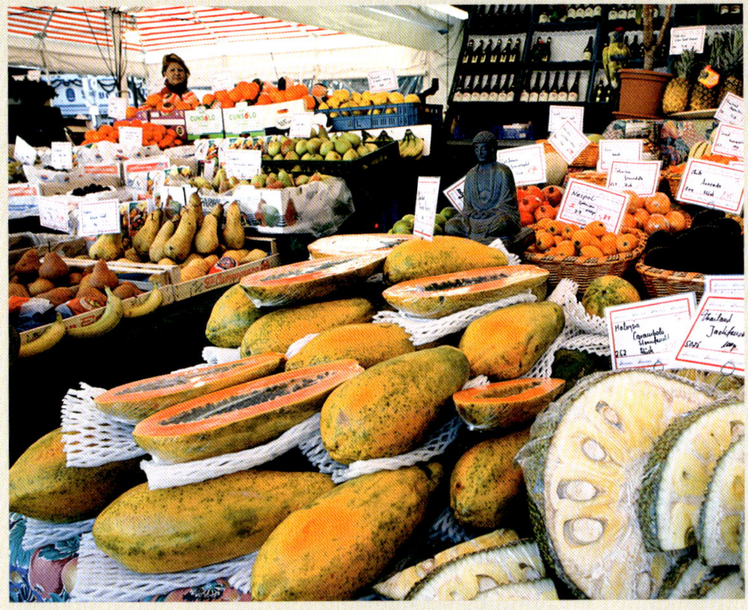

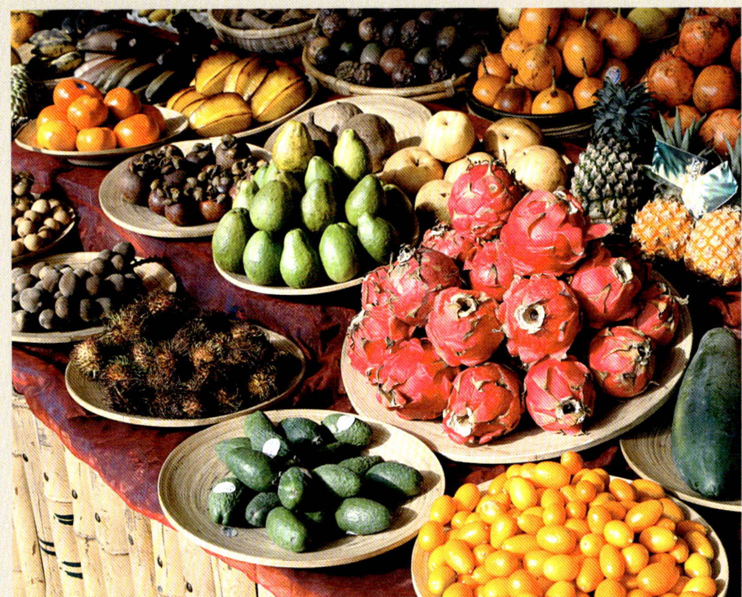

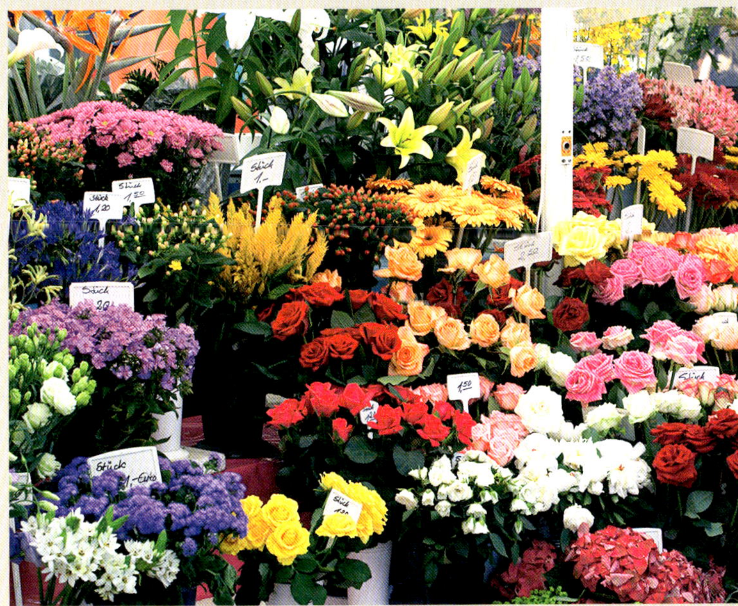

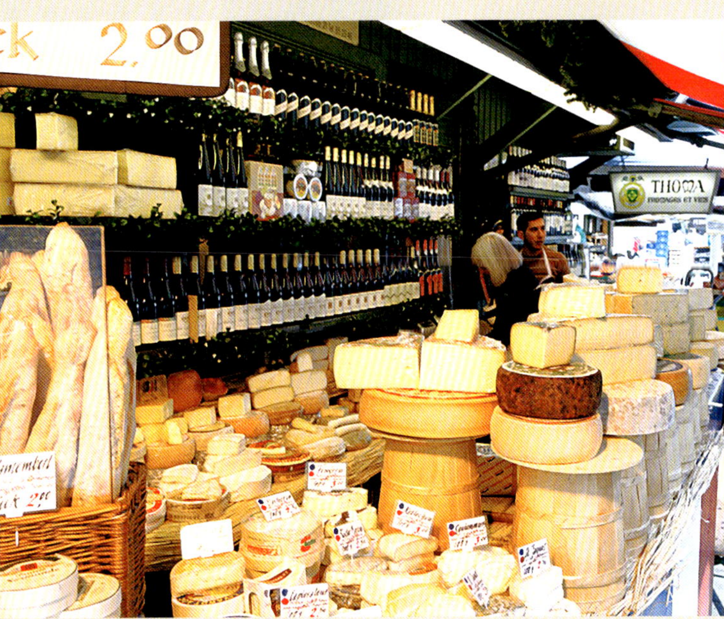

Right:
The entrance to the late baroque Asamkirche of St John Nepomuk on Sendlinger Straße stand proud of its neighbouring edifices.

Far right:
The Städtisches Hochhaus (the old technical town hall) on Blumenstraße dates back to 1928/29.

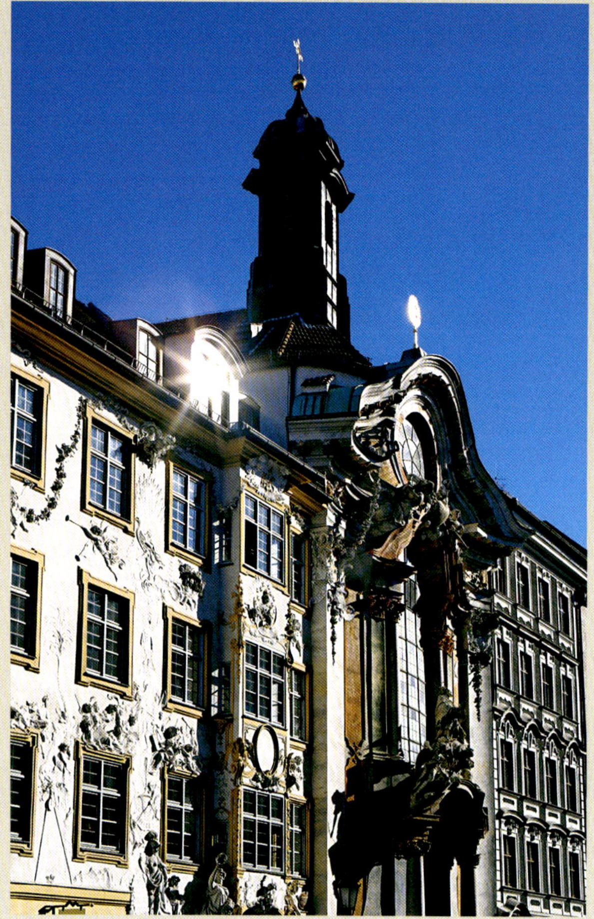

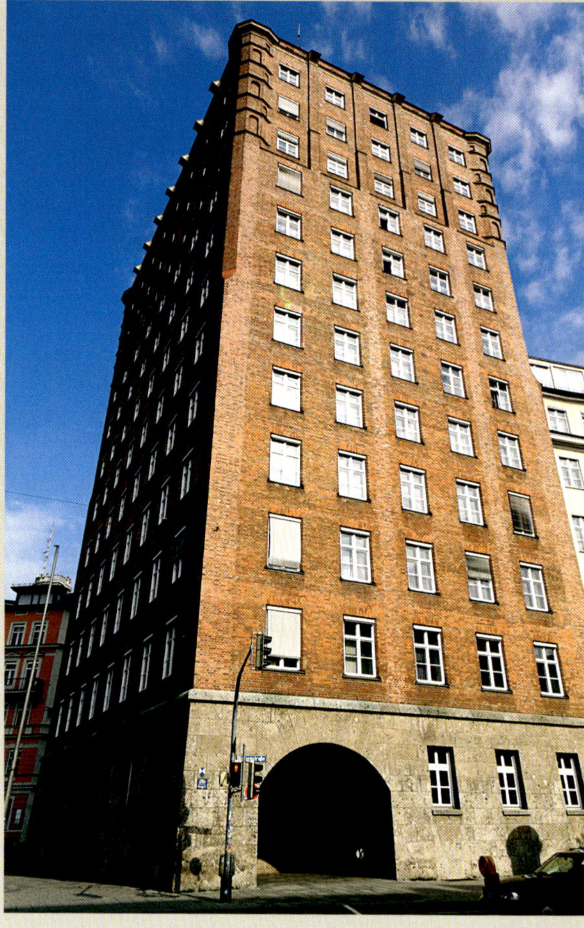

Right:
The Orag-Haus was built on Jakobsplatz by the Bavarian cooperative of tailors at the turn of the 19th century.

Far right:
In 2006 a new synagogue was opened on Jakobsplatz. The synagogue, Jewish Museum and new hall for the religious Israelite community of Munich and Upper Bavaria now make up the Jakobsplatz Jewish Centre.

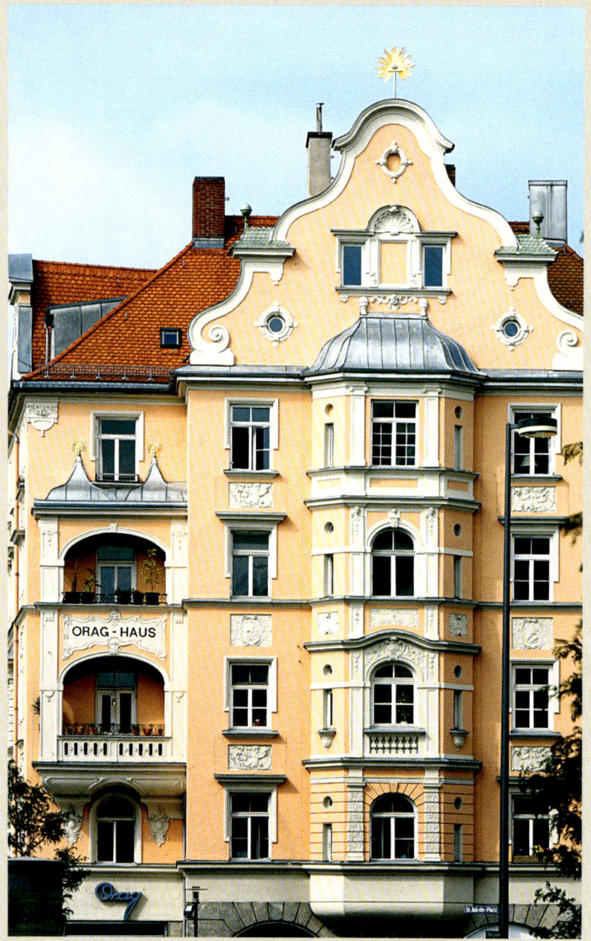

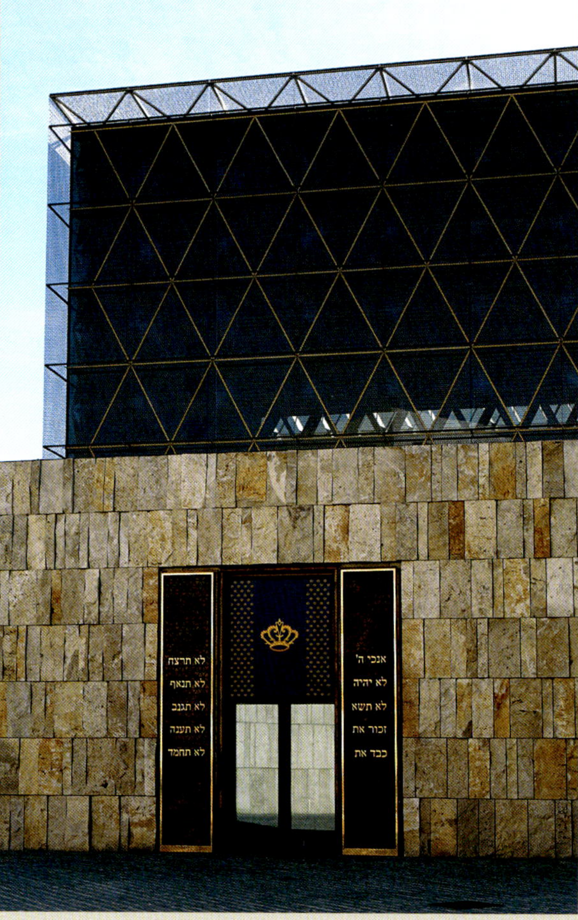

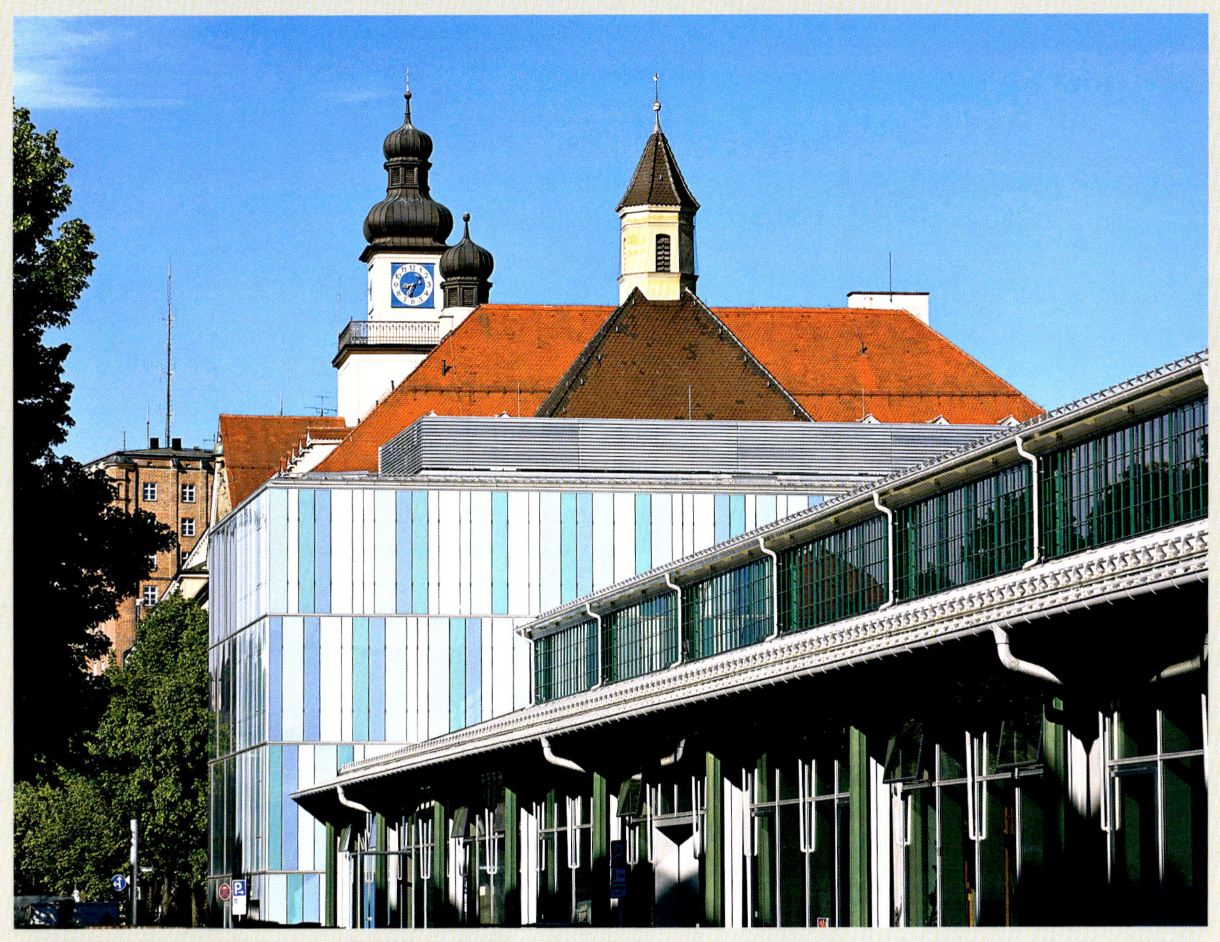

The first Schrannenhalle (officially known as the Maximilian grain hall) was erected by Karl Muffat on the edge of Viktualienmarkt between 1851 and 1853. The present hall, erected some years ago, services a number of small shops, crafts outlets and pubs and cafés.

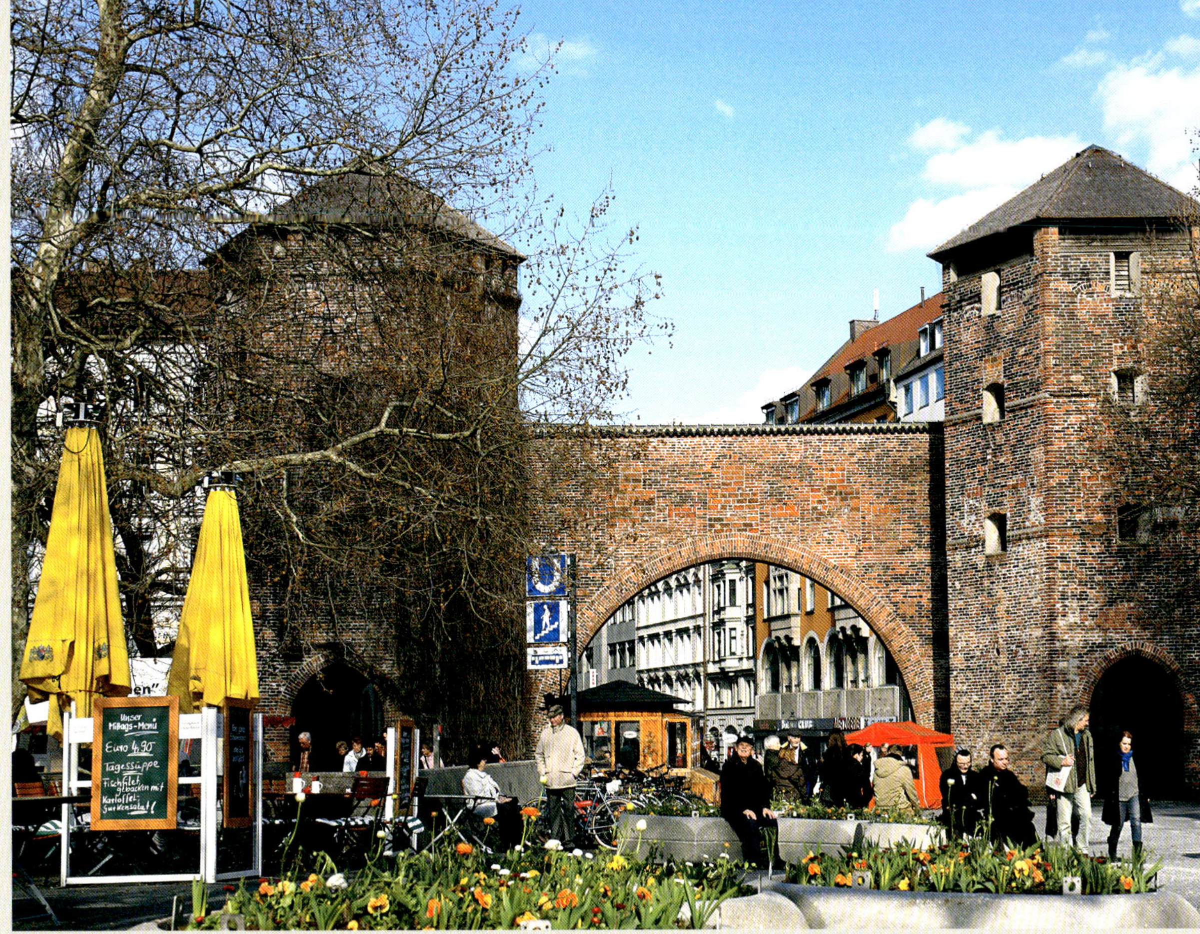

Sendlinger Tor from 1308 was originally much the same as the Isartor until in 1810 the central tower was removed and in 1906 the three arches between the flanking towers were turned into one.

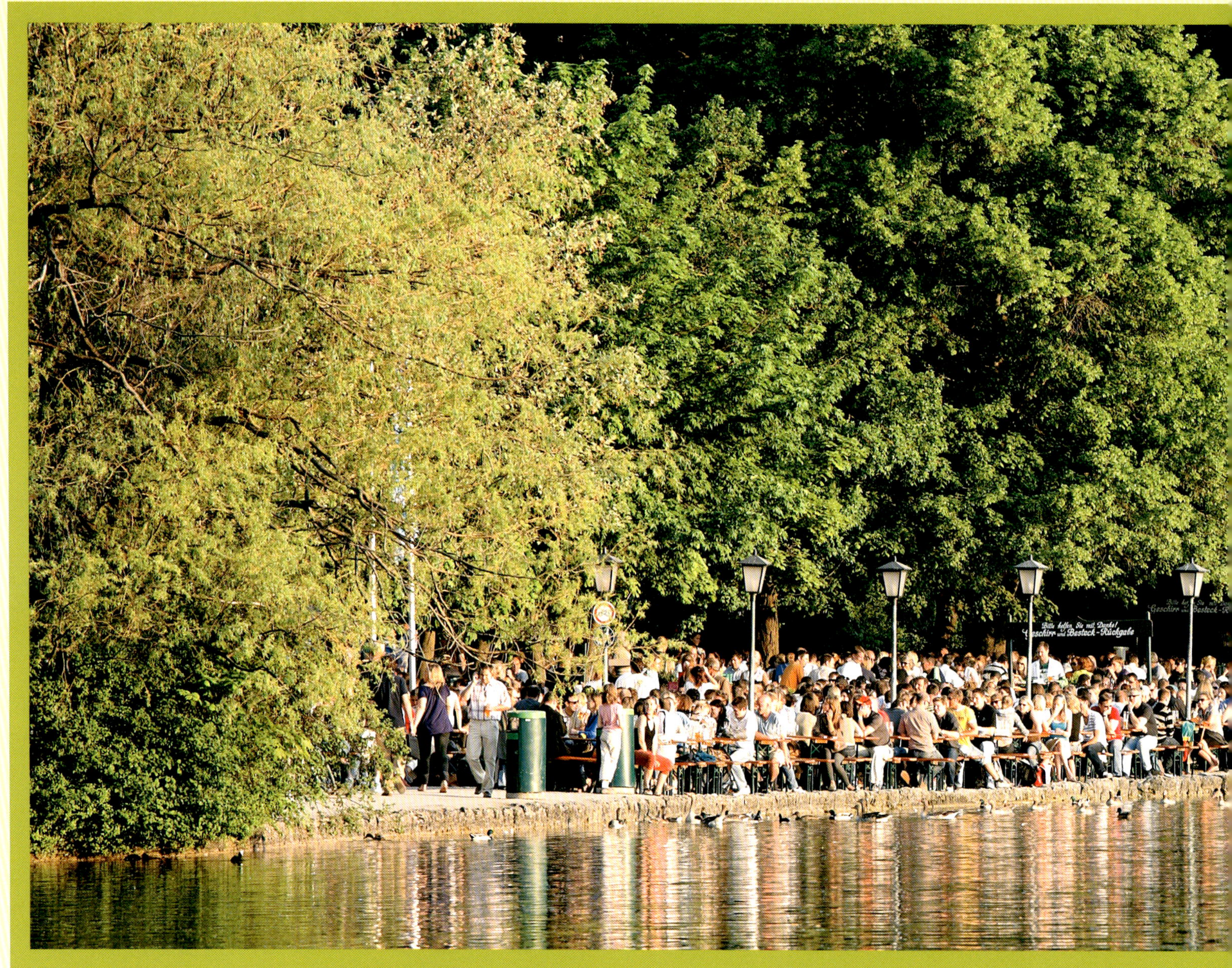

TOWN GATES, CHURCHES AND PARKS – BEYOND THE CITY CENTRE

There's also plenty of interest to entice you beyond the confines of Old Munich. In the 14th century Emperor Ludwig the Bavarian ordered that an extended set of fortifications be built which should enclose the then new areas of the "outer town". Three of his historic city gates still survive.

To the east is the Isartor; with its central gate and two flanking towers it gives us a good impression of what the town walls must have looked like in the late Middle Ages. A museum dedicated to Karl Valentine and Liesl Karlstadt was installed here in 1959. In honour of the two comedians the clock on the west facade has its

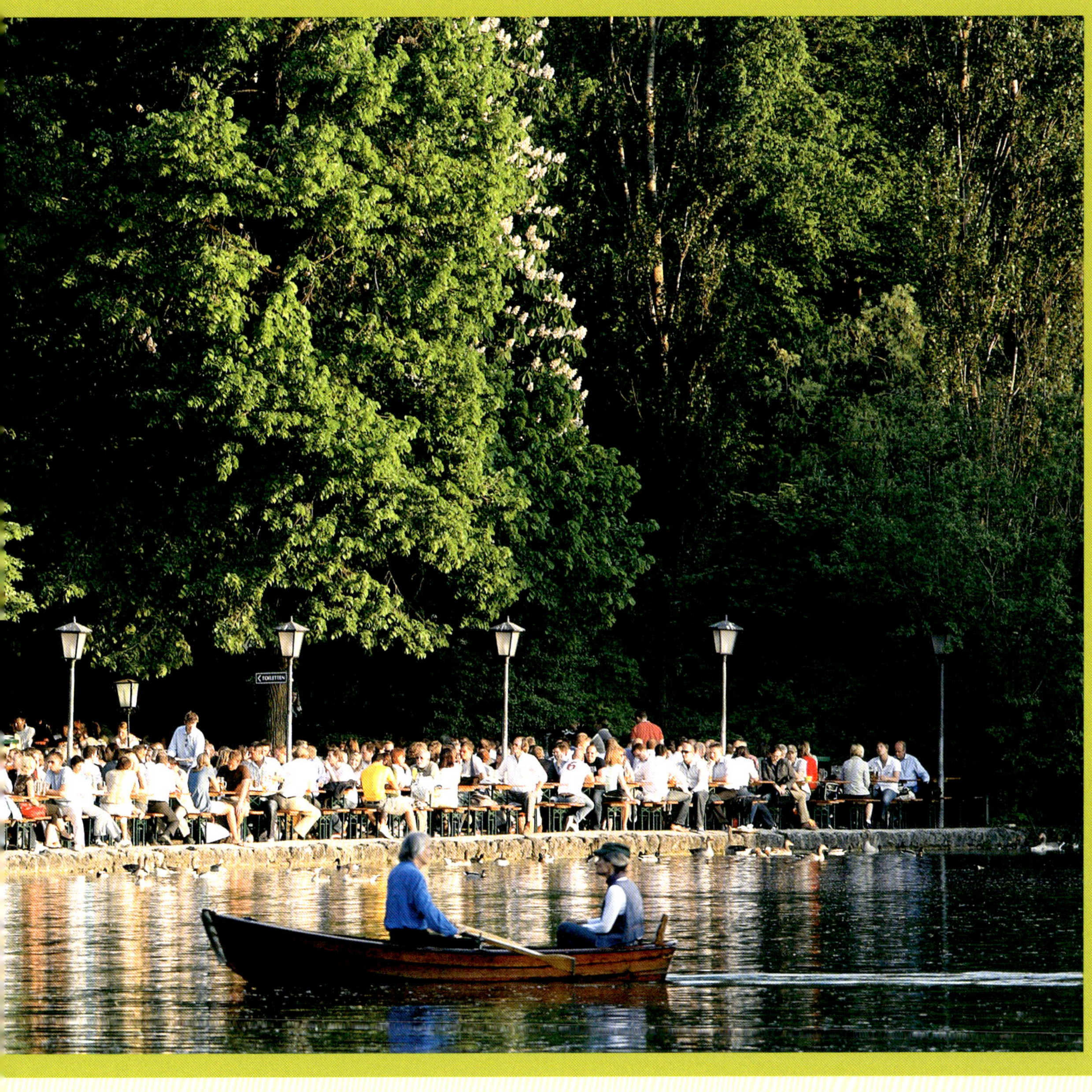

The most idyllic beer garden in Munich is perhaps this one, the Seehaus on the Kleinhesseloher See in the middle of the Englischer Garten.

numbers reversed and runs anticlockwise; as Willy Brandt once observed: "Clocks in Bavaria tick differently".

THE GATES

The southernmost city gate is the Sendlinger Tor where the long route to Italy once commenced. It was refurbished several times between 1808 and 1906. The western edge of the old town is marked by the Karlstor. It was originally called Neuhauser Tor and was renamed in honour of Elector Karl Theodor in 1791 ("Karlstor" = Karl's gate). It opens out onto Karlsplatz – known in Munich as Stachus – one of the busiest squares in Europe. The old north gate, the Schwabinger Tor, was torn down in 1817 to enable an unhindered view of the Siegestor which welcomed visitors arriving from the north. The triumphal arch was erected between 1843 and 1852 in the vein of the Arch of Constantine in Rome and dedicated to the glory of the Bavarian army. A statue of Bavaria sits atop it, riding out of town on a quadriga drawn by four lions. Between the Siegestor and Odeonsplatz is the showy Ludwigstraße; the distance between the Feldherrenhalle and the Siegestor is exactly one kilometre.

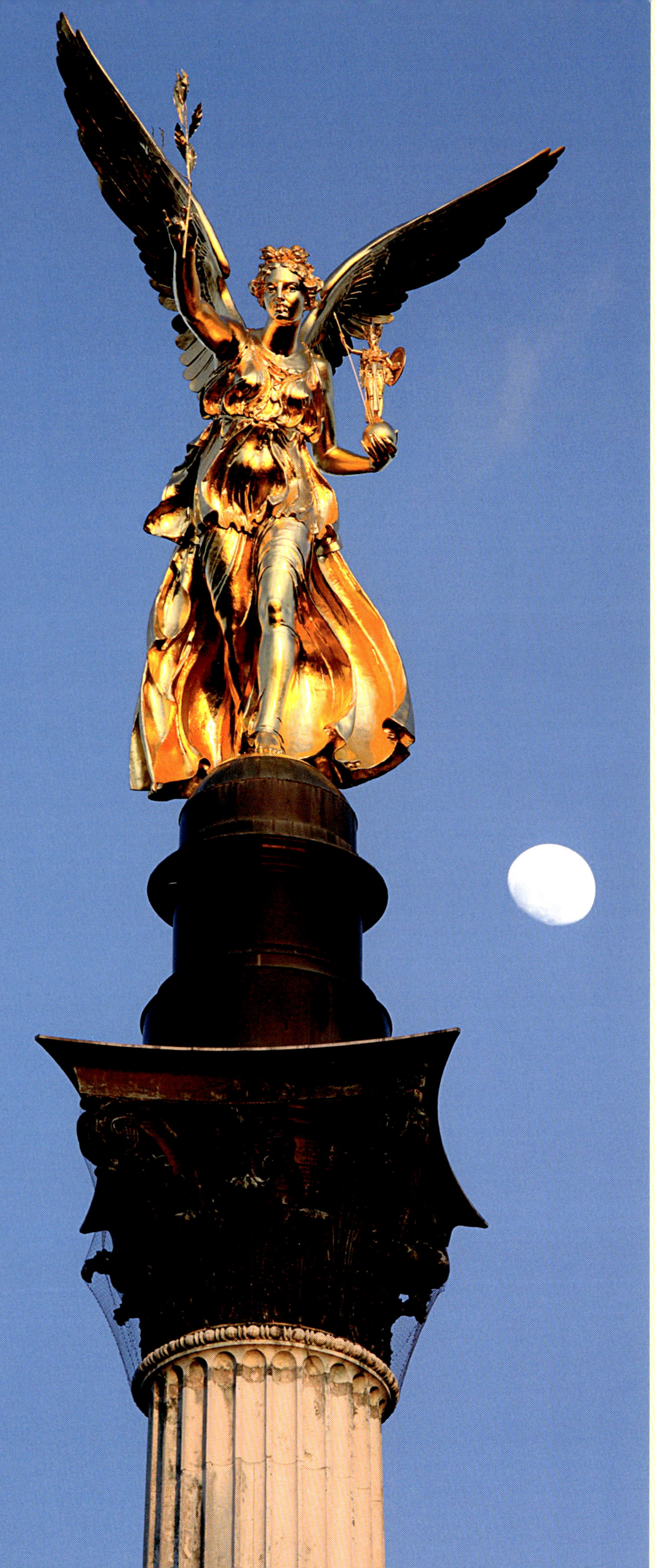

ROYAL SPLENDOUR

Another good example of royal splendour is the Maximilianeum. King Maximilian Joseph II (1811 – 1864) had this "national building" put up between 1857 and 1874 on the eastern banks of the River Isar. Since 1876 it has housed a foundation for gifted students from Bavaria and the Palatinate. Those who pass their Abitur (A level or high school diploma) with a straight 1.0 (A grade) can apply to be accepted by the association. Women were only admitted in 1980. In 1949 the complex was made the seat of the Bavarian state parliament.

The unique neoclassical design of Königsplatz in Maxvorstadt has earned Munich the epithet of Isar Athens. Its architect Karl von Fischer (1782 – 1820) copied the ensemble from the Acropolis in the Greek capital. Königsplatz is supposed to show Bavaria's affinity with Greece, especially on 16-year-old Prince Otto, a son of King Ludwig I, being crowned monarch of the new kingdom of Greece in 1832.

Leo von Klenze (1784 – 1864), Ludwig I's royal architect, continued Fischer's work in adherence to the latter's original plans, building the Ionic Glyptothek on the north side of Königsplatz between 1816 and 1830 and the Doric Propylaea to the west, also based on the Greek edifice, from 1854 to 1862. The gallery of antiquities, erected in the Corinthian style in 1838 – 1848 on the south side of the square, is the work of Georg Friedrich Ziebland from Regensburg (1800 – 1873) and was first used as a venue for exhibitions of art and industry.

Several of the churches in the area are worth popping into. The Ludwigskirche, to name but one, is the first monumental church to be fashioned in neo-Romanesque – a masterpiece by Friedrich von Gärtner (1791 – 1847) who after Klenze was King Ludwig I's chief architect. The second largest altar fresco in the world, The Last Judgement, was crafted by Peter von Cornelius (1783 – 1867) here in the Nazarene style. Religious philosopher and theologian Romano

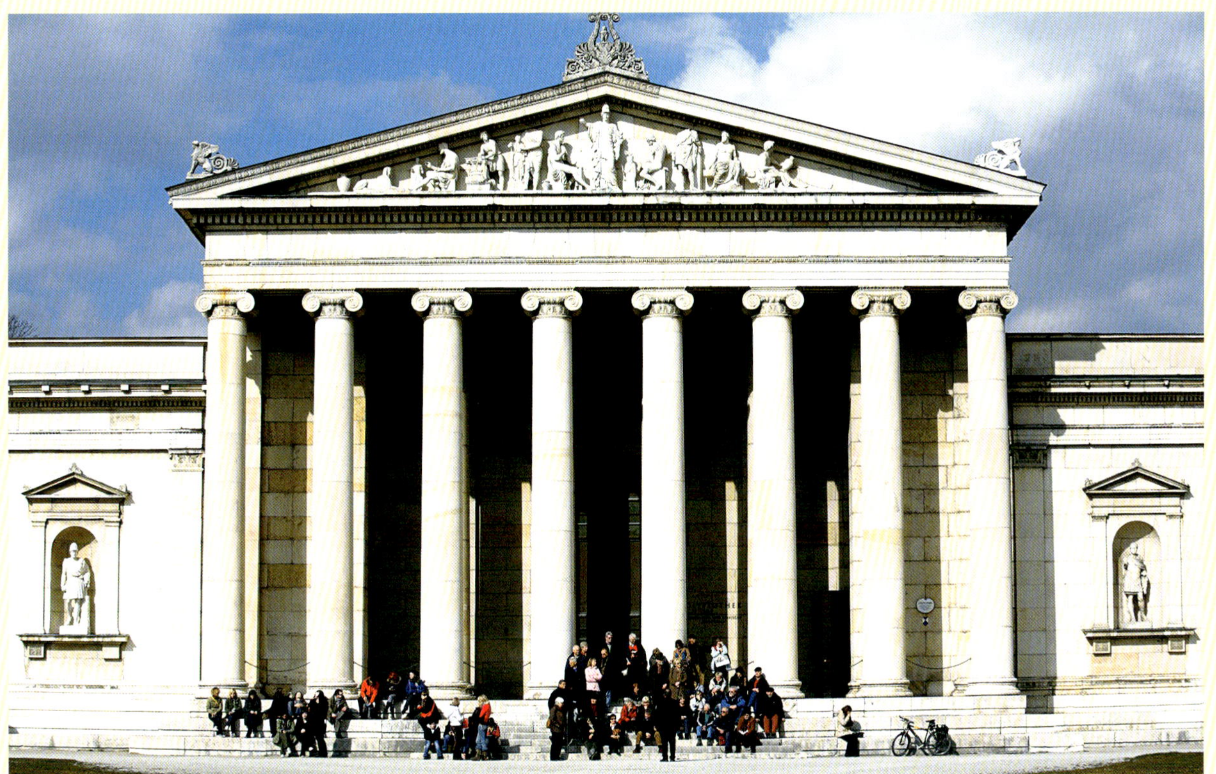

Left page:
Since 1899 an angel of peace has watched over Prinzregentenstraße on the right bank of the Isar, erected to celebrate 25 years of peace following the Franco-Prussian War of 1870/71. Despite its glittering gilt exterior, the angel is made of simple wood.

Left:
King Ludwig I commissioned Leo von Klenze to build the Glyptothek (1816–1830) to house his collection of ancient sculptures. The name Glyptothek comes from the Greek gluptos for "carved".

Guardini (1885–1968) preached in the Ludwigskirche before he was laid to rest here in 1997.

JEWEL OF THE BAVARIAN ROCOCO

The Catholic filial church of St George, a jewel of the Bavarian Rococo, was once the village church of Bogenhausen. Royal architect Johann Michael Fischer (1692–1766) was commissioned with the refurbishing, with Balthasar Trischberger (1721–1777) succeeding him on his death. The pulpit and Corbinian Altar are by Ignaz Günther (1725–1775). Member of the Resistance Father Alfred Delp (1907–1945) was active in the parish until he was arrested and executed by the Nazis. The cemetery is also worth seeing and is where many famous names have found their final place of rest, from Liesl Karlstadt and Erich Kästner to conductors Hans Knappertsbusch and Rudolf Kempe to Rainer Werner Fassbinder, Helmut Fischer and Walter Sedlmayr.

The abbey church of St Boniface forms the nucleus of the Benedictine monastery founded by King Ludwig I in 1835. Consecrated in 1845, the church by Georg Friedrich Ziebland is based on an early Christian aisled basilica. It was badly damaged during World War II and only the southern half has been reconstructed with modest means. King Ludwig I had himself interred in "his" basilica in 1868 in a simple sarcophagus.

Many other museums and cultural sites lie beyond the Altstadtring. Visitors to Munich can relax in one of the many parks, the largest being the Englischer Garten. A few restful hours are also guaranteed in the Leopoldpark in Schwabing and the Maximiliansanlagen on the right banks of the Isar. The Alter Südfriedhof and Alter Nordfriedhof cemeteries have not been used for decades and are a great place for a romantic stroll amongst old trees and weathered tombstones, some of which still bear traces of damage from the Second World War.

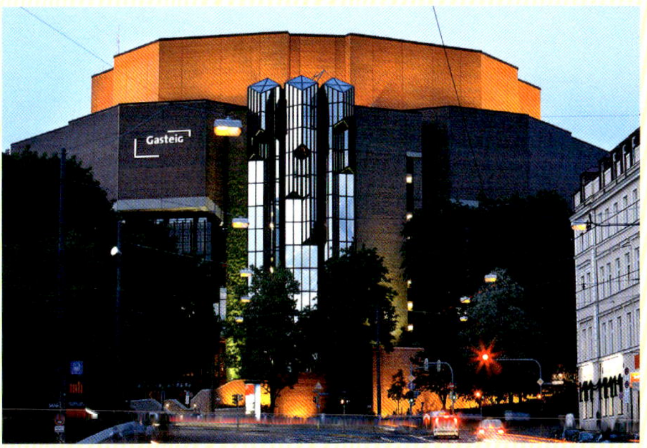

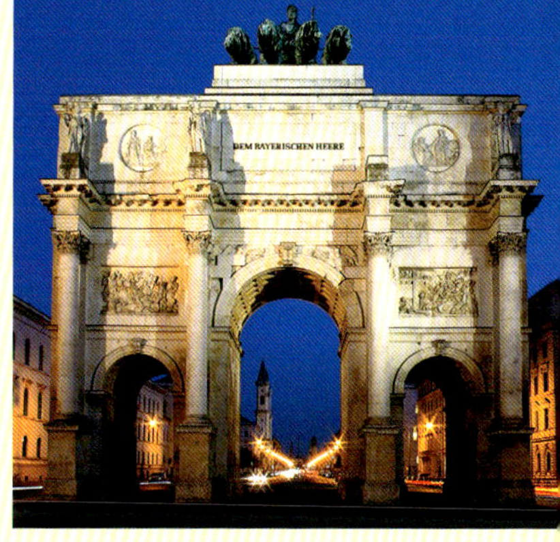

Above left:
The Gasteig is Munich's huge centre of the arts, used by several thousand visitors a day. The word is derived from the German gacher Steig or "steep track" which once led from what's now the Ludwigsbrücke up to the church of St Nikolai on the banks of the River Isar.

Above:
Following heavy damage inflicted by WWII air raids the Siegestor, which separates Maxvorstadt from Schwabing, was deliberately only partially rebuilt. It now admonishes the visitor with the inscription: "Dedicated to victory, destroyed by war, devoted to peace".

Right:
The Propylaea was the last neoclassical building in Munich, erected between 1846 and 1862 on the west side of Königsplatz by Leo von Klenze.

Far right:
The abbey church of St Boniface built by King Ludwig I was designed in the style of an early Christian basilica by Georg Friedrich Ziebland. The king also gave the Benedictine monks the monastery of Andechs which had been secularised in 1803.

Below:
The building which now houses the state collection of antiquities is also by Ziebland, with the abbey of St Boniface backing onto it. The main body of the collection comprises the Greek vases procured by King Ludwig I.

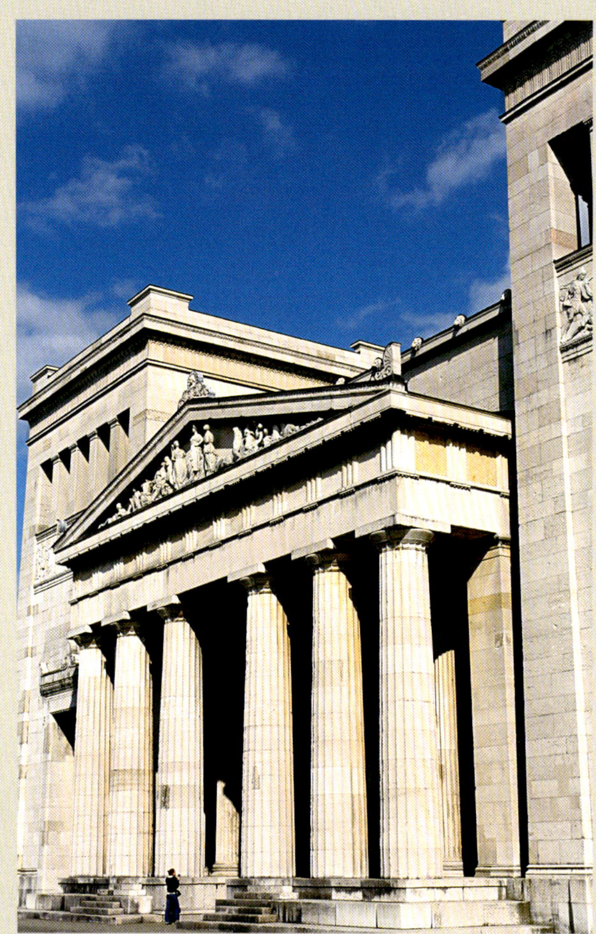

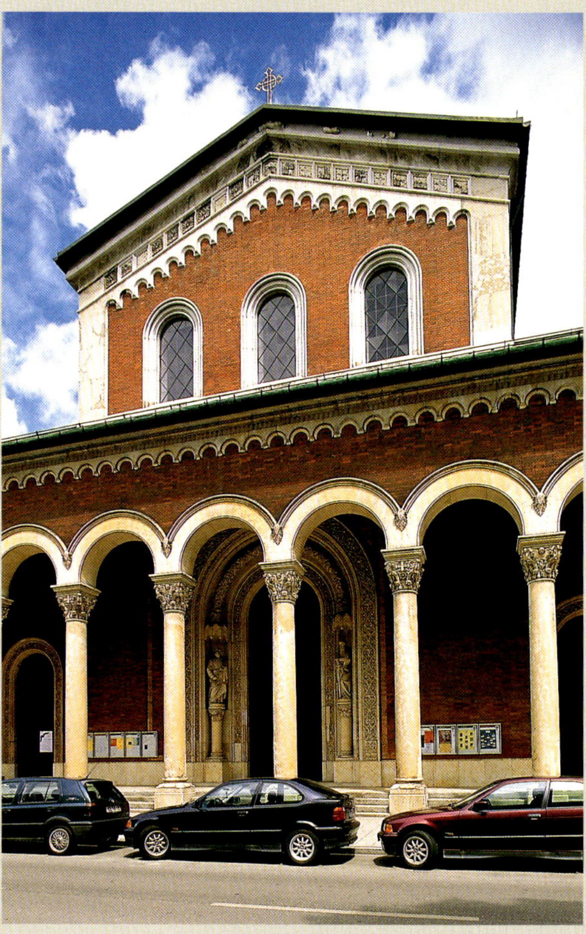

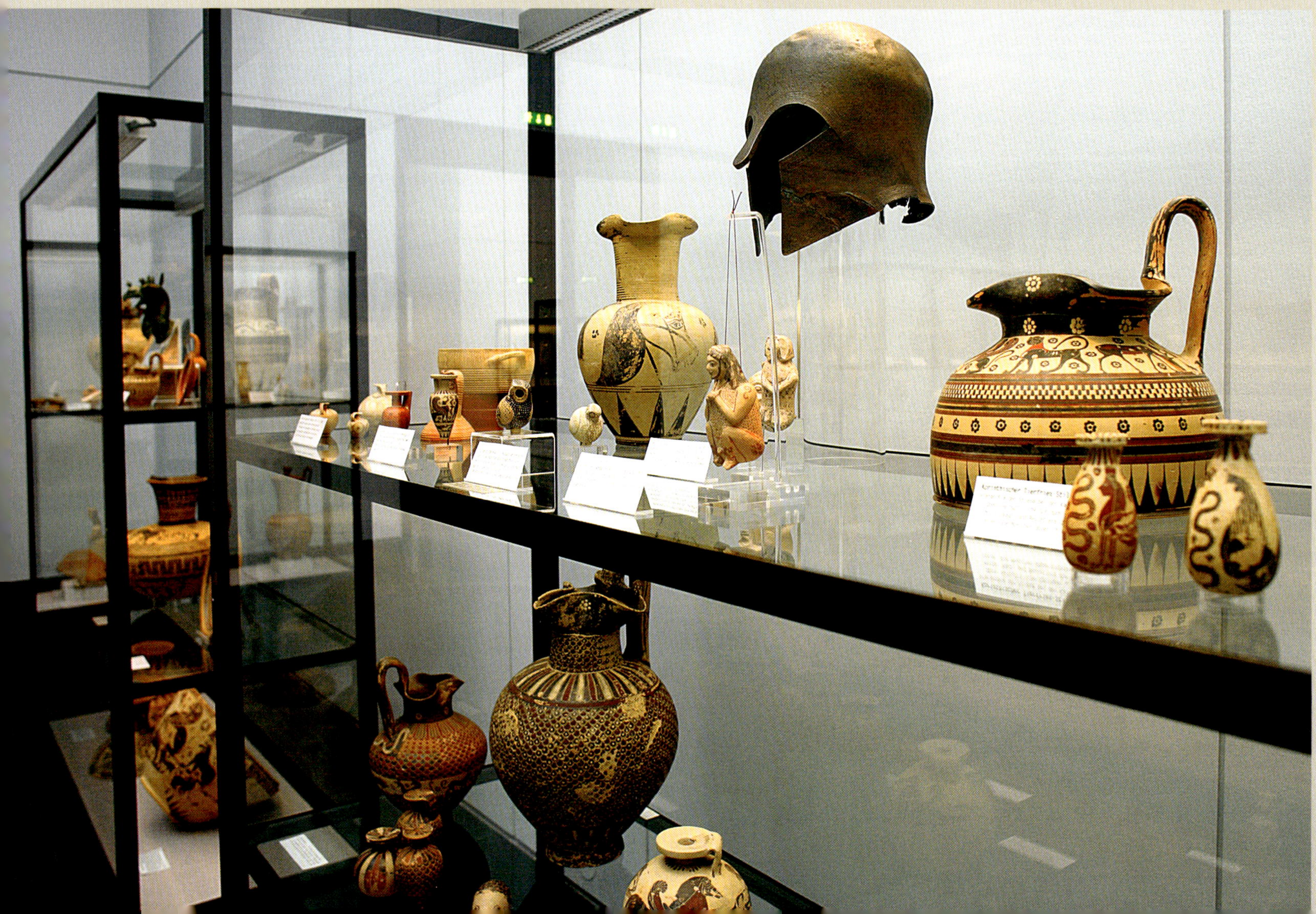

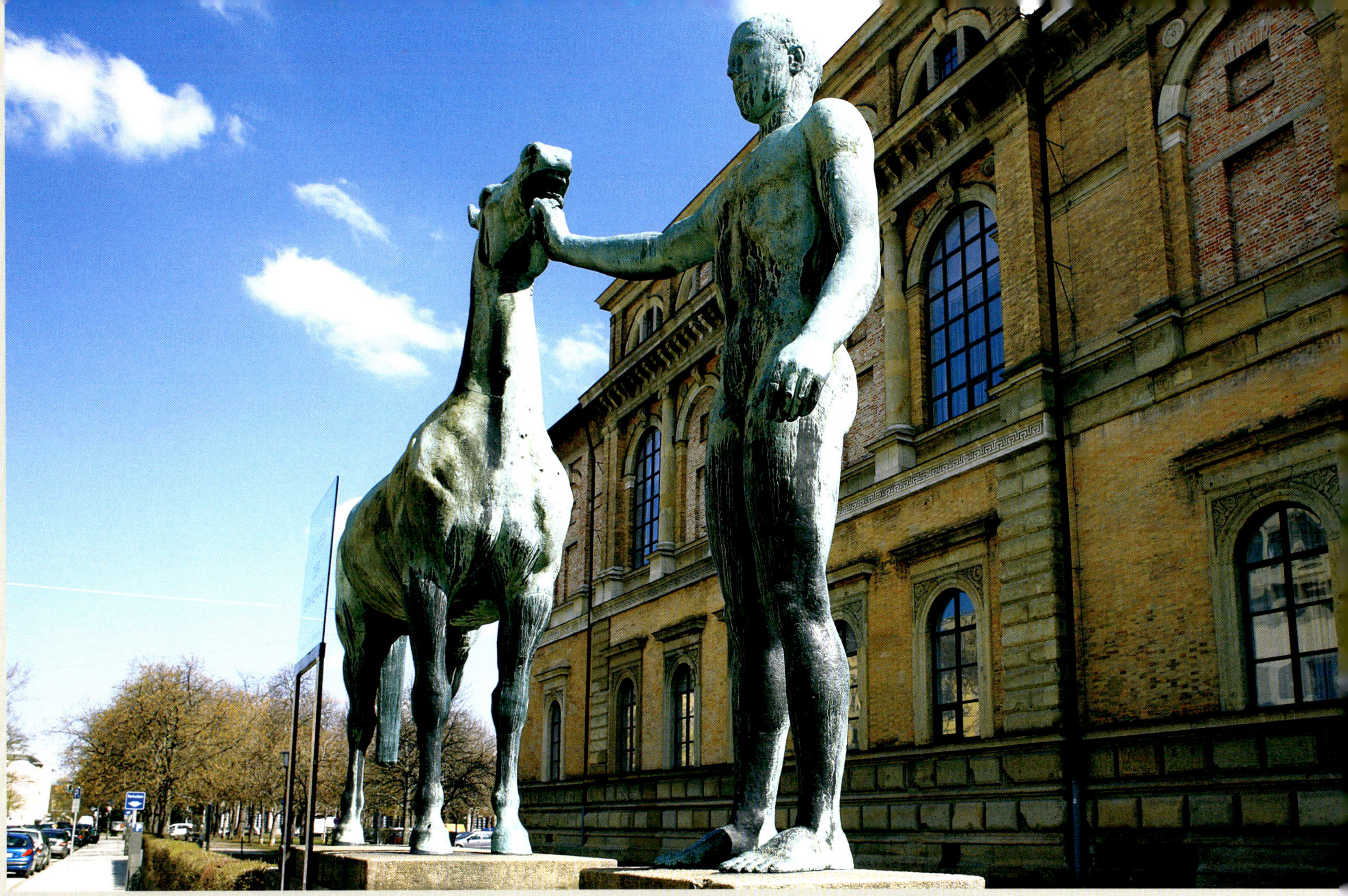

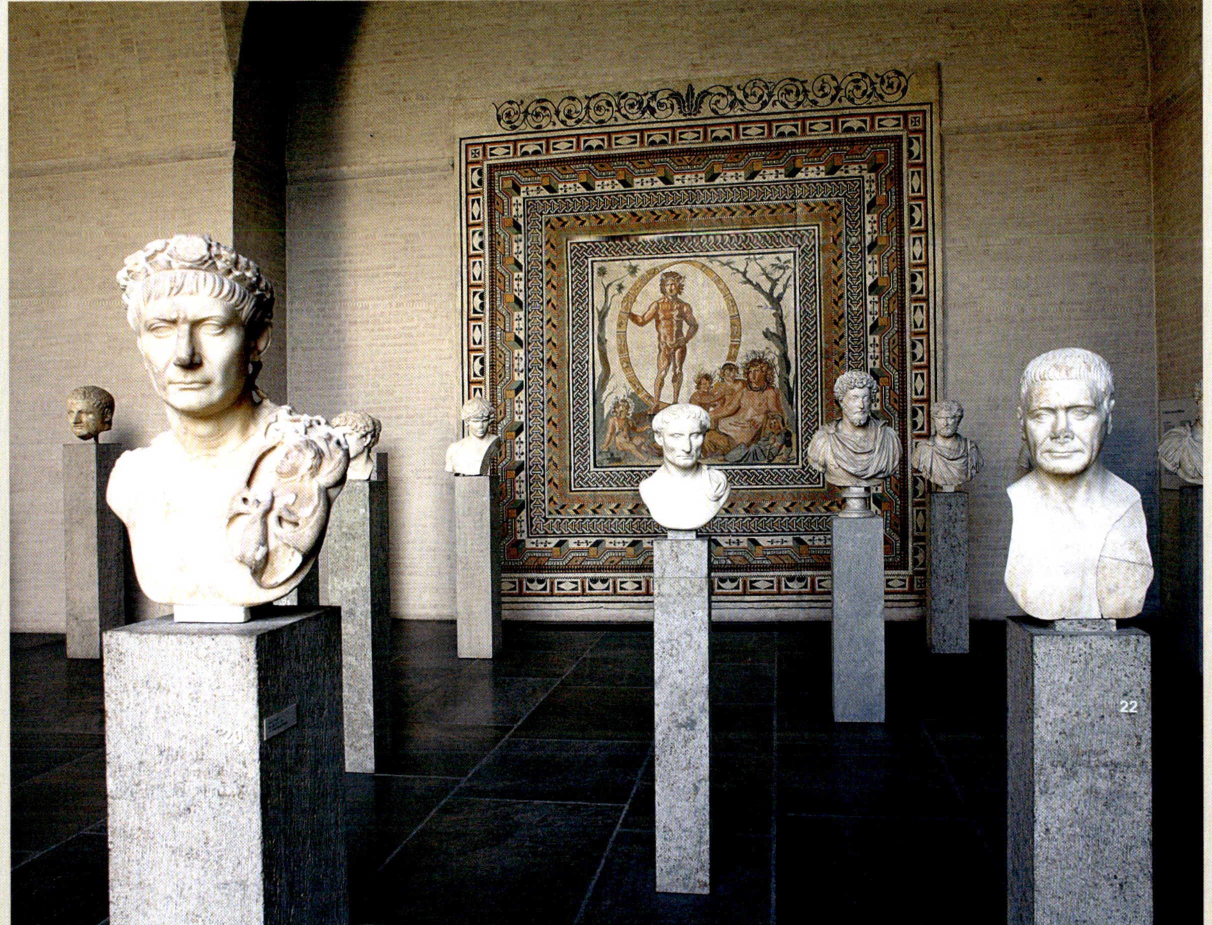

Above:
This horse tamer by Hermann Hahn (1868–1942) stands outside the Alte Pinakothek.

Left:
King Ludwig I began systematically collecting ancient carvings when he was crown prince. The Glyptothek contains sculptures, mosaics and reliefs from the archaic period (c. 650 BC) to the late Roman (c. 550 AD). At the time of their creation many of them were not pure white marble, as we know them today, but painted in bright colours.

Right page:
Franz von Lenbach's house, now a listed building, has all the charm of a Tuscan villa. It was erected from plans by Munich architect Gabriel von Seidl (1848–1913) from 1887 to 1891 and has been extended and rebuilt several times in its history.

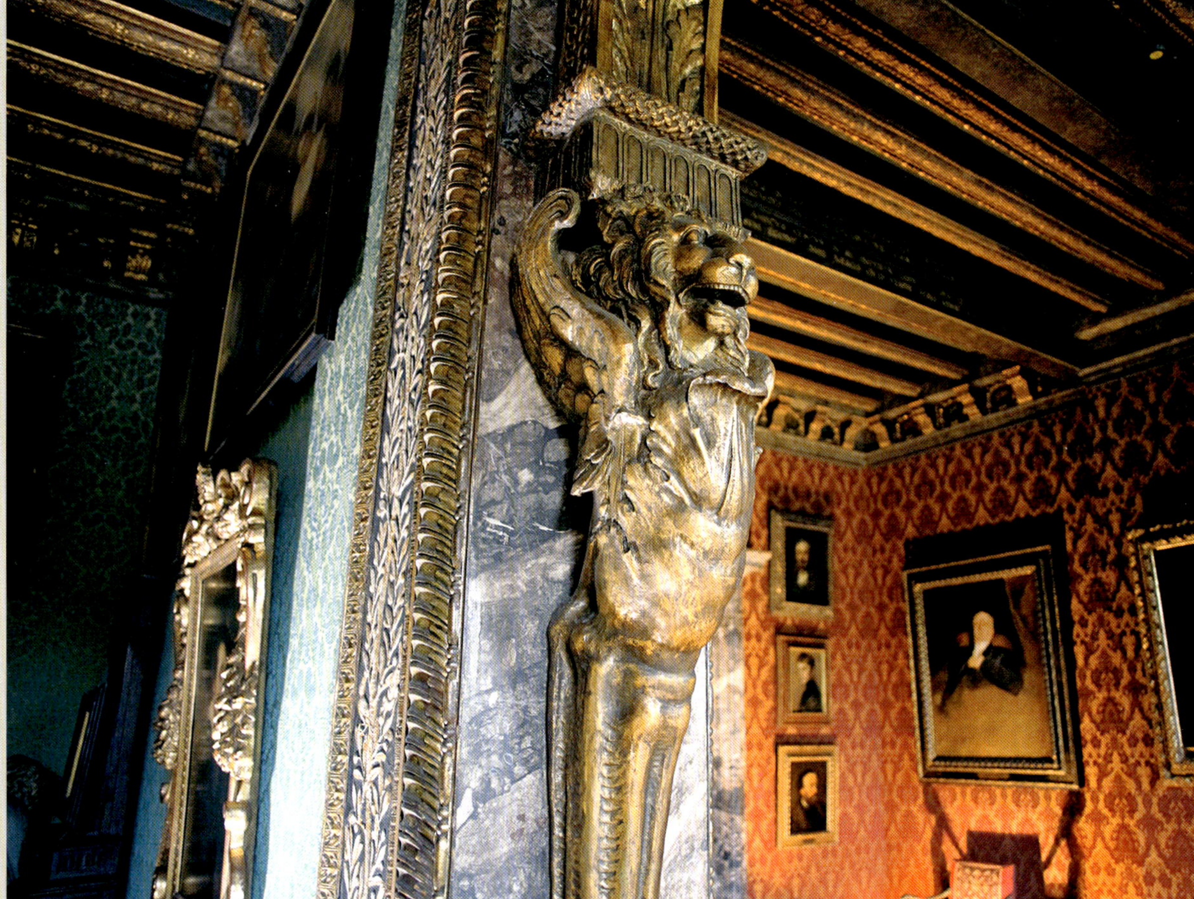

The villa belonging to prince of painters Franz von Lenbach (1836–1904), built between 1887 and 1891, now accommodates the state art gallery. The rooms on the first floor have been left as they were originally and are open to the public.

Right:
The Lenbachhaus owes its world fame to its unique collection of works by Der Blaue Reiter. Here the tiny bronze statue of The Panther (1908) with The Tiger (1912) behind it, both by Franz Marc.

Far right:
Franz von Stuck (1863–1928) made this bronze sculpture of a dancer in 1897, giving her the face of his wife Mary.

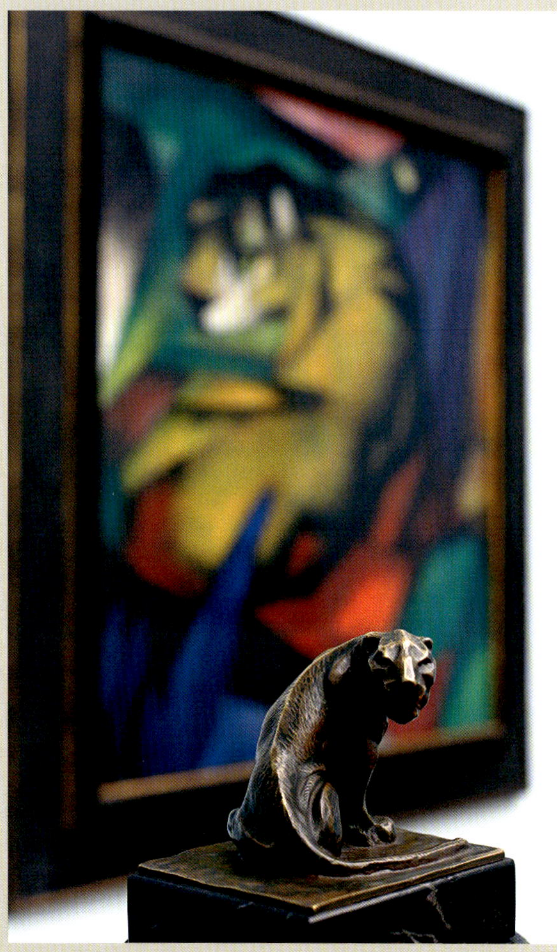

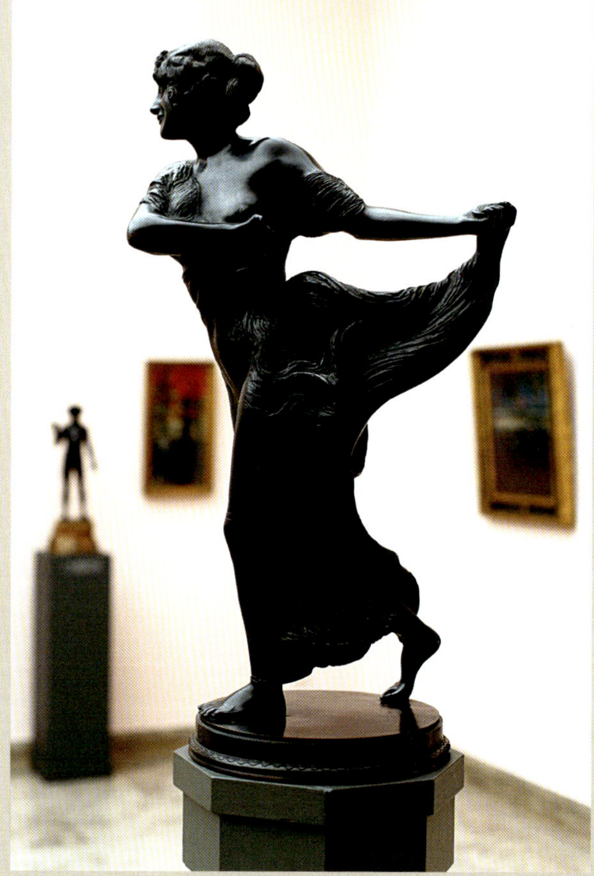

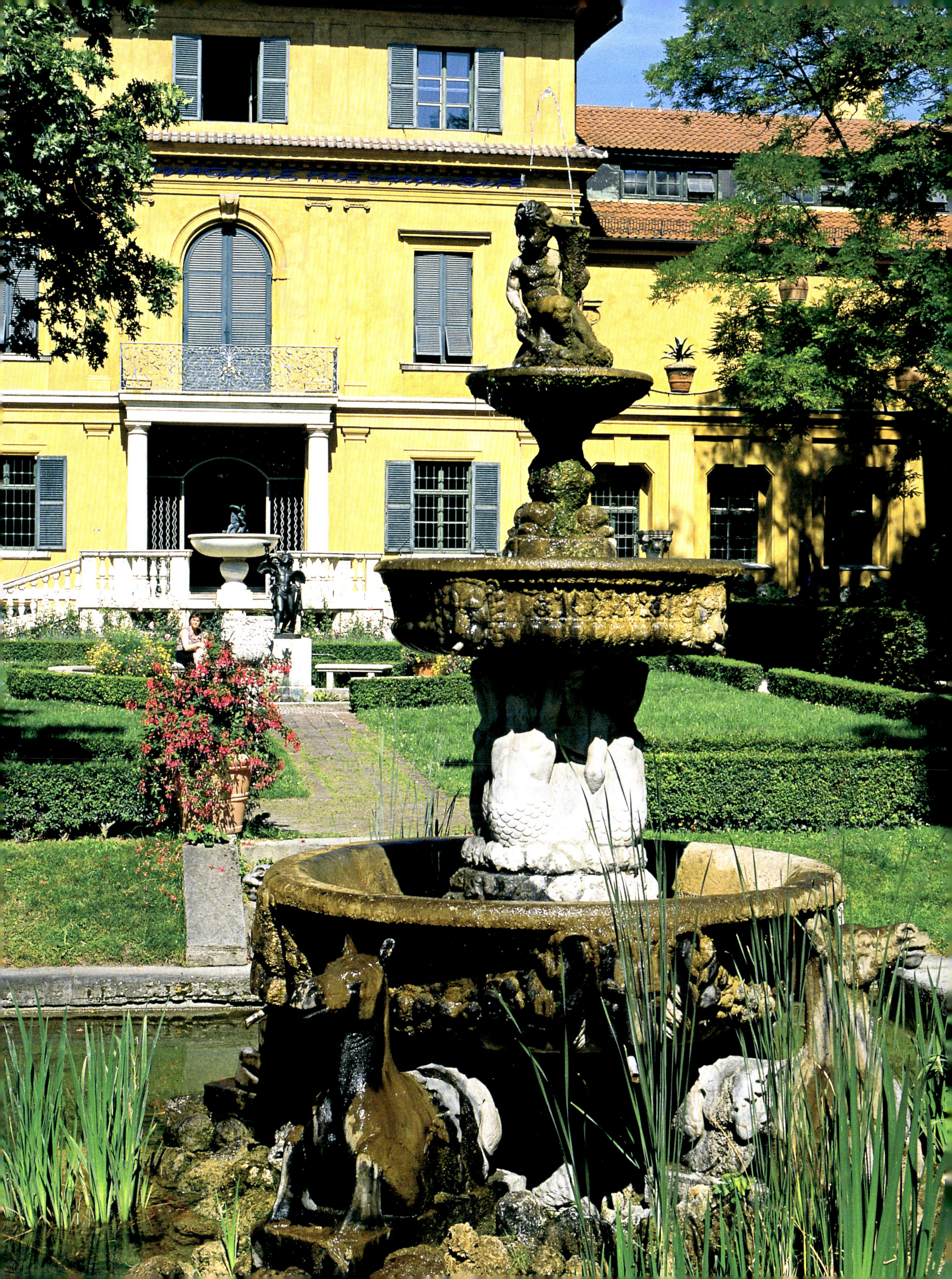

NEW ARTISTIC AVENUES –

DER BLAUE REITER

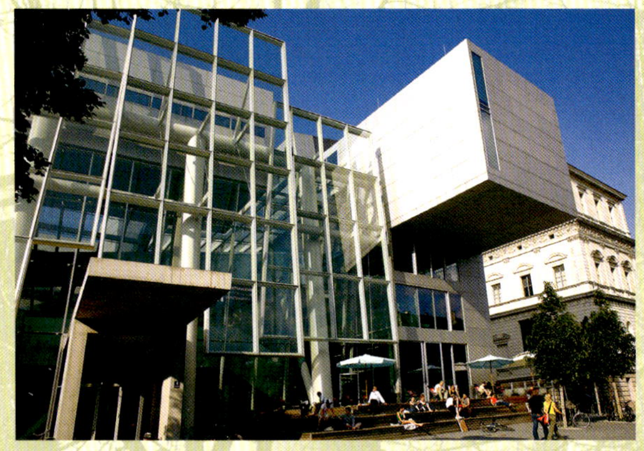

At the close of the 19th century the undisputed capital of the art world may have been Paris but Munich also had a lot to offer. The Bavarian capital was a magnet for writers, painters and sculptors of all persuasions; students came in droves from home and abroad to the art academy and school of the applied arts and curious observers of the latest artistic trends positively filled galleries and museums. Munich was a base for various groups, some members of a Secession akin to the one in Vienna, and the decidedly arty suburb of Schwabing was famous for its legendary happenings.

Above:
This extension was added to the academy of fine arts in 2005 by avantgarde architects Coop Himmelb(l)au from Vienna.

Centre:
In 2006 this mural by Franz Ackermann (*1963) was painted around a display of pictures by Franz Marc, both on show at the Lenbachhaus.

Below:
Königsplatz underground station has been decorated with motifs from famous paintings. Passengers on this line can gaze upon one of Franz Marc's blue horses while waiting for the tube.

In 1896 Munich was visited by a young artist from Russia who quickly became a leader in his field: Wassily Kandinsky (1866–1944). He first studied at the art academy under Franz von Stuck. He later joined an association entitled Phalanx where he met his later partner Gabriele Münter. He travelled widely between 1904 and 1908 and spent a year in the French town of Sèvres where he turned to Expressionism. As a result conservative artistic groups refused to include his work in their exhibitions.

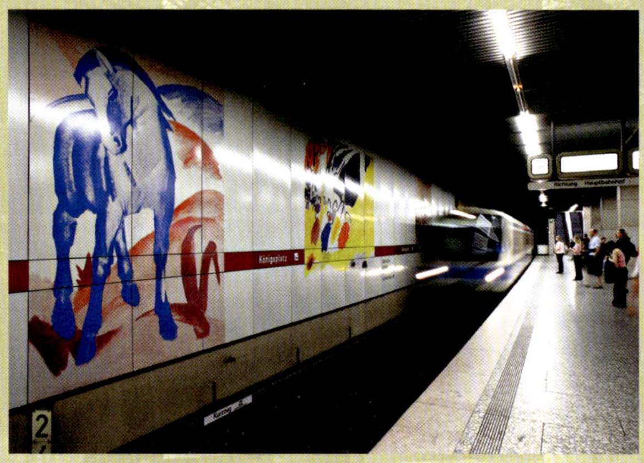

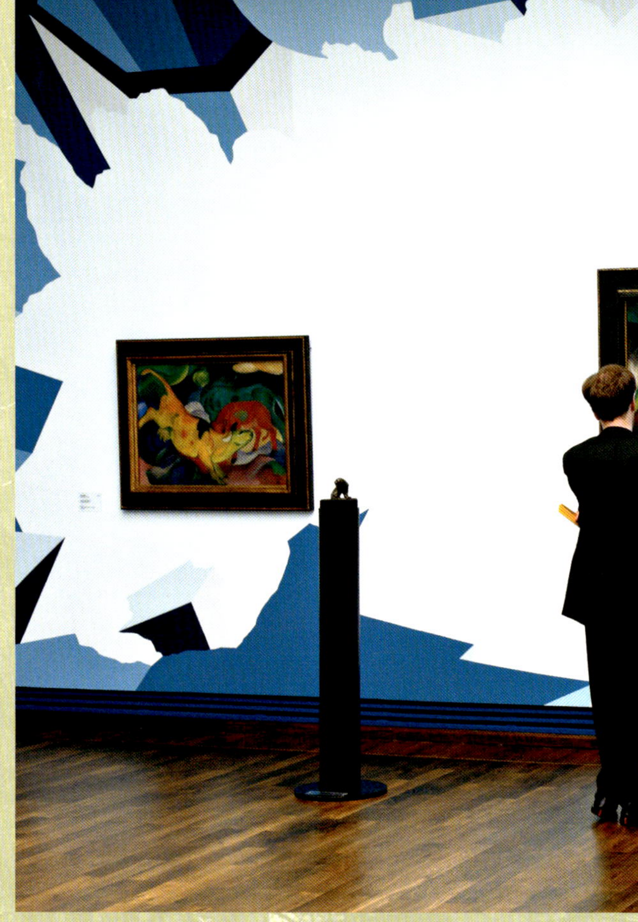

In 1909 Kandinsky and a few friends thus formed their own society which they called the Neue Künstlervereinigung München.

In 1909, 1910 and 1911 they put on joint exhibitions. After the first one the local press was moved to comment: "Either the majority of the members of this association is incurably mentally ill or we are dealing with a group of scrupulous fraudsters..."

Kandinsky's pictures became more and more removed from the representational, triggering a huge row within the group. In 1911 they split. In the same year a handful – among them

Gabriele Münter, Franz Marc, August Macke, Alfred Kubin, composer and artist Arnold Schönberg and of course Kandinsky – reformed as Der Blaue Reiter (The Blue Rider). The epithet was concocted over coffee in Sindelsdorf in Upper Bavaria by Kandinsky and Marc; as the Russian explained: "Both of us loved blue, Marc horses, I riders. Thus the name came about."

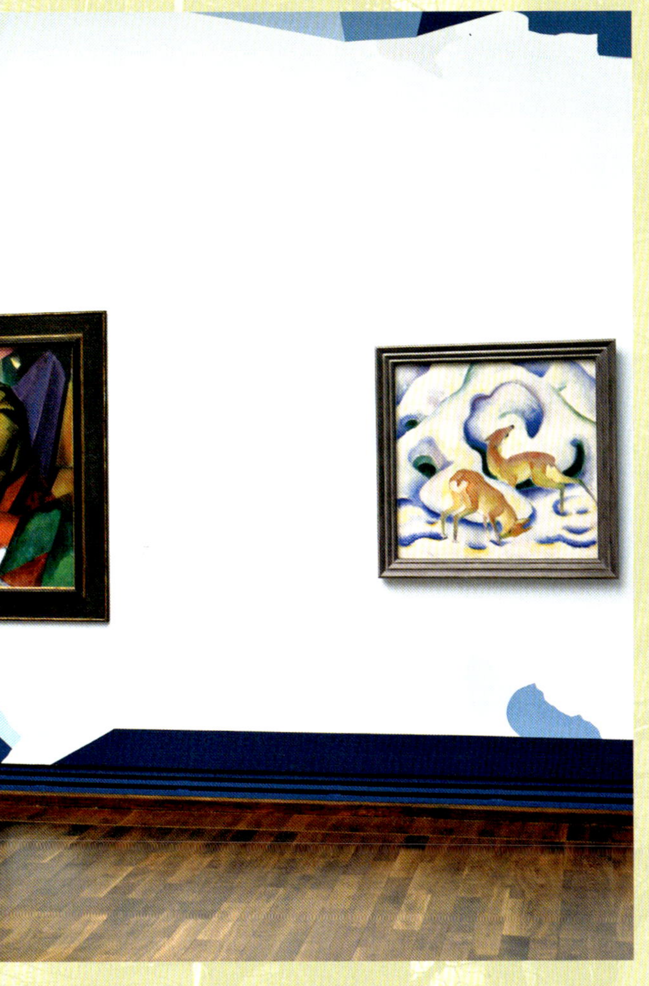

LIBERATION FROM STAGNANT TRADITIONS

In their exhibitions and with the publication of an almanac containing illustrations and theoretical treatises the group wanted to liberate painting from the stagnant traditions of academic art. Art historian Horst Richter describes their objectives thus: "To empathise with the secrets of nature instead of unmasking [it]; complete dematerialisation and the conquering of the corporeal instead of clinging to the tangible (...); to discover one's own self instead of arousing social sympathies. To this end the Munich artists

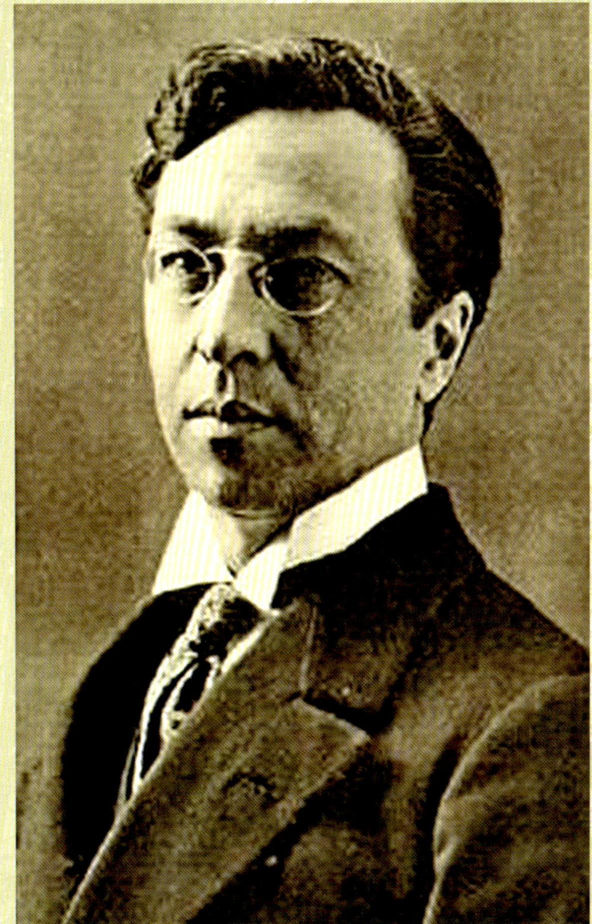

chose harmony of colour over dissonance of colour (...) and they scrutinised and analysed shape instead of breaking it apart."

Yet this consortium was also destroyed by inner conflict, their end brought about by political unrest. At the outbreak of the First World War Kandinsky had to return home to Russia. Marc and Macke lost their lives on the battlefields of France.

The oeuvre of Der Blaue Reiter is well documented by the Städtische Galerie at the Lenbachhaus in Munich. The splendid villa which once belonged to prince of painters Franz von Lenbach also boasts the largest collection of works by Kandinsky in Germany. This was bequeathed by his partner Gabriele Münter who in 1957 gave the city of Munich 90 oils and 300 watercolours by the great man and also 25 works of her own. It's thus hardly surprising that the Lenbachhaus has become something of a place of pilgrimage for aficionados of this truly unique artistic movement.

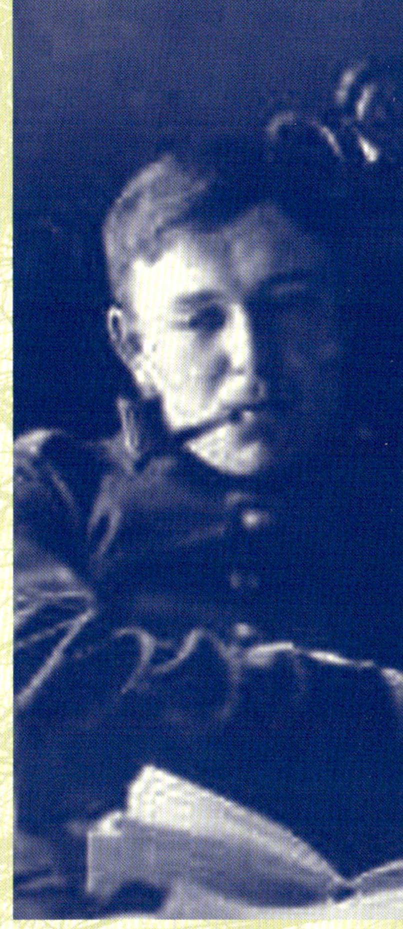

Above left:
Wassily Kandinsky (1866–1944) moved to Munich in 1896 and studied at the art academy under Franz von Stuck. He later lectured at the Bauhaus in Weimar, Dessau and Berlin.

Above:
August Macke (1887–1914) grew up in Cologne and Bonn. He was a member of Der Blaue Reiter and for a while lived on the shores of the Tegernsee. At the age of 27 he fell in France – just eight weeks after the outbreak of the First World War.

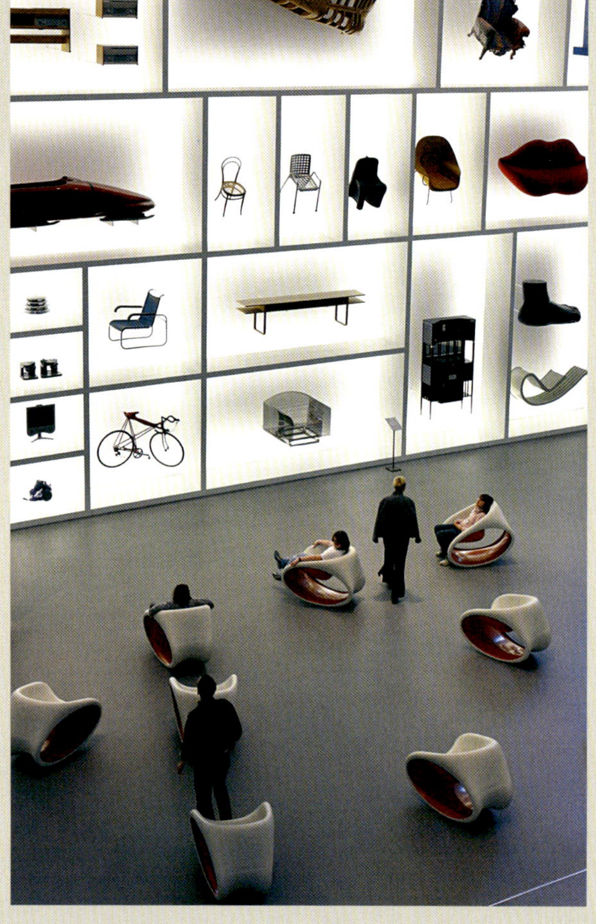

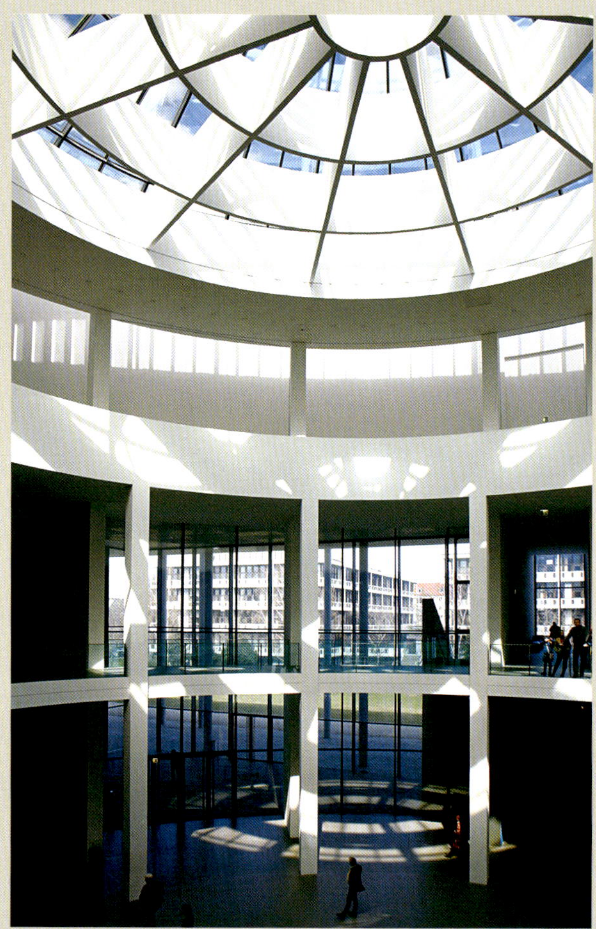

The Pinakothek der Moderne in Maxvorstadt contains four separate museums devoted to art, graphics, architecture and design. The modern building is the perfect addition to the Alte and Neue Pinakothek which together make up Munich's impressive arts complex. It was constructed between 1996 and 2002 by architect Stephan Braunfels (*1950).

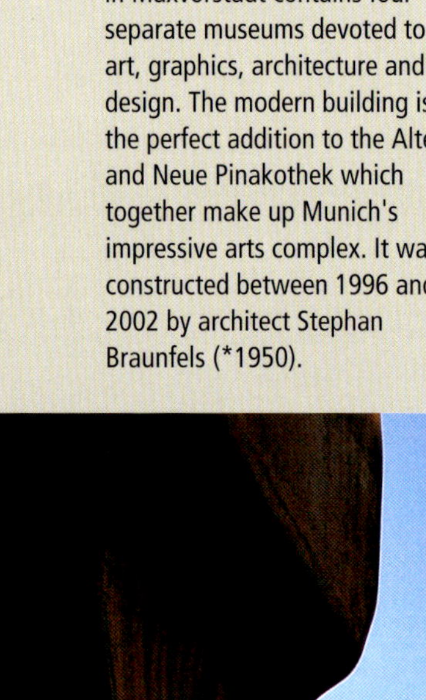

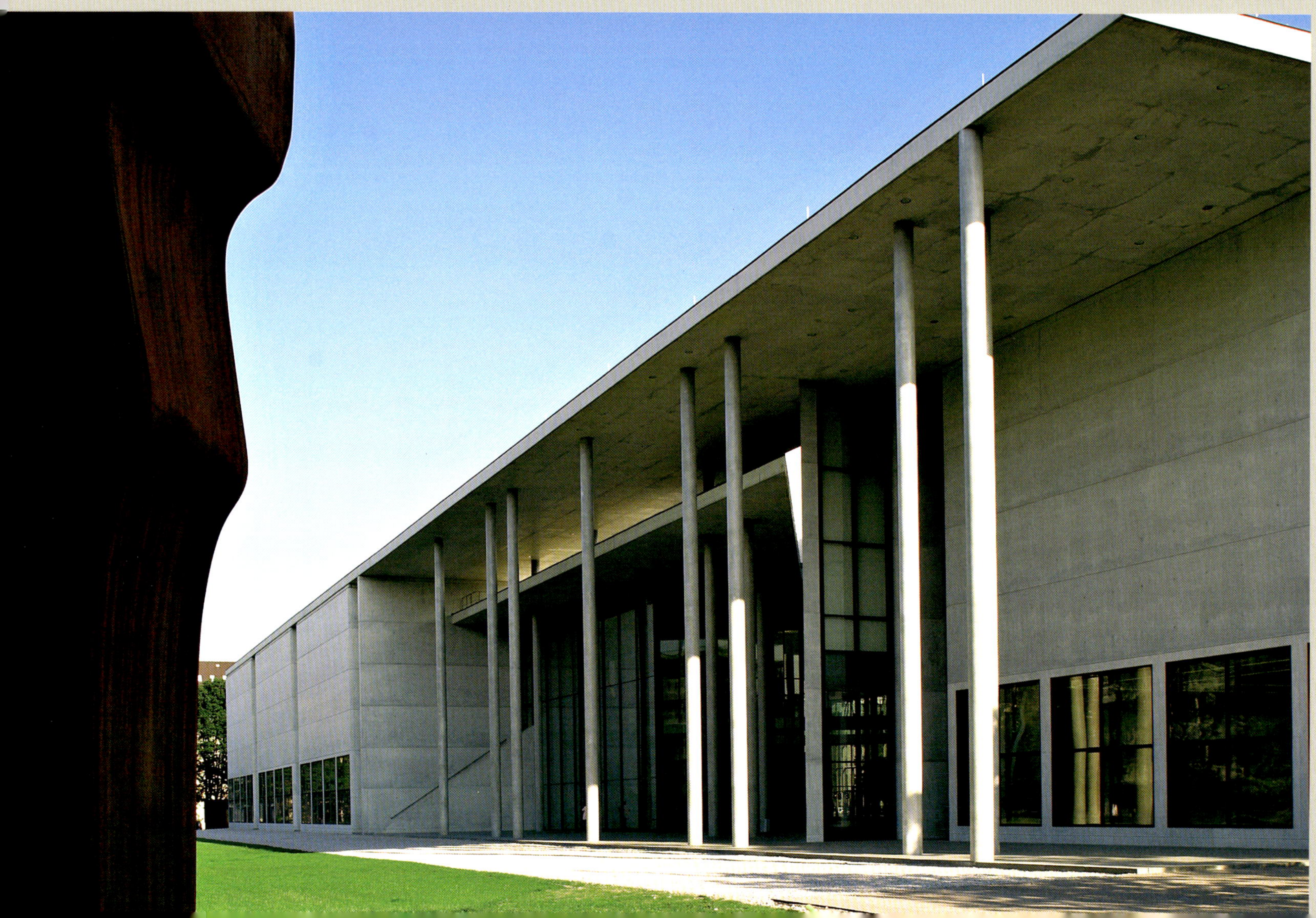

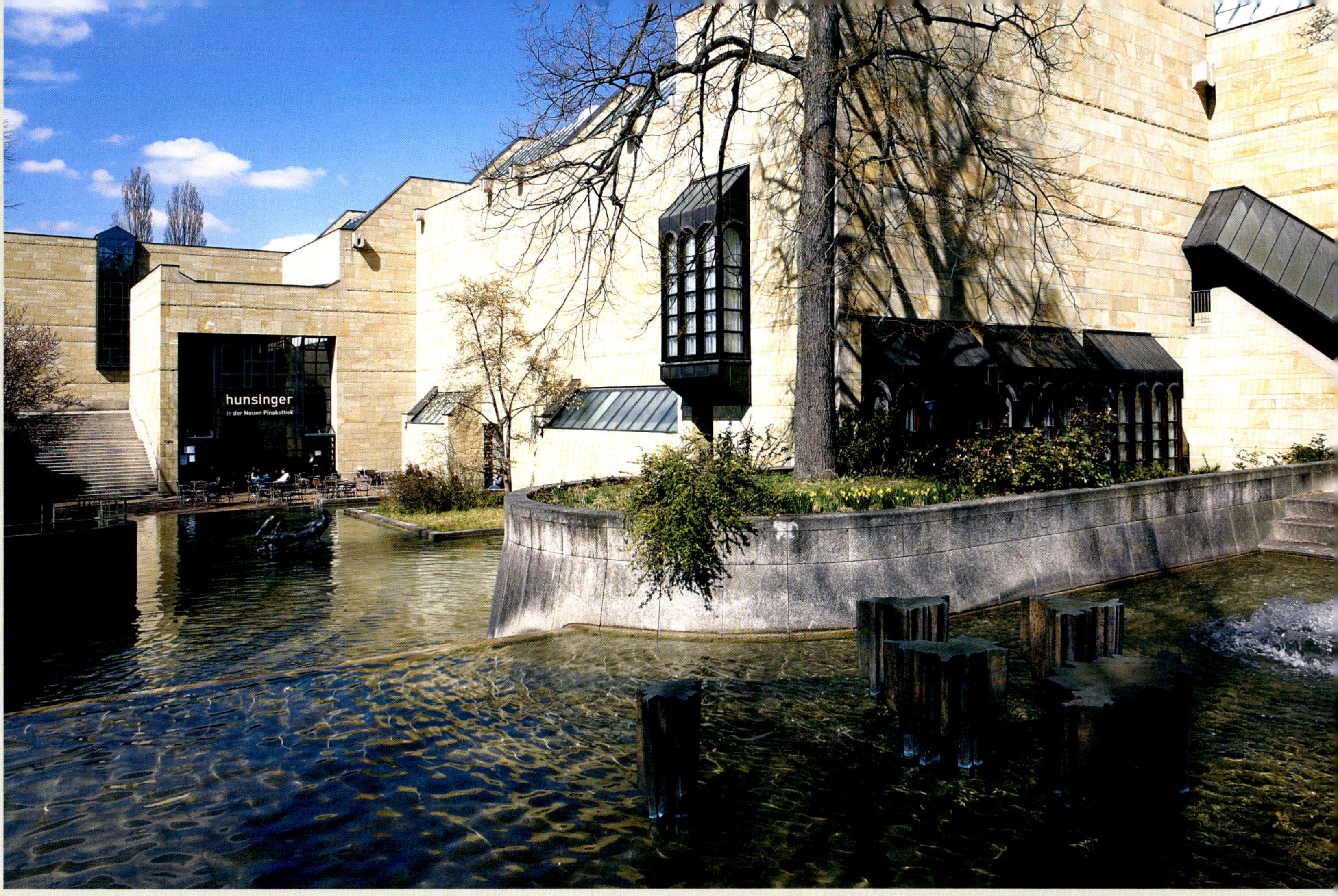

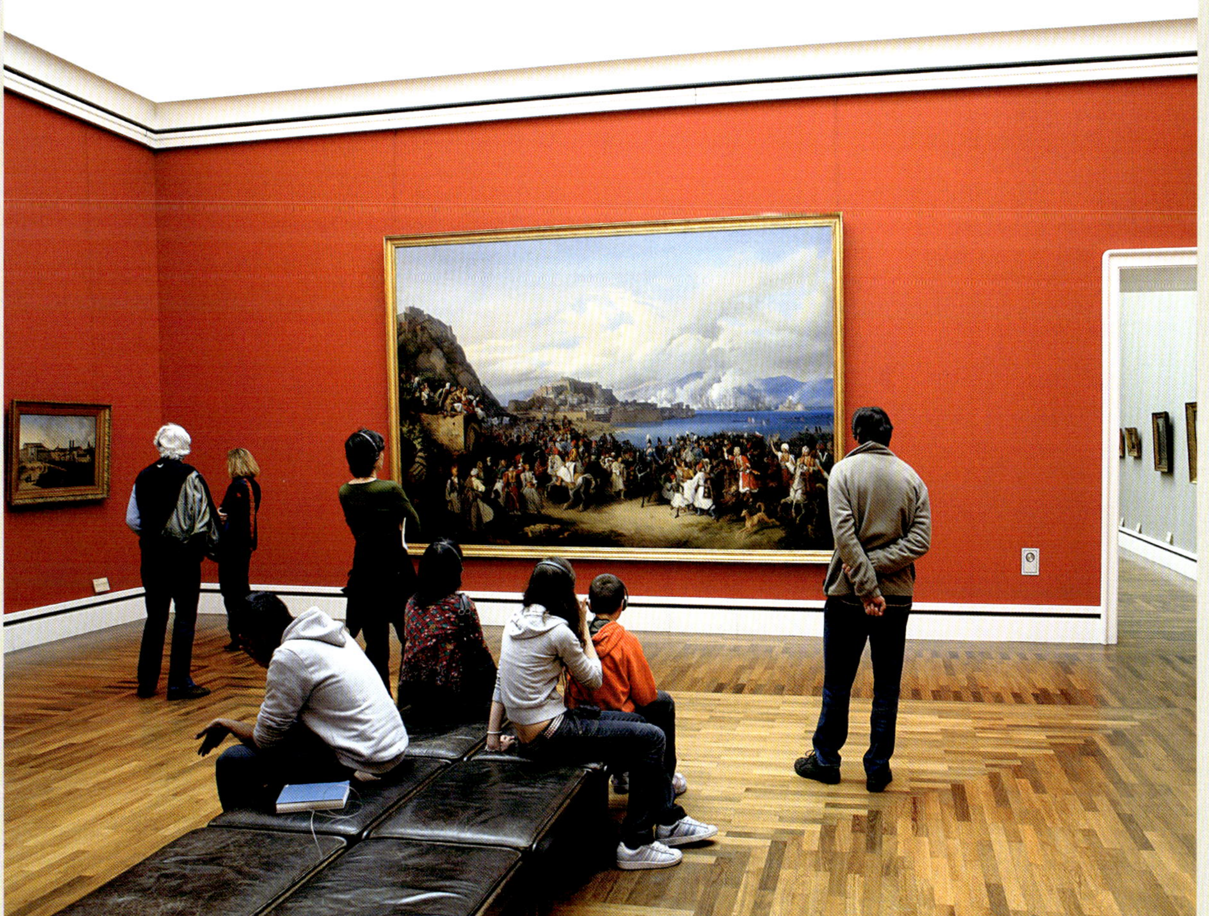

Above:
The focus of the Neue Pinakothek is on European art from neoclassicism to Jugendstil. The first museum was completely annihilated in the Second World War and the ruins torn down. In 1975 the foundations were laid for the current postmodernist edifice which opened its doors in 1981.

Left:
Visitors to the Neue Pinakothek studying the enormous Entry of King Otto of Greece in Nafplion by Peter von Hess (1792–1871). King Ludwig I bought it from the artist in 1835; Otto I of Greece was one of the king's sons.

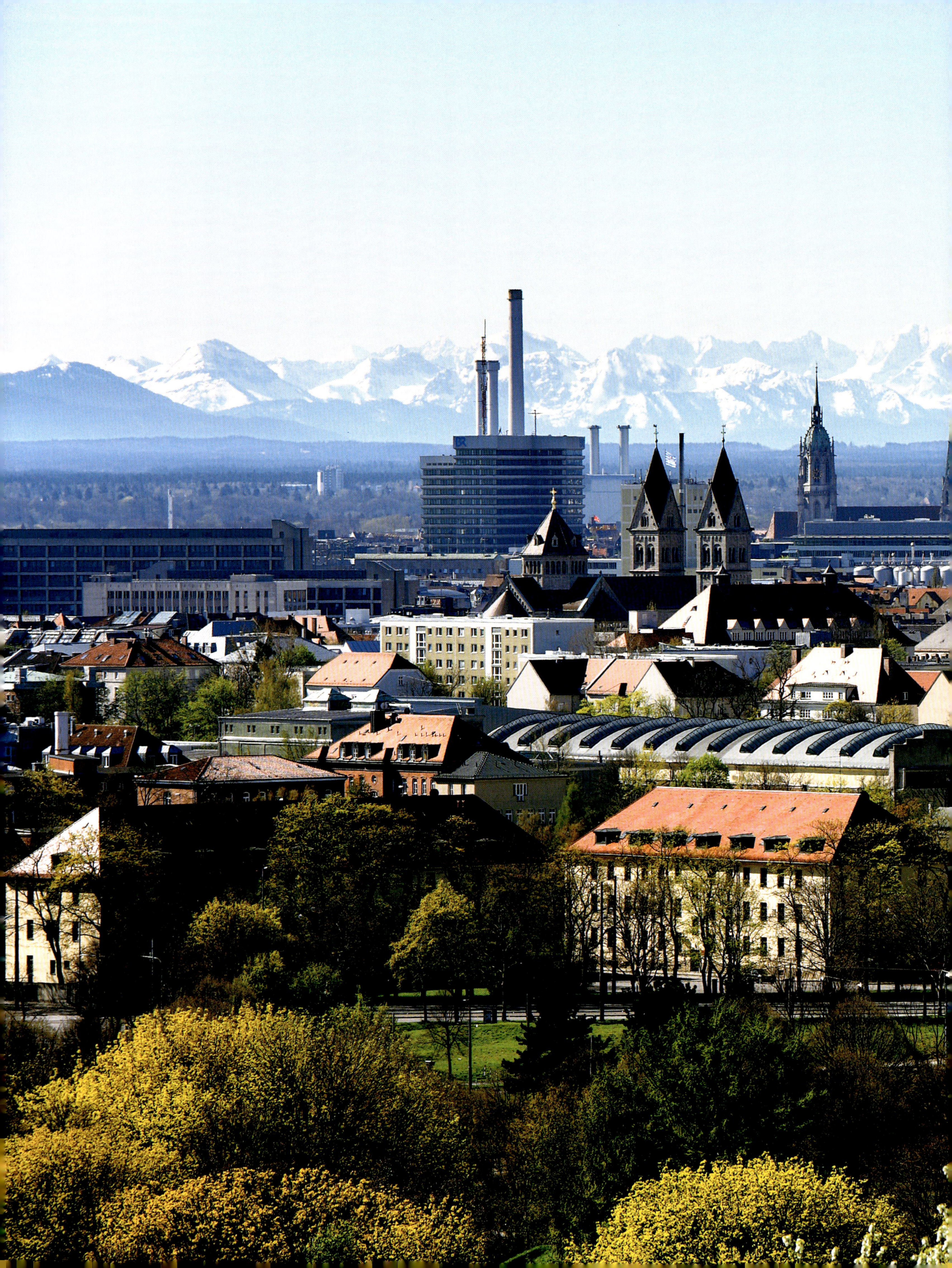

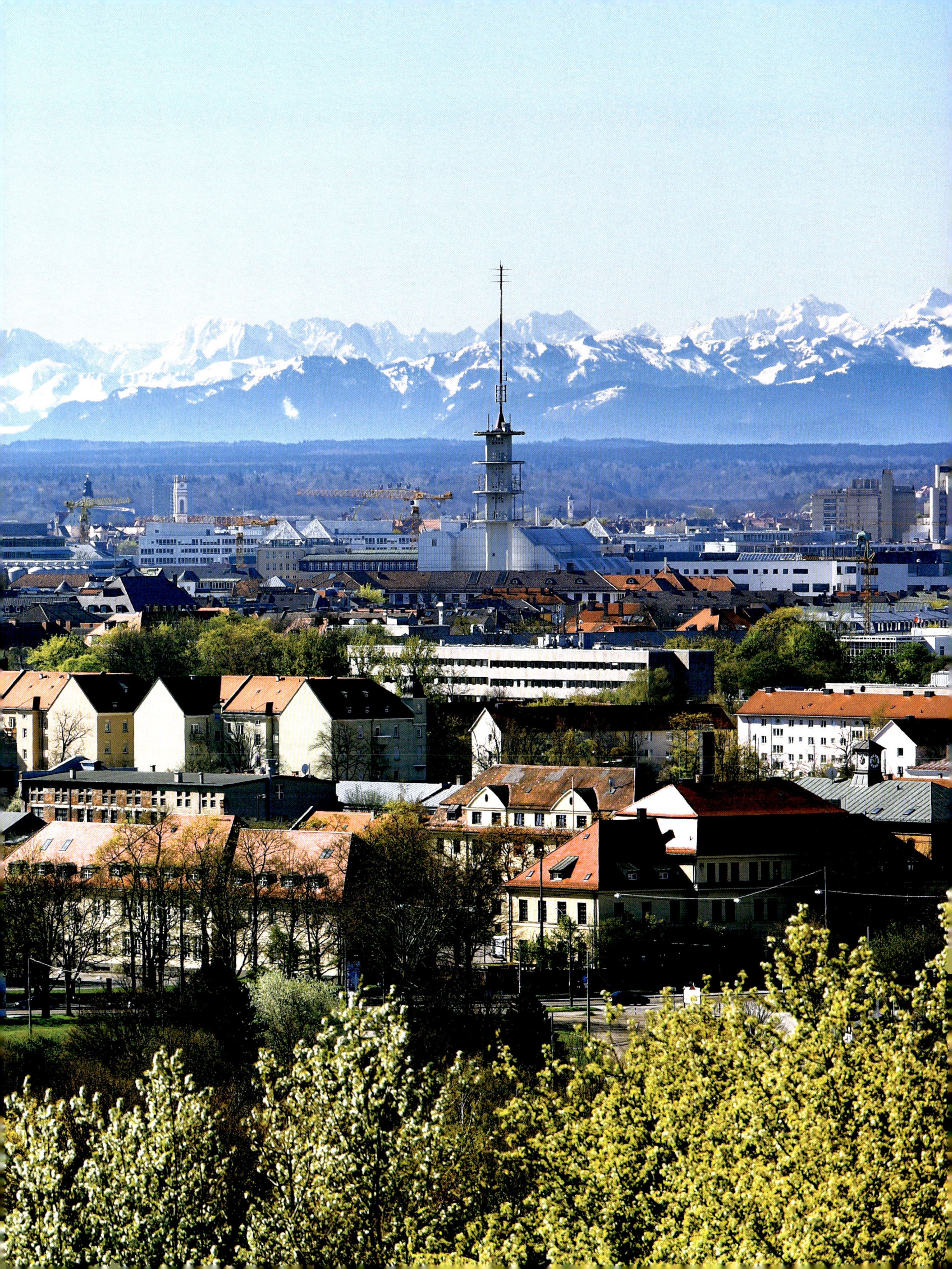

Page 102/103:
View south from Olympiaberg of the churches of St Benno and St Paul and the Alps. The hill is made of the ruins of the city, deposited here between 1947 and 1958, and is also called Schuttberg or rubble mountain.

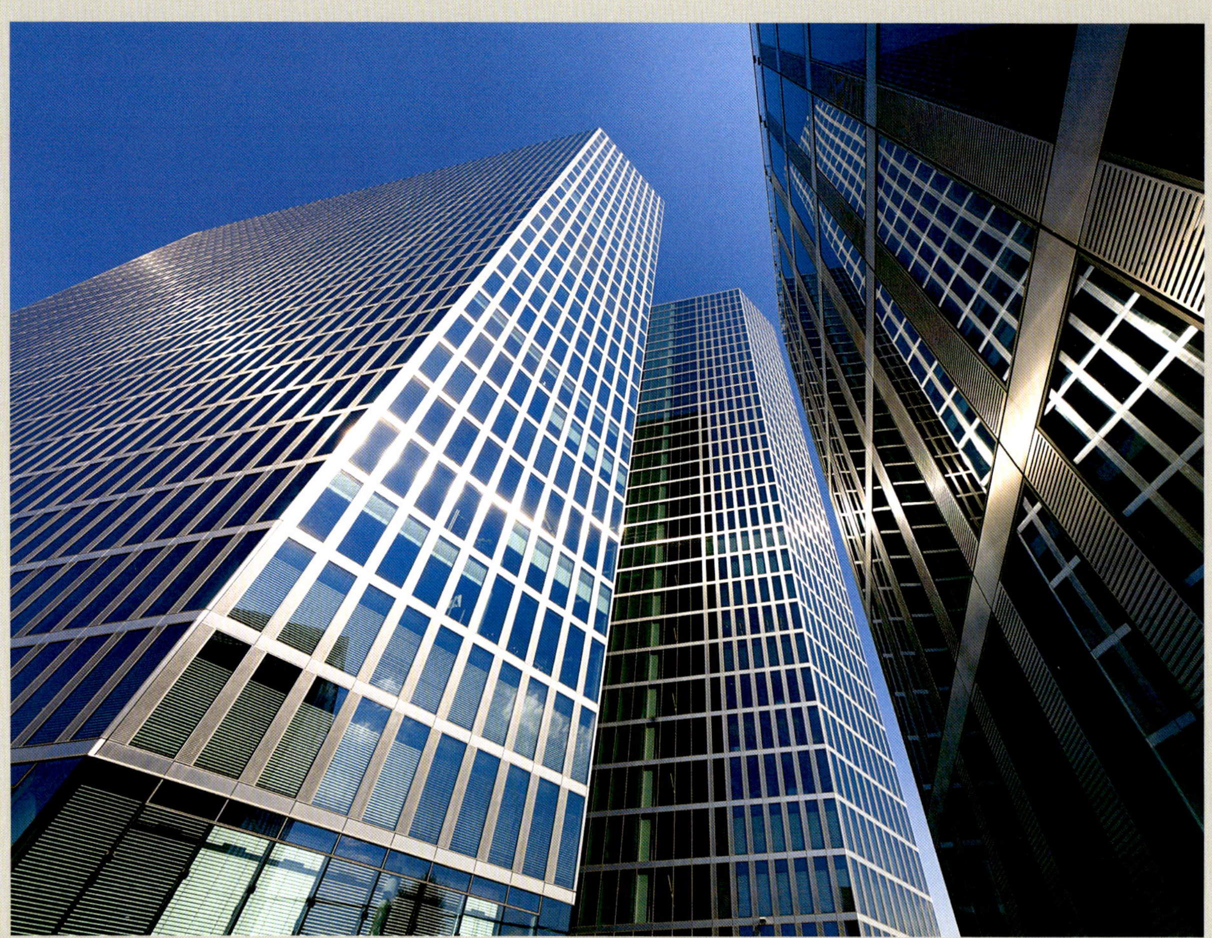

Right:
Highlight Towers in Schwabing, completed in 2004, are 126 m (413 ft) and 113 m (370 ft) tall and thus amongst the highest buildings in Munich. The towers are linked by three bridges made of steel and glass.

Below:
The architectural avant-garde is also manifested in BWM-Welt created by the Coop Himmelb(l)au partnership between August 2003 and autumn 2007. The exhibition within centres on motor vehicles, motor sport and technology.

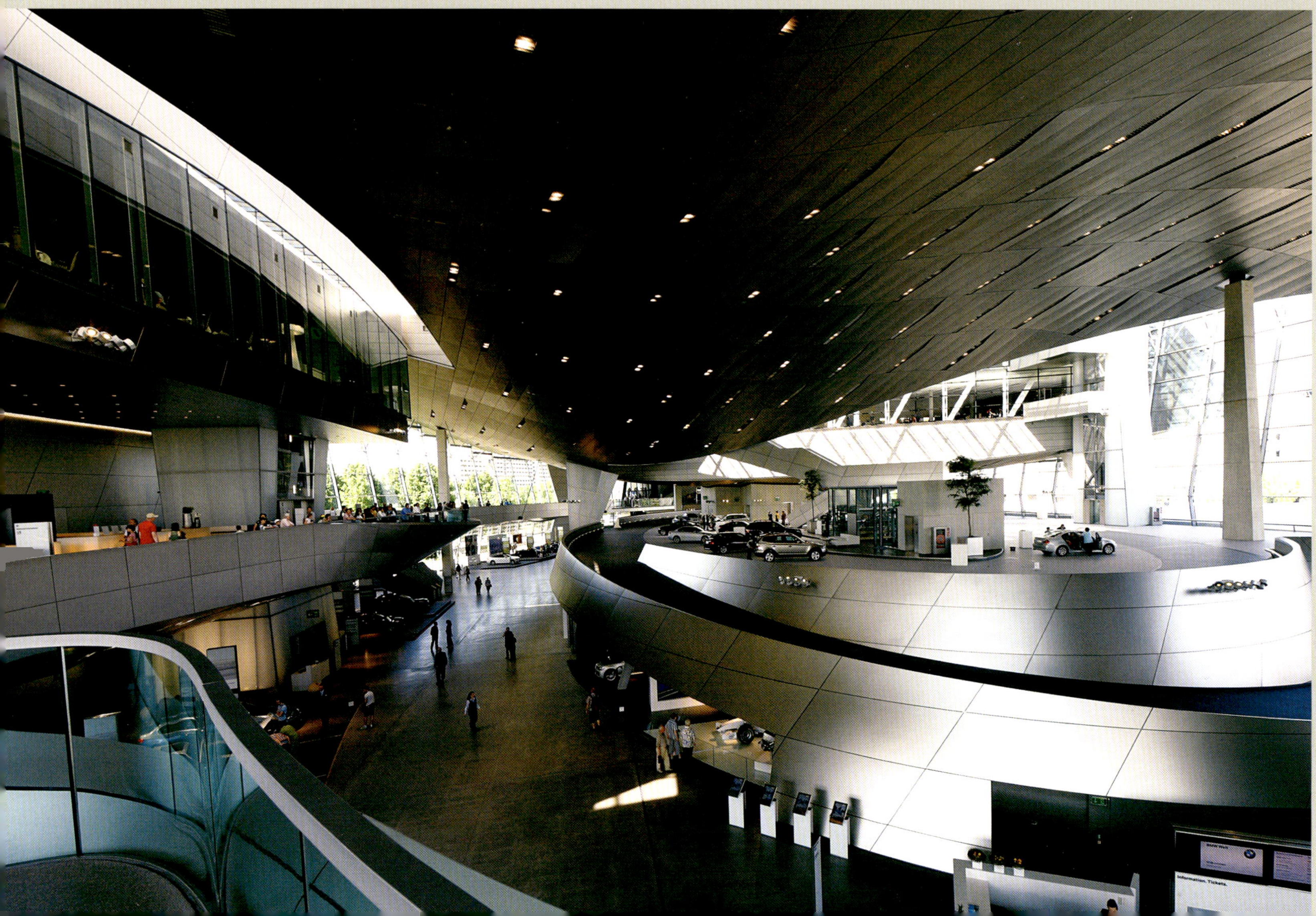

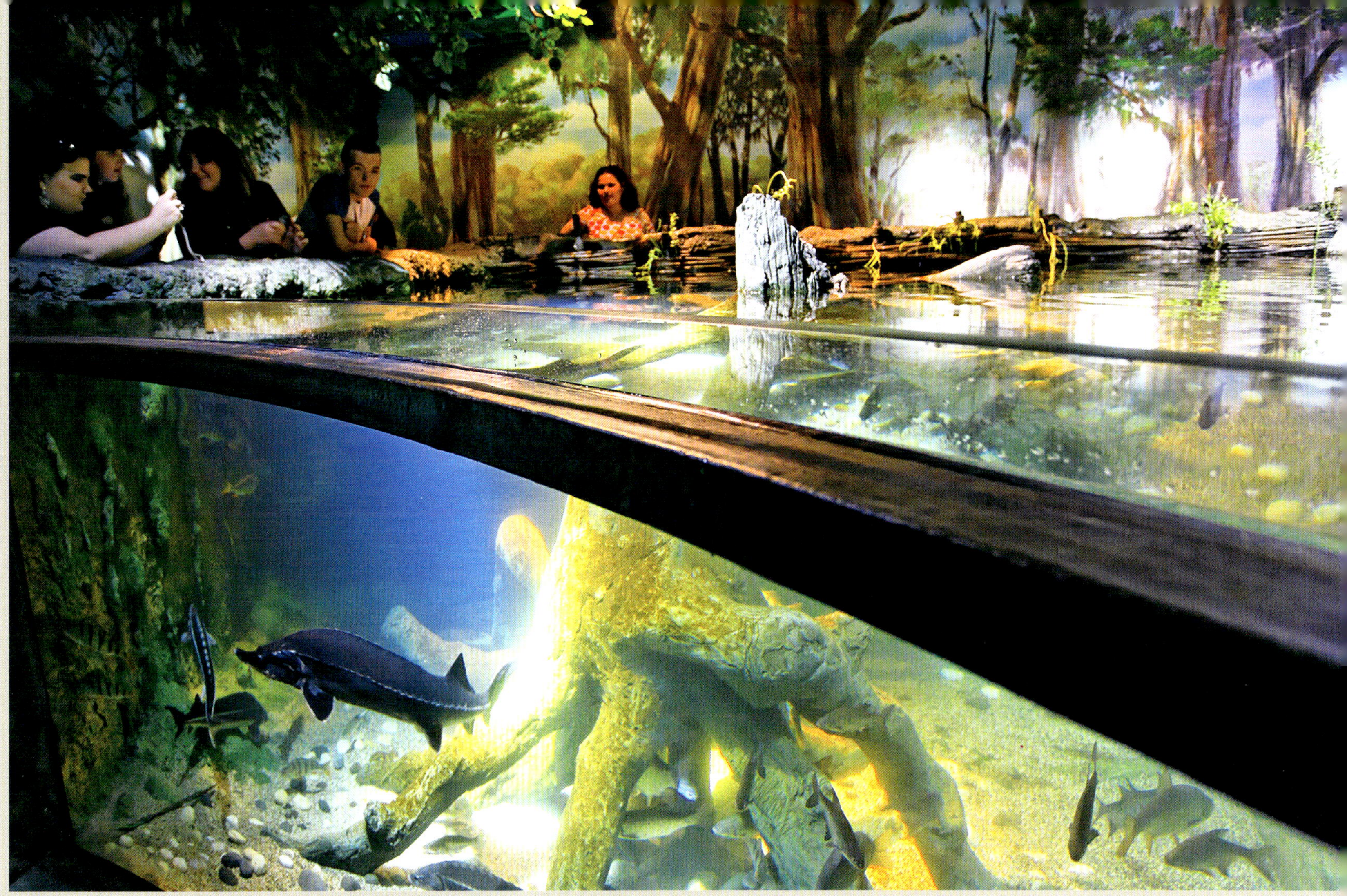

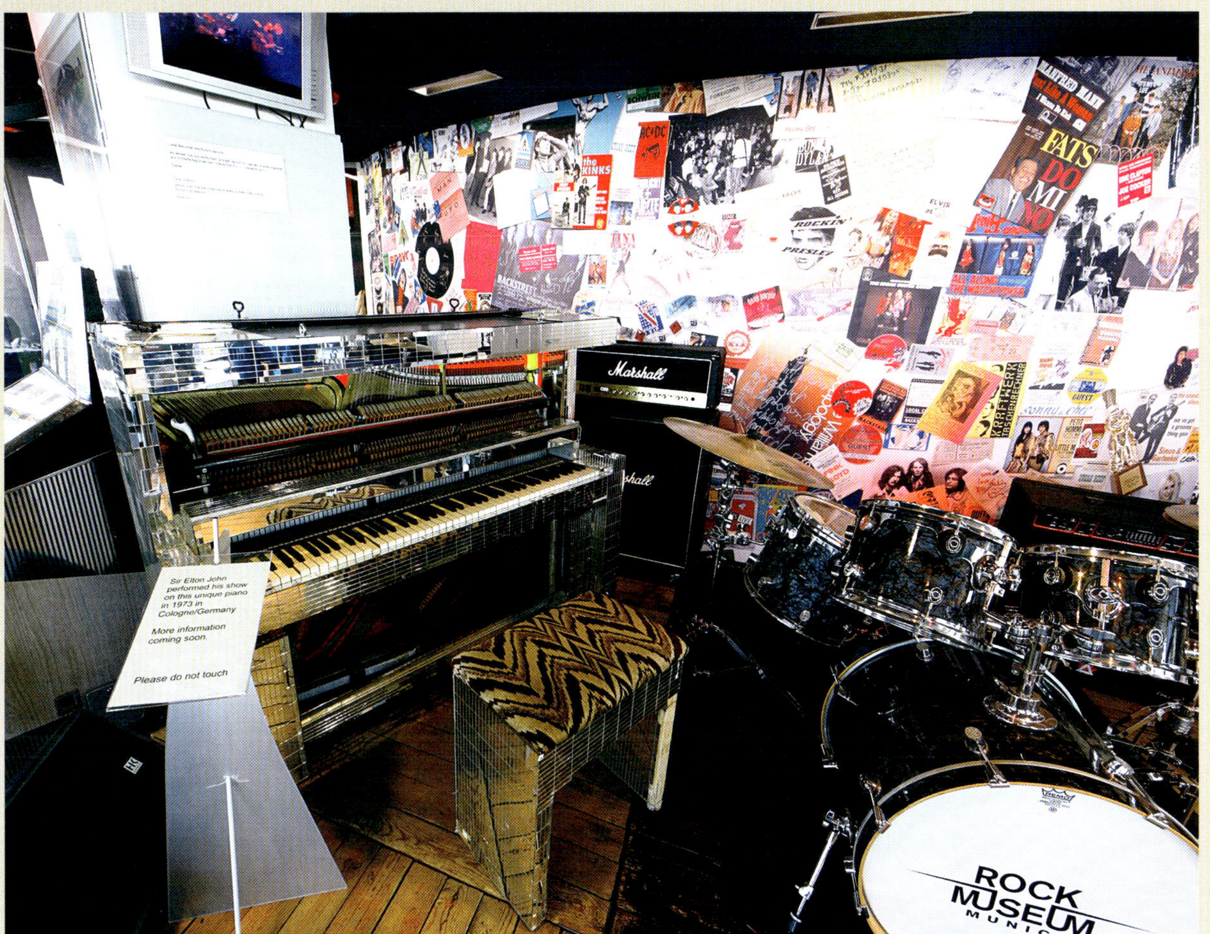

Above:
On April 6, 2006, a new Sea Life Centre opened in Munich in the Olympiapark. One of a commercial enterprise of big-time aquariums, the Munich branch studies underwater life in the Isar and Danube, Black Sea and Mediterranean. Everything can be closely observed underwater from a long glass tunnel.

Left:
In 2004 the Olympic Tower was turned into a museum of rock and pop. The enormous viewing platform is now home to memorabilia to die for: guitars signed by Frank Zappa, the Rolling Stones and others, gold discs, clothes, records, autographs and much more.

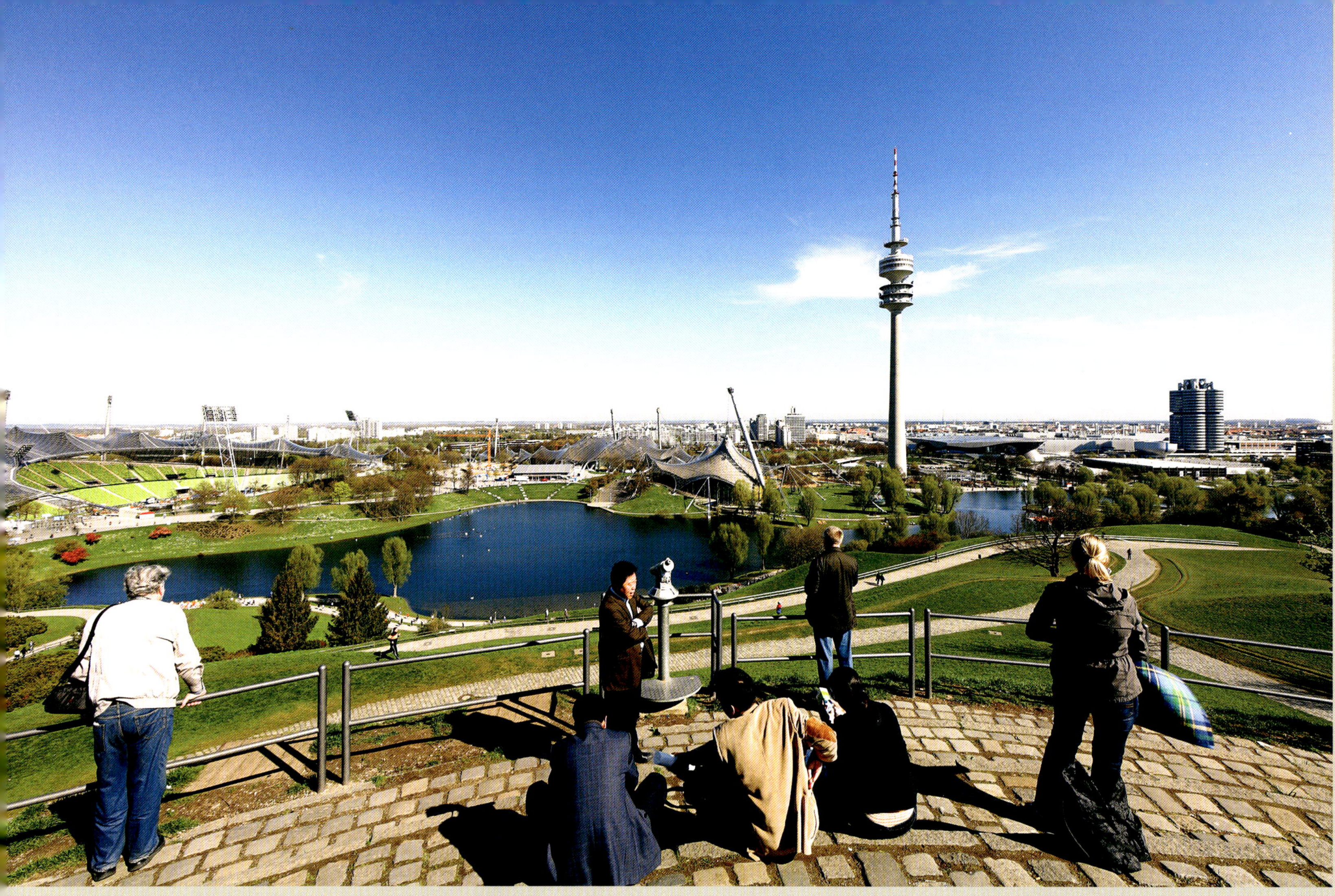

Above:
From Olympiaberg you look out across the Olympic Village with its lake, stadium, hall and tower. At 160 hectares (395 acres) the park is one of the largest green spaces in Munich.

Right:
In hot competition with the Frauenkirche for the place of most famous landmark in Munich is the enormous Plexiglas tent roof of the Olympic Stadium which hangs on no less than 58 steel masts. In summer guides take intrepid visitors up on special roof top tours.

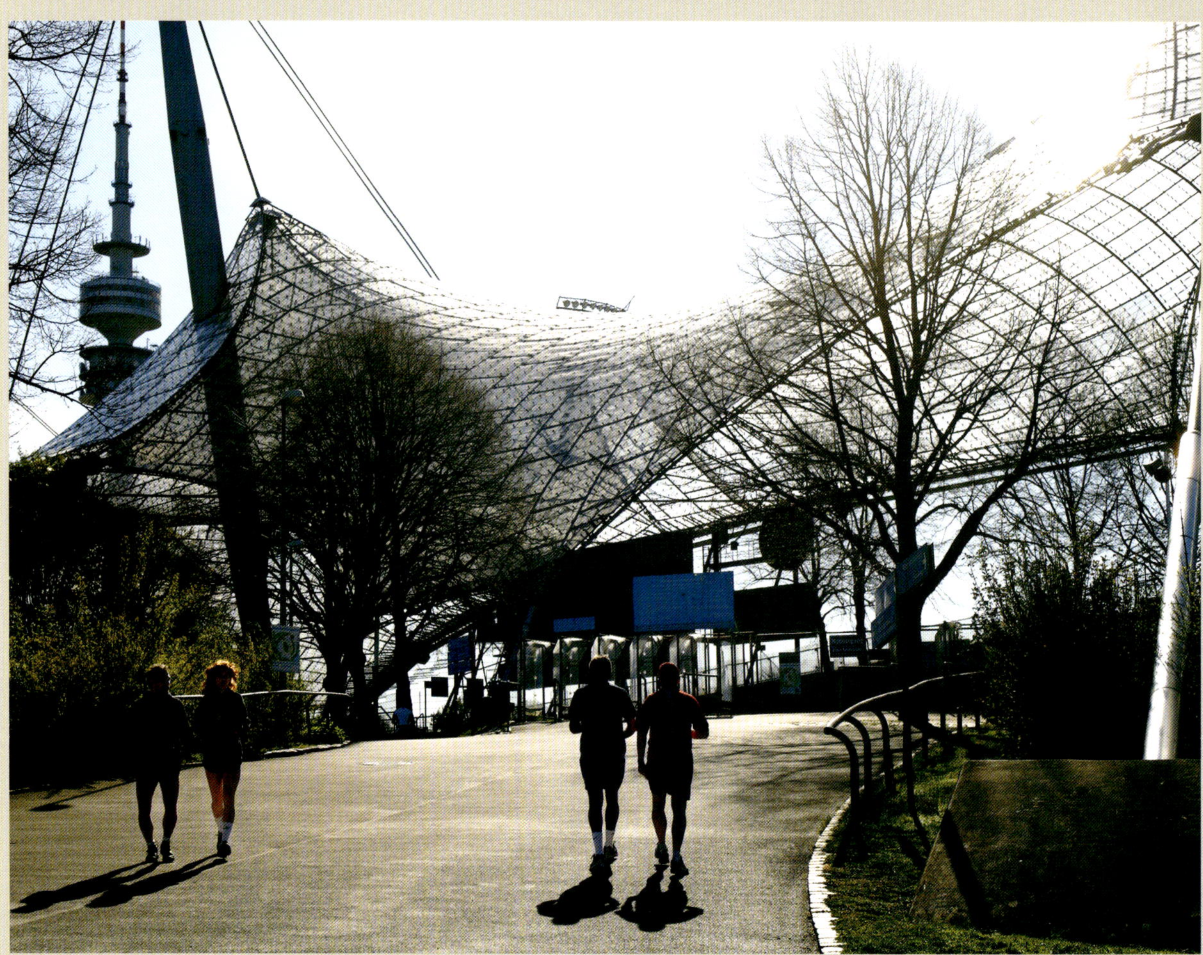

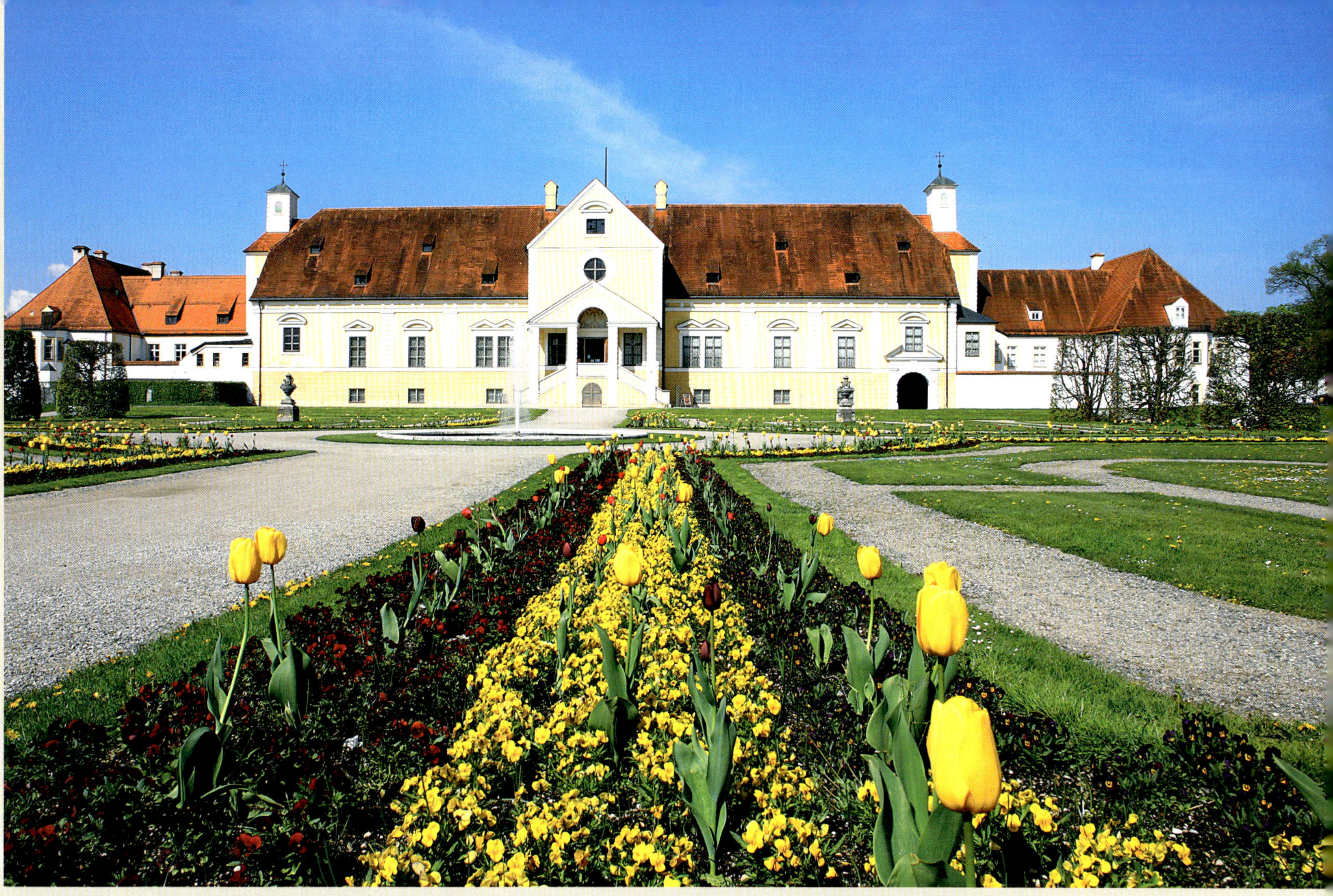

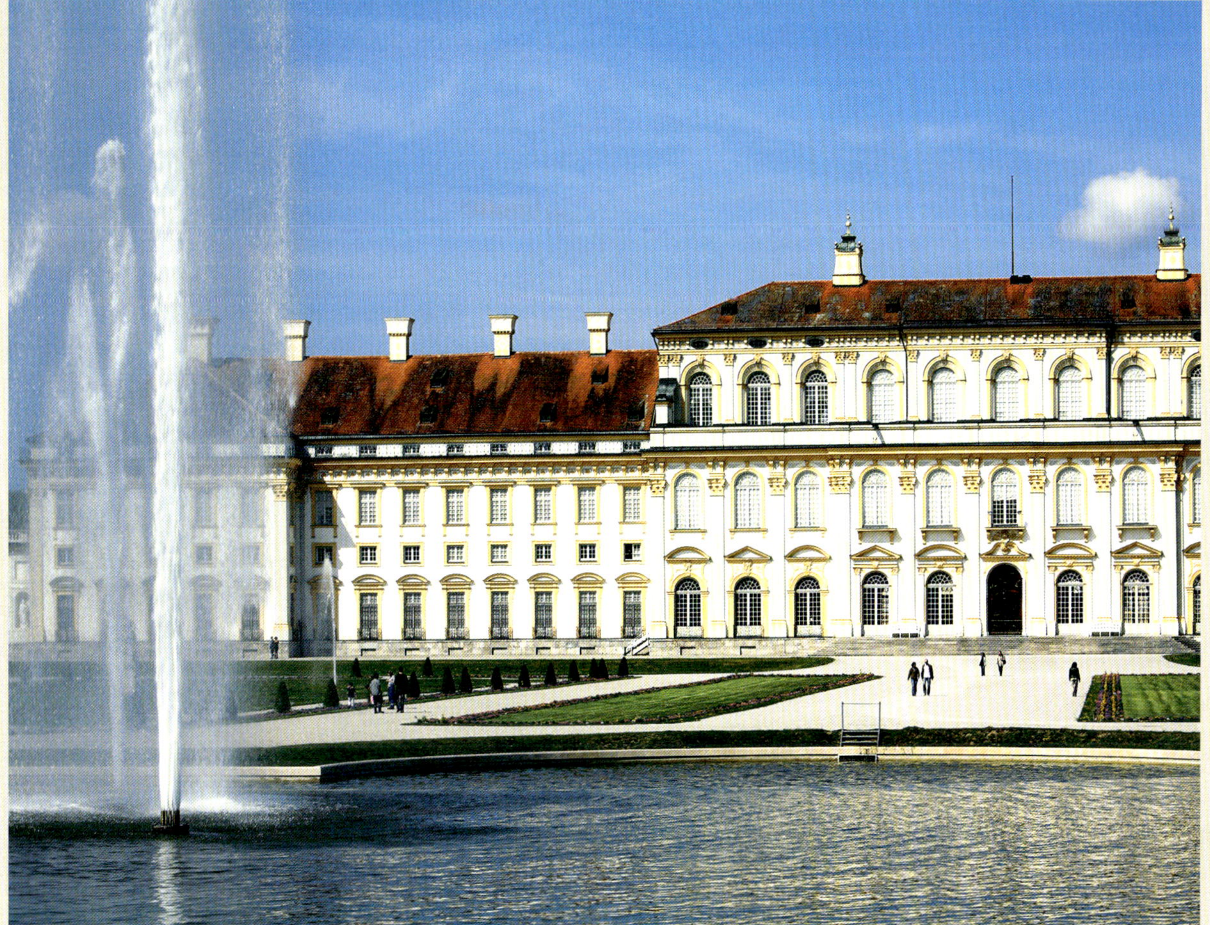

Above:
The Altes Schloss in Schleißheim was erected in the style of the late Renaissance for Duke Maximilian I by Heinrich Schön the Elder between 1616 and 1623. Flemish artist Peter Candid was responsible for the paintings on the walls and ceilings.

Left:
The Neues Schloss in Schleißheim was the new palace built for Elector Max Emanuel between 1701 and 1726 from plans by Enrico Zuccalli from Graubünden in Switzerland (1642–1724). It was to be the regent's summer residence but was hardly used and by the beginning of the 19th century was opened to the public.

Right:
Detail of the art academy extension in the university suburb of Schwabing.

Far right:
In 1995 Jonathan Borofsky's Walking Man strode right up to the offices of the insurance company Münchener Rückversicherungs-Gesellschaft on Leopoldstraße where he towers 17 m (56 ft) up above the mere mortals below.

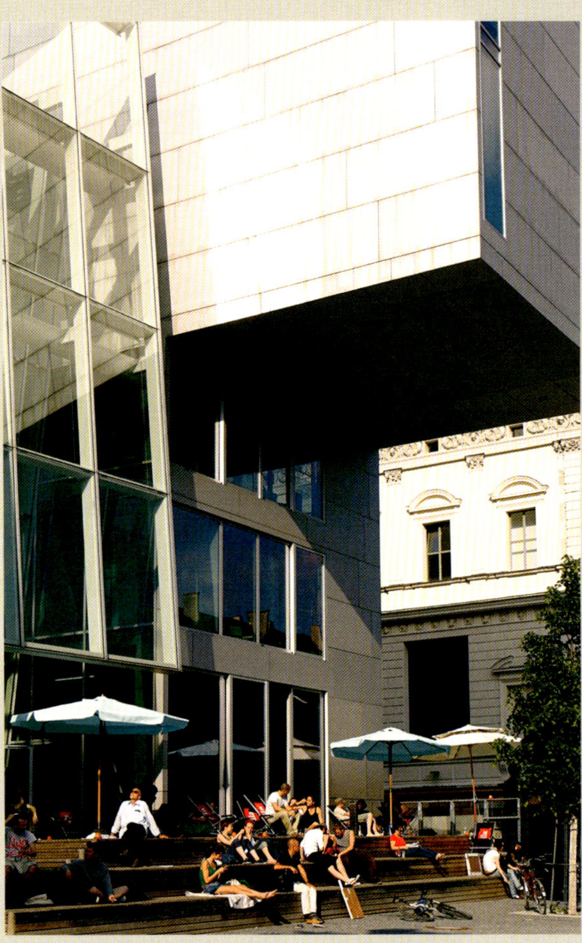

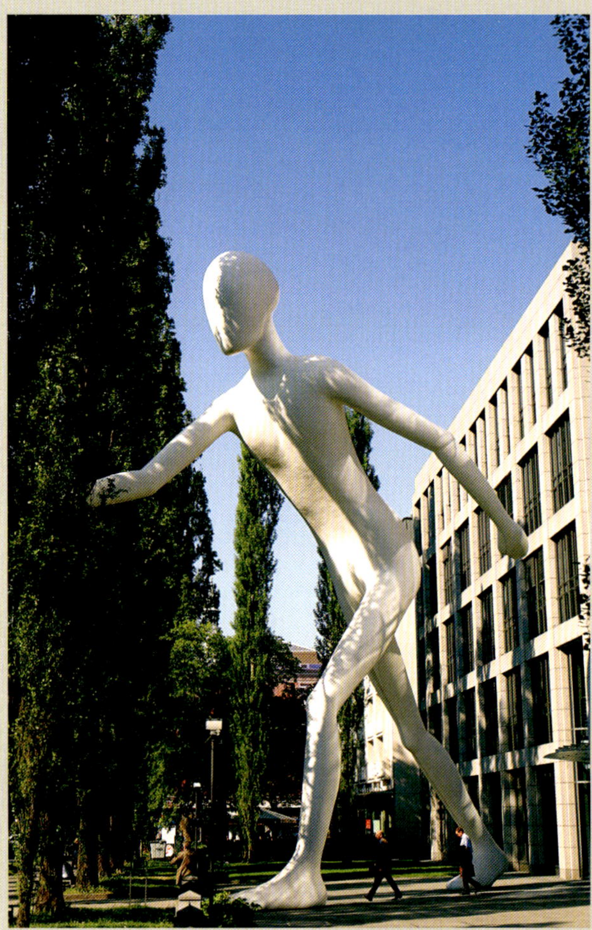

Below:
Stone leaflets set into the ground outside the main building of the university remember the Scholl siblings and the other Resistance members of Die weiße Rose (The White Rose) who were executed by the Nazis in 1943.

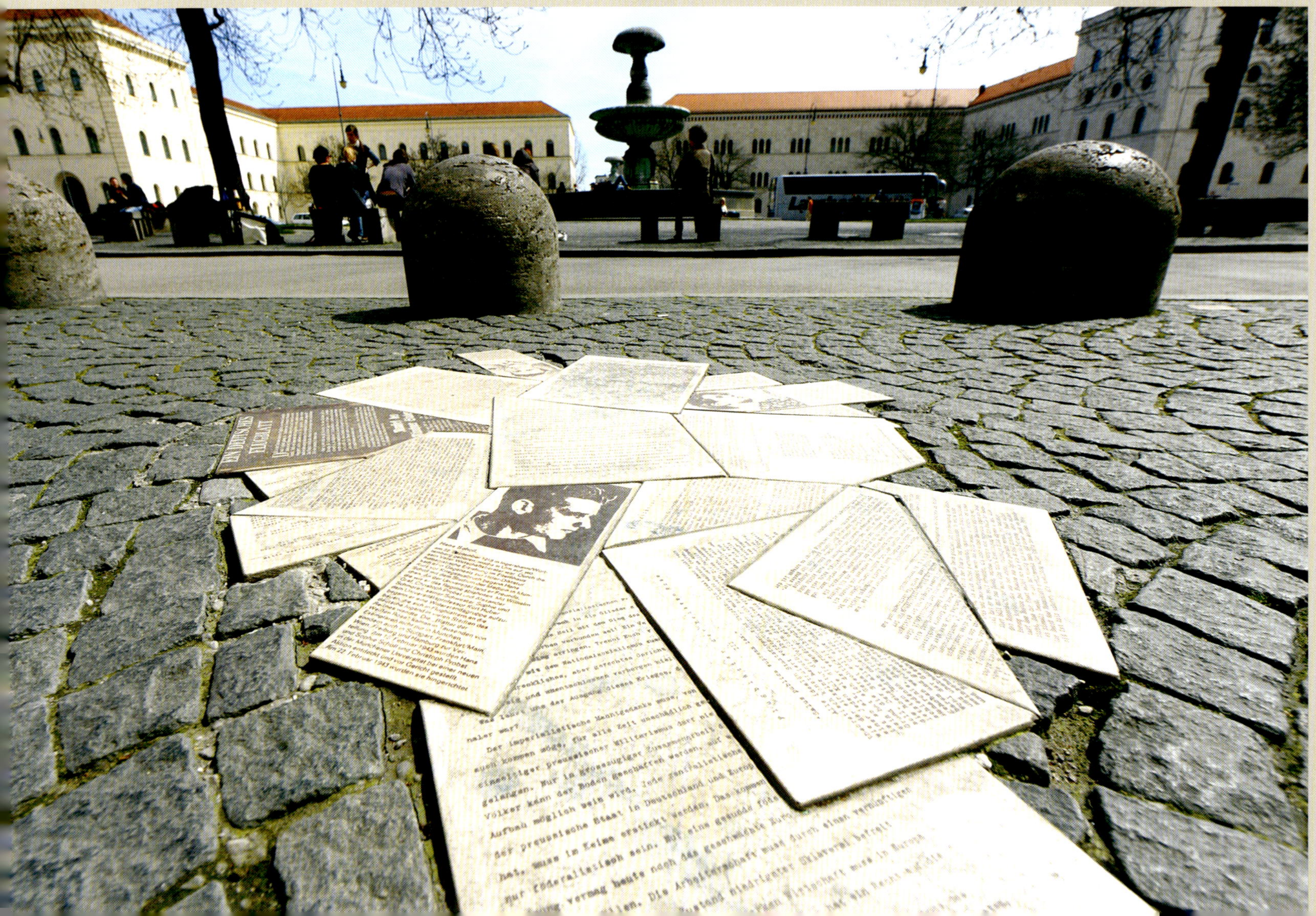

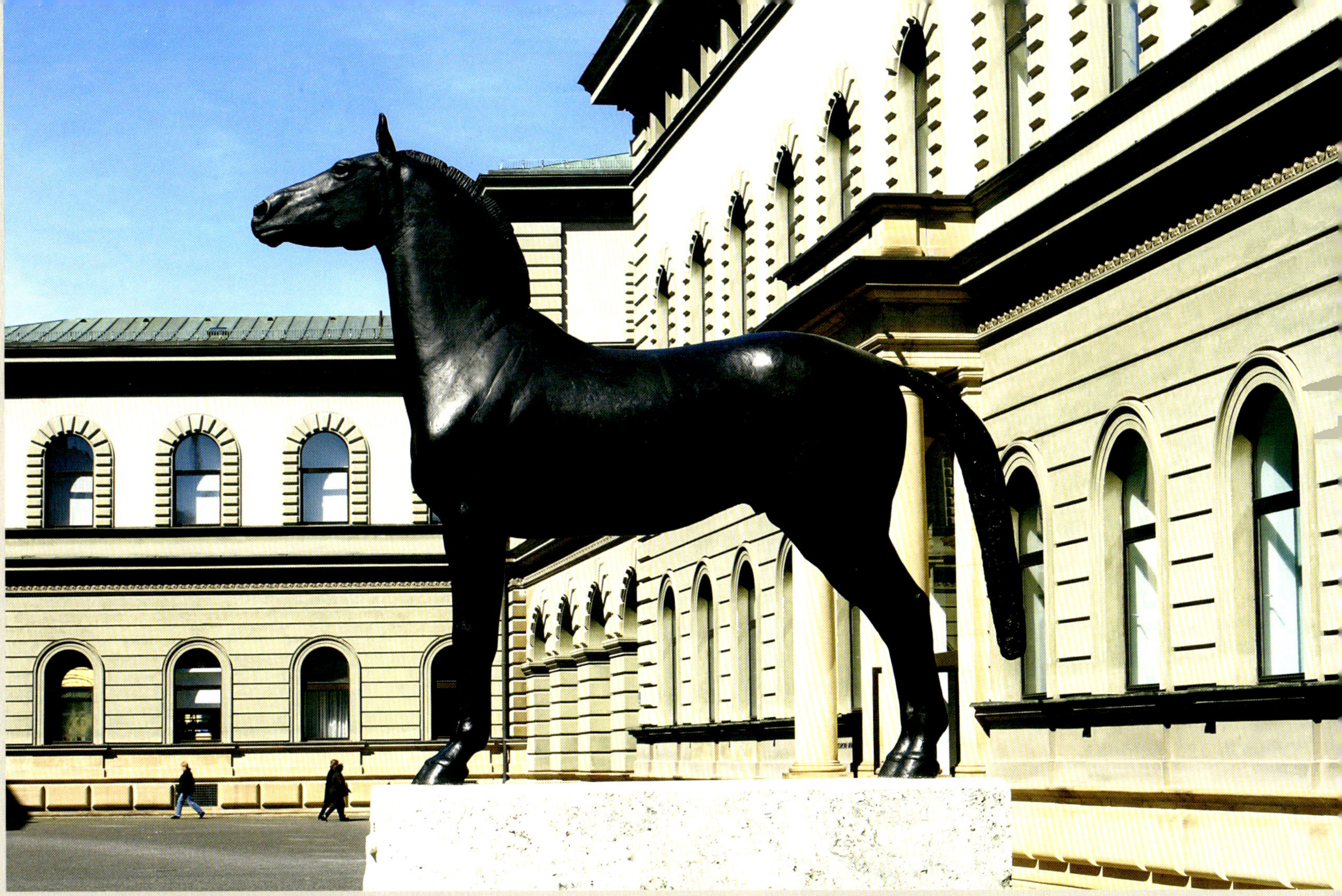

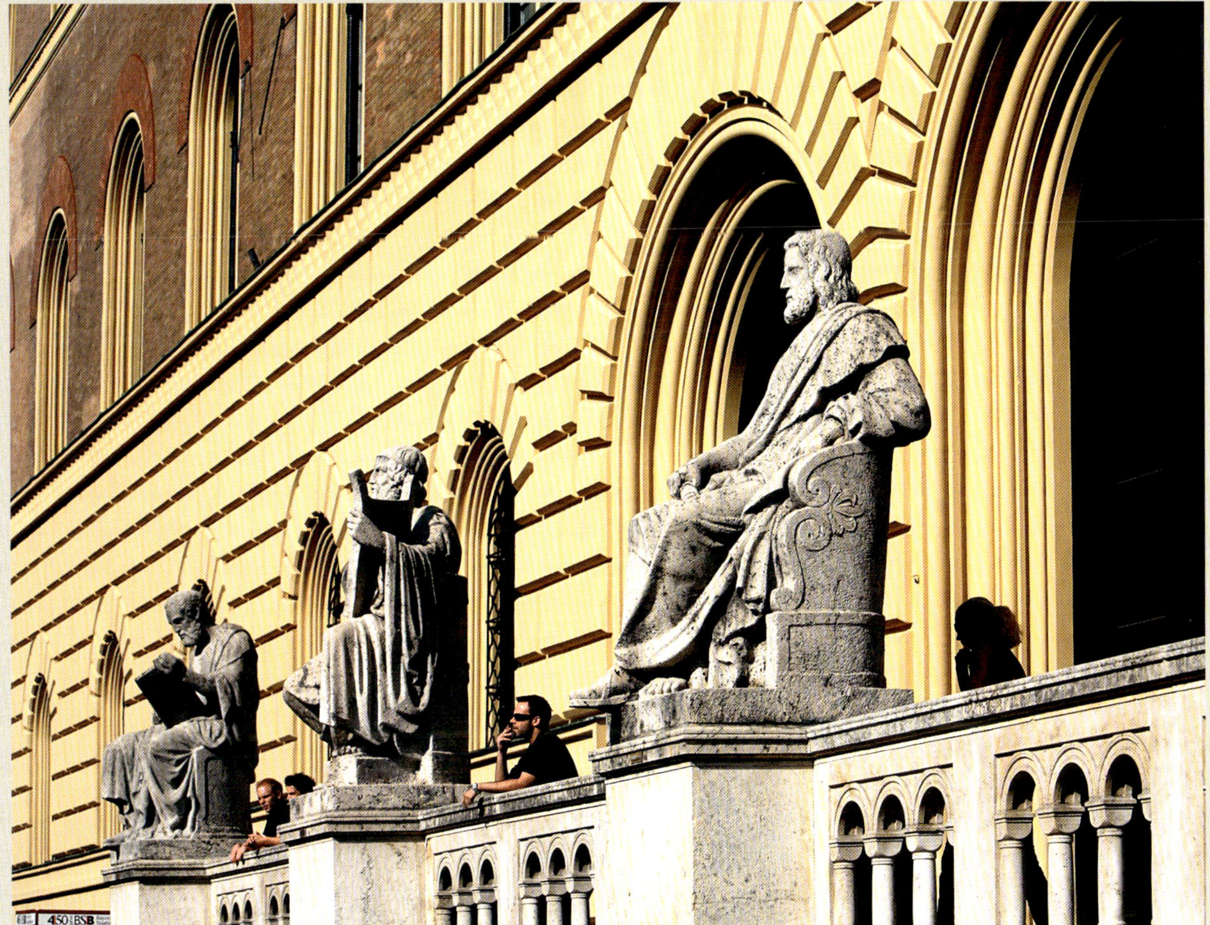

Above:
Monument to the cavalry outside the Bayerisches Hauptstaatsarchiv on Schönfeldstraße, erected in 1960 by Bernhard Bleeker (1881 – 1968). The biggest state archives in Bavaria, the building holds records, certificates, maps and plans issued by the authorities over several centuries.

Left:
With ca. seven million books the Bayerische Staatsbibliothek on Ludwigstraße is one of the largest general libraries in Germany. The architect was Friedrich von Gärtner. The main entrance is carefully monitored by statues of Aristotle, Homer, Thucydides and Hippocrates.

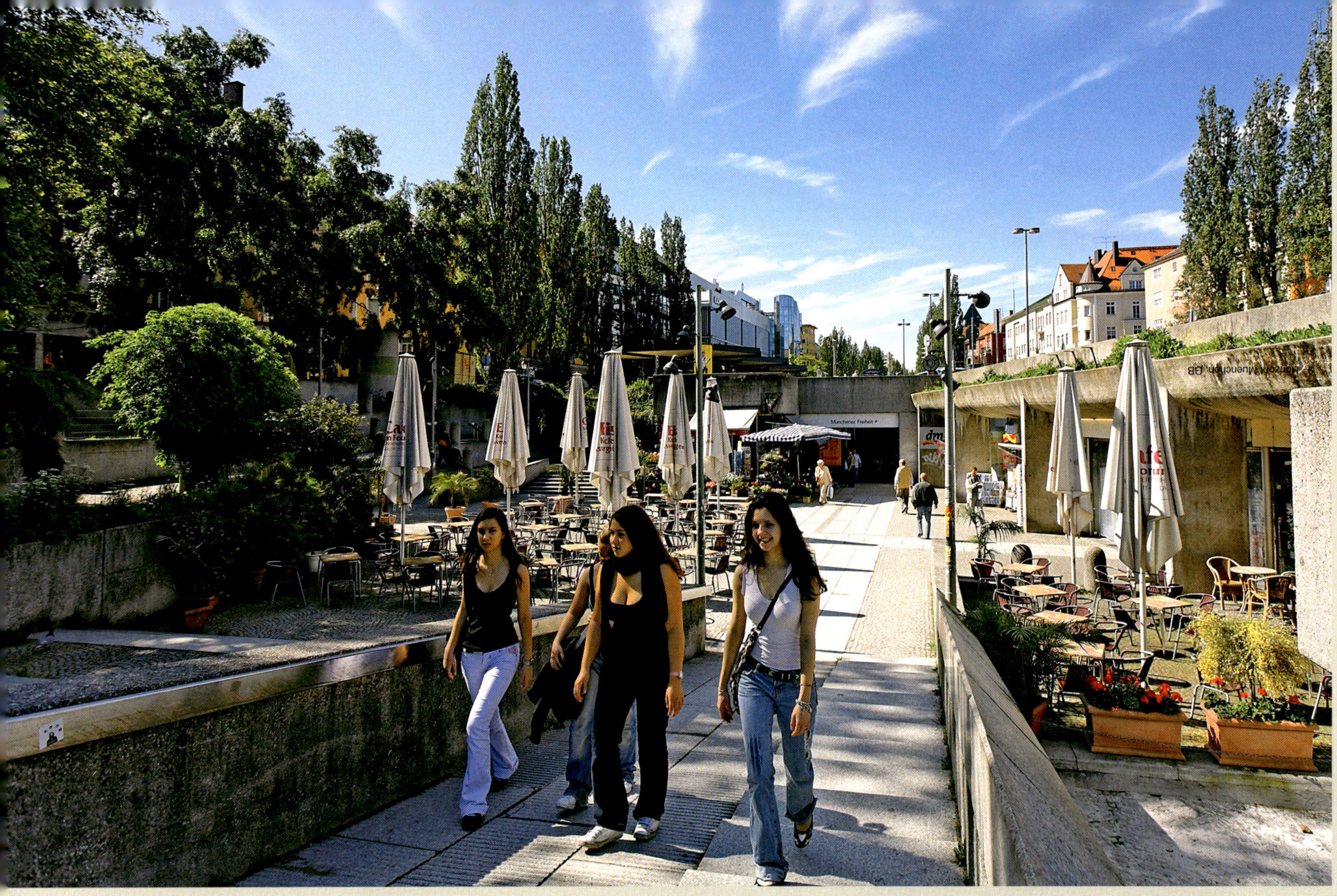

Above:
This square on Leopoldstraße in Schwabing is called Münchner Freiheit or the freedom of Munich, named after the Resistance group Freiheitsaktion Bayern in 1947. The same name was used by a famous German pop band in 1980.

Right:
Outside the Café Münchner Freiheit, also on the square, a statue of Schwabing actor Helmut Fischer (1926–1997) smiles benignly into the camera. Fischer played Monaco Franze in the TV series of the same name by Helmut Dietl.

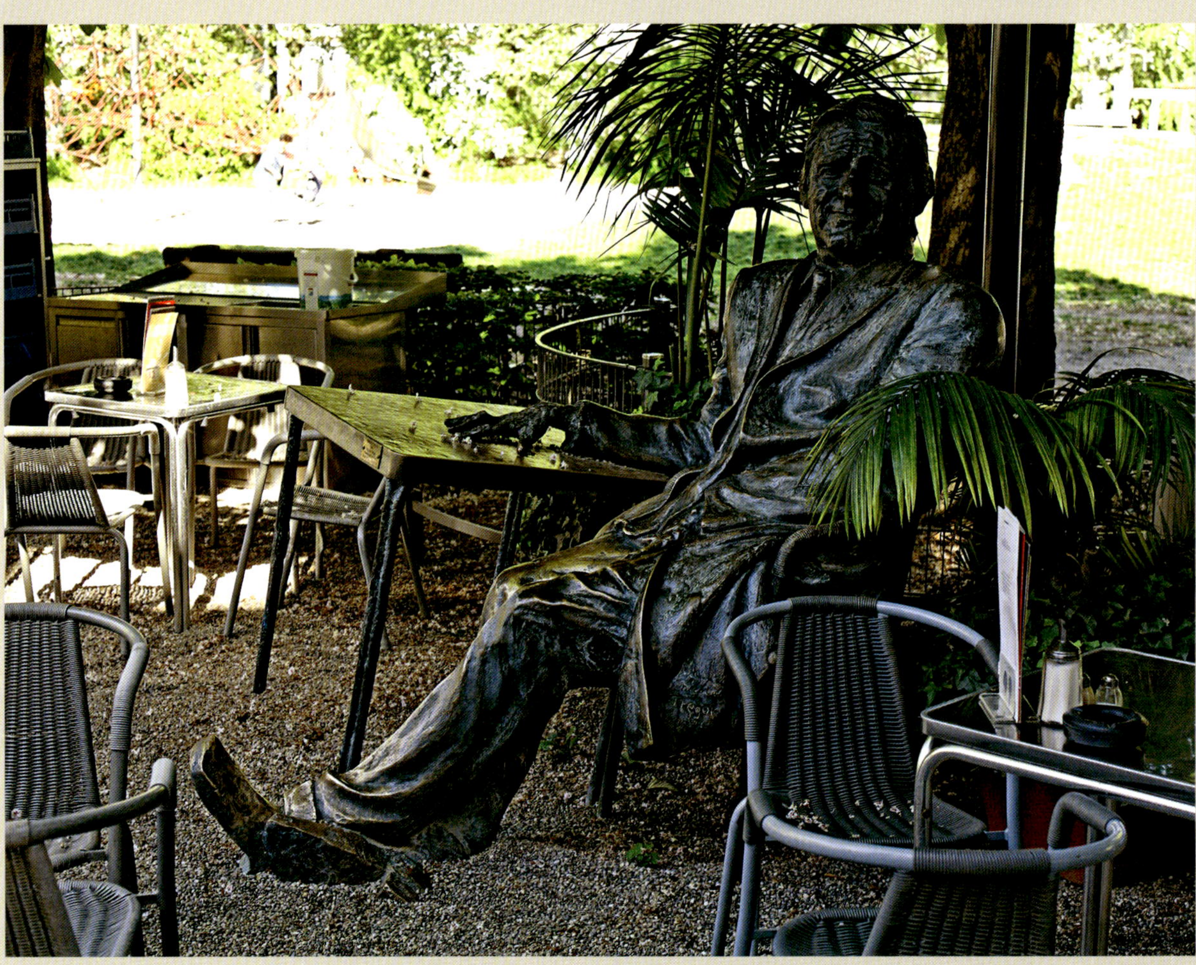

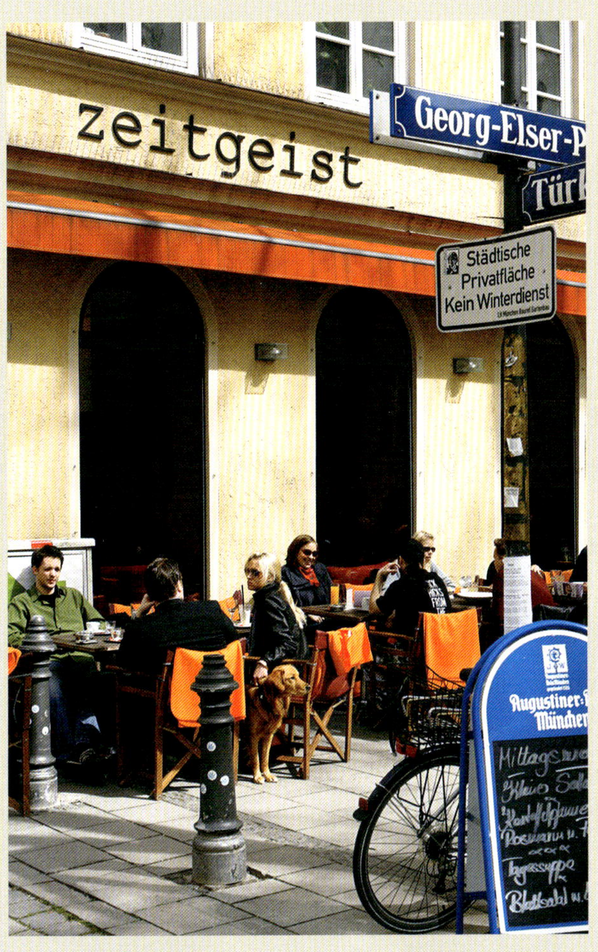

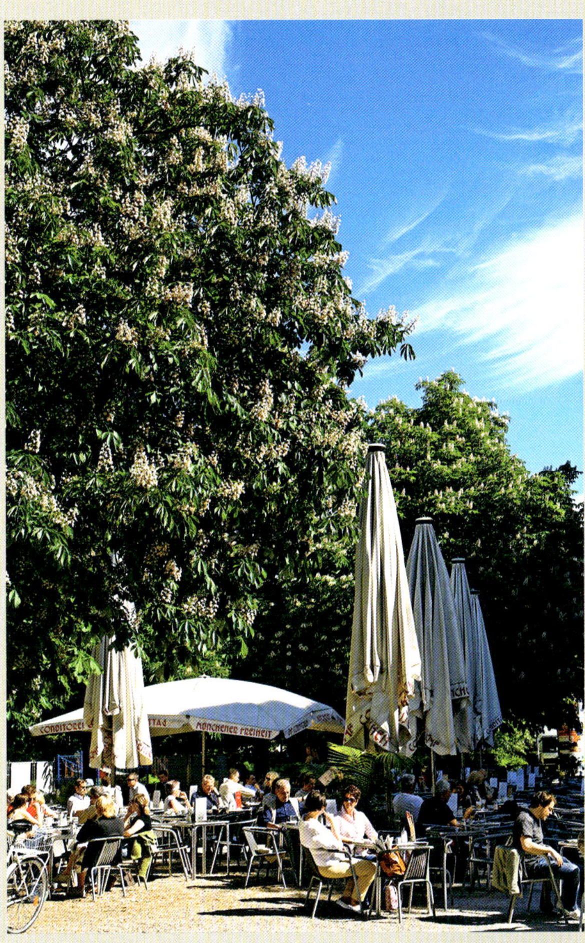

Far left:
Popular with students both young and old: Café Zeitgeist on Georg-Elser-Platz in Maxvorstadt.

Left:
With a coffee in front of you and a newspaper spread out on your lap, where finer to while away a few sunny hours than at the humming café on Münchner Freiheit?

Below:
Schall & Rauch, a student pub on Schellingstraße. You can order breakfast here until 4 pm – a not imprudent service if your main clientele has a bit of trouble getting up in the mornings ...

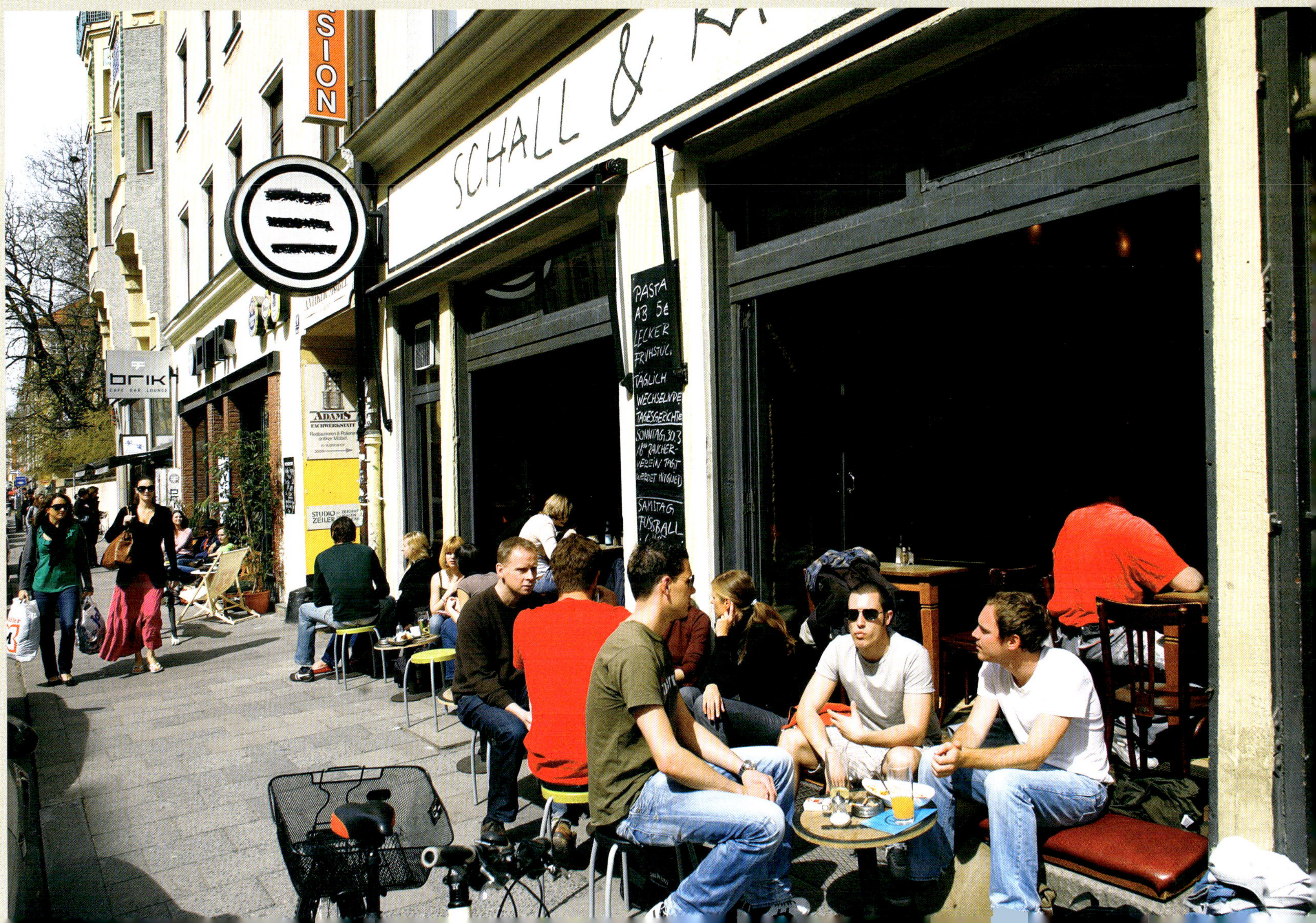

OASIS IN THE HEART OF TOWN – THE ENGLISCHER G

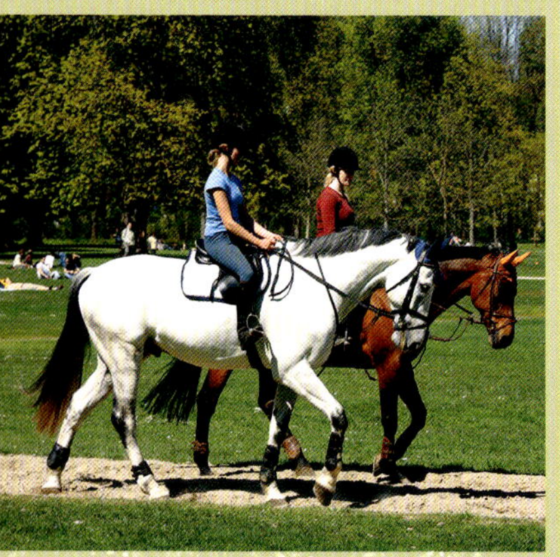

Above:
This oasis in the heart of the metropolis can also be explored on horseback, with bridleways kept separate from the paths and trails for pedestrians.

Middle:
View of the inside of the Monopteros. In the English gardens of the day mock temples such as these were popular places to sit and think – or take afternoon tea and cake.

It's bigger than Hyde Park in London and Central Park in New York; over 4 square kilometres (1.5 square miles) in size, the Englischer Garten or English Garden in the northeast of Munich is one of the biggest municipal open spaces in the world. It was also the first park open to the public on the Continent. In 1789 Elector Carl Theodor was inspired by Benjamin Thompson, the count of Rumford, to implement one of the ideals of the Enlightenment, namely to make palace and military gardens accessible to the general public "for the purpose of exercise and respite from work, social interaction and the rapprochement of the classes."

The planning was largely down to Friedrich Ludwig von Sckell (1750–1823), one of the great garden designers of Germany together with Prince Hermann von Pückler-Muskau and Peter Joseph Lenné. Sckell trained as a landscape gardener in both Versailles and England, among other places, designing the gardens in Munich as an informal landscaped park akin to those of the Fair Isle, hence the name "Englischer Garten". In the spring of 1792 the doors of Theodor's Park, as it was originally called, were thrown open.

At the time about 40,000 people lived in Munich. Today more than twice this number come to

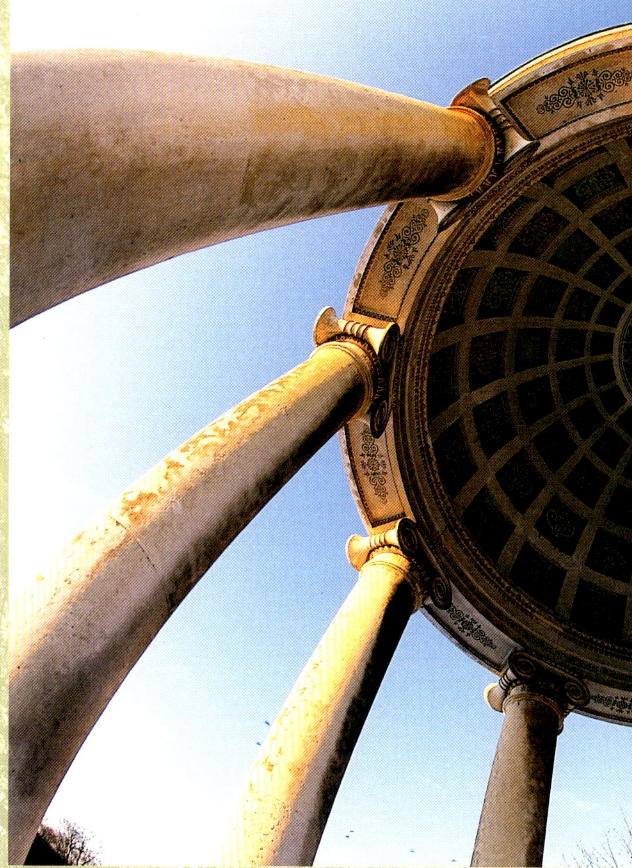

the south end of the park on sunny days to spend a few hours away from it all. 78 kilometres (30 miles) of hiking paths, cycle tracks and bridleways provide plenty of recreation. The system of streams laid out by Sckell is 8.5 kilometres (5 miles) long and on the expansive Kleinhesseloher See with its three islands you can fish or even hire a pedalo.

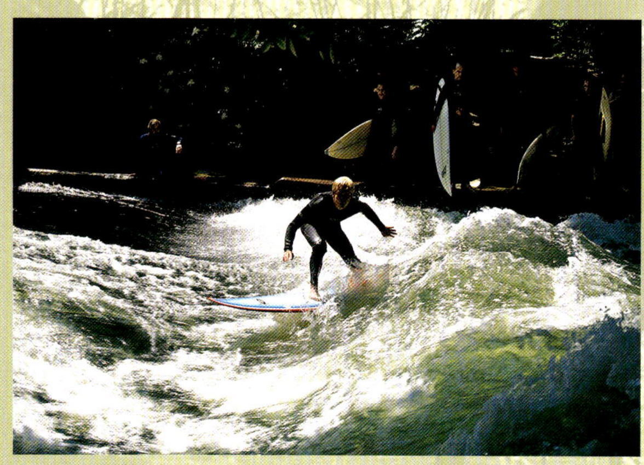

The Eisbach is part of the system of streams running through the Englischer Garten, the informal 'English' gardens landscaped by Friedrich Ludwig von Sckell. Due to the risk of accident swimming and surfing in the Eisbach are officially forbidden.

BEAUTIFUL BUILDINGS AND BEER GARDENS

The park is dotted with several suitably picturesque edifices, including the wooden Chinesischer Turm modelled on the Pagoda in the Royal Botanic Gardens of Kew in London. The shorter Munich version dates from 1789/90 and has been rebuilt

ARTEN

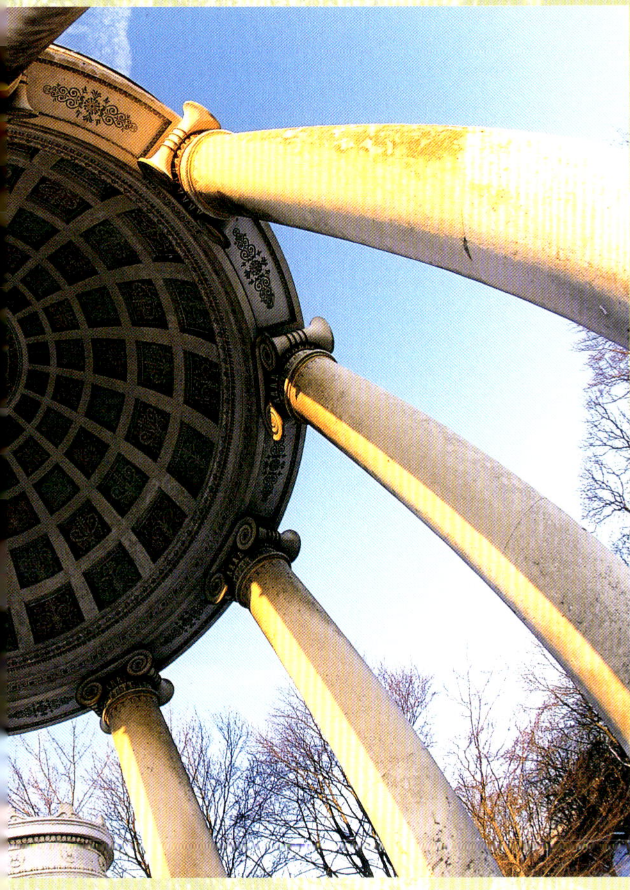

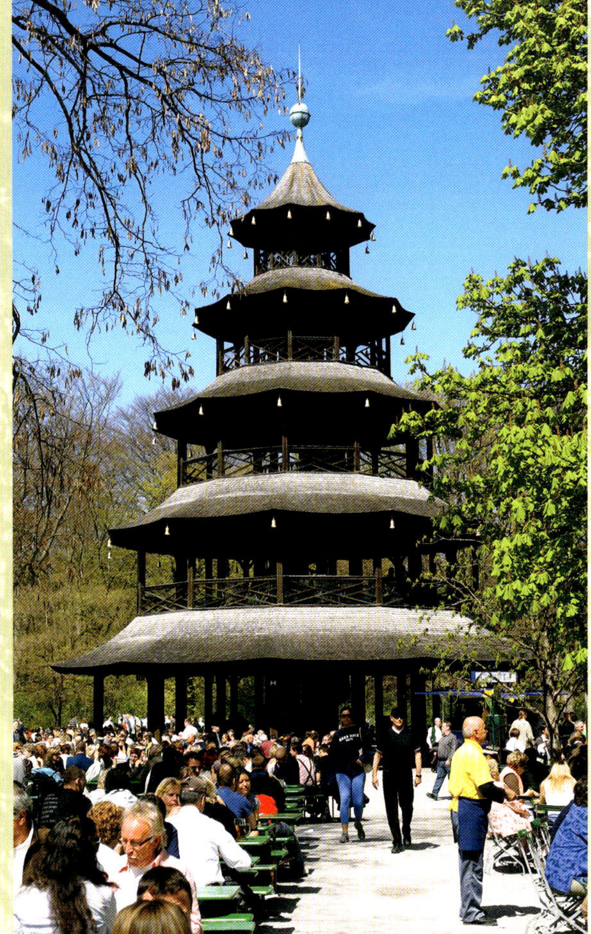

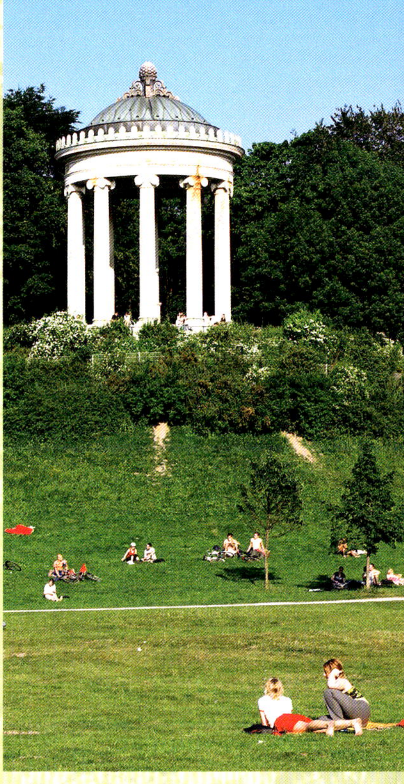

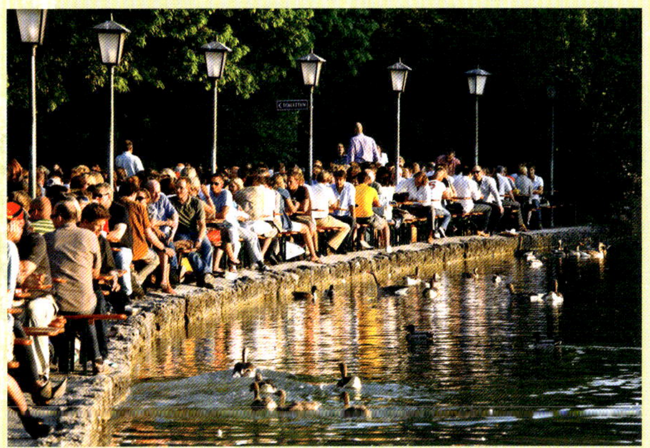

Above left:
The wooden Chinesischer Turm from 1789/90. Destroyed in the Second World War, it was reconstructed in 1951/52.

Above:
The Monopteros was erected from plans by Leo von Klenze on a manmade hill in 1836/37. It's one of the best known landmarks in the Englischer Garten.

Left:
Where else in Munich can you sup a glass of beer and feed the ducks at the same time?! The Seehaus beer garden on the Kleinhesseloher See.

several times in its history. Beneath it is the second largest beer garden in Munich, seating 7,000. Not far away is a Biedermeier merry-go-round, popular in fair weather with the park's smallest visitors.

The Japanisches Teehaus or Japanese tea house with its matching gardens is much younger, constructed in honour of the Summer Olympic Games of 1972 on a man-made island in the Schwabinger Bach. The Monopteros, a mock Greek temple, was erected in 1836 by the famous neoclassical architect Leo von Klenze (1784–1864). At the northern end of the gardens is an amphitheatre where classical comedies have been performed for free every July since 1990. There are also monuments to the park's initiator Count Rumford and the designer Sckell, plus a bit of the now defunct Berlin Wall.

Several restaurants and beer gardens make the Englischer Garten popular among both the people of Munich and their guests from further afield. About 3.5 million a year take a well-earned breather in this oasis in the heart of town – leaving several tons of rubbish behind a day. No less than 60 employees administer to the city gardens. Most of us merely come here to visit; others, such as hedgehogs, squirrels, rabbits, badgers, foxes and hares, live here permanently. The park also has 50 to 60 species of nesting birds and grass carp, tench and pike in the lake, the latter fished in autumn by keen anglers for the local tables of Munich.

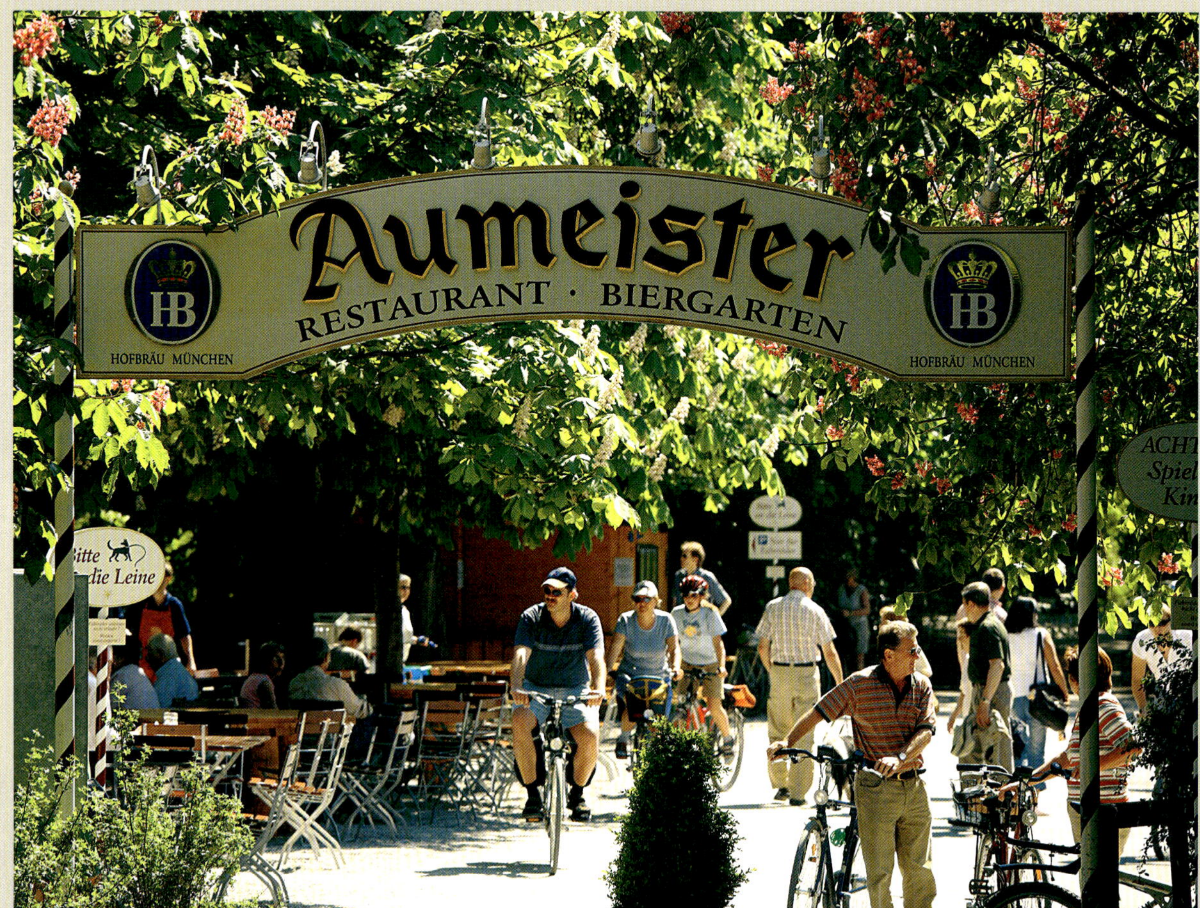

Right:
The Aumeister beer garden at the northern end of the Englischer Garten was once a royal hunting lodge built in 1810. Here you can tuck into some hearty Bavarian fare under shady chestnut trees.

Below:
The Kleinhesseloher See with its three islands, Seehaus beer garden and pedalo hire is the pulsating heart of the Englischer Garten and the perfect place to switch off, relax and unwind.

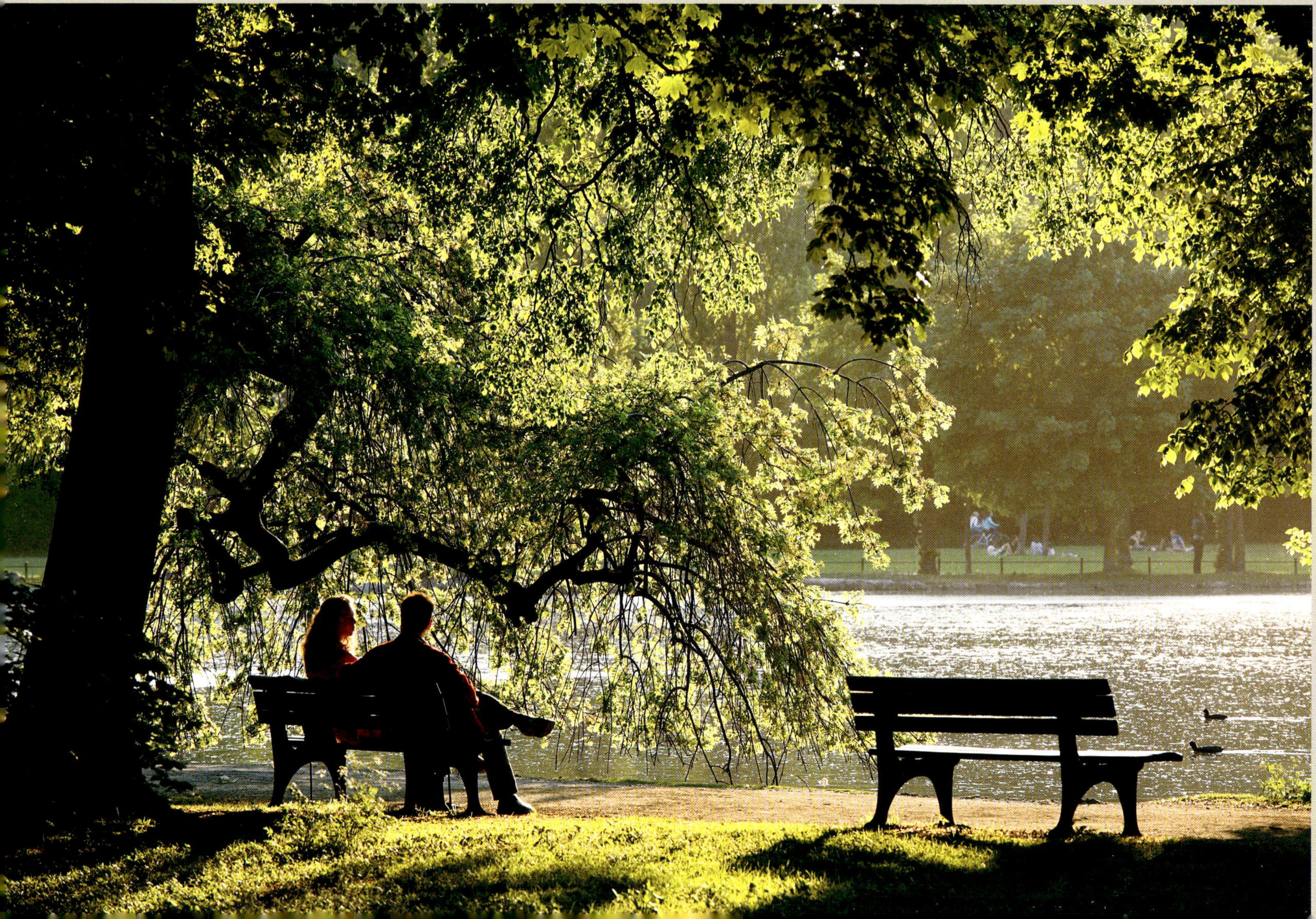

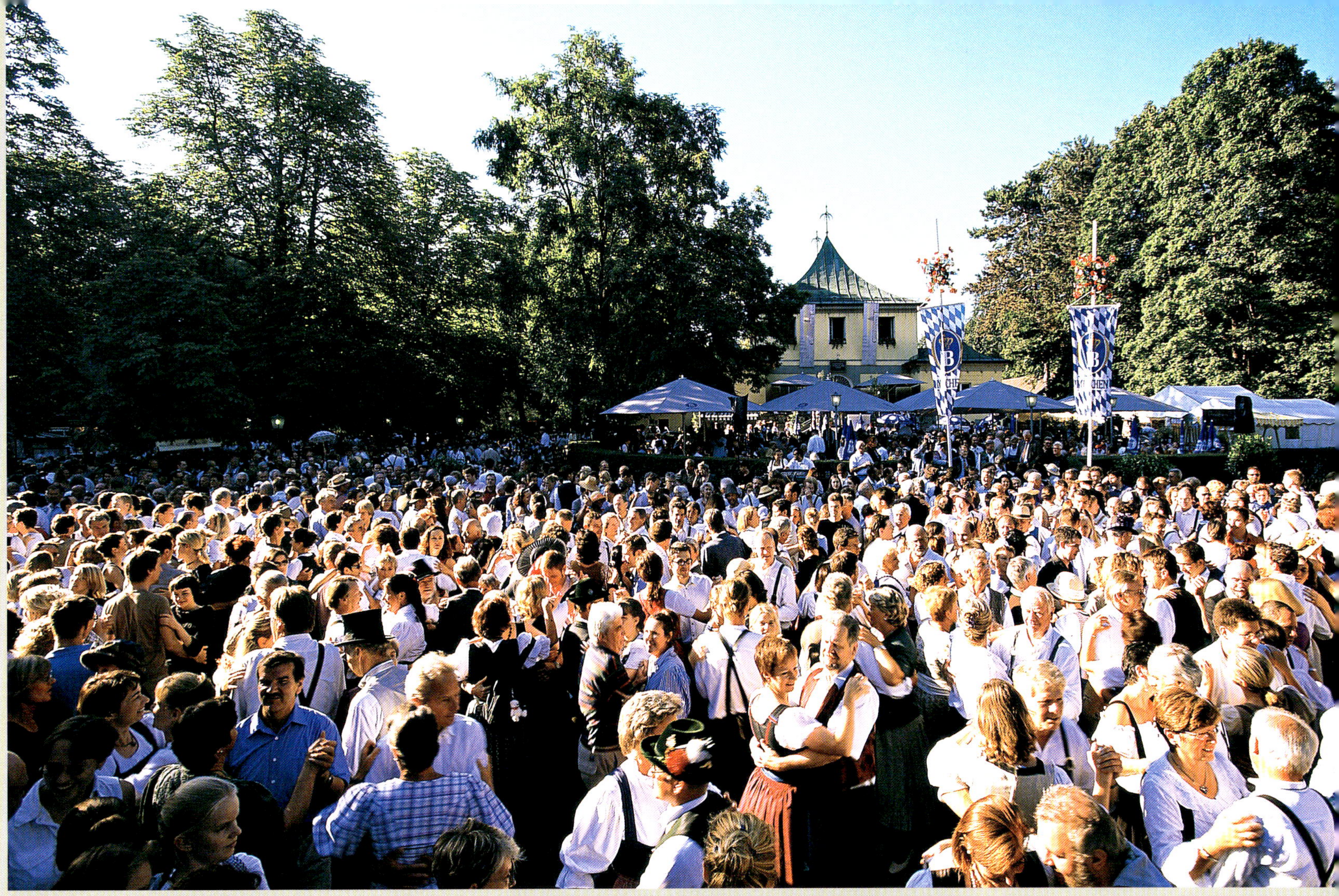

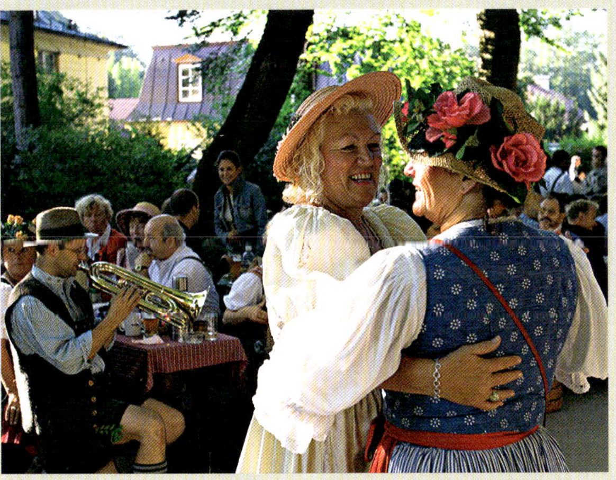

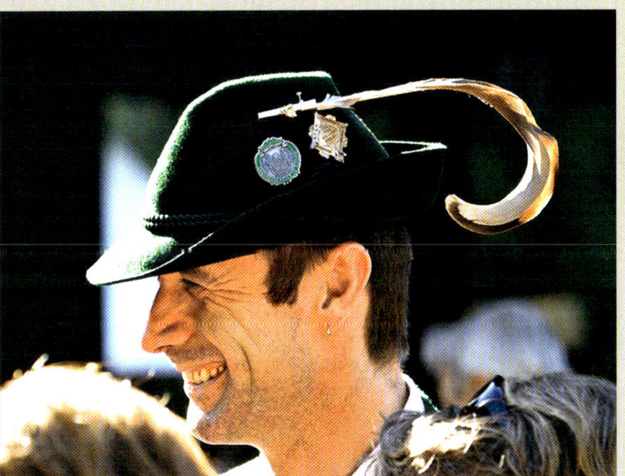

Above:
Thousands flock to the Kocherlball held in the beer garden beneath the Chinesischer Turm every year. It takes place on the 3rd Sunday in July when the crowds gather as early as 6 o'clock in the morning.

Left:
The Kocherlball is based on an ancient Munich tradition. In the old days servants couldn't get the evenings off to go out so they partied in the early hours while their lords and ladies were still abed. By 1904 the Kocherlball had got so out of hand it was banned for "lack of decorum". It was only reintroduced in 1989 to celebrate the Englischer Garten's 200th anniversary. Many of the ball-goers come in local dress or in costumes from the turn of the 19th century.

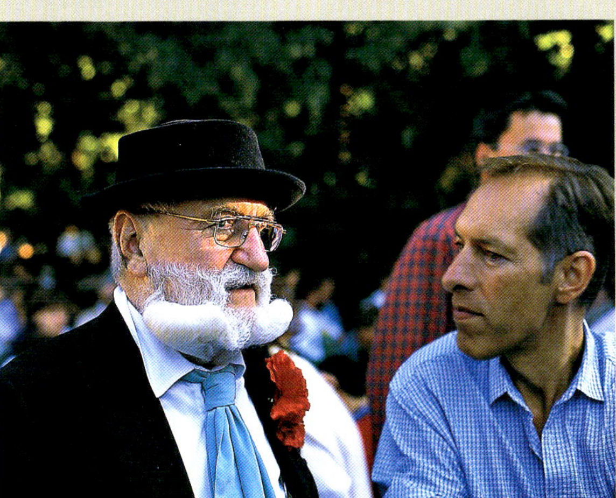

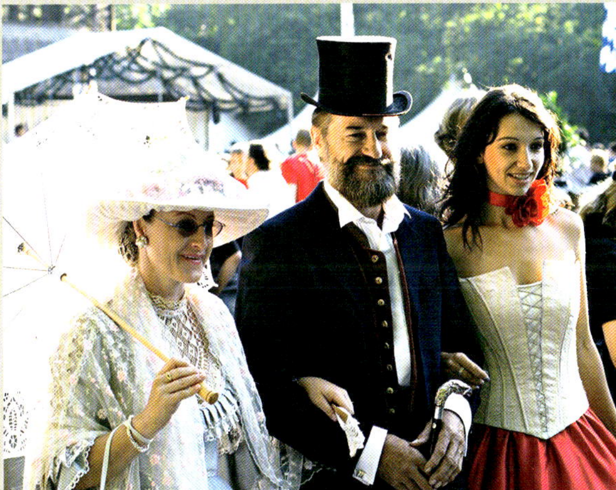

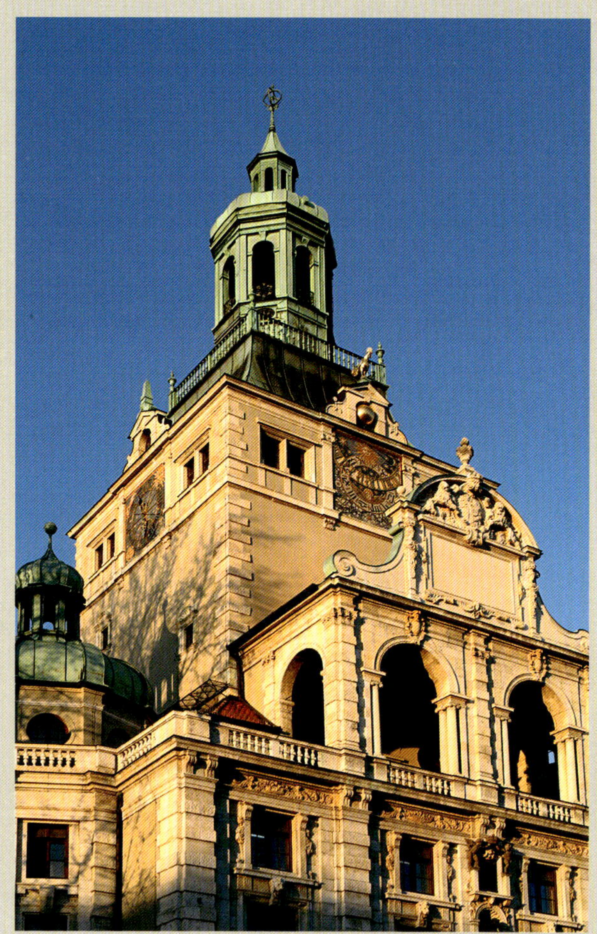

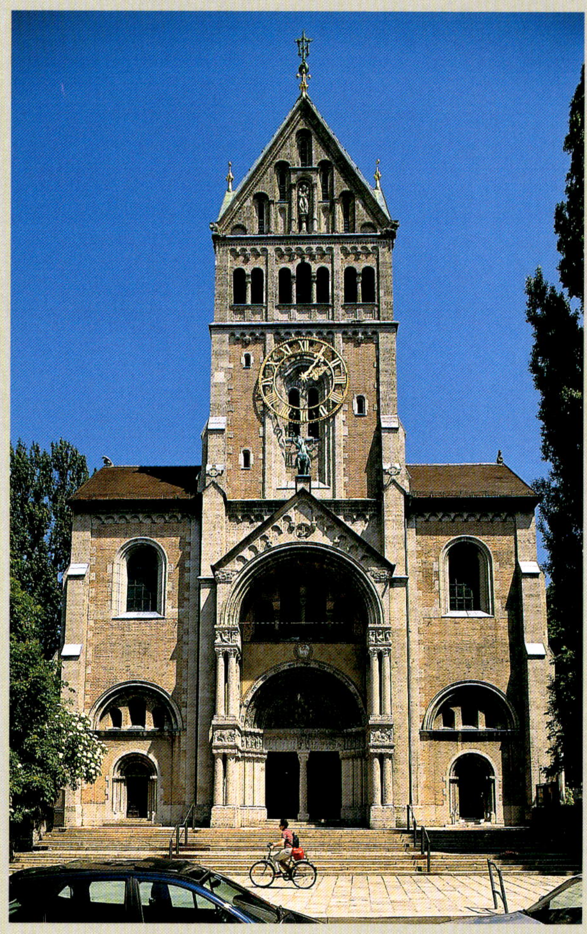

Right:
The Historicist Bayerisches Nationalmuseum was put up between 1894 and 1899 by Munich's royal architect Gabriel von Seidl (1848–1913).

Far right:
Gabriel von Seidl also built the Catholic parish church of St Anna in Lehel from 1887 to 1892. It's one of the best examples of Historicist architecture in Munich.

Below:
The Haus der Kunst on Prinzregentenstraße was opened as an exhibition of German art in 1937. For over 60 years now it has had works on display that the Nazis excluded from the original exhibition on the grounds that they were "degenerate". The gallery is a true manifestation of the triumph of free artistic expression over despotic propaganda.

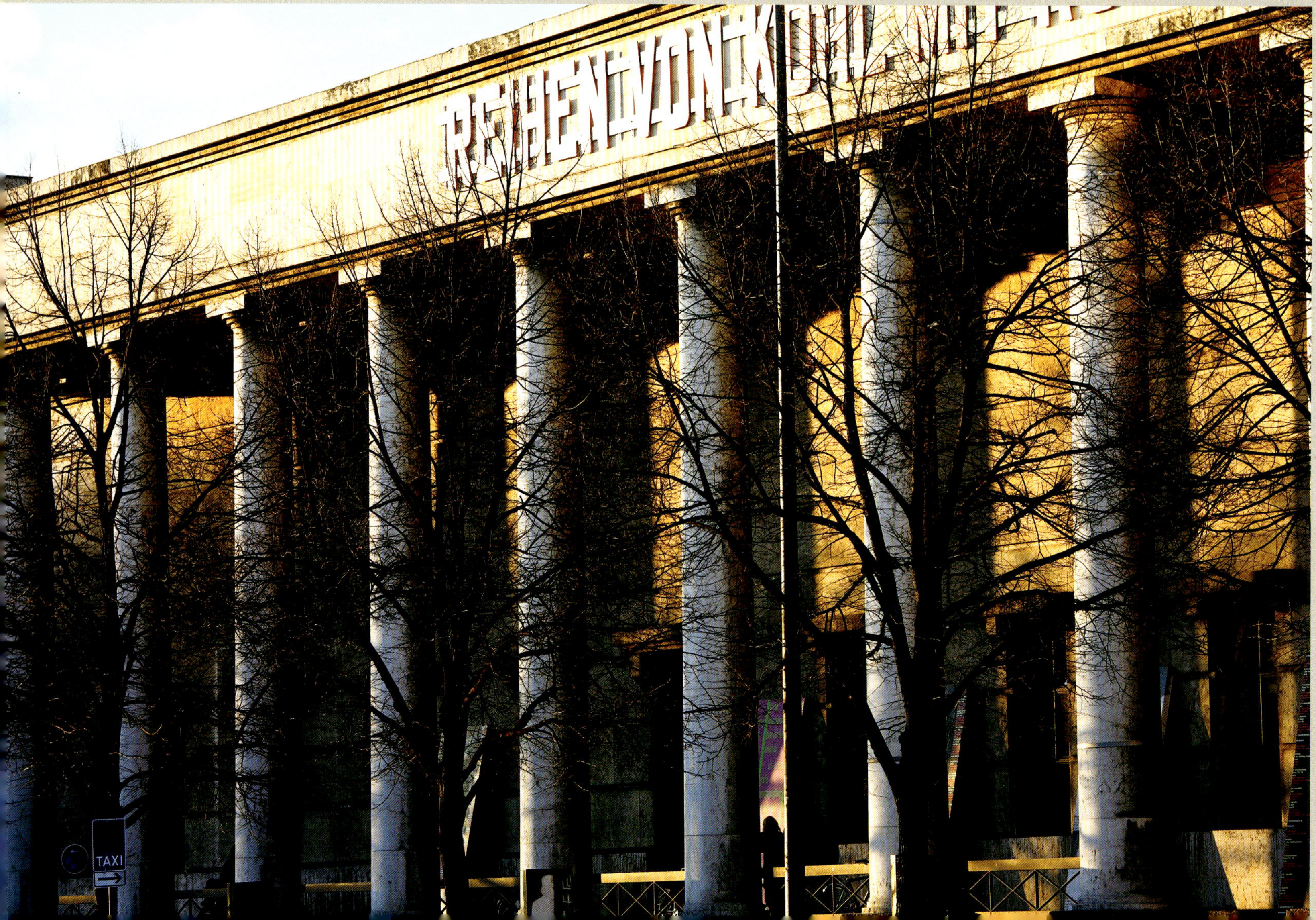

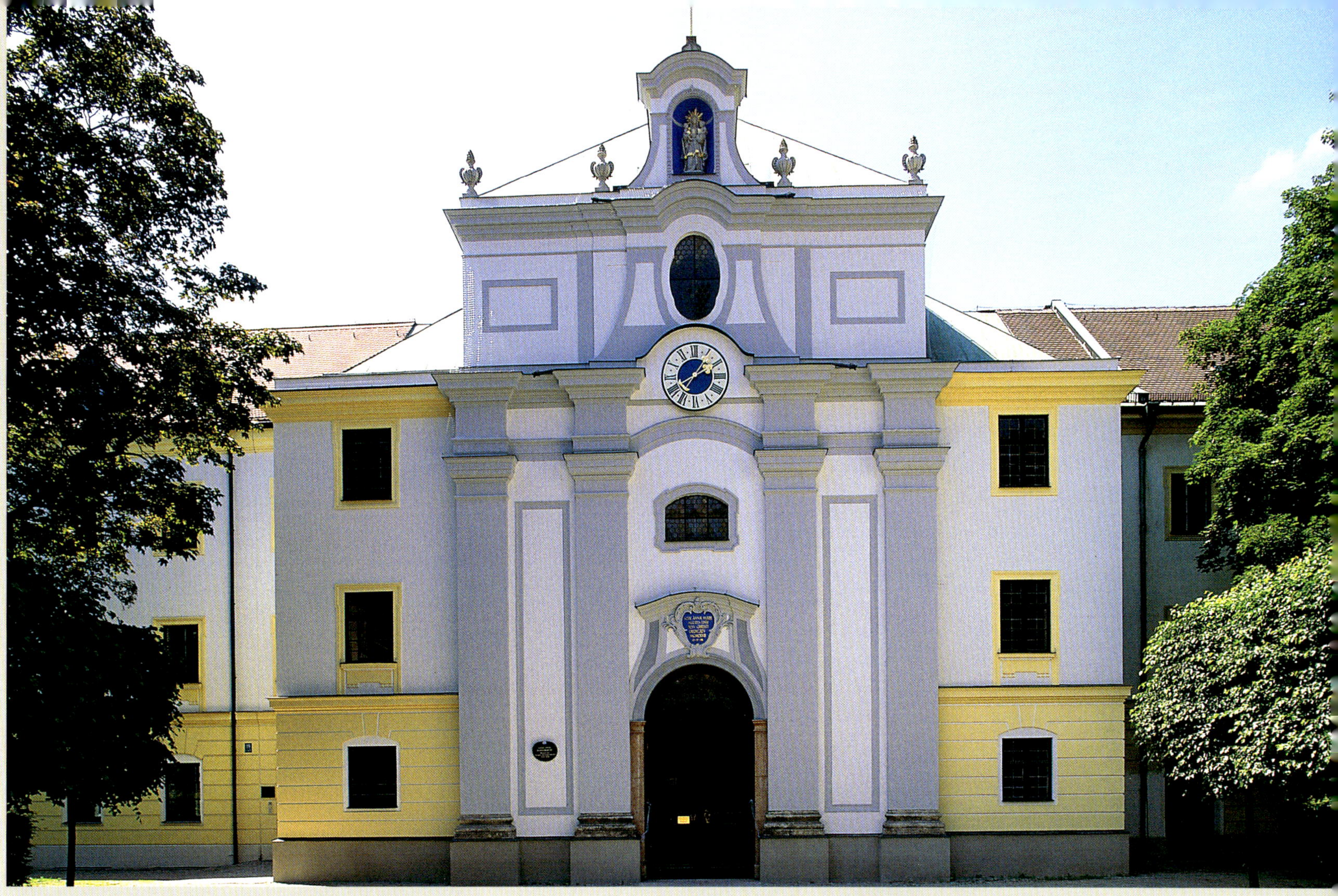

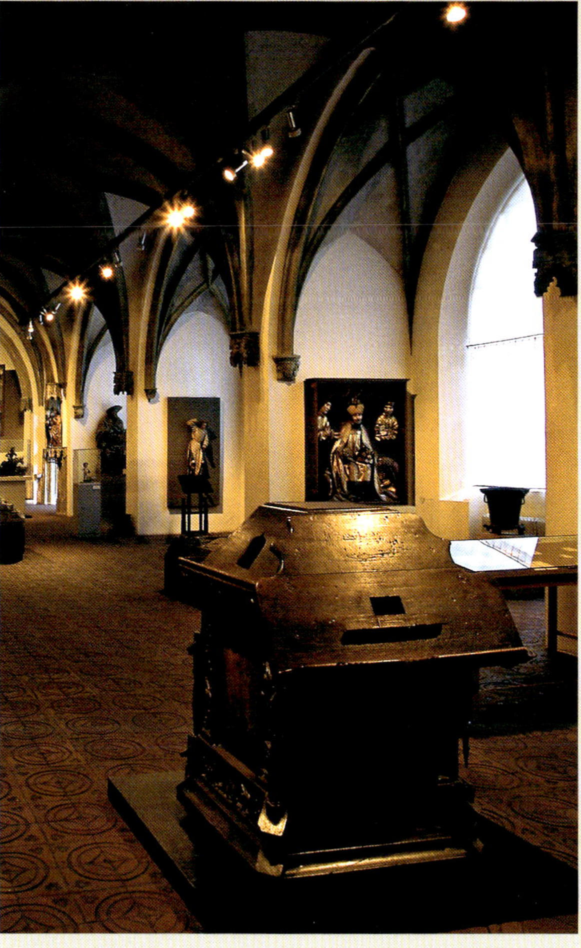

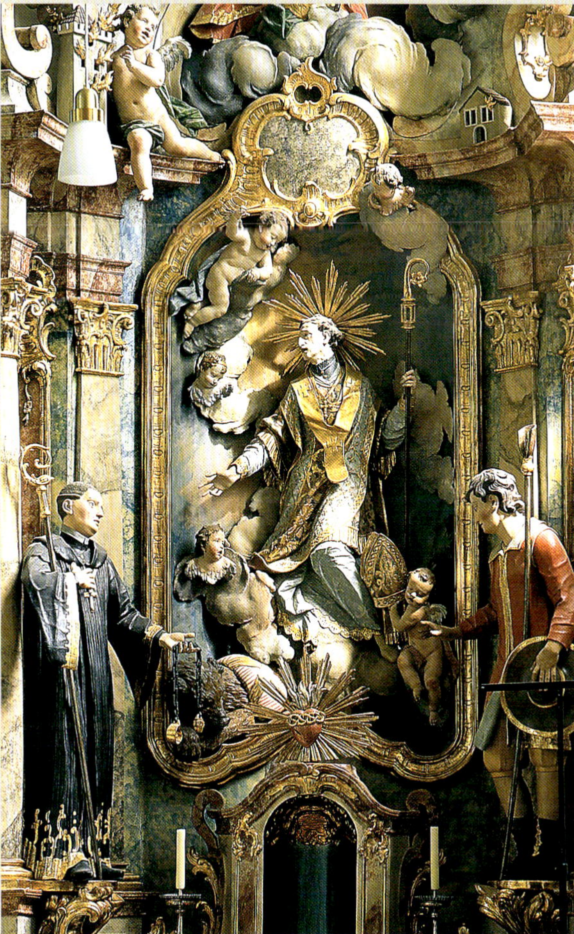

Above:
Opposite the parish church of St Anna in Lehel is the monastic church of St Anna. The latter is the first Rococo church in Old Bavaria and was built by Johann Michael Fischer between 1727 and 1733. The interior was designed by Cosmas Damian Asam, Egid Quirin Asam and Johann Baptist Straub.

Far left:
The exhibits in the art and culture section of the Bayerisches Nationalmuseum document the history of both in Bavaria and Southern Germany from the Middle Ages to the present day.

Left:
The Catholic daughter church of St Georg was once the village church of Bogenhausen. Many famous names are laid to rest in its graveyard. The pulpit and two side altars are by Ignaz Günther (1725–1775); here the altar dedicated to St Corbinian.

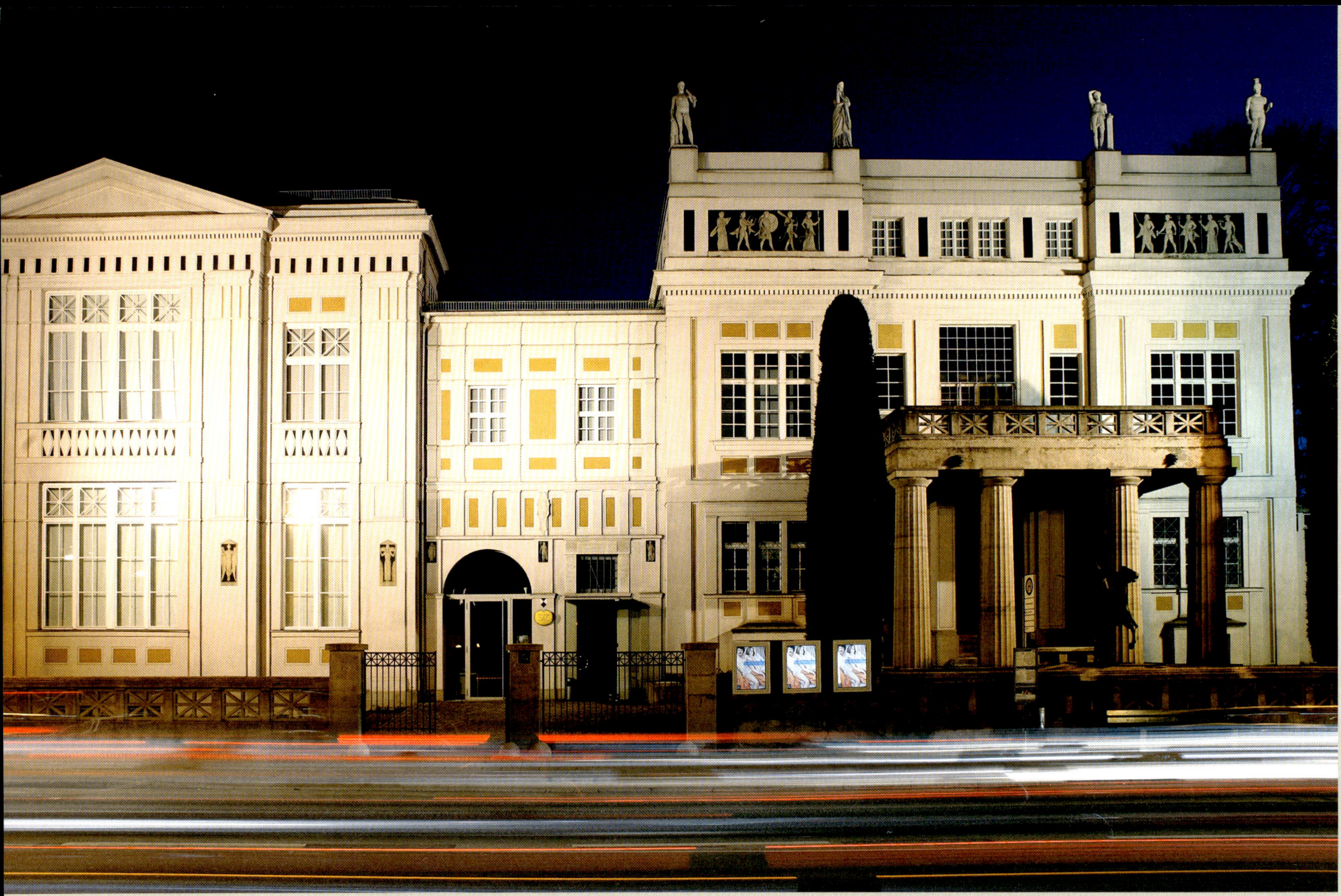

Above:
Neo-classical Villa Stuck on Prinzregentenstraße from 1897/98 once belonged to and was designed by painter Franz von Stuck. The house is now used as a city museum.

Right:
The music room is one of the highlights of Villa Stuck. Much of the furnishing is original. The wall paintings were copied from murals in Pompeii; the ceiling is supposed to represent the sky at night.

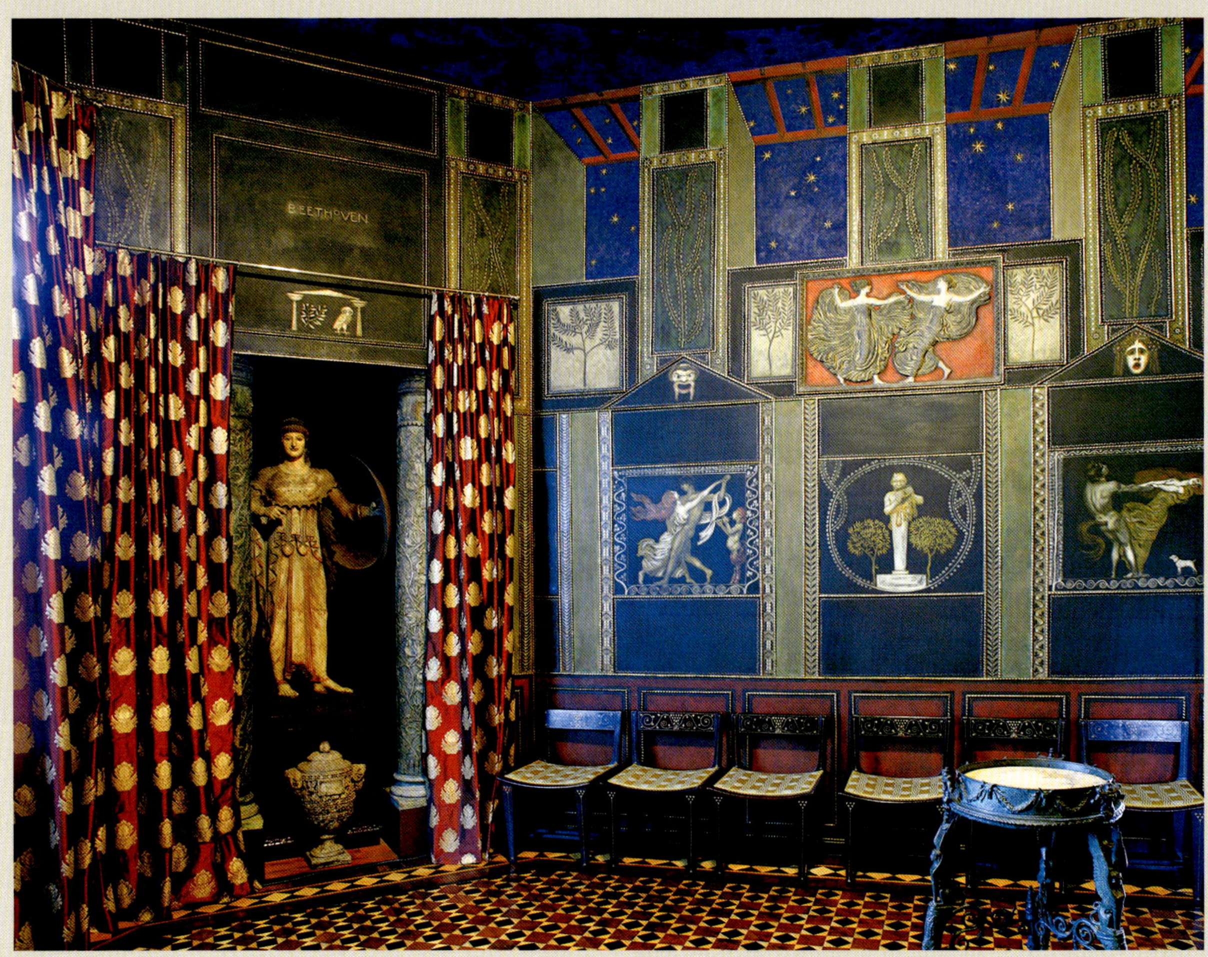

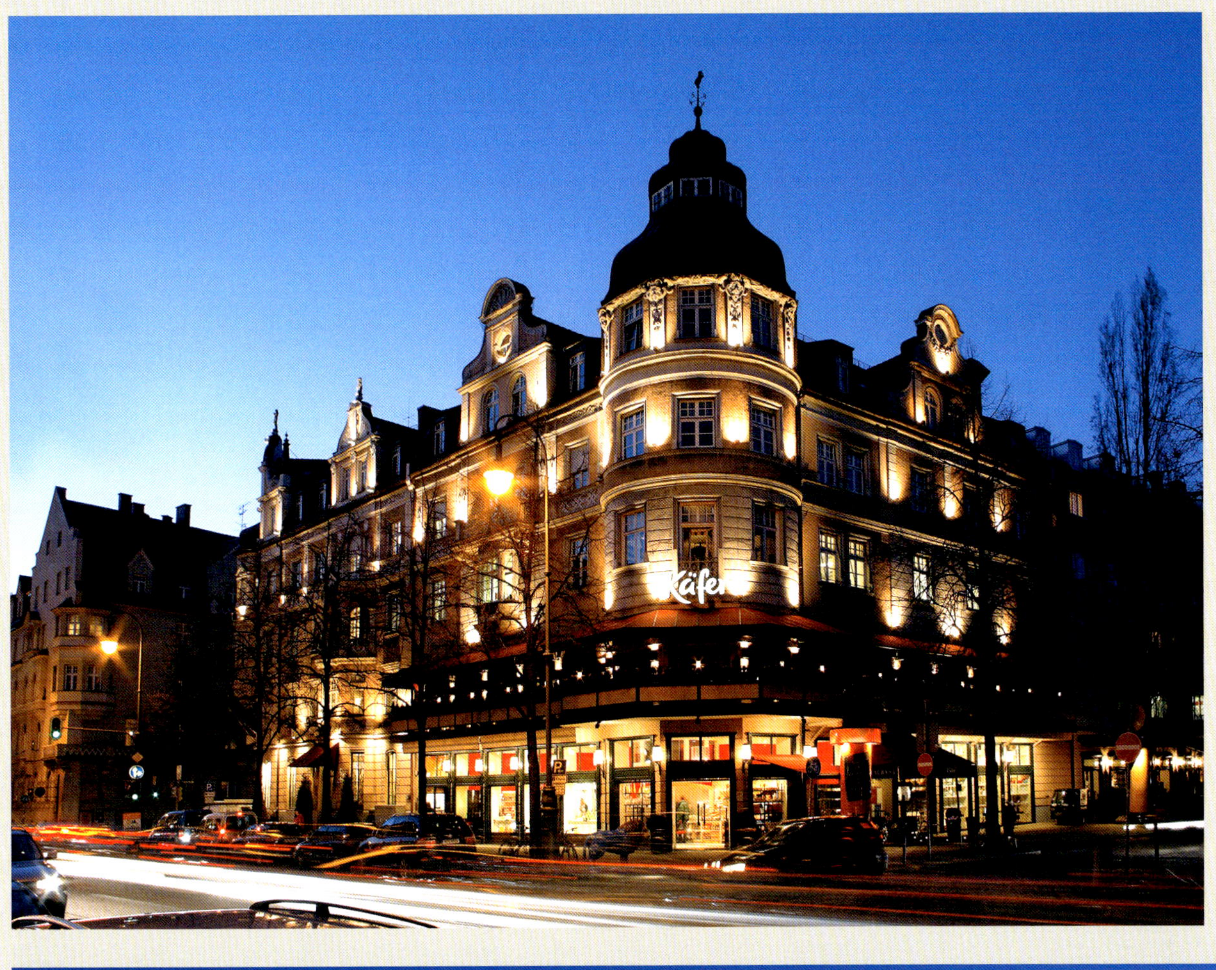

Left:
This edifice on the corner of Prinzregentenstraße is the parent branch of the famous Käfer delicatessen.

Below:
The Jugendstil Prinzregententheater was built in 1900/01 from designs by Max Littmann (1862 – 1931). From 1944 to 1963 it acted as a venue for the Bavarian state opera who had been bombed out of their own premises. The Bayerische Theaterakademie set up shop here in 1993.

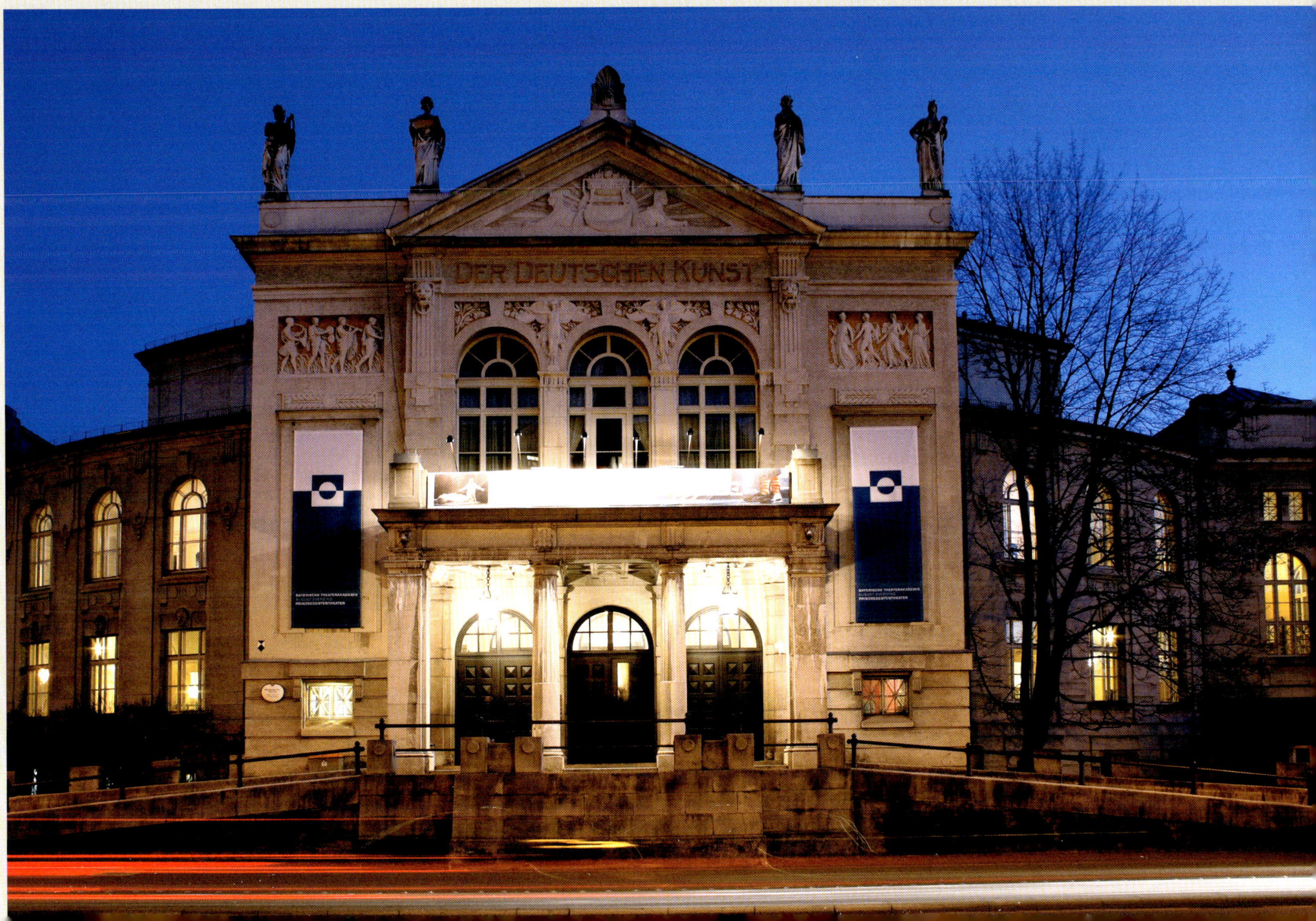

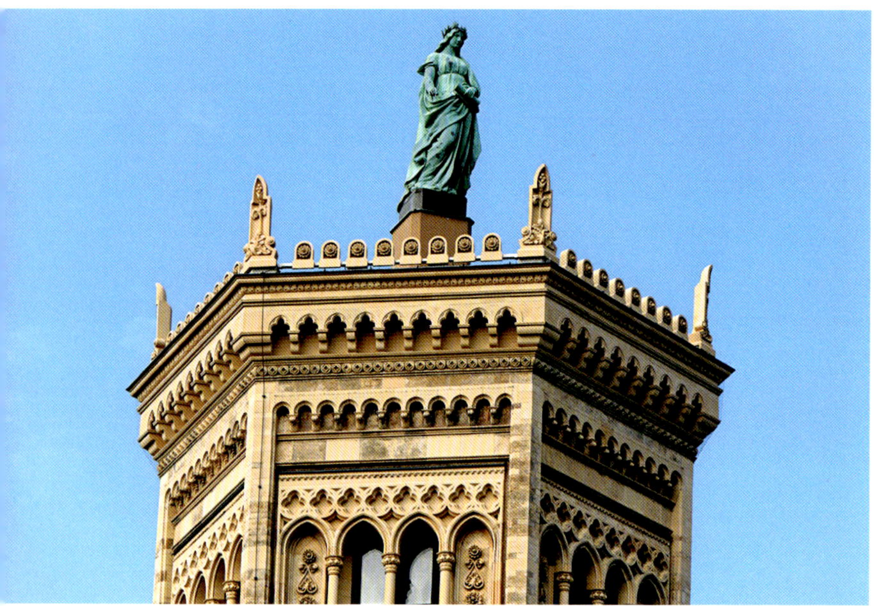

Top left:
The seat of the local government of Upper Bavaria on Maximilianstraße was designed by Georg Friedrich Christian Bürklein (1813–1872) between 1856 and 1864. The elongated complex , crowned by a statue of Justice, is a big example of the Maximilian style.

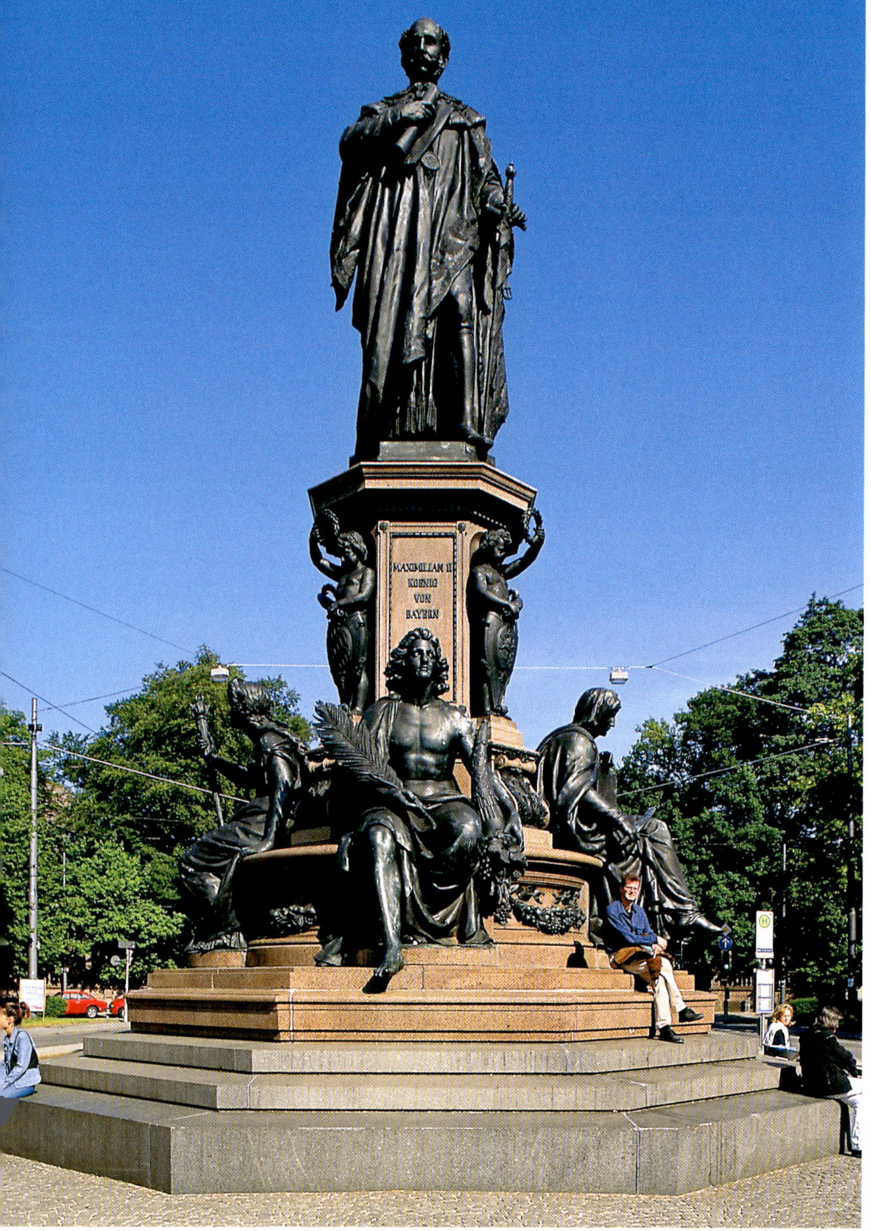

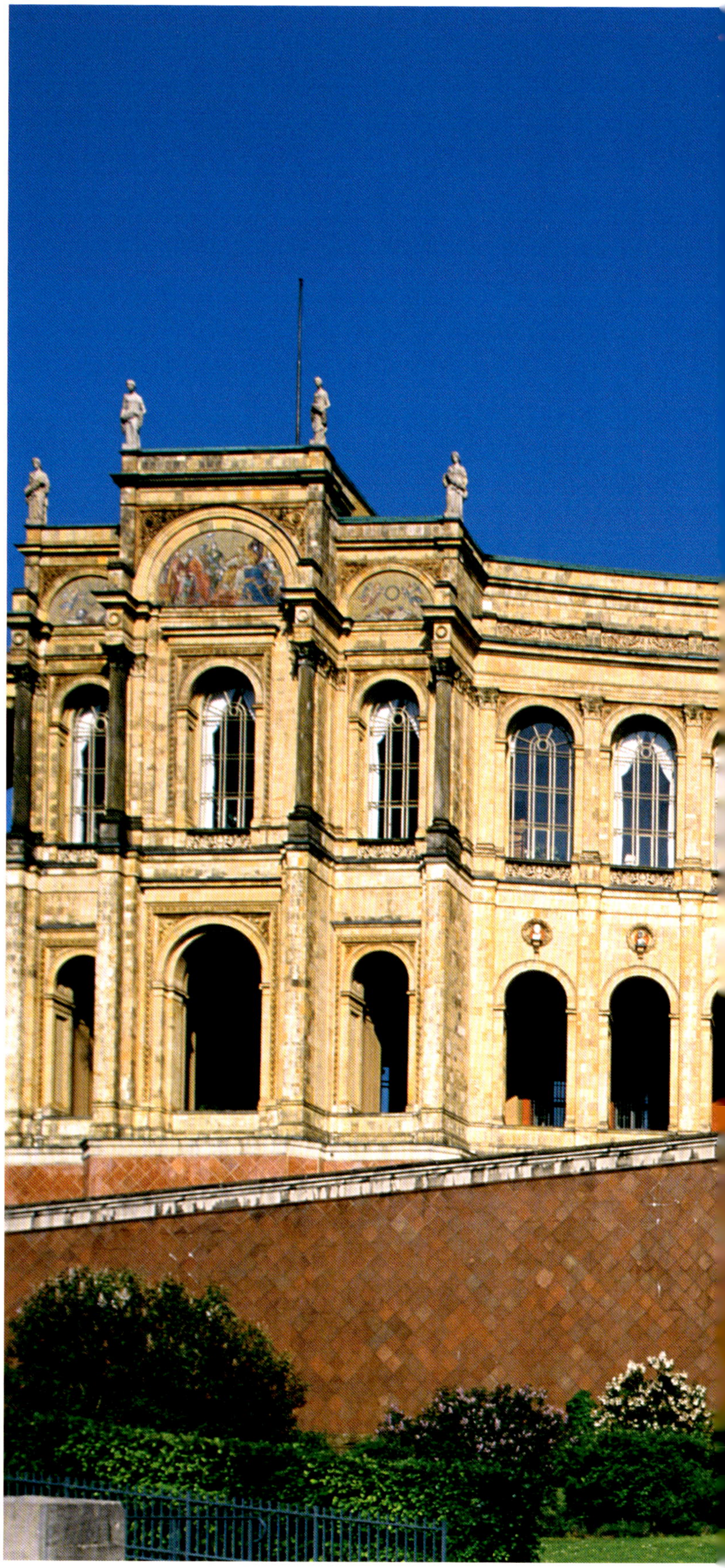

Bottom left:
Maximilian architecture combined elements of the neo-Gothic and Renaissance, making Maximilianstraße, conceived by Bürklein, an absolutely unique example of urban development. The impressive statue of King Maximilian II depicted here is by Kaspar Clemens von Zumbusch (1830–1915) who was chiefly active in Vienna.

Below:
The magnificent apex of Maximilianstraße is formed by the Maximilianeum, also by Friedrich Bürklein. Since 1876 it has housed a foundation for gifted students from Bavaria. It's also the seat of the Bavarian state parliament.

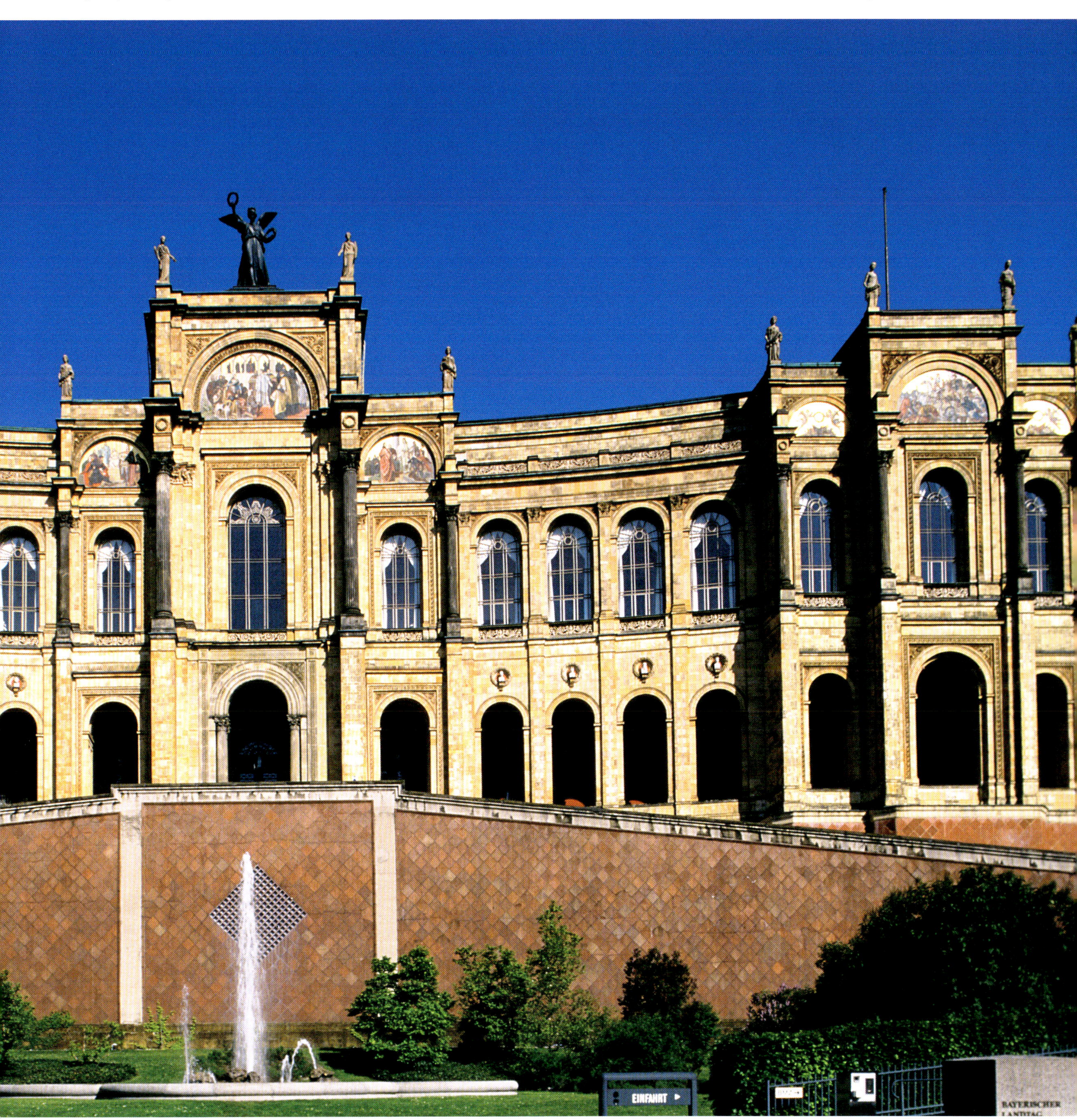

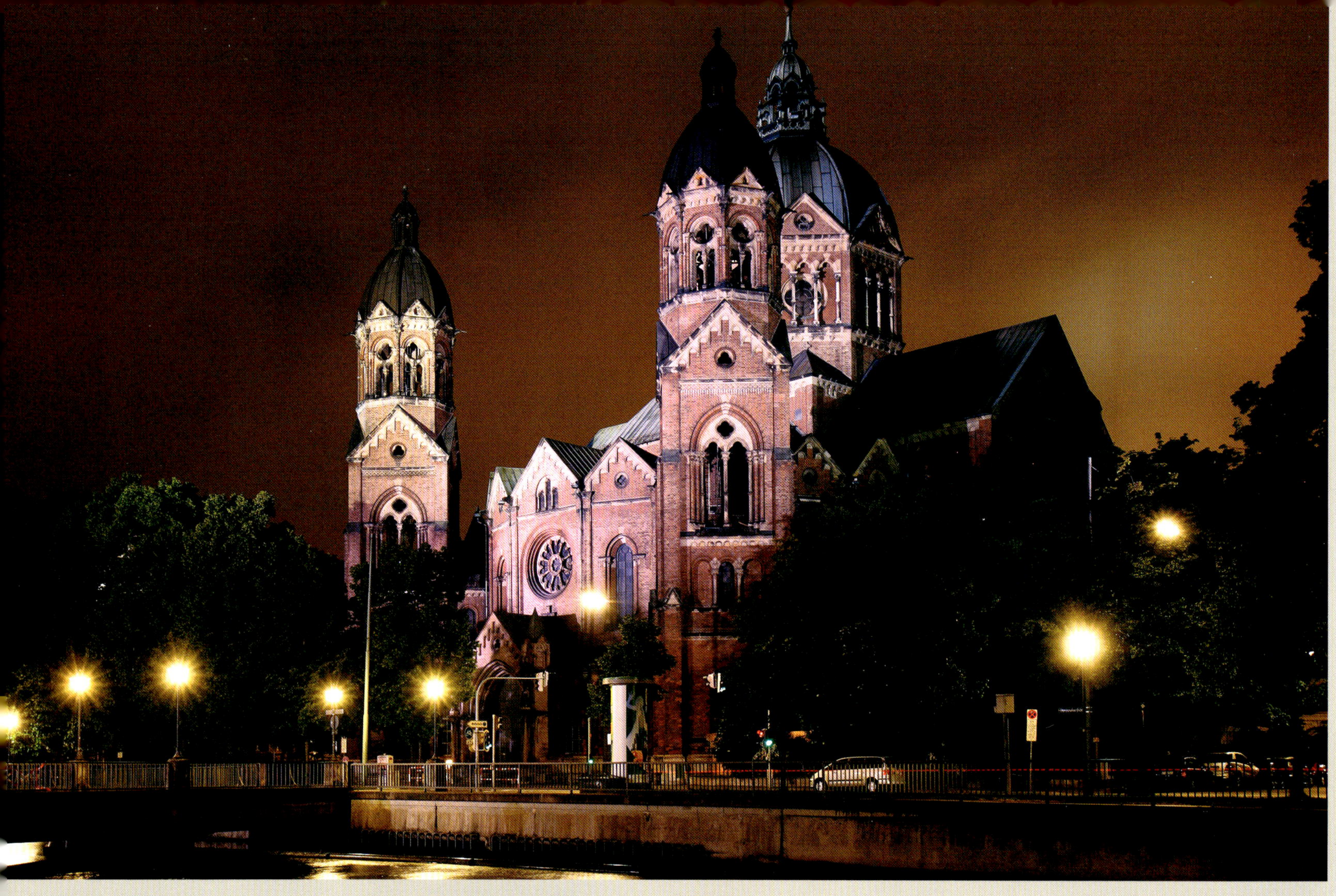

Above:
The parish church of St Lukas on Mariannenplatz in Lehel (1893–1896) is the third Evangelical Lutheran building in Munich. The exterior pays homage to the Romanesque; inside early Rhineland Gothic prevails.

Right:
With its mighty dome St Lukas' is something of a Munich landmark. The choir here is one of the city's leading amateur vocal ensembles. It consists of about 90 singers and puts on two to three big concerts a year in the church.

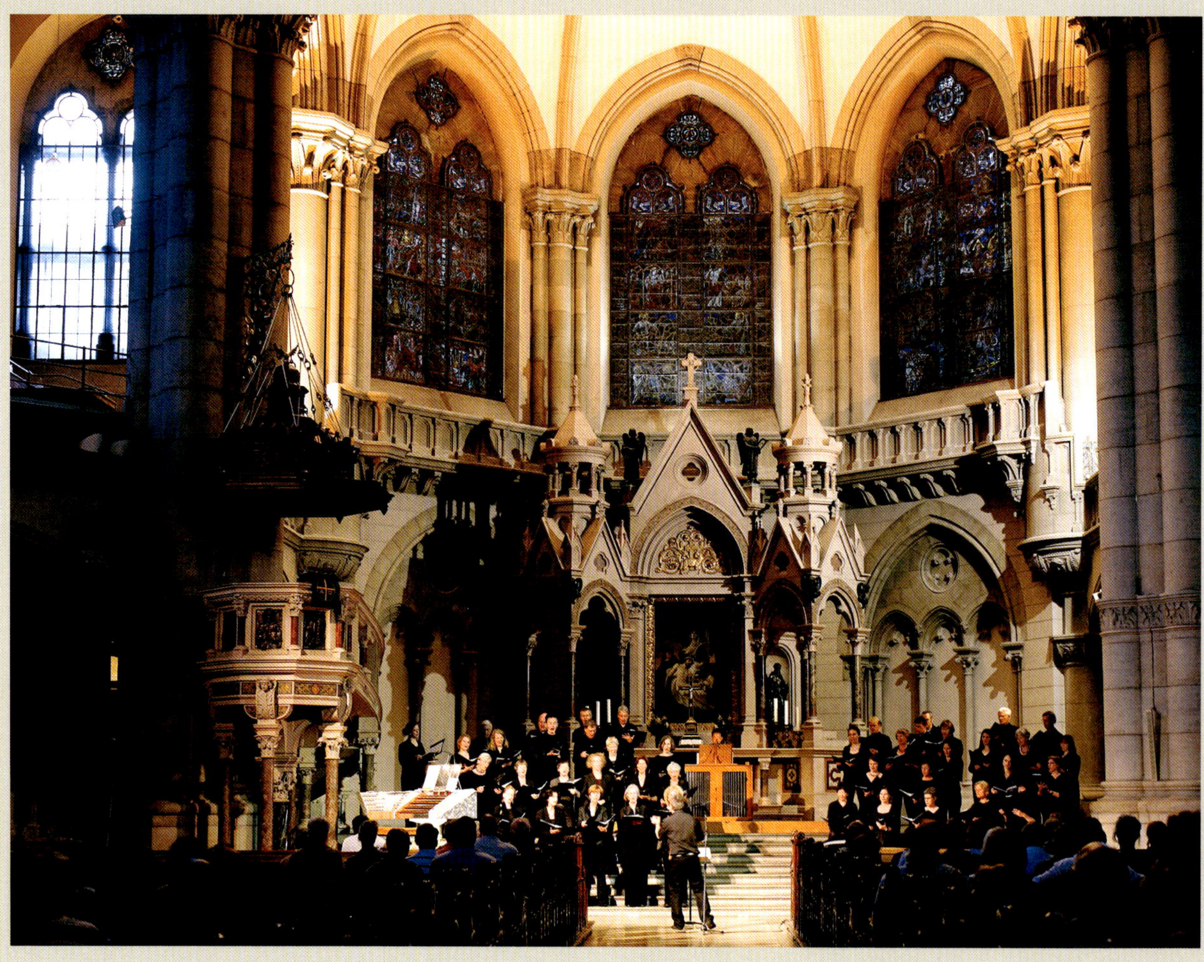

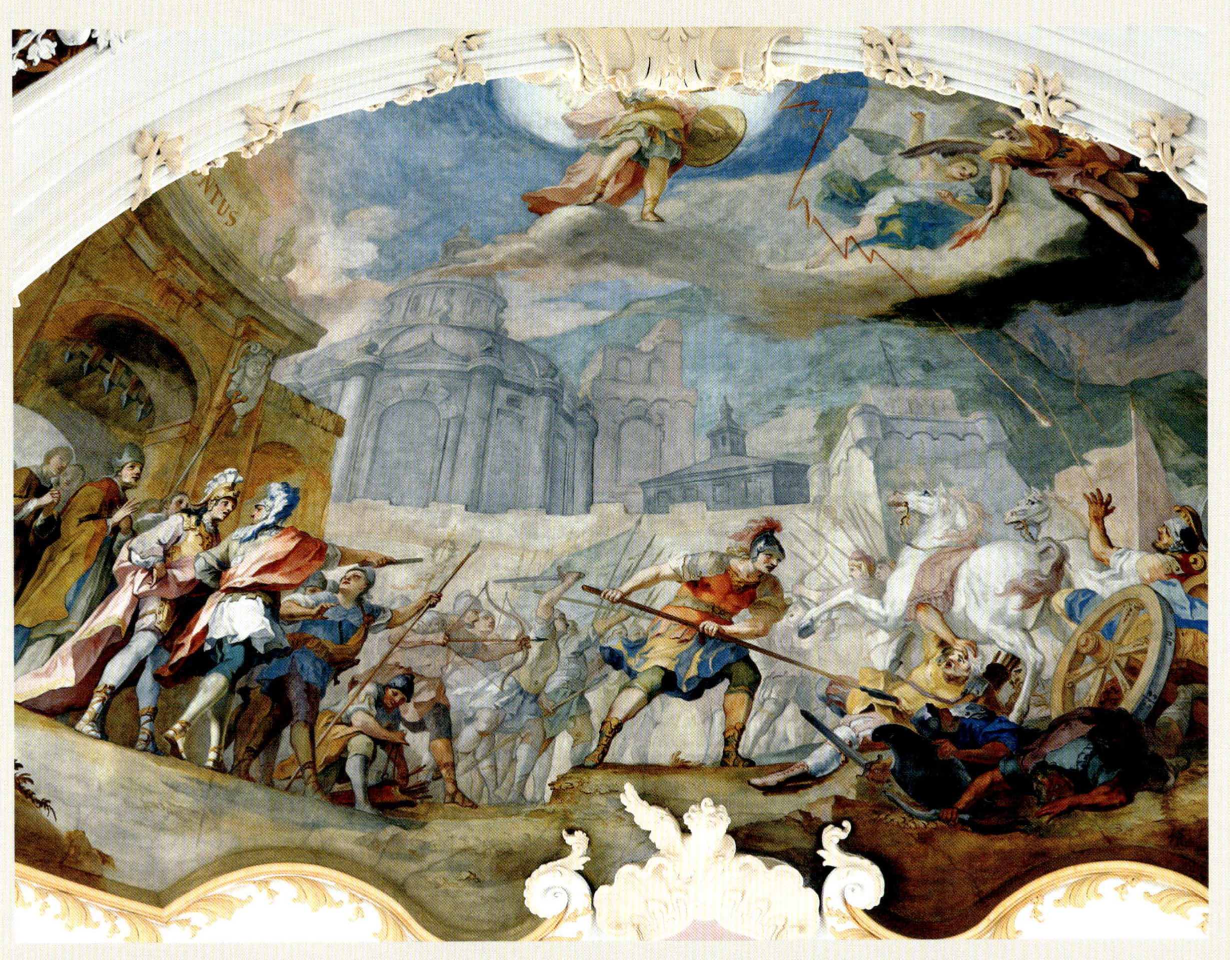

Left:
The late baroque church of St Michael in Berg am Laim is a prime example of the Southern German Rococo. Painter and royal stucco artist Johann Baptist Zimmermann from Wessobrunn did the ceiling frescoes and stucco in 1743/44.

Below:
The church of St Maria in the suburb of Ramersdorf was a place of pilgrimage in the 14th century. Erasmus Grasser (1450–1518) and Jan Polack (~1435–1519) both worked on the interior. The high altar was built from plans by Munich architect Constantin Pader in c. 1660.

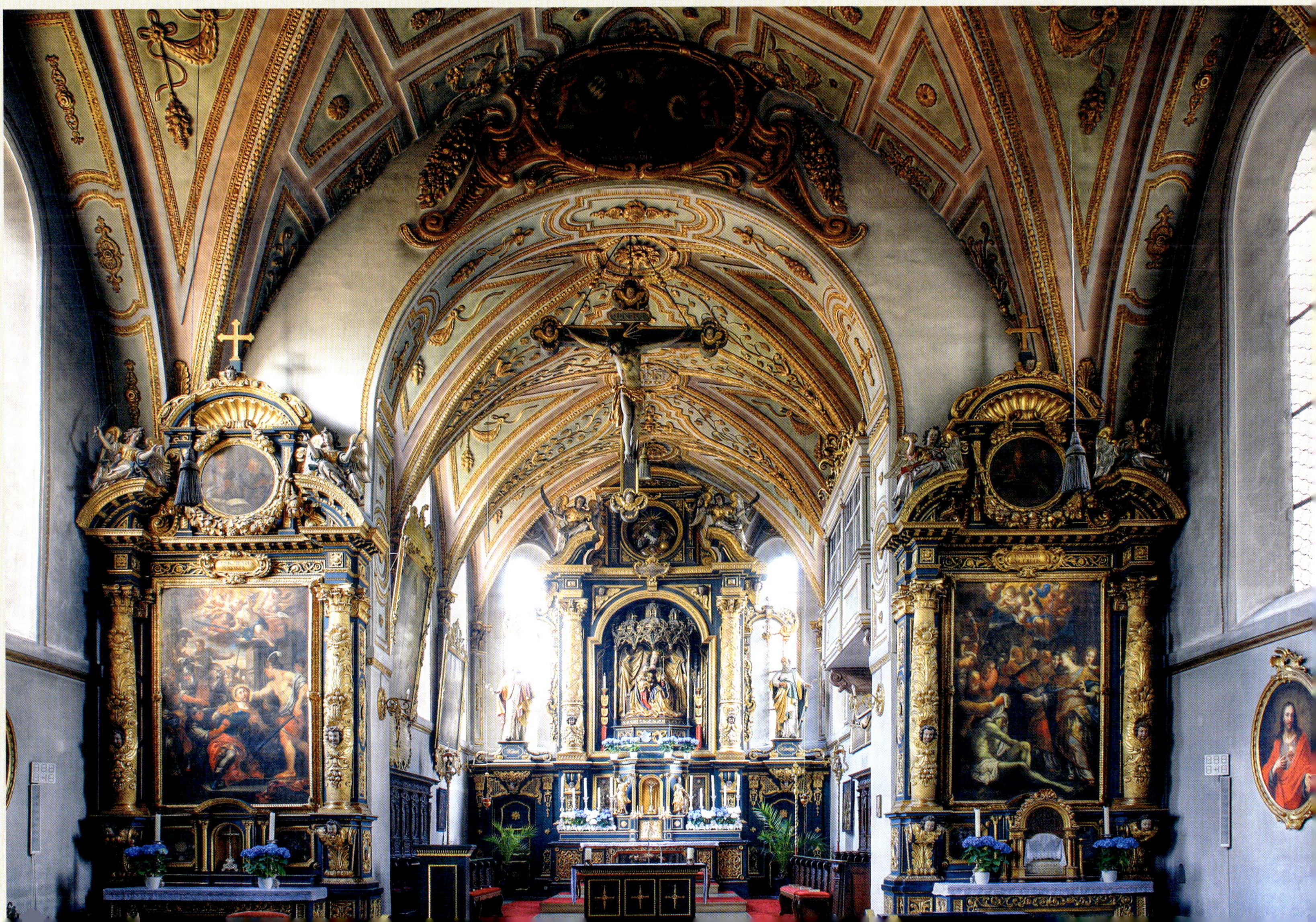

Right page:
Many suburbs of Munich have their own Maypole. This one adorns Wiener Platz in Haidhausen. In the background is the neo-Gothic church of John the Baptist on Johannisplatz, built by Matthias Berger of Munich (1825–1897) between 1852 and 1874. Its west tower is 97 m (318 ft) tall, making it the third-highest steeple in Munich.

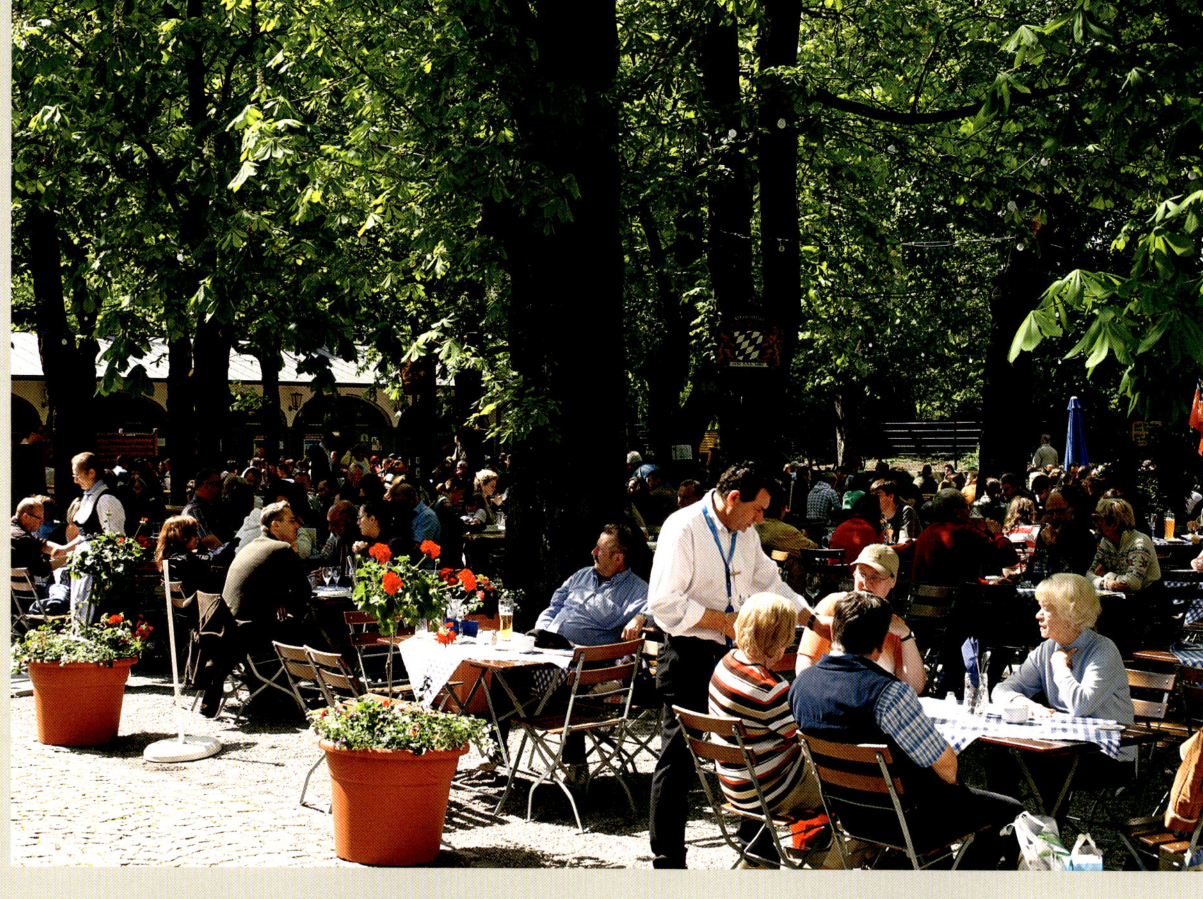

The Hofbräukeller on Wiener Platz in Haidhausen has been open for business since 1892. Behind its Gründerzeit facade is an idyllic beer garden which opens out onto a lush green meadow.

Right:
The Fischerbuberl fountain on Wiener Platz from 1910 is by sculptor and graphic designer Ignatius Taschner (1871–1913). The little boy and his endless supply of drinking water originally stood on Viktualienmarkt; they were moved when the Schrannenhalle was rebuilt.

Far right:
The Fortuna-Brunnen on Isartorplatz was created by Munich sculptor Karl Killer (1873–1948) in 1907. The octagonal basin of red marble depicts scenes from farming. In the middle is a bronze statue of Fortune with four small mermaids at her feet.

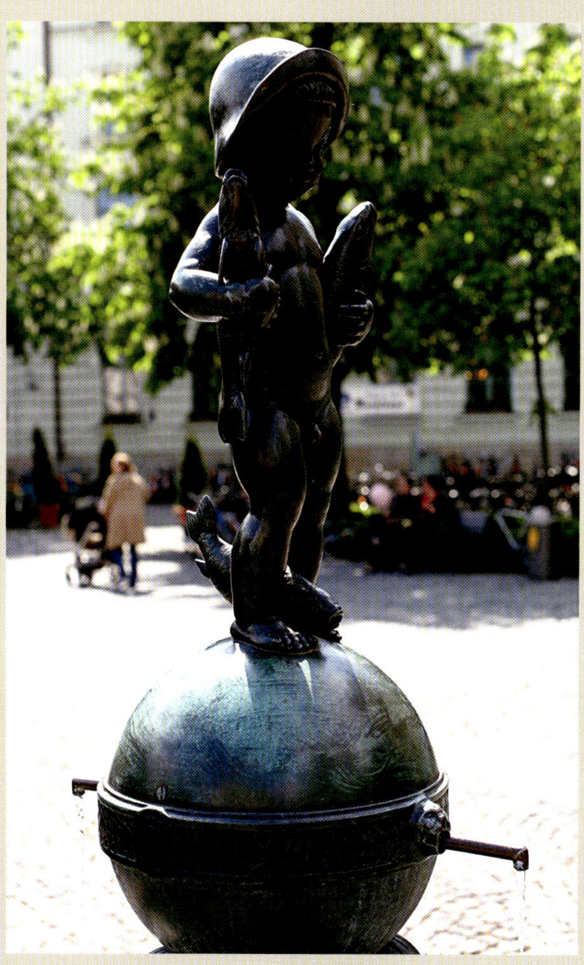

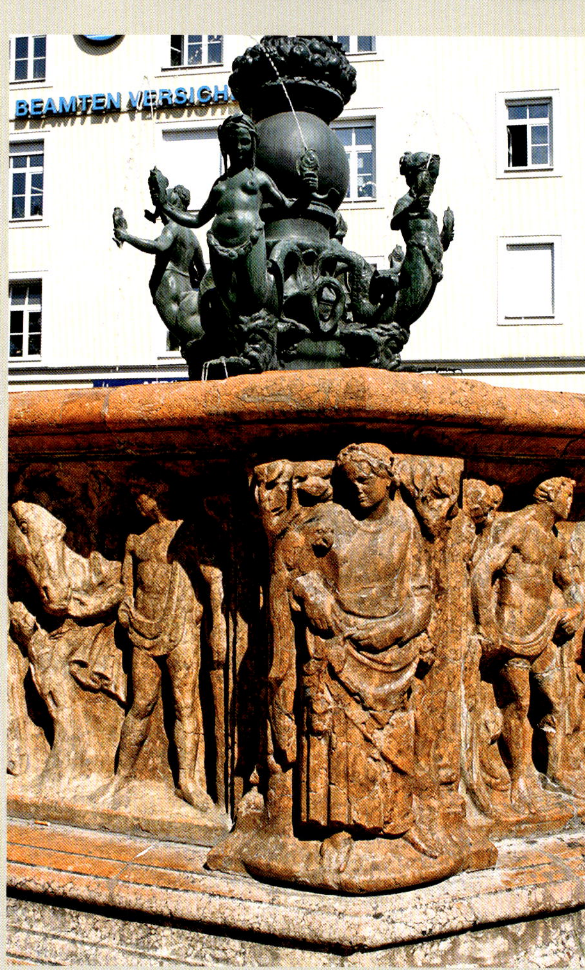

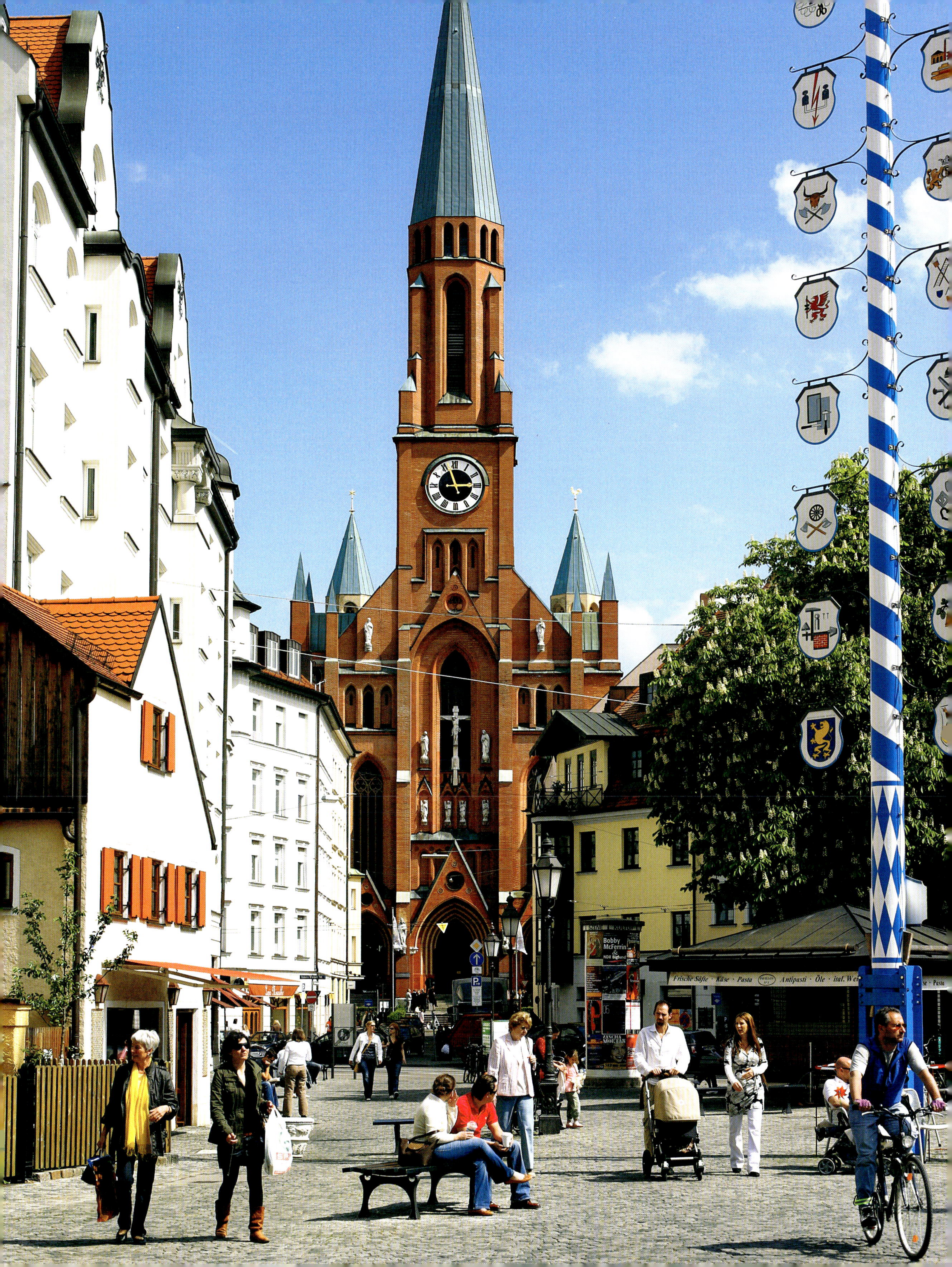
Bobby McFerrin
Frische Säfte · Käse · Pasta
Antipasti · Öle · ital.

Right page:
Not far from the Gasteig is the little church of St Nikolai. It used to service the 13th-century leper house which was built well outside the city walls. The building was later used as a hospital and torn down in 1861–1863.

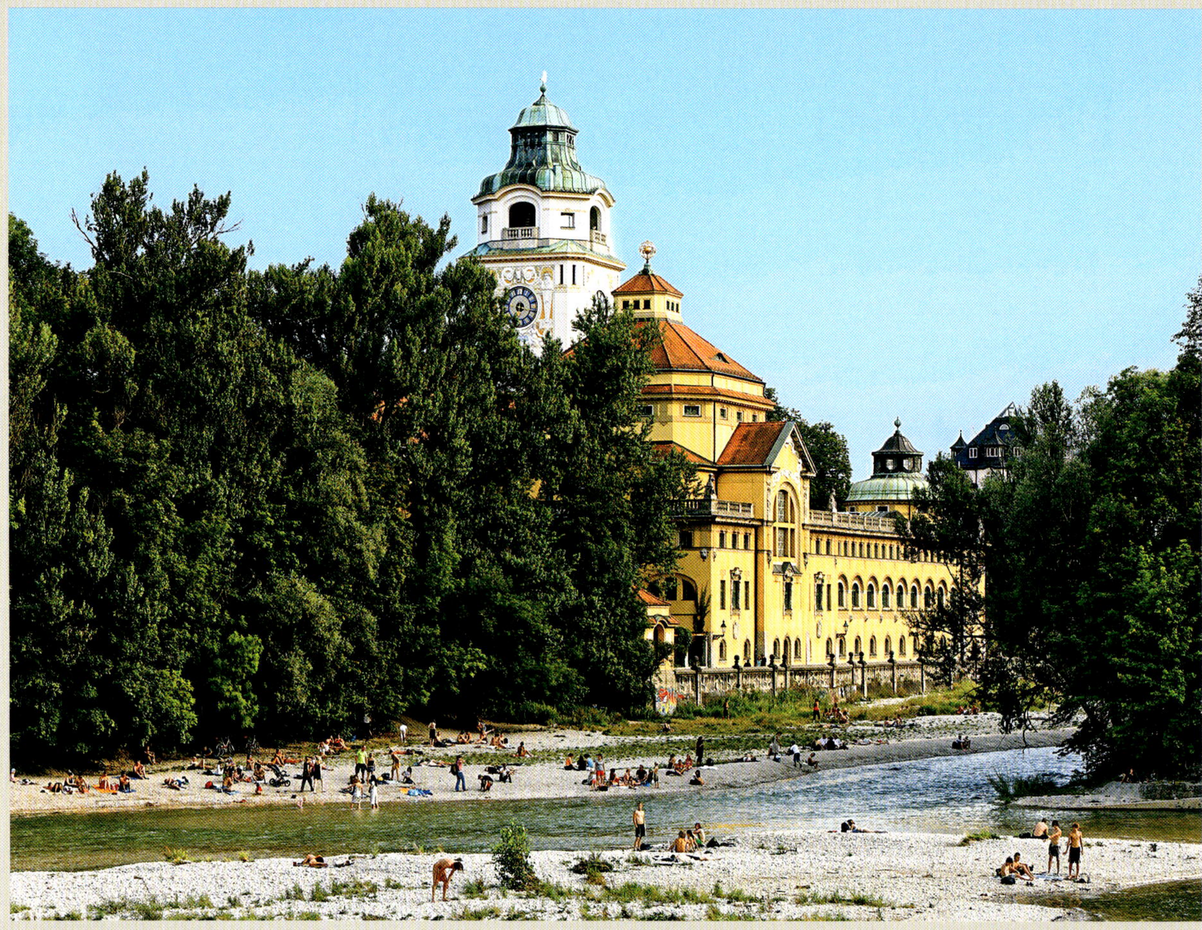

On its completion in 1901 the Müllersches Volksbad in Au on the right bank of the Isar was the first public baths in Munich and the biggest and most expensive swimming pool in the world. It's named after its generous sponsor, Munich engineer Karl Müller.

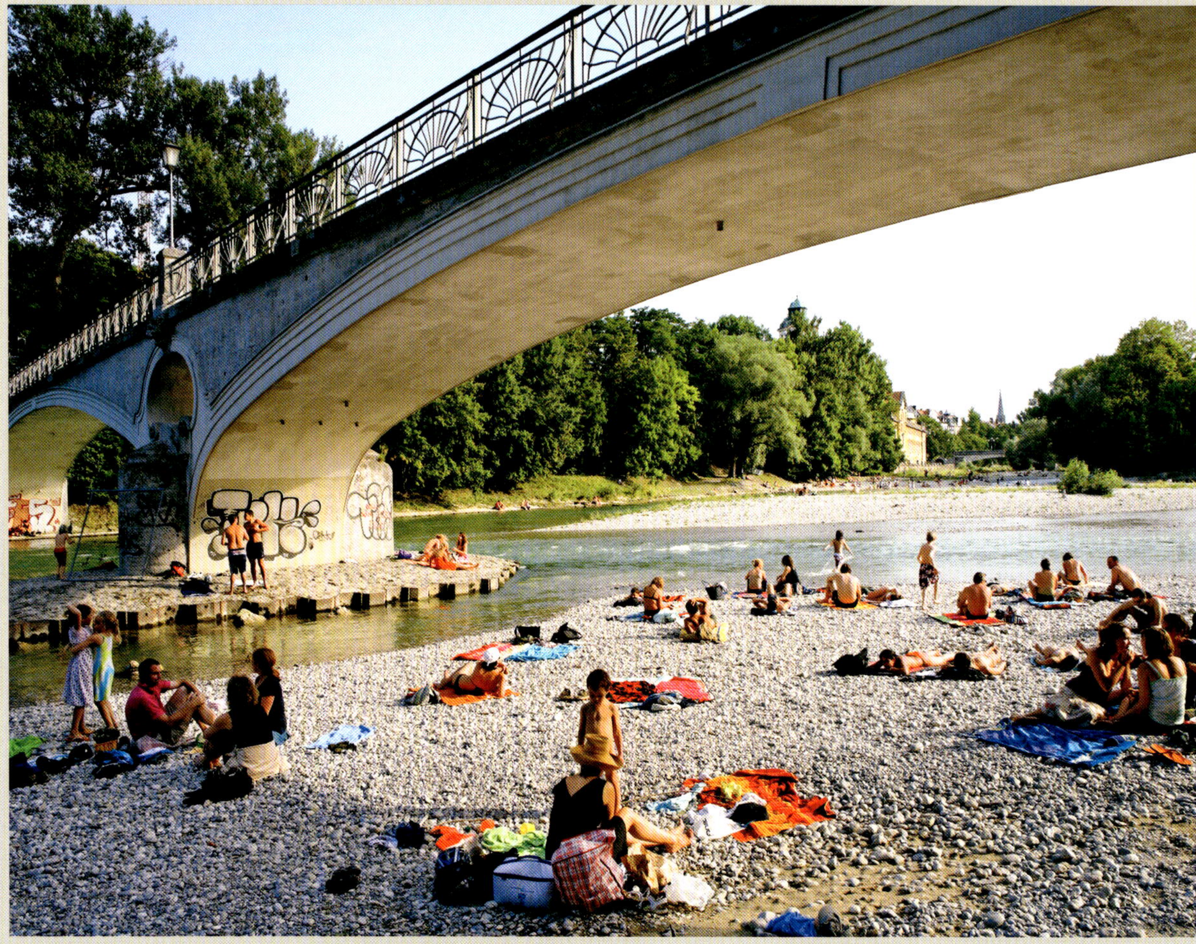

Jugendstil ornaments decorate the iron balustrade of the Kabelsteg, built in 1898. The footbridge joins the Praterinsel with the right bank of the Isar at the church of St Lukas. In summer the bridge provides welcome shade for swimmers and sunbathers.

Page 128/129:
The Munich Philharmonic playing at home at the Philharmonie in the Gasteig. In 1901 and 1910 Gustav Mahler conducted the orchestra, which was founded in 1893, at the premieres of his 4th and 8th symphonies. The orchestra has had its own philharmonic hall here since the opening of the Gasteig in 1985.

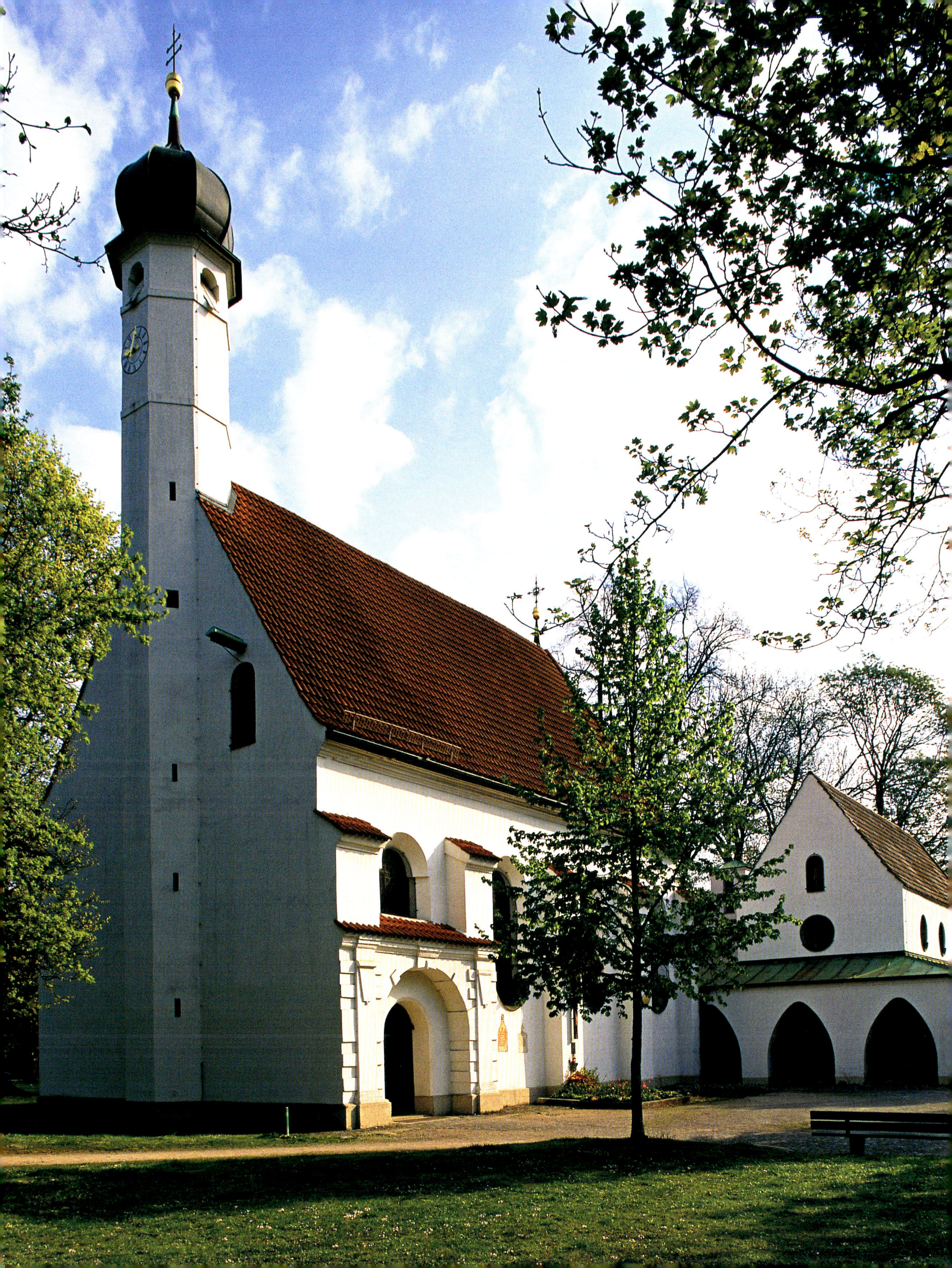

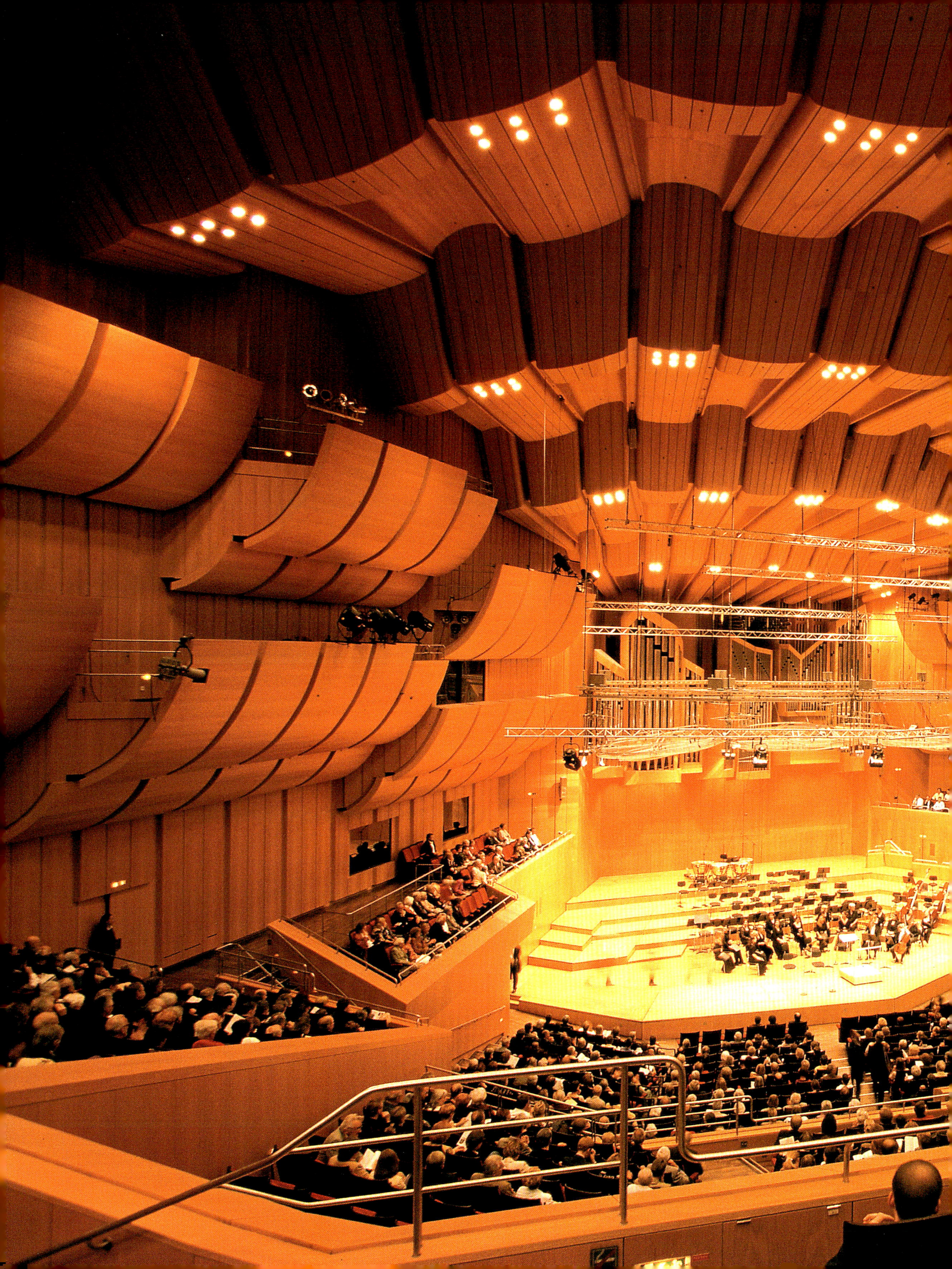

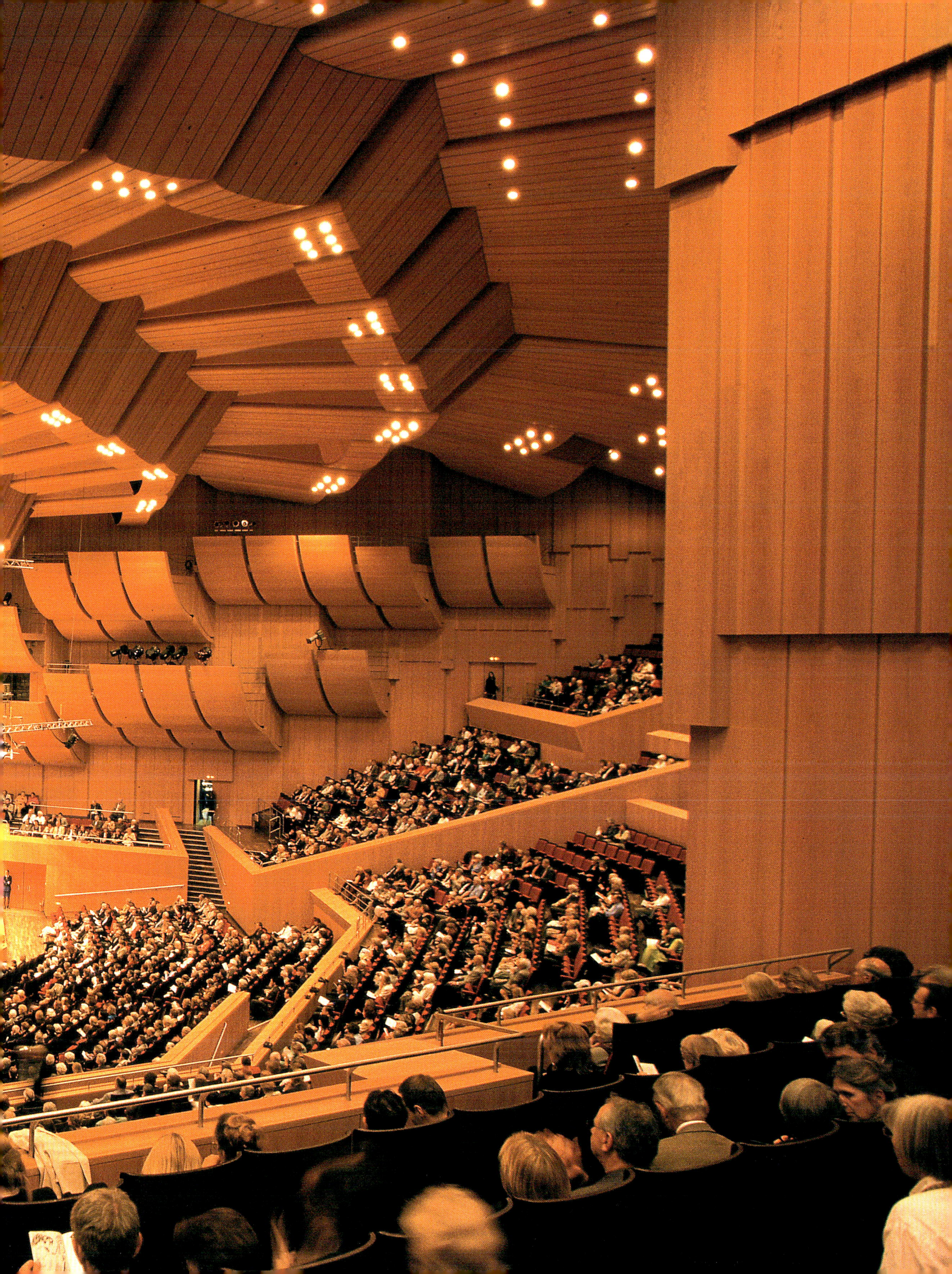

Below:
The German museum of masterpieces of science and technology, as the Deutsches Museum is officially called, fills a large island in the middle of the River Isar. Over the past 850 years the sand bank has served a number of different purposes, acting as a landing stage for river craft, a toll booth and a store for wood and coal. In 1906 the foundations were laid by none other than King Wilhelm II; after almost twenty years of construction the museum was finally opened on May 7, 1925.

Top right:
At various locations throughout Munich the Deutsches Museum demonstrates just what intellectual curiosity and inventive genius are capable of producing. On the Theresienhöhe is the museum of transport whose three halls are split into the categories of urban transport, travel and mobility and technology. Here, Hall II.

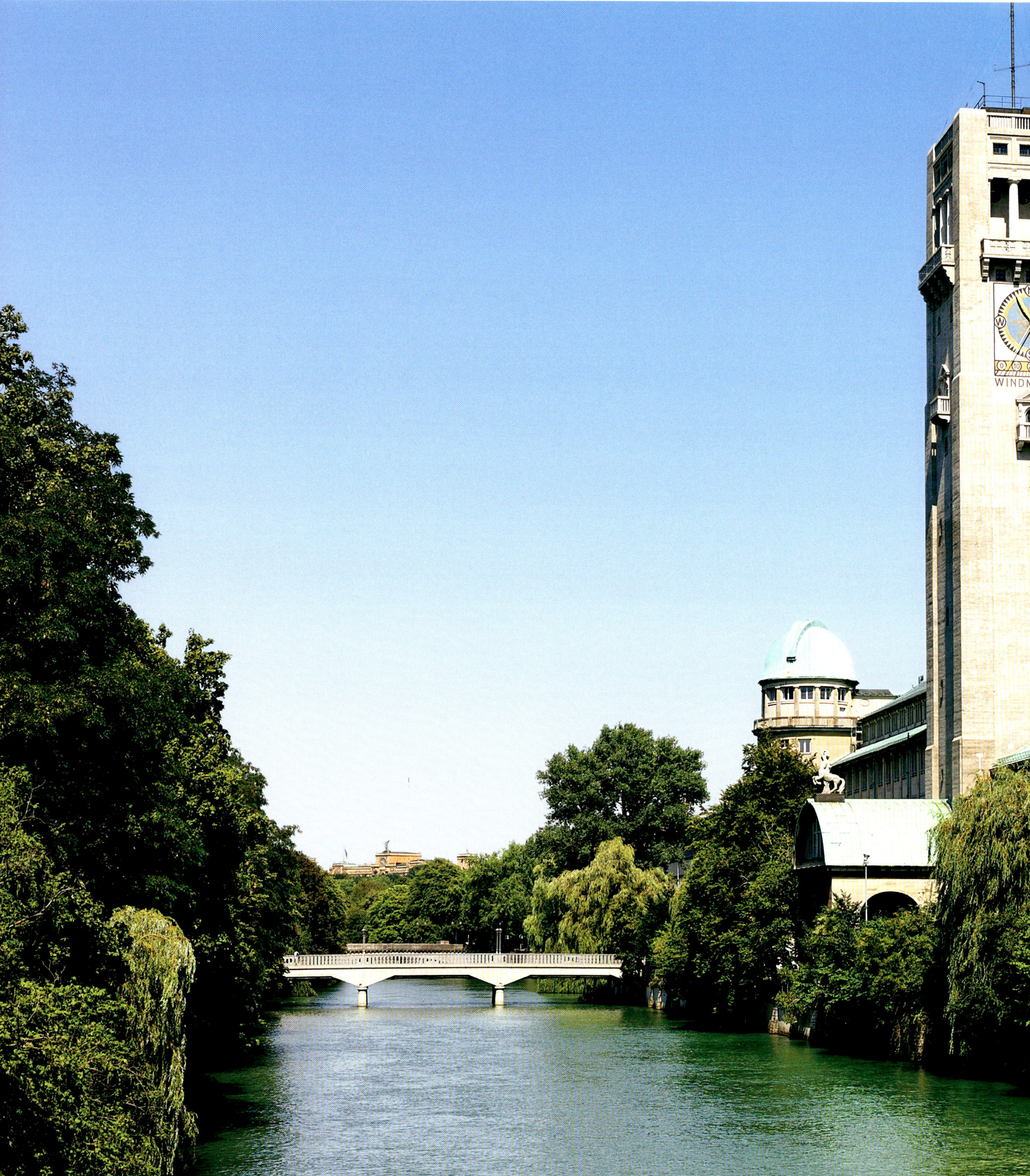

Centre right:
Musical instruments from replica Germanic lyres to the synthesiser are on display in the relevant section of the Deutsches Museum.

Bottom right:
Topics under scrutiny in the museum's pharmacy section range from circulatory disorders and infectious diseases to contraception and the development of medicines. Here visitors can walk into a giant human cell.

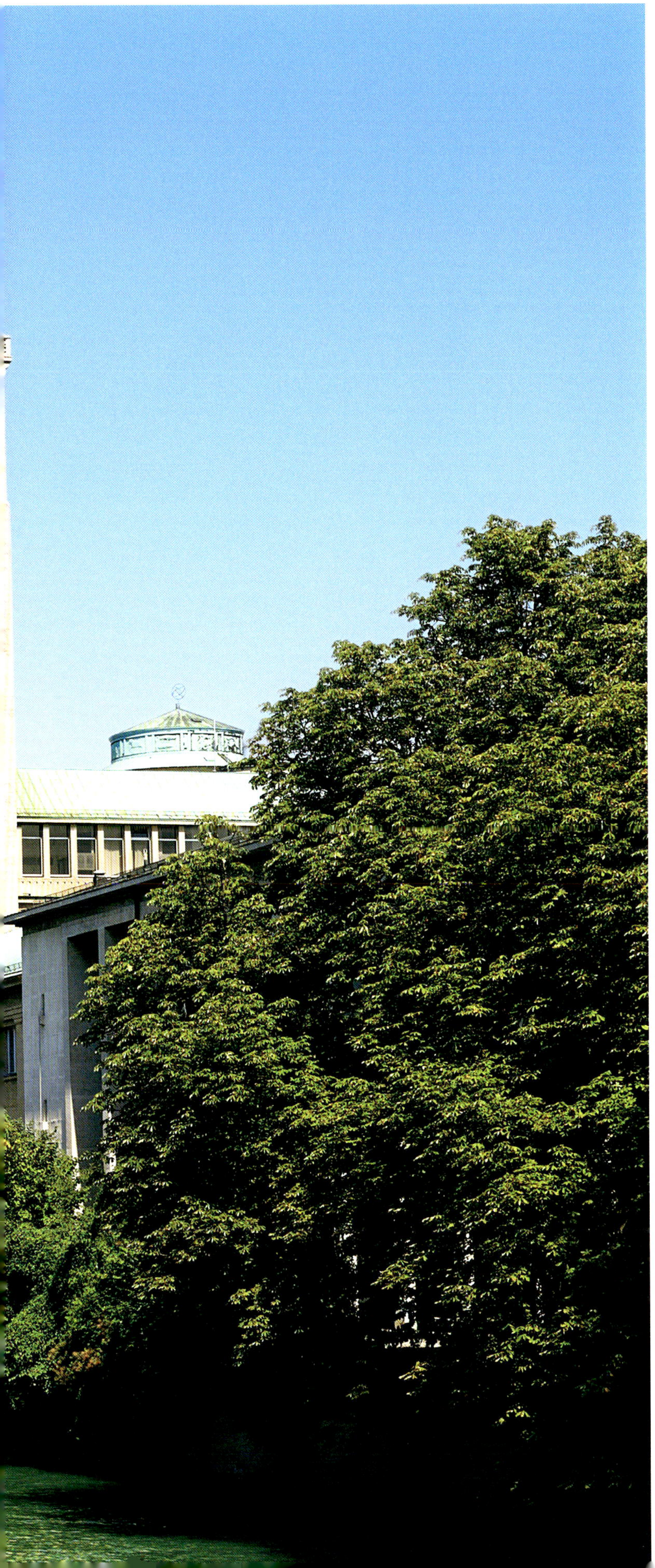

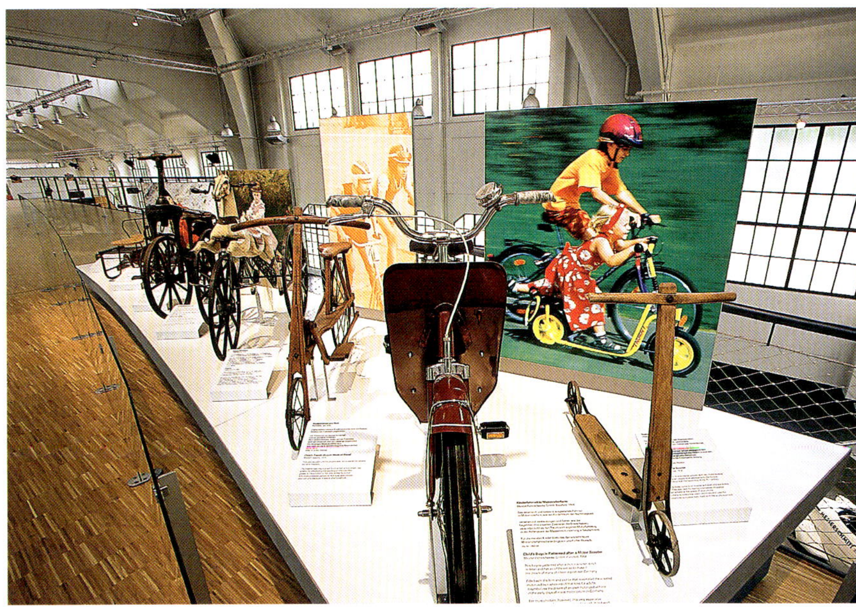

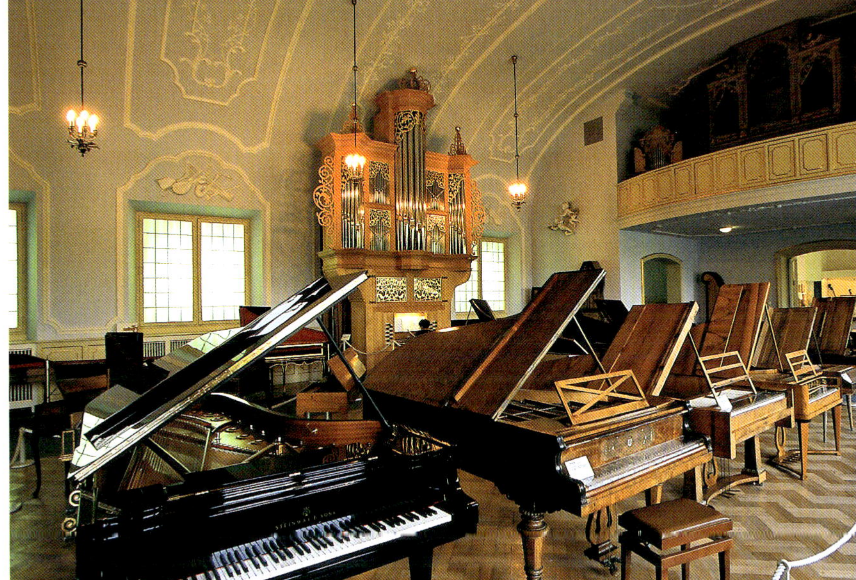

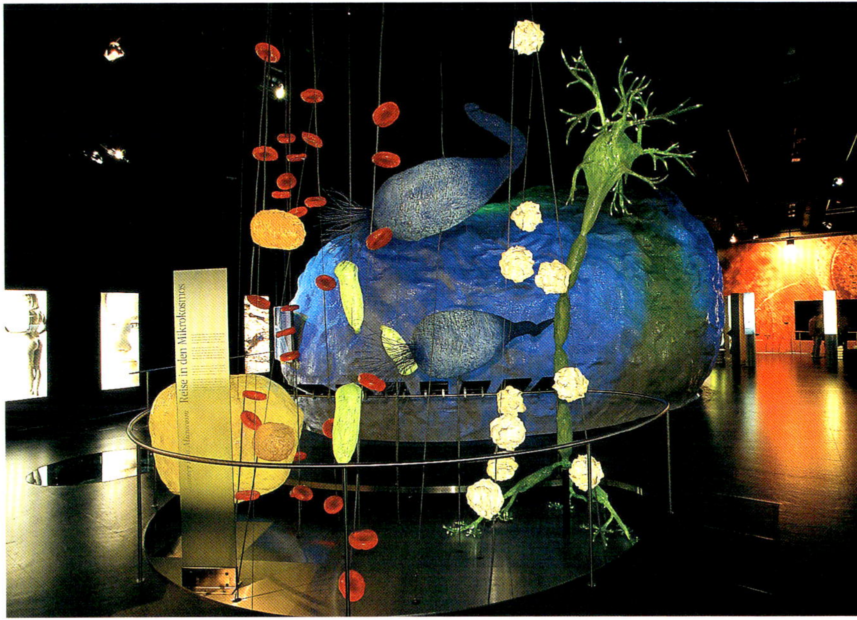

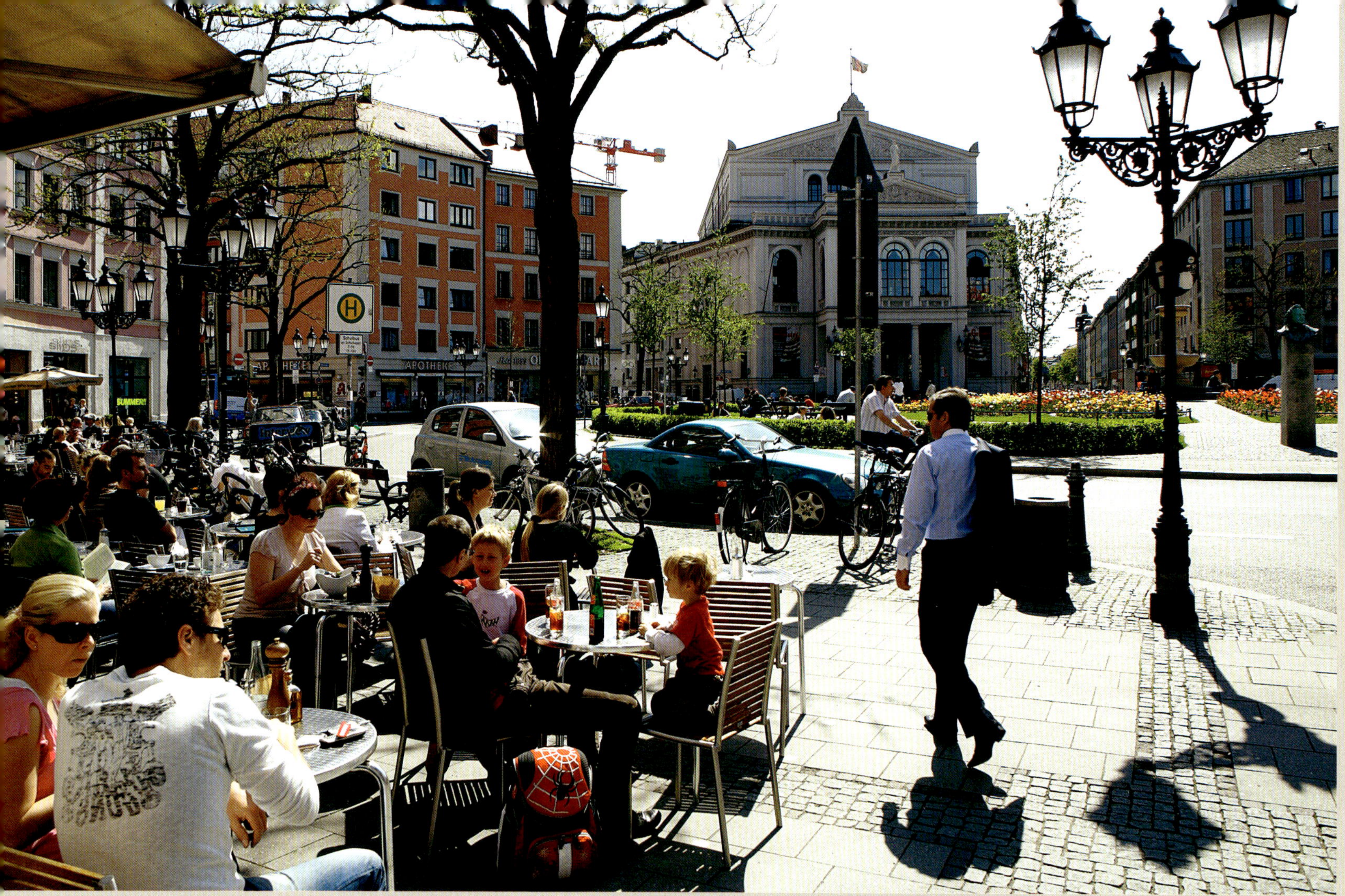

Above:
The Staatstheater on Gärtnerplatz (in the background) was founded in 1864 in Isarvorstadt. Folk theatre was on offer here right from the beginning which, according to Bertolt Brecht, was tantamount to "crude and down-market drama [...] Here there are rude jokes mixed with sentimentality, there outrageous morals and cheap sexuality. The bad are punished and the good will marry, the diligent come into an inheritance and the lazy go empty handed."

Right:
In 1866 Gärtnerplatz was the first purely decorative square in Munich. Its redesign a few years ago was based on the historic plan, with a round bed of flowers, a fountain and monuments to Friedrich Wilhelm von Gärtner and Leo von Klenze at its centre.

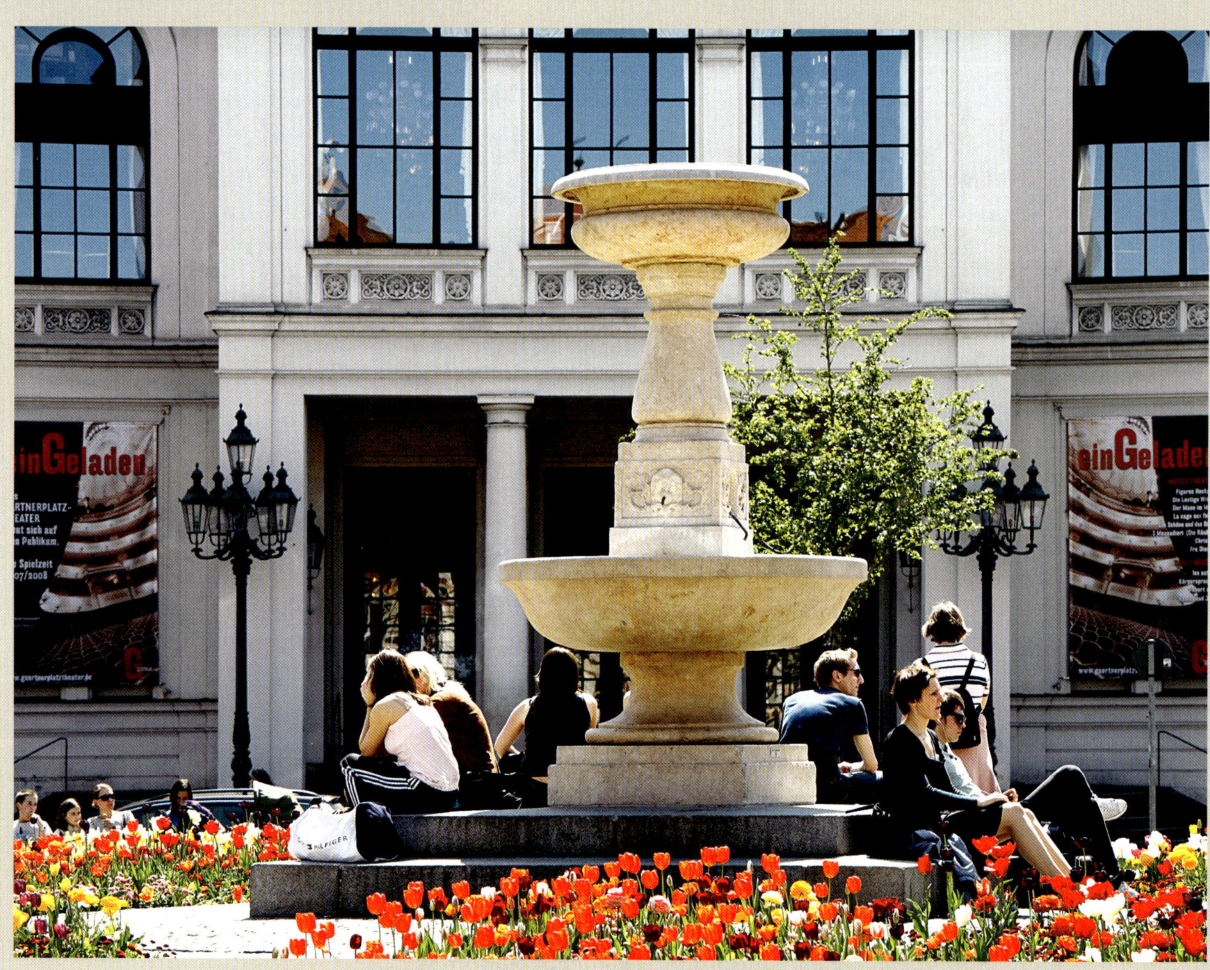

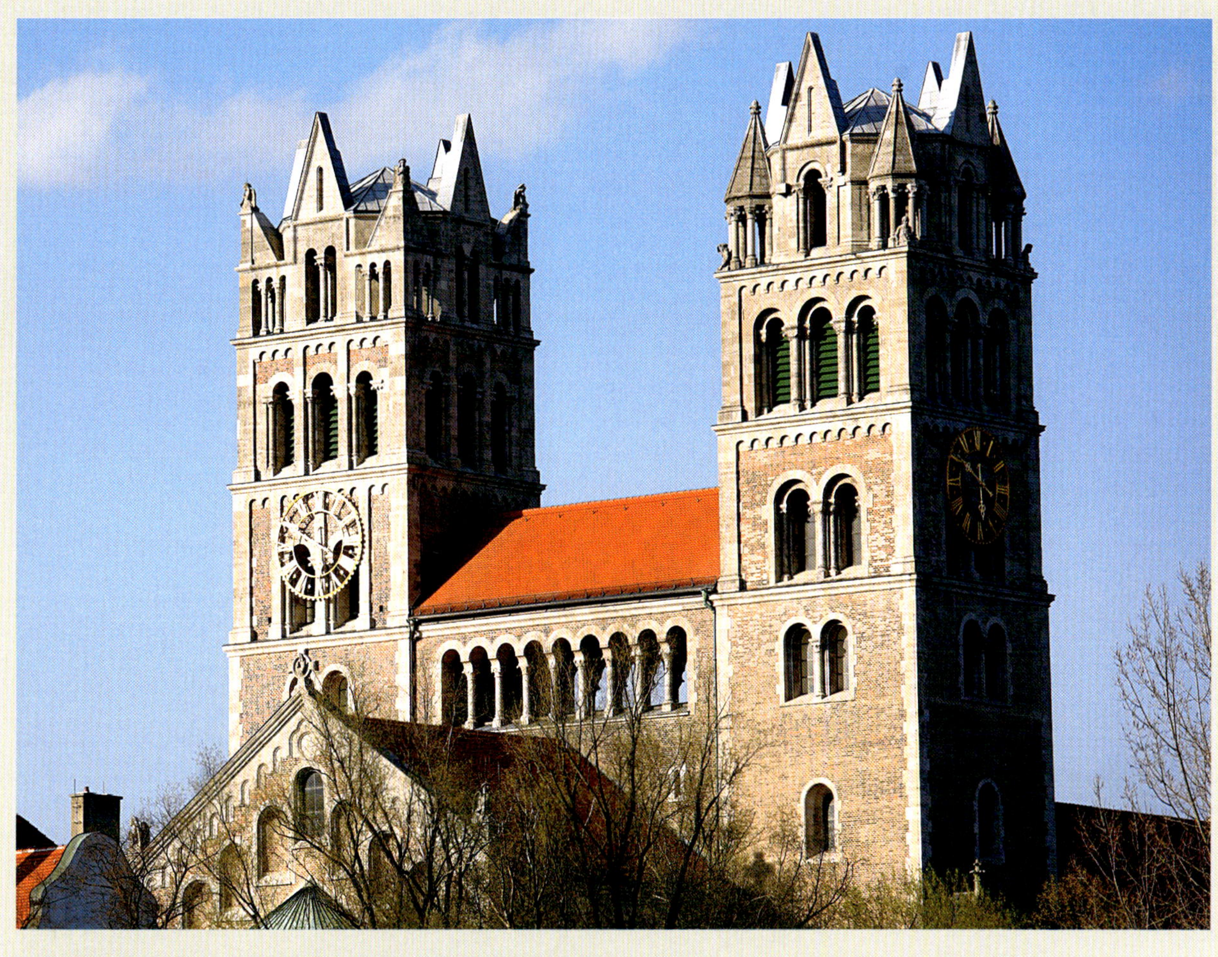

Left:
The church of St Maximilian in the Glockenbachviertel was built in neo-Romanesque by Heinrich von Schmidt between 1892 and 1908.

Below:
Path running alongside the Glockenbach, one of the streams which used to power the town mills and iron hammers and dispose of refuse and human waste. Up until the 1970s most of these rivulets had been drained or boxed in; now efforts are being made to restore them.

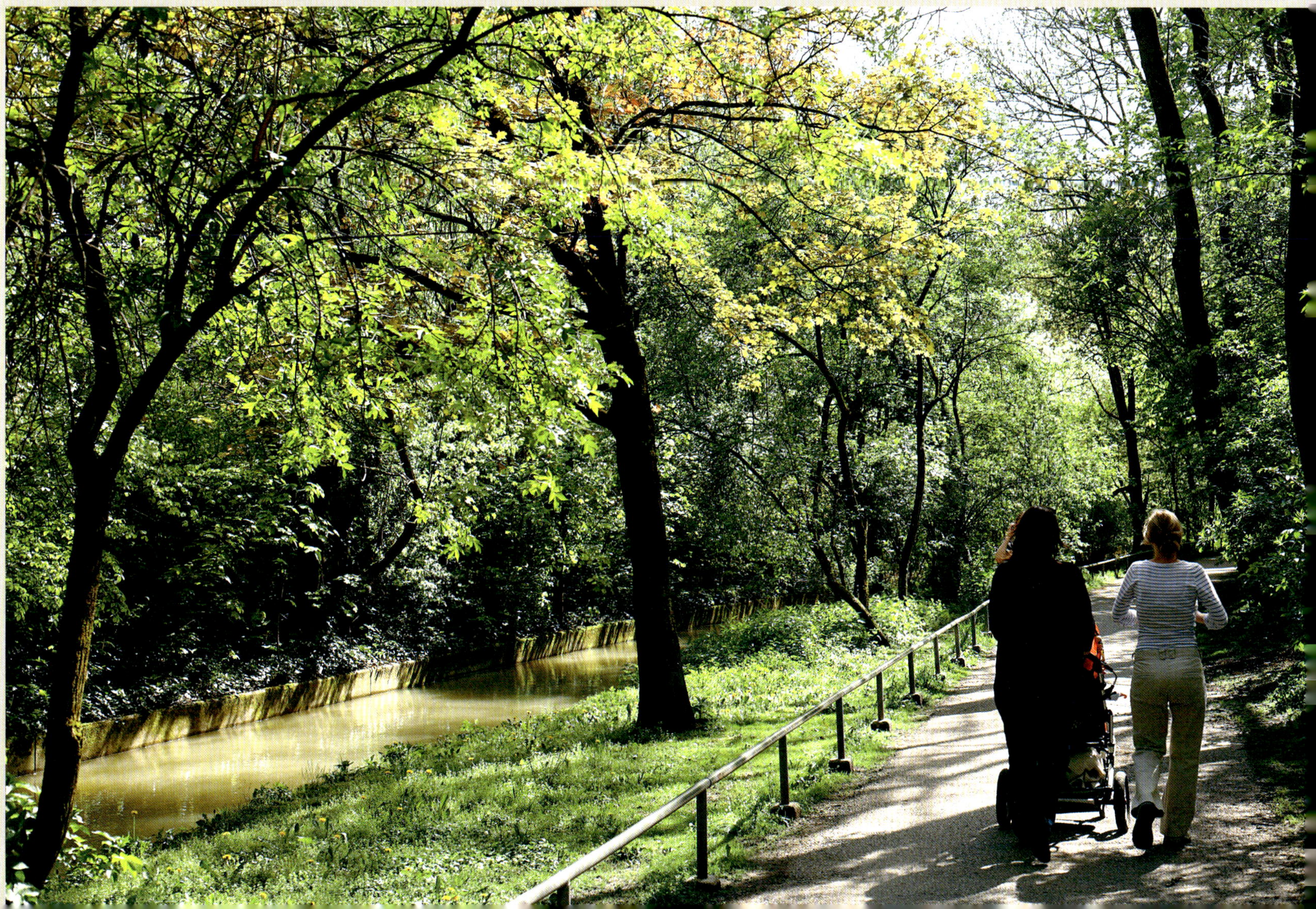

Below:
The Auer Dult is a traditional fair which is held three times a year on Mariahilfplatz near Maria Hilf church in Au. The Maidult takes place around the first weekend in May, the Jakobidult in July and the Kirchweihdult in the week following the church fete in October. Each event lasts nine days.

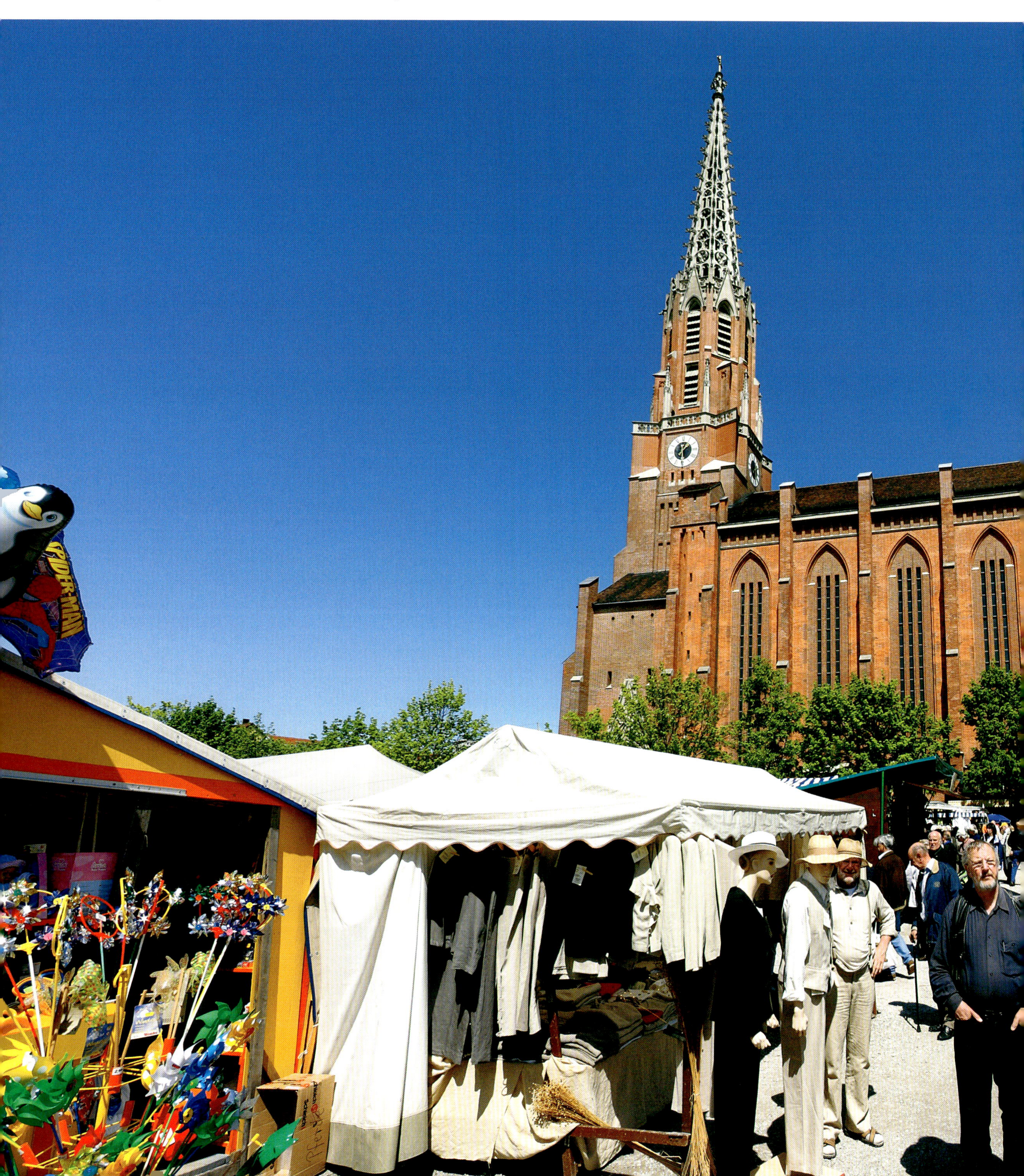

Small photos, right:
The Jakobidult was first held in 1310. Today the huge market sells crockery, pots, clothes, second-hand books and antique furniture.

The market comes complete with a funfair offering various rides and amusements: here a merry-go-round, fun for the little ones and a good old Bavarian brass band.

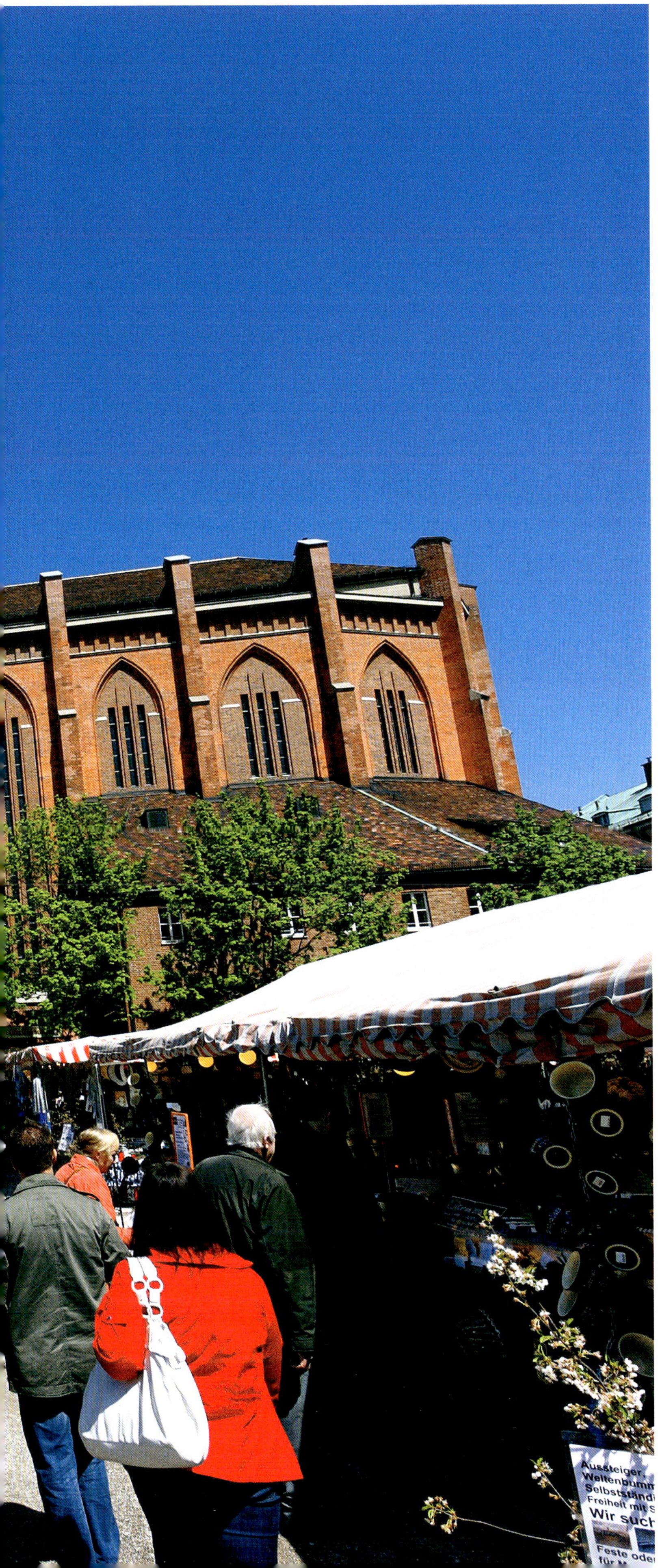

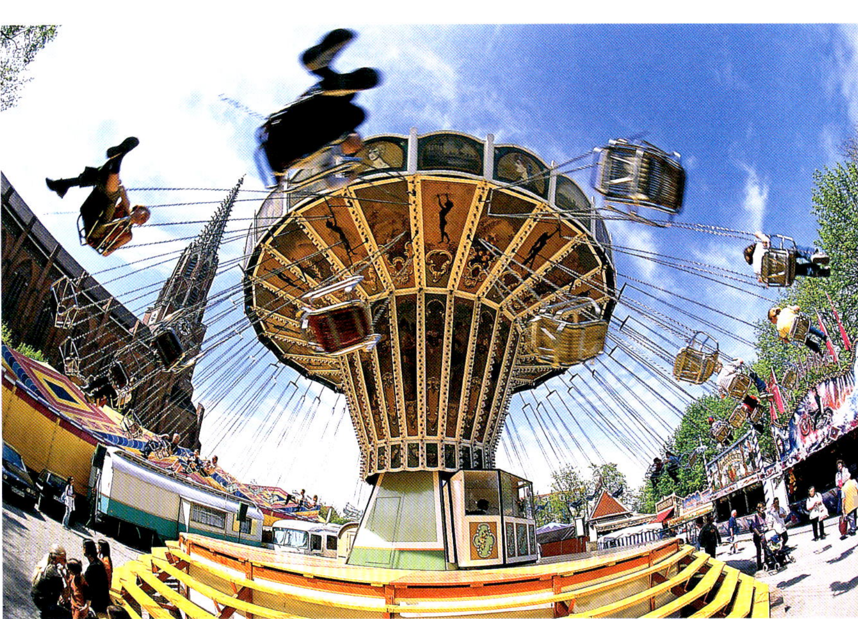

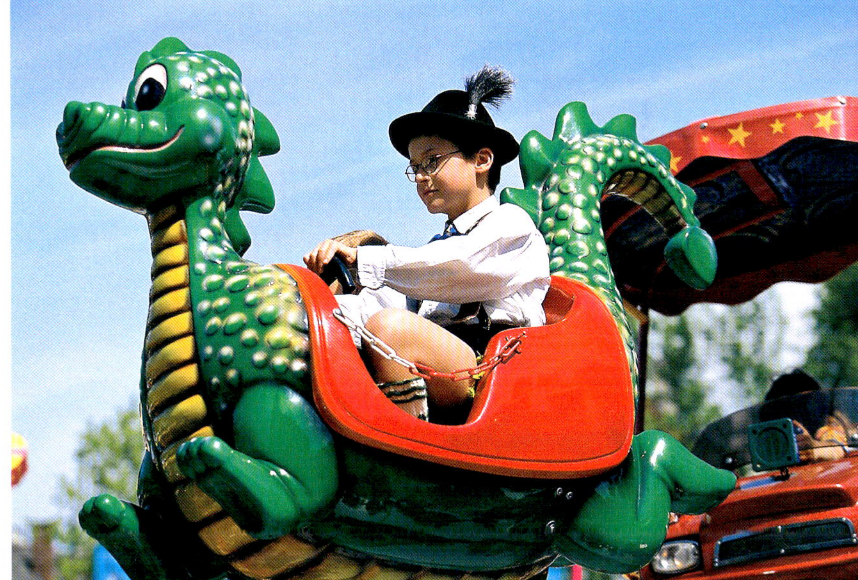

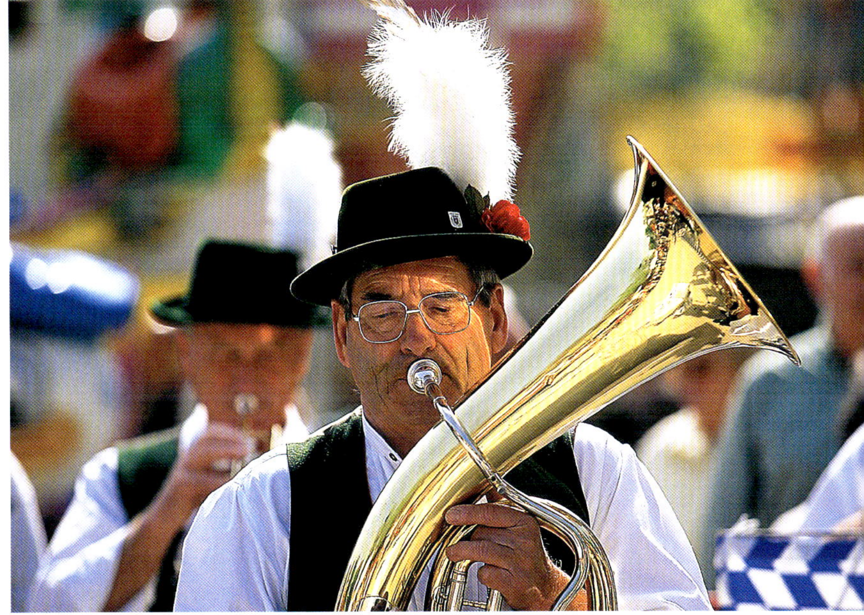

Tierpark Hellabrunn is Munich's zoo. It's in the suburb of Thalkirchen, tucked away in the East Isar conservation area. Opened on August 1, 1911, it now has about 7,700 vertebrates from 340 different species. Hellbrunn tries to house its residents in surroundings which are as close to their natural habitat as possible, its large enclosures often full of old trees and largely devoid of ugly fencing. Above is the terrarium, below the giraffe enclosure.

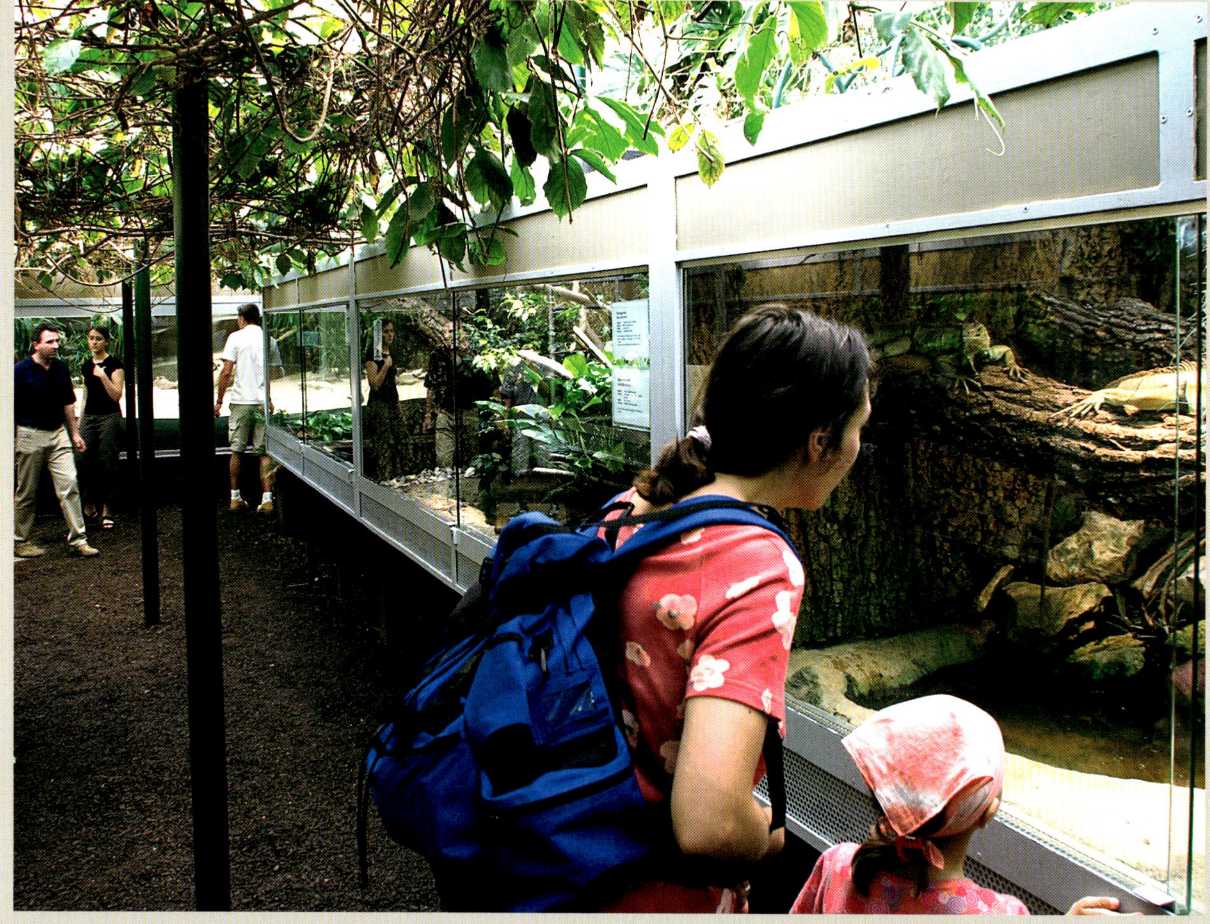

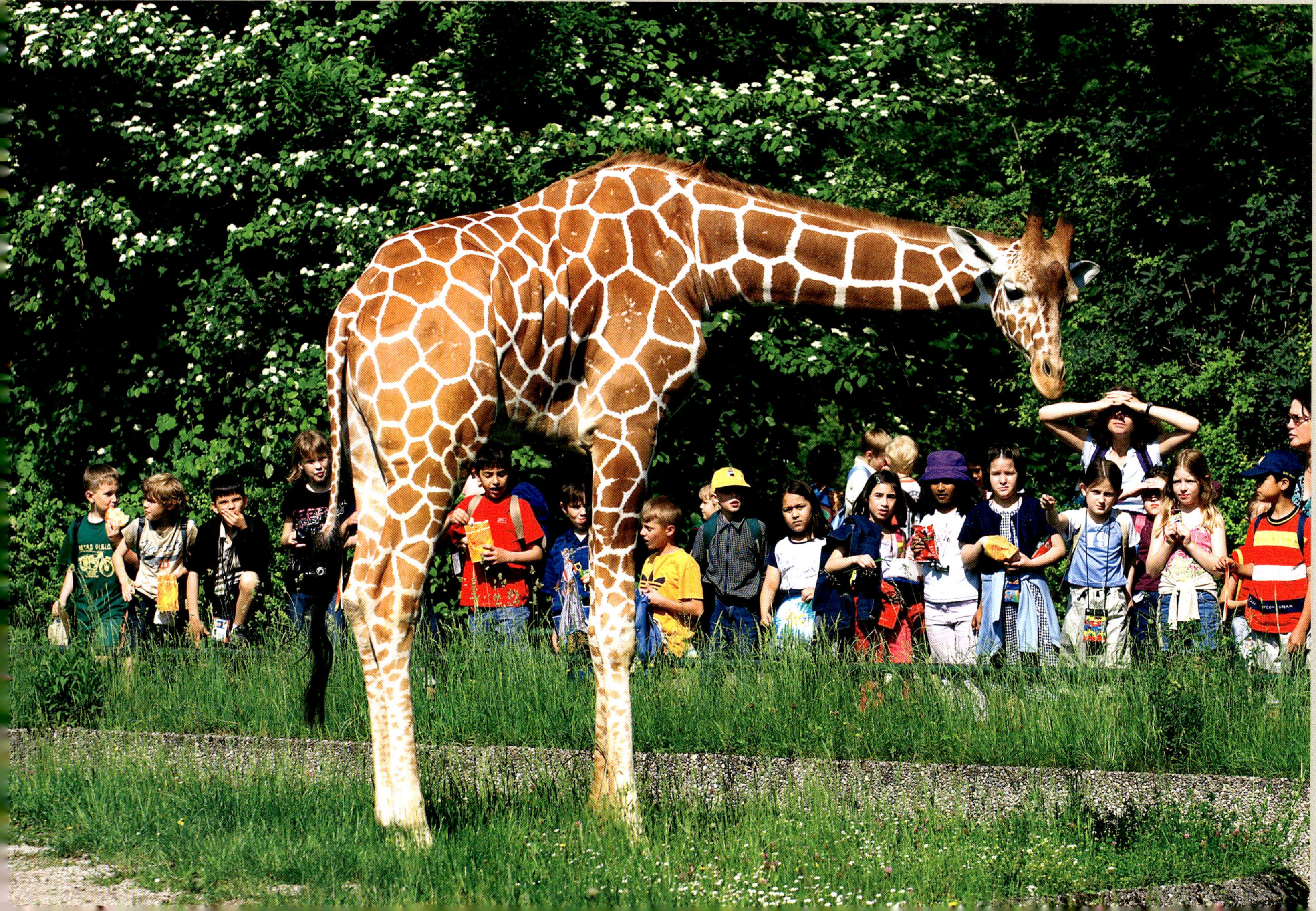

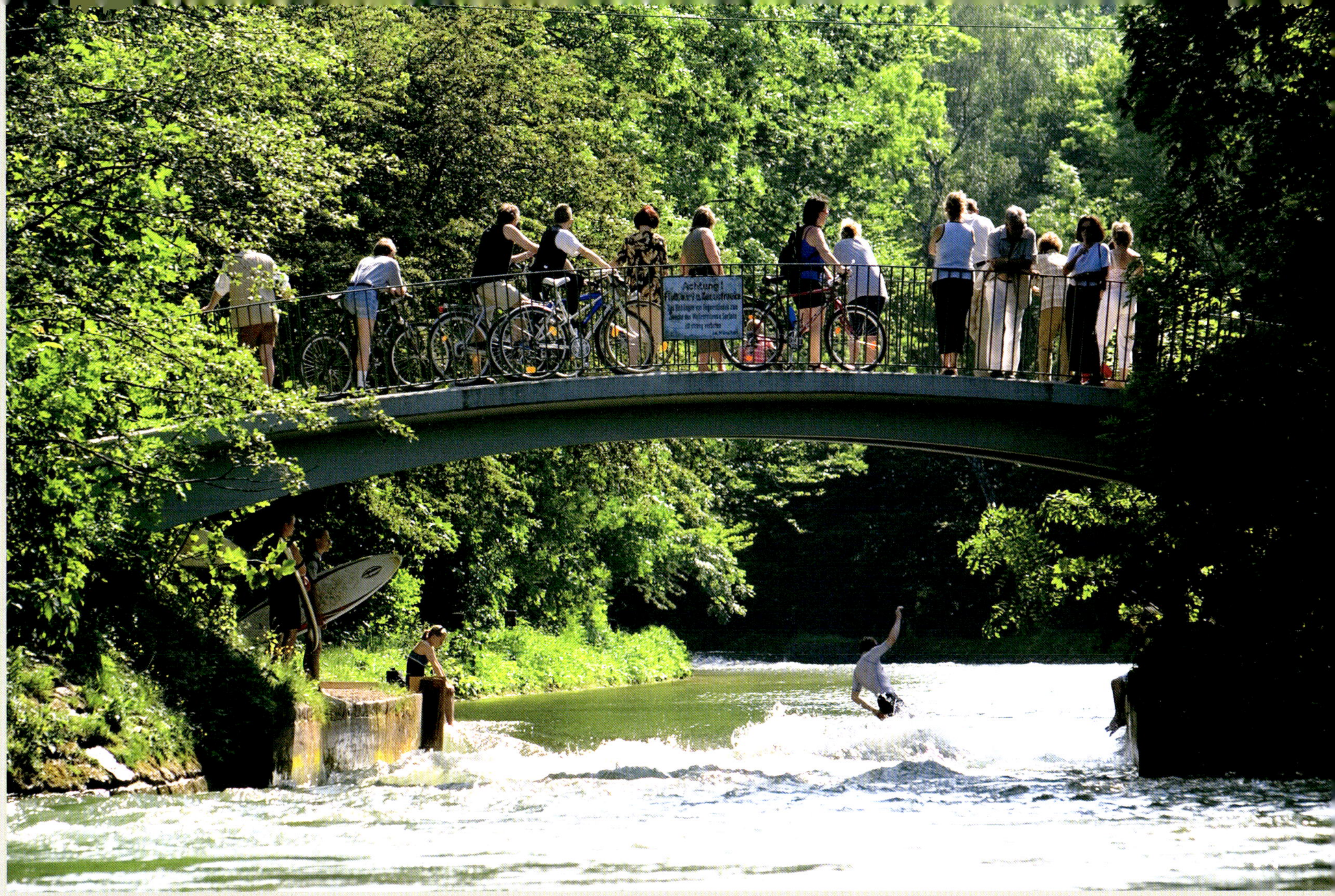

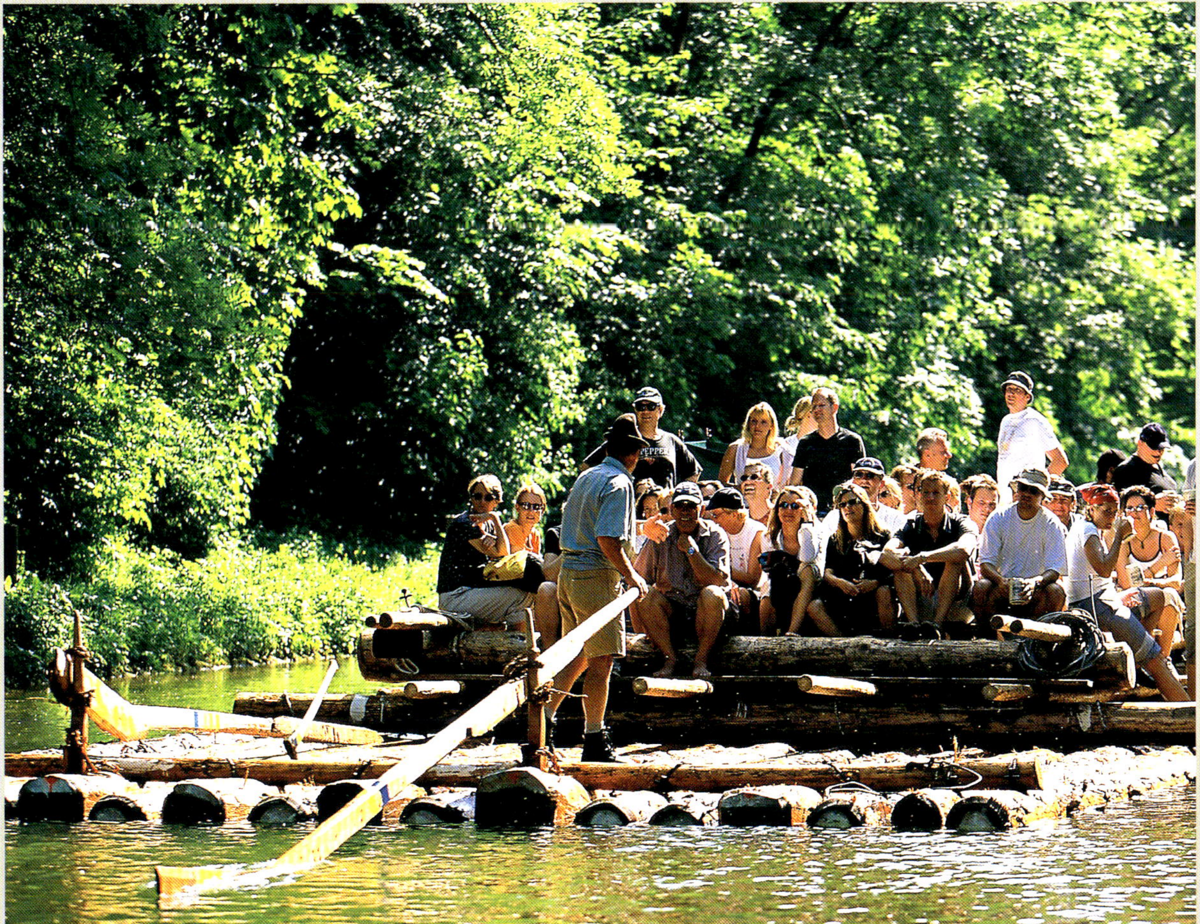

Above:
The "standing wave" on the Flößland canal in Thalkirchen is one of the most famous in Europe and the second hottest surfing venue in Munich after the Eisbach in the Englischer Garten. The exploits often draw a crowd.

Left:
The canal in Thalkirchen is also where big tourist rafts made of thick tree trunks terminate their sedentary journey from Wolfratshausen down the River Isar. Once the guests have disembarked the rafts are dismantled, taken back upstream on a lorry and put back together in time for the next trip.

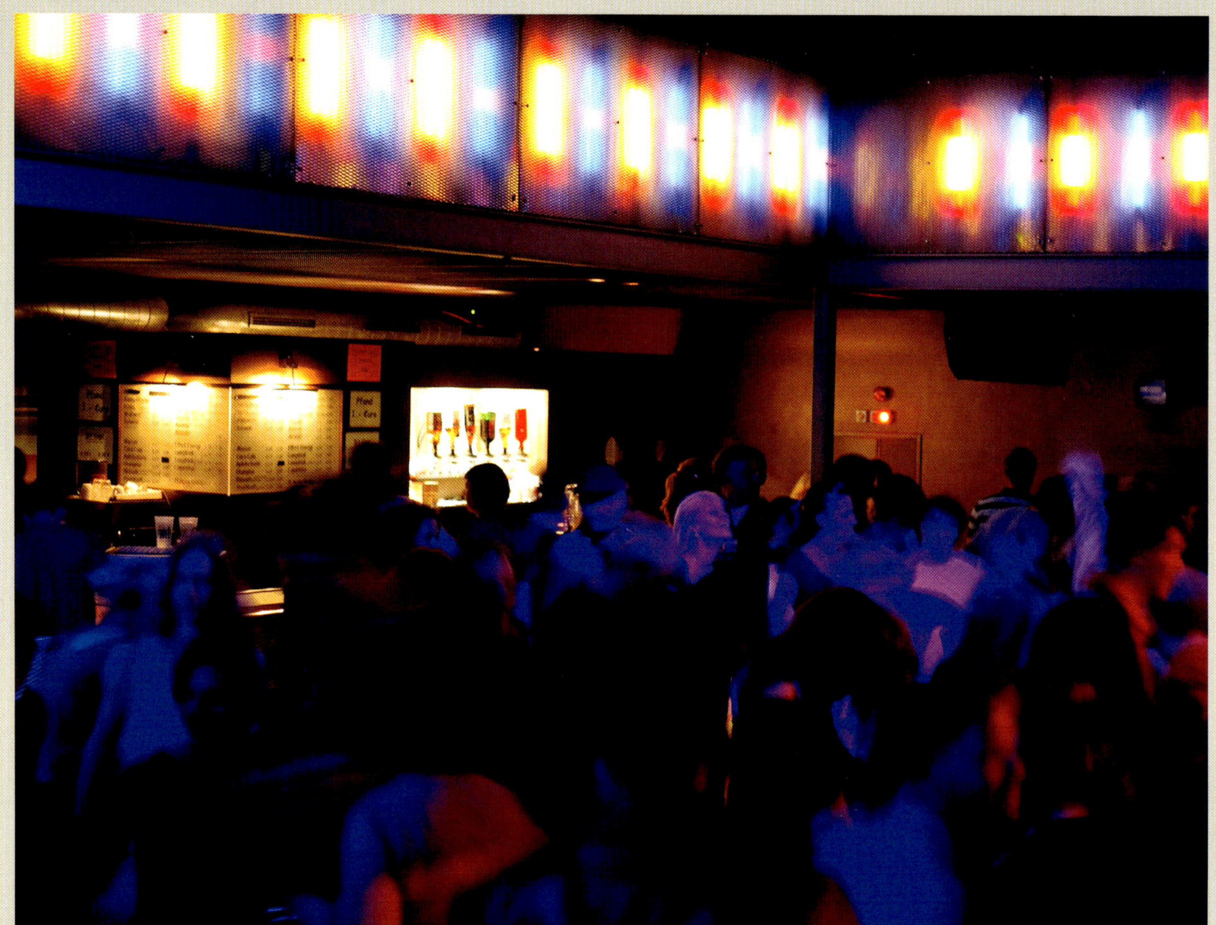

Right:
Nightlife at Club Ampere at the Muffatwerk in Au-Haidhausen. In a heady combination the Muffat hall, café, night club and beer garden have created a cultural biosphere on the banks of the Isar whose very special atmosphere makes it a popular hangout for arts freaks and night owls.

Below:
Jazz band The Boperators with Annette Neuffer at the Unterfahrt club in the suburb of Haidhausen. The venue has daily concerts featuring musicians on the local and international modern jazz scene and is included on the list of the 100 Great Jazz Clubs.

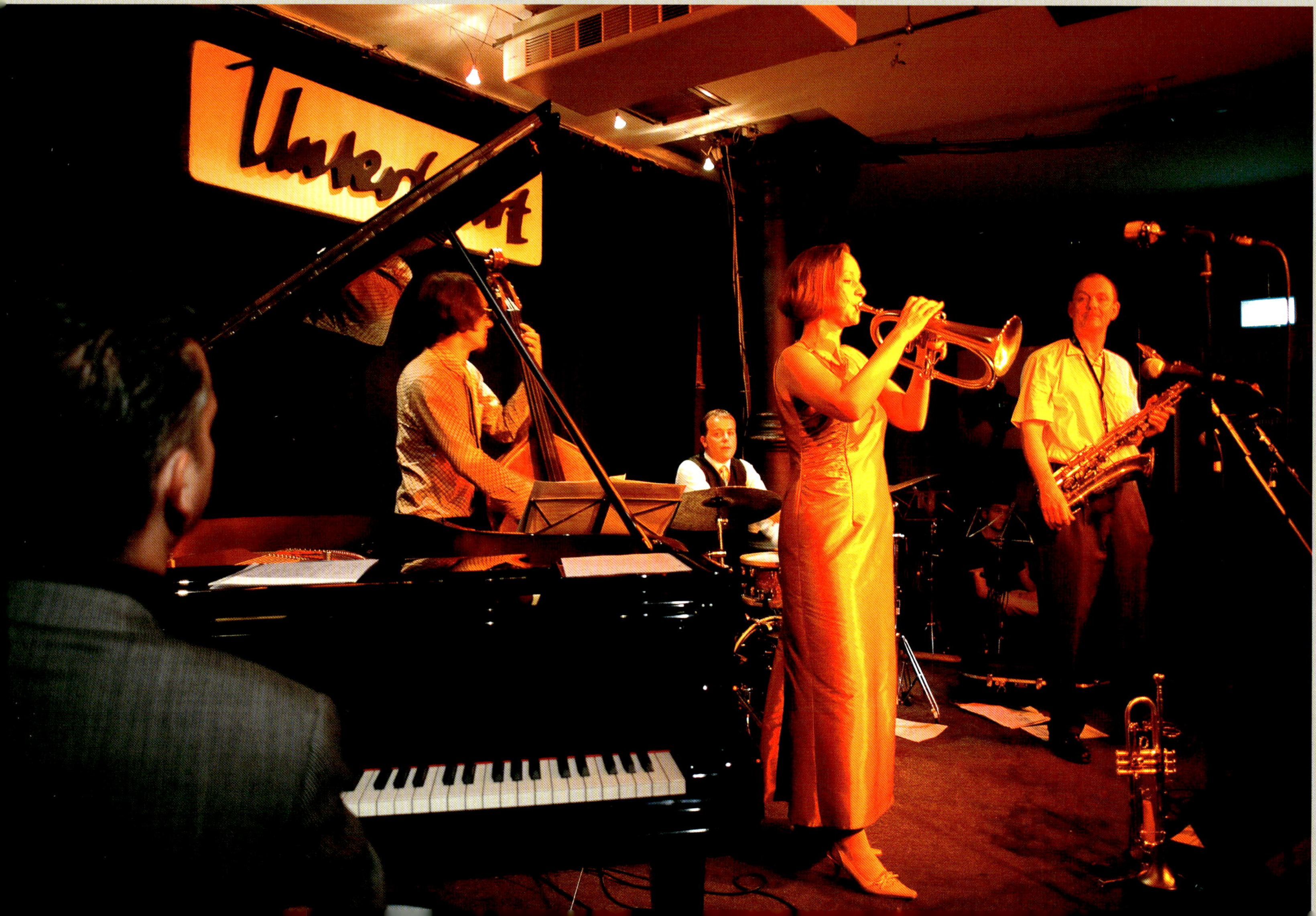

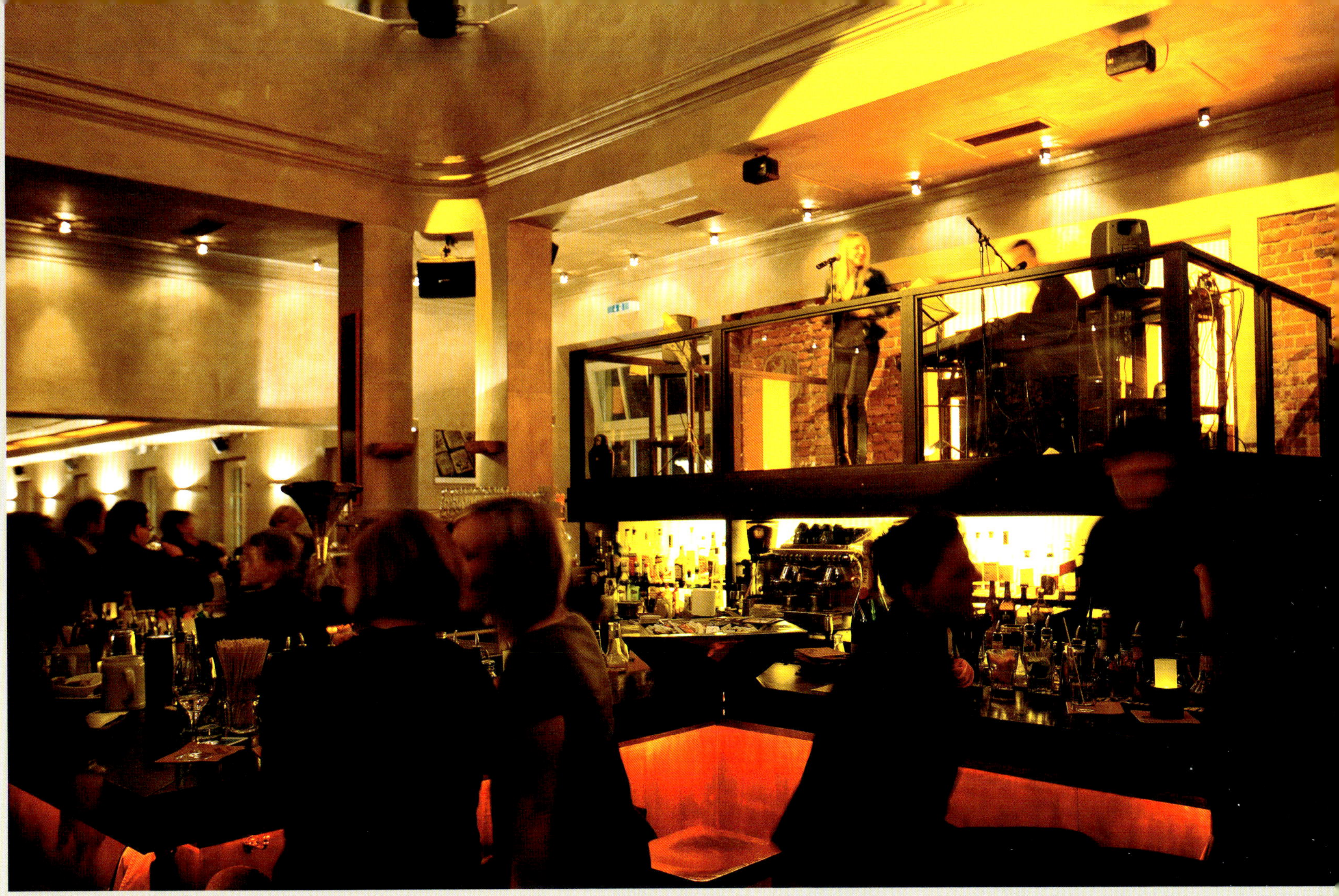

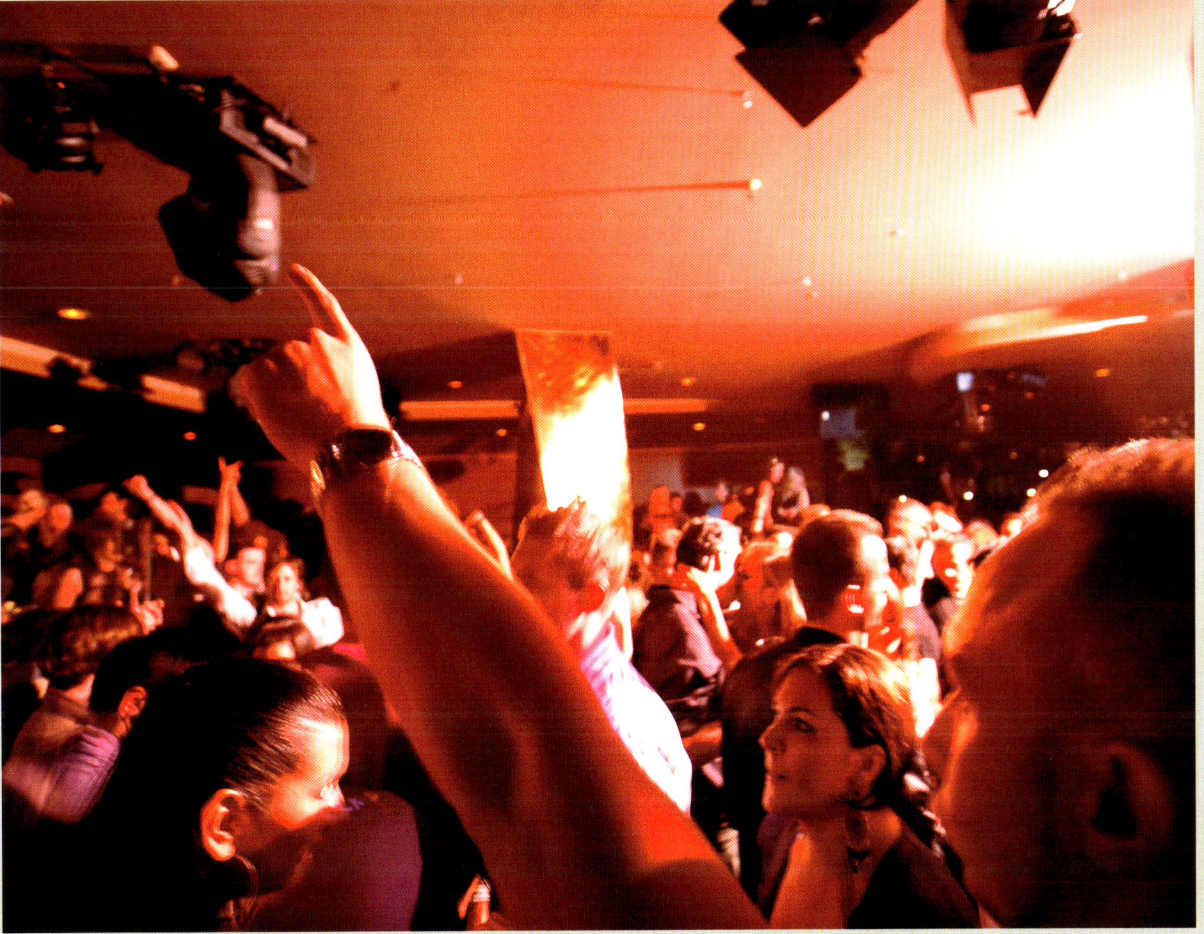

Above:
Live music with dena acoustic at the Park Café restaurant and dance venue on Sophienstraße 7 in the old botanical gardens. Park Café was an institution during the 1960s and 1970s and one of the hottest dives on the Munich disco scene. Over the years it's become one of the biggest clubs in town.

Left:
Partying at Club Pacha, a disco which has several franchises across the globe. The club logo and trademark consists of two cherries. The Pacha on Maximiliansplatz in Munich was opened in November 2000.

Right:
On its opening in 1857 the Großhesseloher Brücke was the second highest railway bridge in the world. In 1983/84 the old bridge was torn down and by 1985 a new one built in its place.

Below:
Gutshof Menterschwaige on the banks of the Isar near Harlaching wouldn't be the same without its idyllic beer garden. King Ludwig I once supped his beer here under the pub's ancient chestnut trees. On a fine day the smell of barbecued fish wafts through the air.

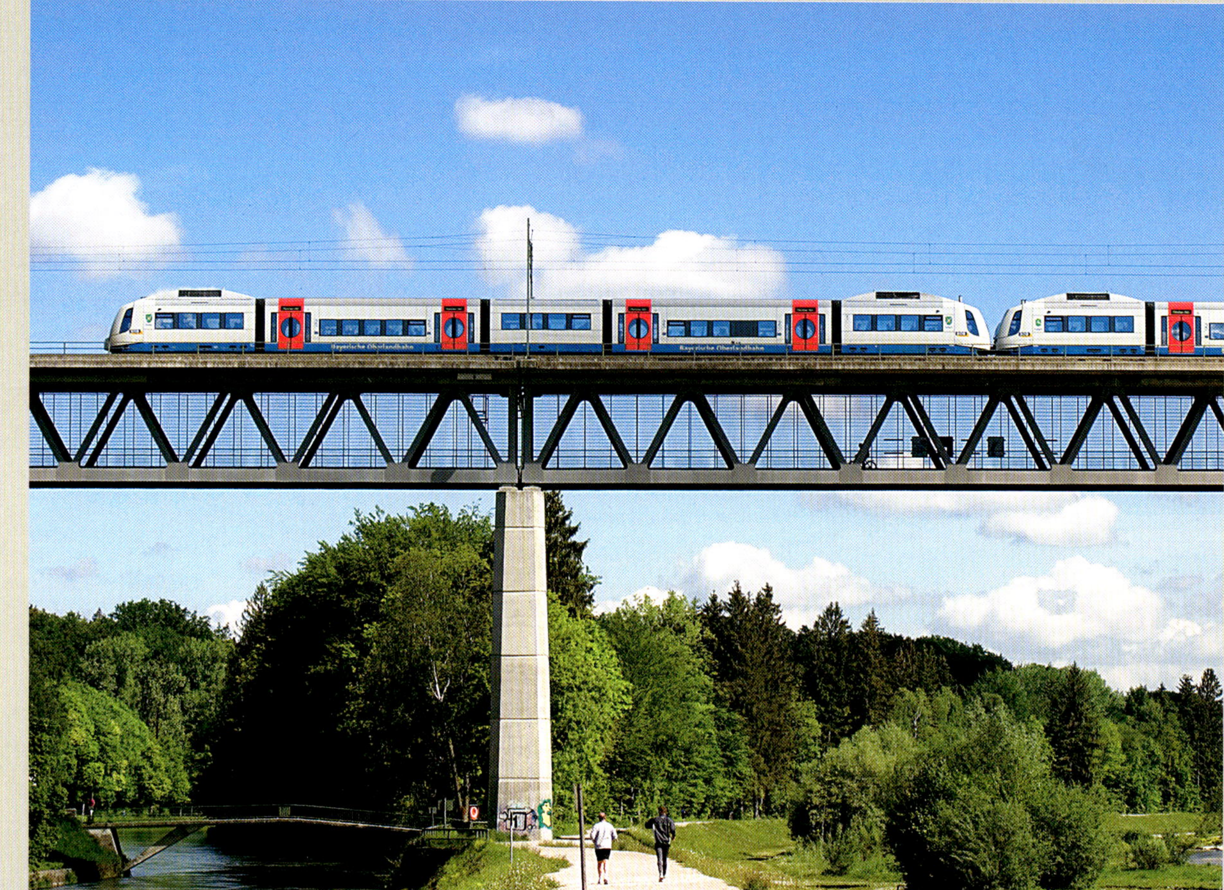

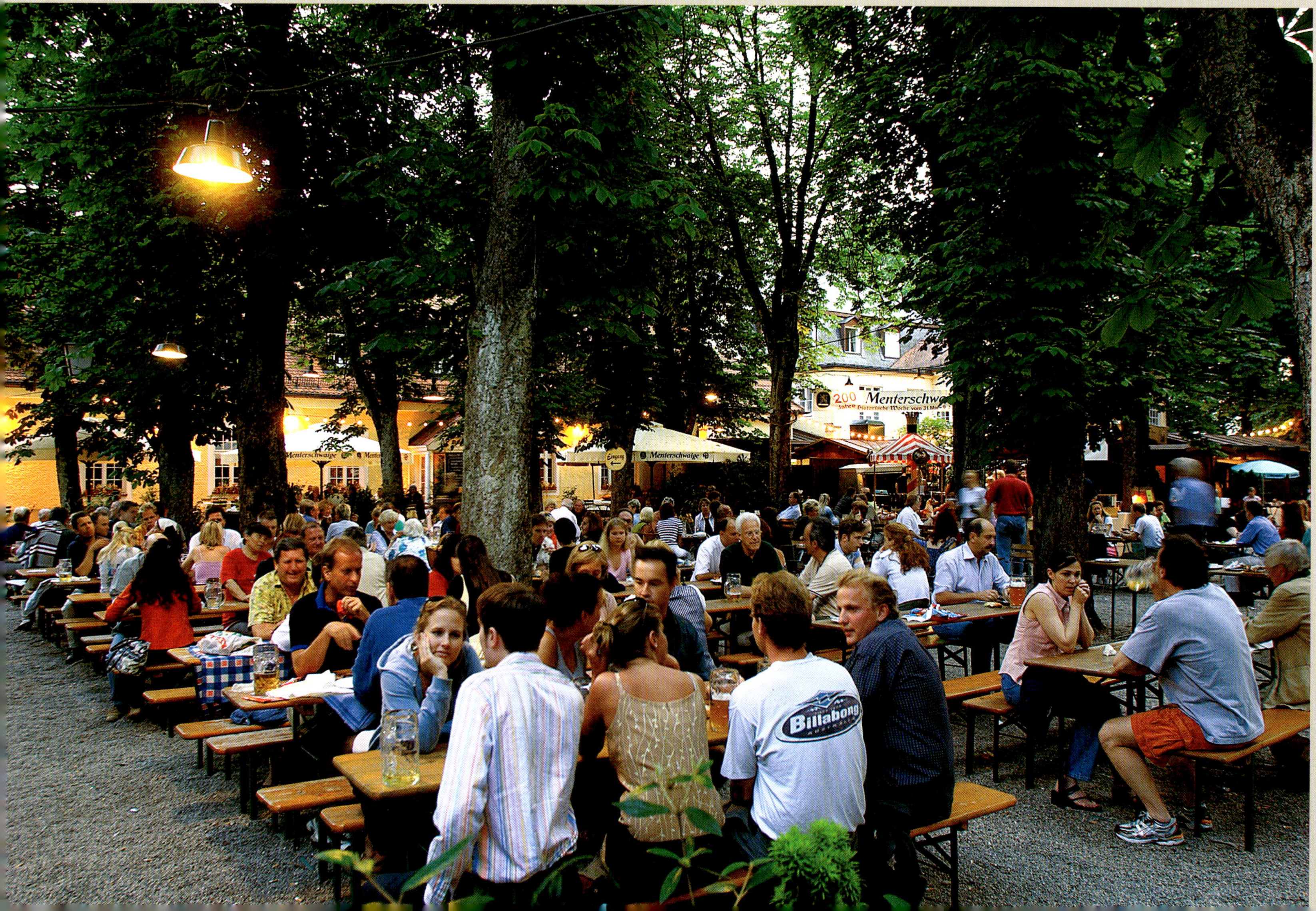

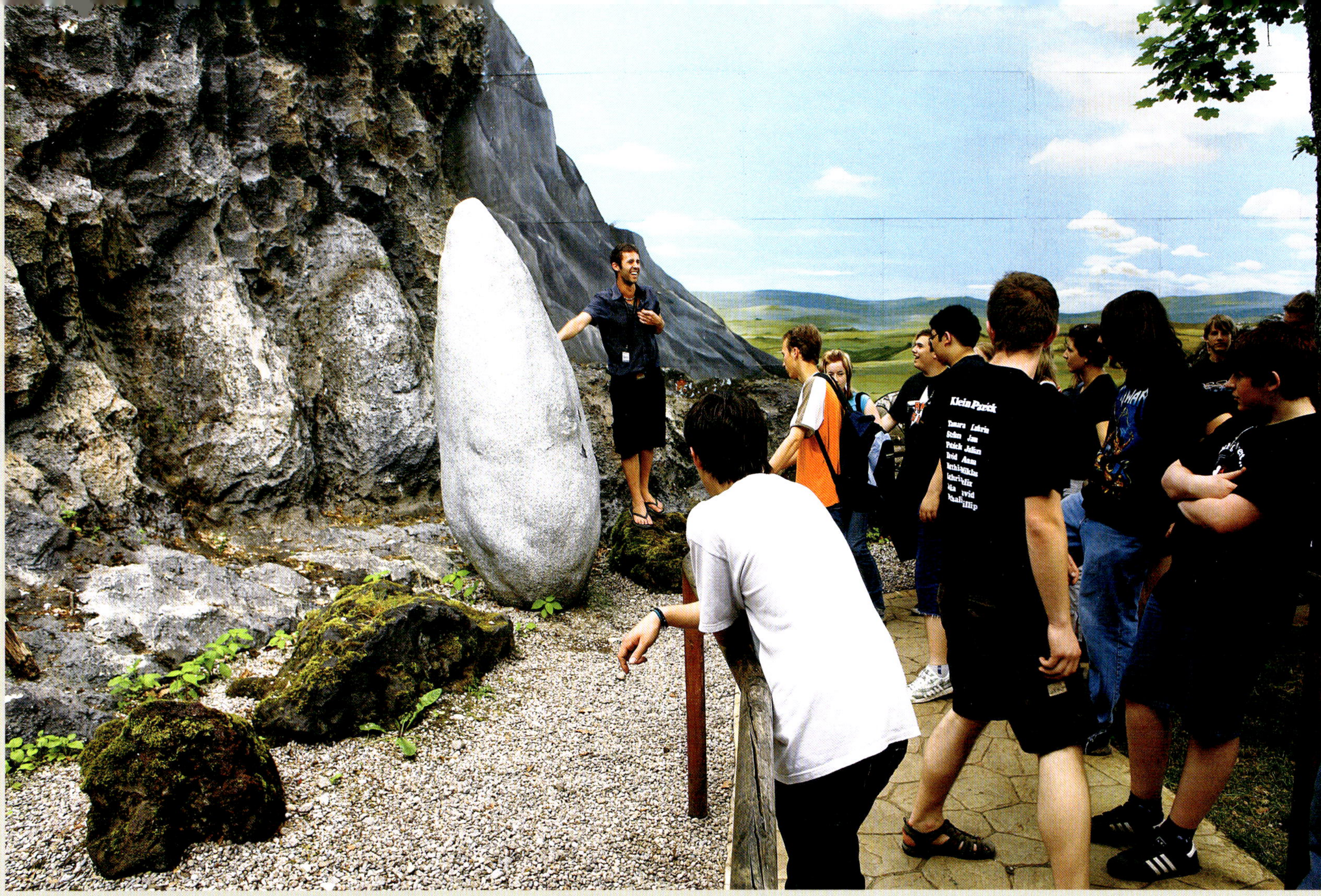

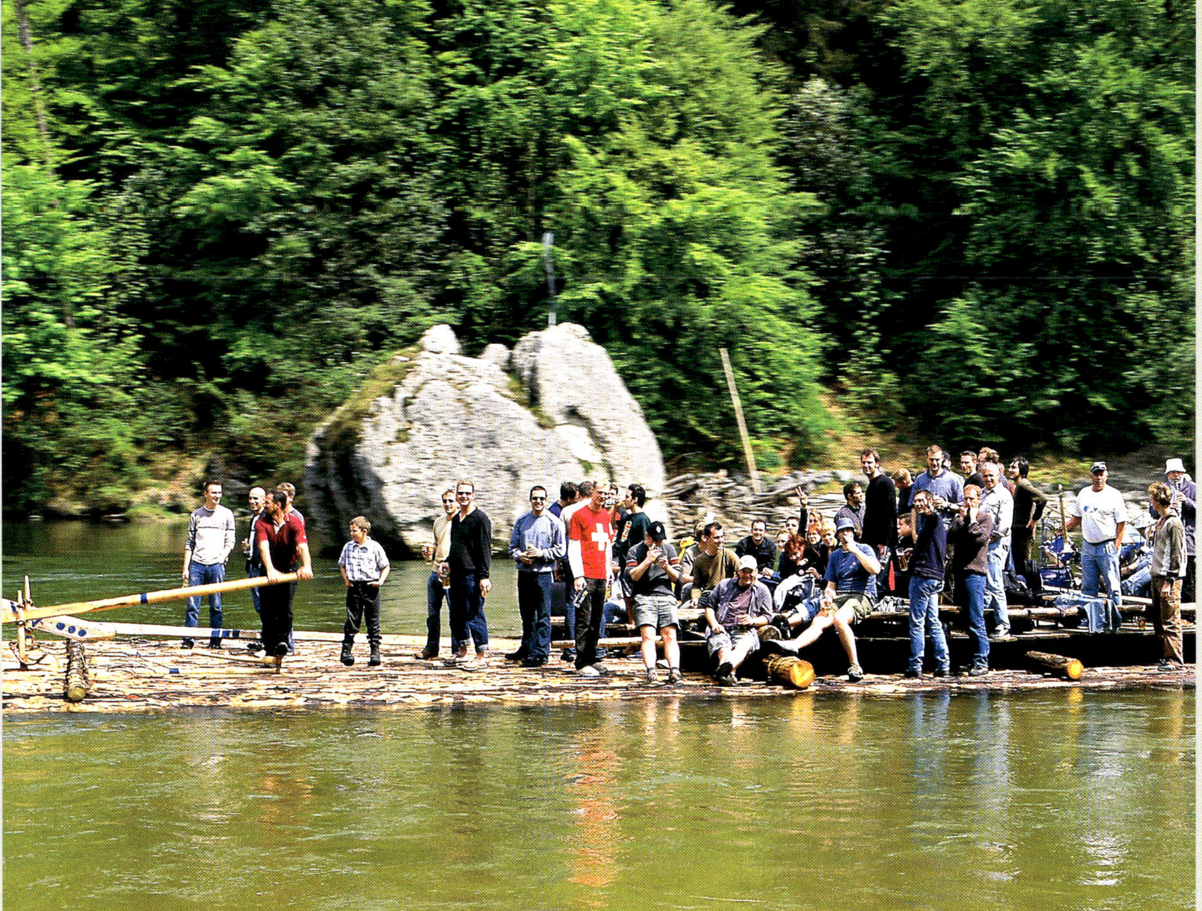

Above:
"The year is 50 BC. Gaul is entirely occupied by the Romans. Well, not entirely ... One small village of indomitable Gauls ..." is just around the corner. Here a set from the film of Asterix at the Bavaria studios.

Left:
The Isar is the fourth longest waterway in Bavaria. In Wolfratshausen, where it joins the Loisach, you can board a raft bound for Thalkirchen. Here rafters pass Georgenstein near Baierbrunn.

Right page:
View of the Oktoberfest from the top of the Big Wheel. The biggest public festival in the world has been held on the Theresienwiese to the west of Munich since 1810 and clocks up over six million visitors a year.

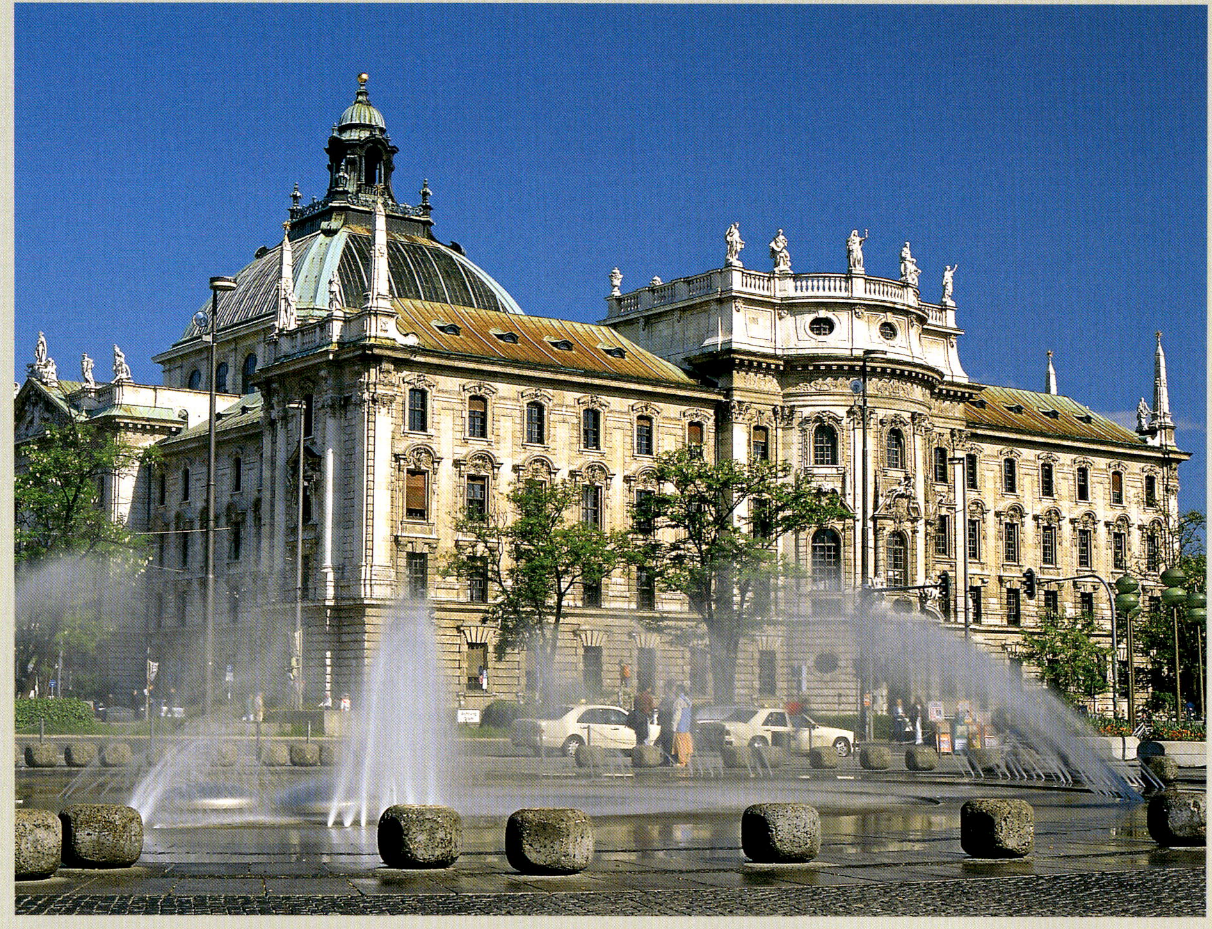

The palace of justice on Stachus (Karlsplatz) was erected in neo-baroque by Munich architect Friedrich von Thiersch (1852–1921) from 1891 to 1898. The glass dome is 67 m (220 ft) high. The palace of justice is the seat of the district and high court. In 1943 this was where the case against the Resistance members of Die Weiße Rose was held.

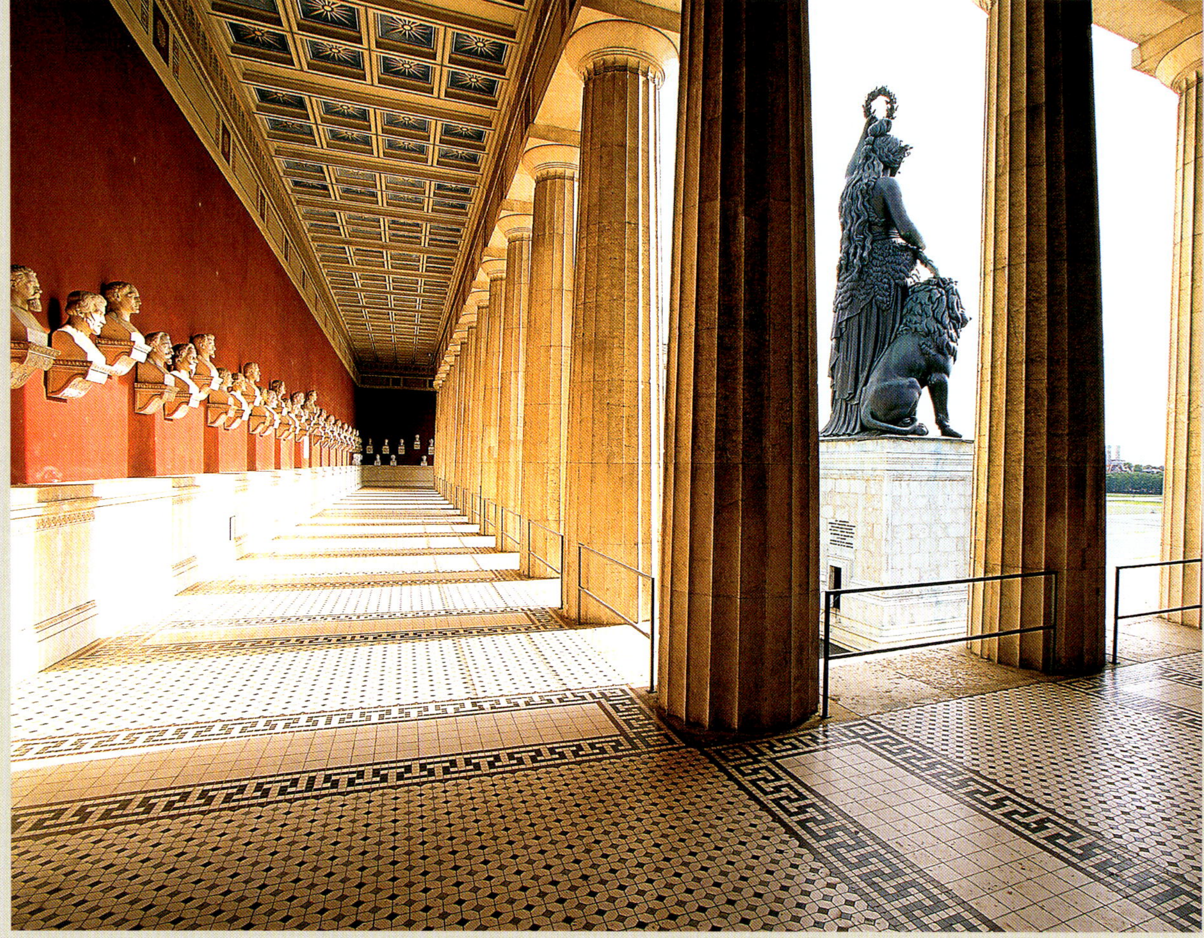

This hill on the western edge of the Theresienwiese is where Leo von Klenze built his hall of fame from 1843 to 1853. The monument contains busts of 95 illustrious Bavarians. The colossal statue of Bavaria outside, unveiled in 1850, was designed by Ludwig Schwanthaler and cast after his death by Ferdinand von Miller. Visitors can go inside it and enjoy the view from the platform inside the head.

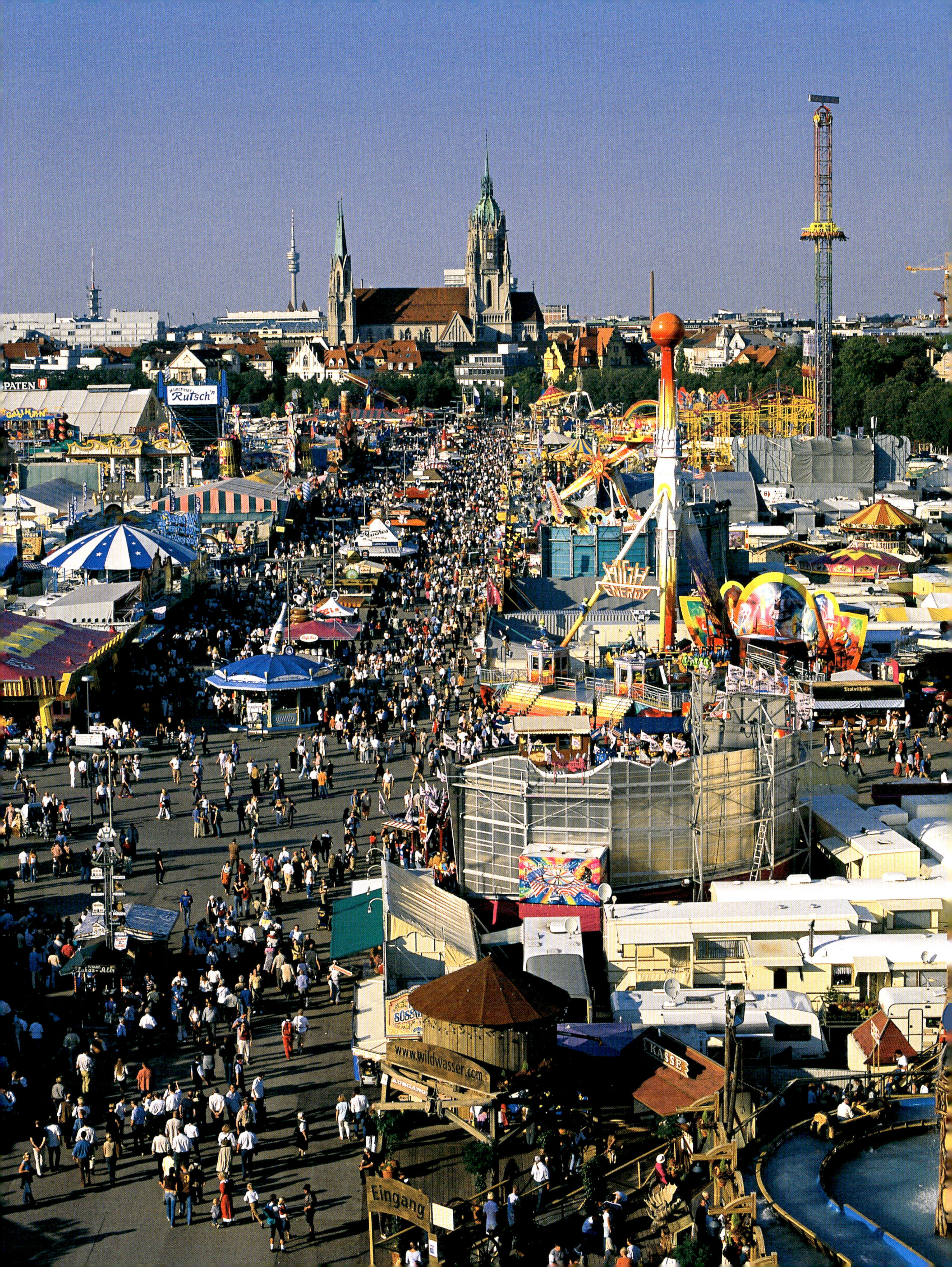
SPATEN
Rutsch'n
HIGH ENERGY
www.wildwasser.com
KASSE
Eingang

THE BIGGEST FESTIVAL OF THEM ALL –

THE OKTOBERFEST

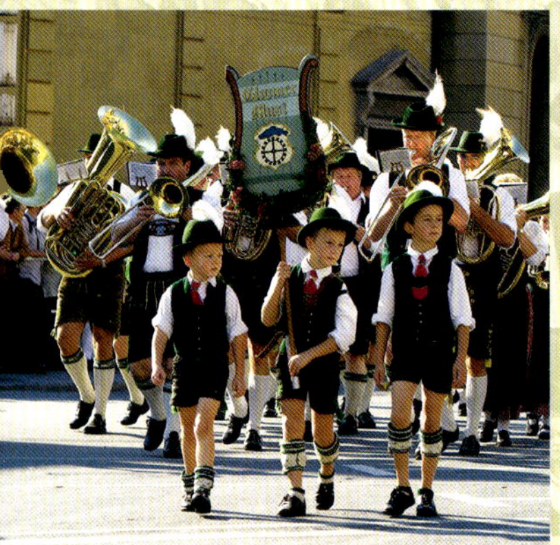

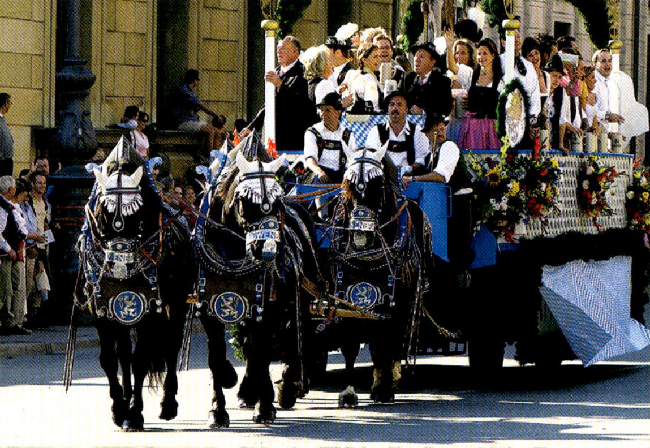

Above:
Among the ca. 9,000 participants are many of Germany's European neighbours, all dolled up in their national costume and many playing their own brand of oompah music.

Above right:
One of the grand highlights of the Oktoberfest is the parade which takes place on the first Sunday of the fair.

Centre:
The "heaven of the Bavarians" is right here, in the Hacker-Pschorr beer tent with its ethereal blue-and-white decor.

The biggest public festival in the world is one superlative after another. Every year over six million people from all corners of the globe positively flock to the Wiesn in droves – from Munich and elsewhere in Germany, from the UK, America, Australia and Japan. To the raucous tones of Bavarian brass bands six million litres of beer are poured down thirsty throats, moistening the remnants of 500,000 fried chickens and 150,000 pairs of pork sausages.

The guests are accommodated in 14 enormous tents – plus a bevy of smaller awnings. There's enough room for about 100,000 backsides and generally you have to be in possession of a seat if you want to be served one of those huge frothing glasses of beer. In between hefty swigs punters test their strength with finger tugs-of-war and beer mug wrestling. Some also try out their personal allure on their fellow visitors, seeing if the recently purchased lederhosen are suitably flattering to ensnare a member of the opposite sex for the duration.

With so many hormones flying about it's hardly surprising that the festival is also visited by a positive army of not-so-welcome callers. The police are on duty round the clock during the 16 to 18 days of the big bun fight, rushing to the aid of women who have been sexually assaulted or even raped. Pickpockets and thieves are in their element and the amount of alcohol consumed often sparks off nasty drunken brawls. Since 2005 the organisers have been trying to tone things down a bit. Under the concept of "ruhige Wiesn" (peace at the Wiesn) traditional band music is only played until 6 pm, with rock and pop to follow but no louder than 85 decibels. The call for last orders is at 10.30 pm.

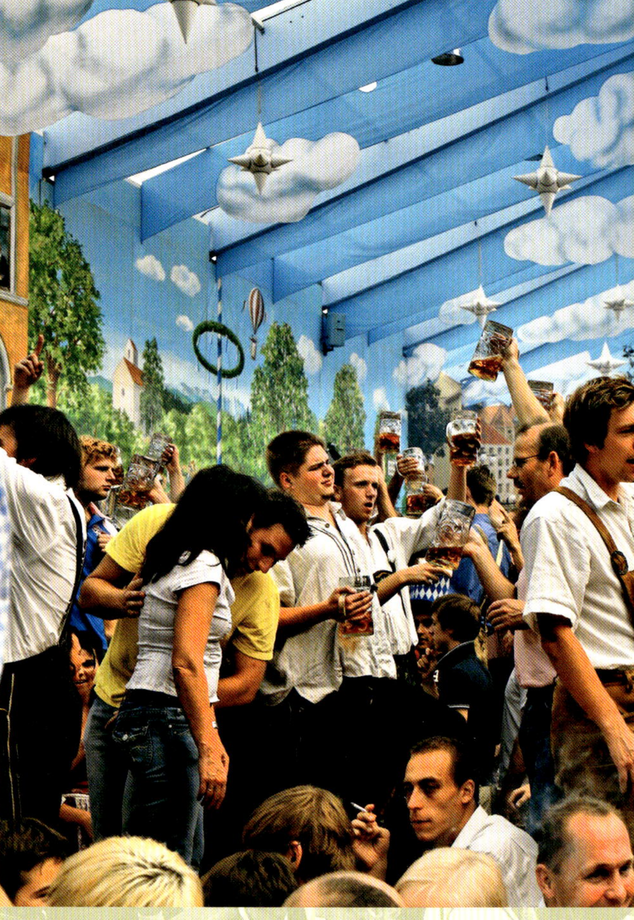

A RIGHT ROYAL WEDDING

The Oktoberfest dates back to 1810. To celebrate the occasion of his son Ludwig's wedding to Princess Therese Charlotte Luise von Sachsen-Hildburghausen king of Bavaria Max Joseph I threw a huge party on the "big field near Sendling", to be staged once a year, hence the name Theresienwiese or Therese's meadow. In

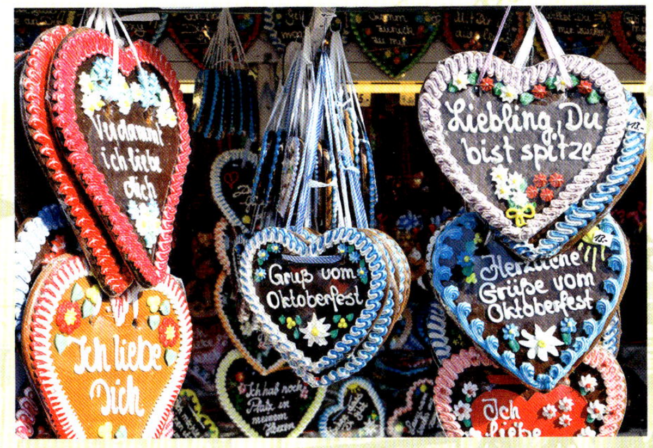

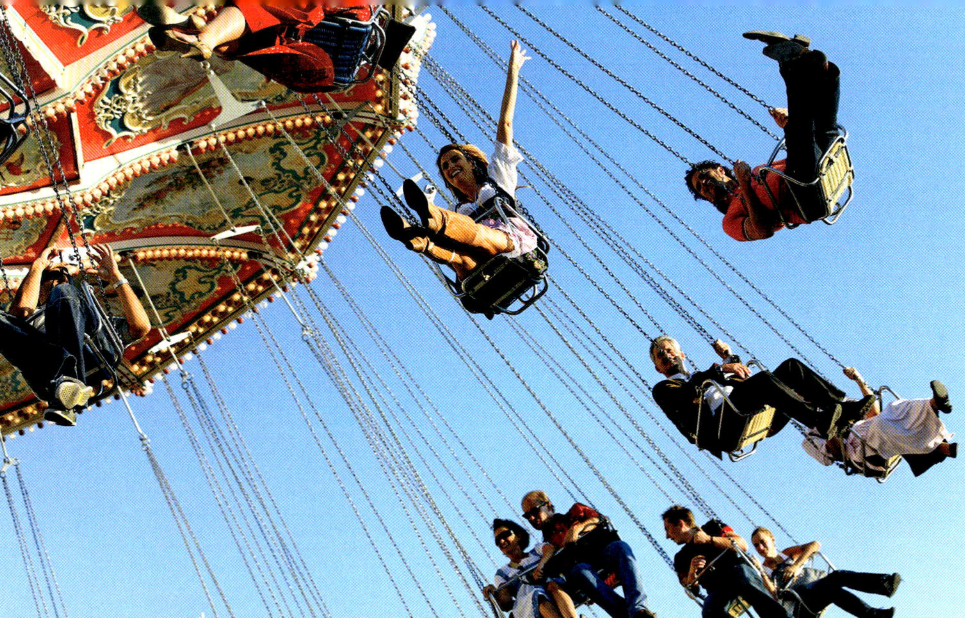

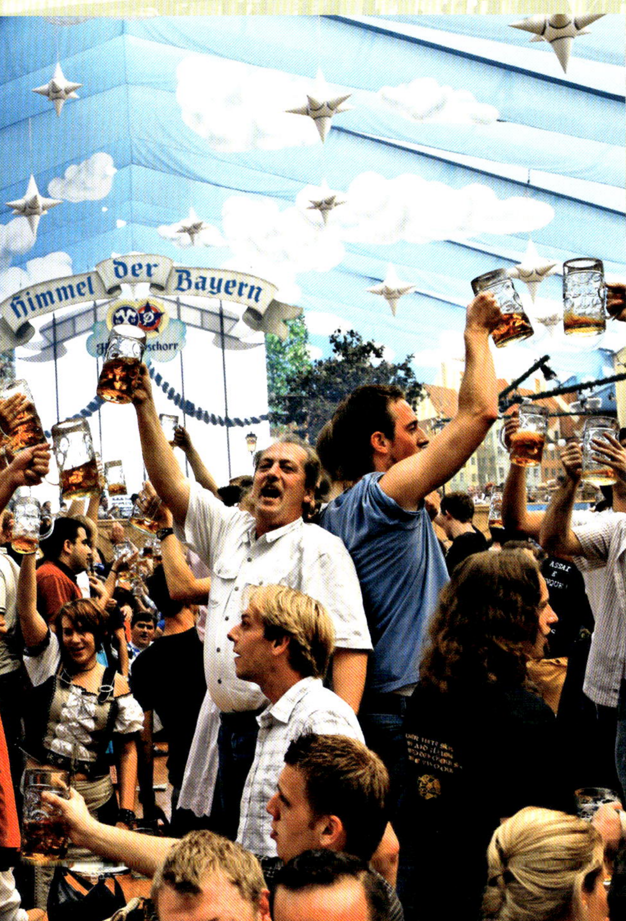

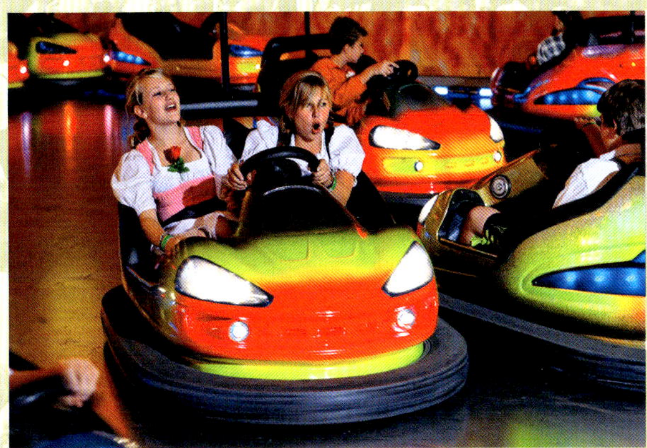

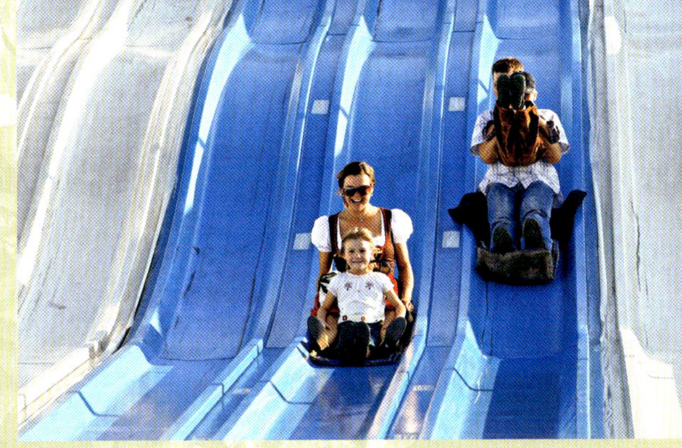

the 200 years since its initiation the festival has been cancelled 24 times – due to the outbreak of war, cholera and the hyperinflation of the 1920s. A bomb set off by right-wing extremists on September 26, 1980, resulted in 13 dead and 211 wounded and was the biggest terrorist attack in Germany since the end of the Second World War. The Oktoberfest wasn't cancelled, however, but merely put on hold for just one day, causing something of an uproar. Bomb or no bomb, the Oktoberfest means business; it has a turnover of around a billion euros and provides 12,000 people with work.

Another bone of contention is the actual amount of beer poured into the mugs; a Maß should hold one litre and not a drop less! Possibly fraudulent levels are controlled by the Verein gegen betrügerisches Einschenken set up in 1899. Glass Maßkrüge were introduced in 1892; traditionalists insist on using the grey steins many of us are familiar with in conjunction with German beer. Tradition is writ large at the Oktoberfest which in 1872 was moved from October to September in the hope of more clement weather. It officially ends on the first Sunday in October or on the Day of German Unity. On the first day of the festival the brewers parade their ornately decorated beer wagons to the Wiesn where on the stroke of midday the lord mayor of Munich ceremoniously broaches the first keg of beer, crying out the words everybody has been eagerly waiting for: *"O'zapft is!"*

Above left:
These gingerbread hearts are always a tricky one: should you eat it now or keep it as a souvenir? Whatever – just don't leave the Oktoberfest without one!

Above:
Tradition may be writ large here but so is all the fun of the fair, with the merry-go-round one of the oldest rides to be had here.

Left:
About 80 fairground rides and booths provide plenty of amusement during the Oktoberfest.

Below:
This positively enormous plastic slide is one of the newer attractions. Carpet, anyone?

The Theresienwiese isn't only used for the Oktoberfest. The Tollwood Festival, for example, is held twice a year, in summer in the Olympiapark and here in the winter.

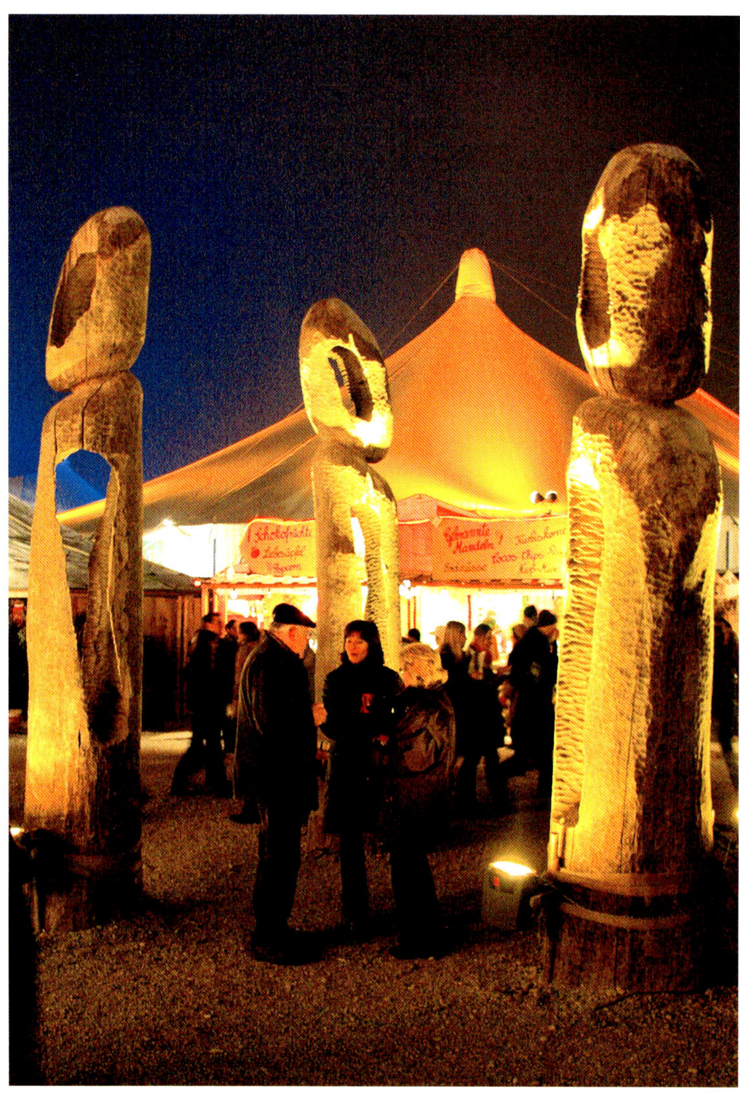

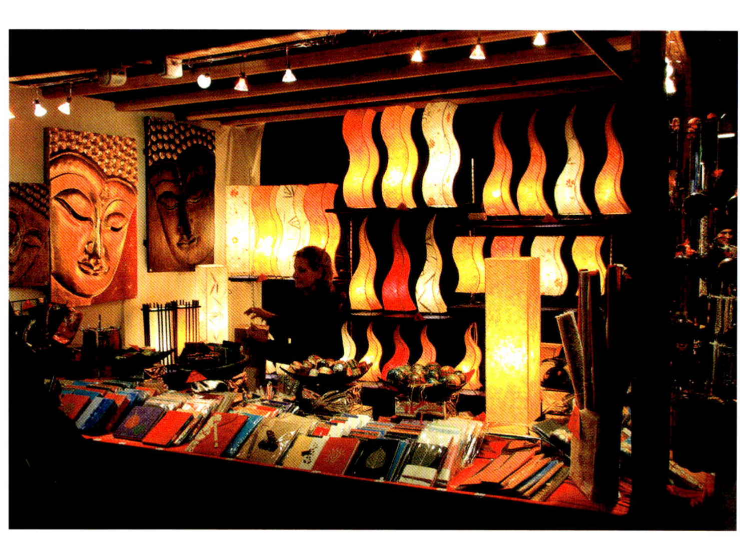

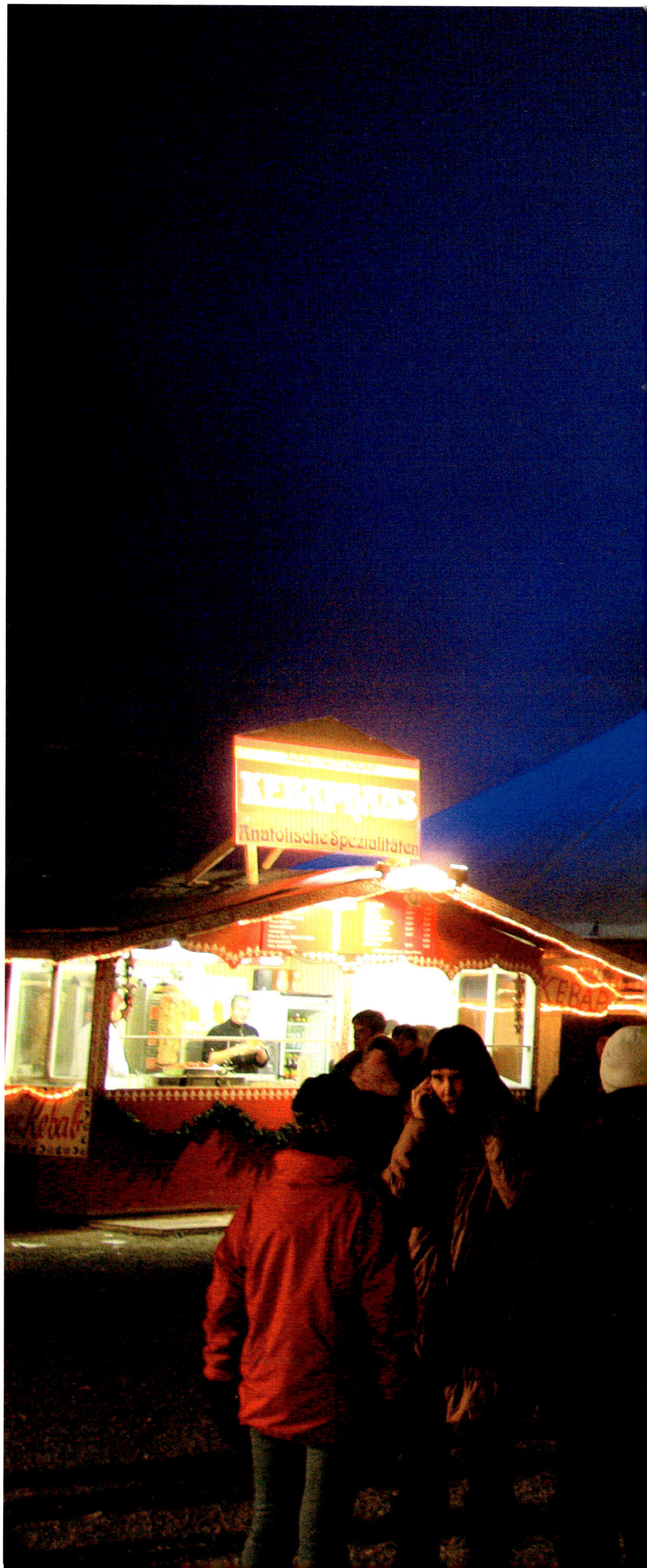

At Tollwood you can mosey on down to music from to rock to singer-songwriter to jazz and blues, take in various theatrical performances or just browse the many interesting artefacts on display and sale here.

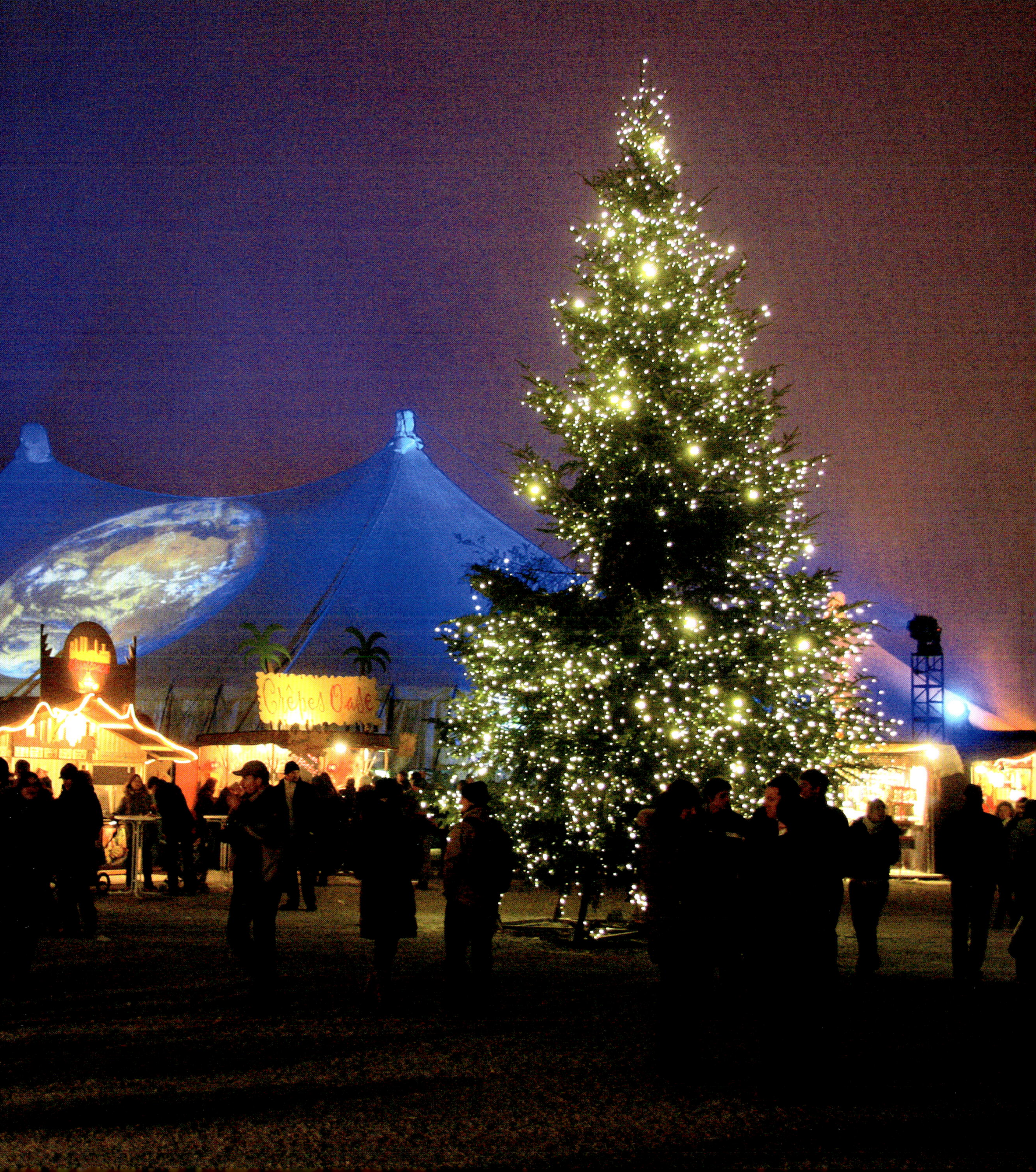
Crêpes Oase

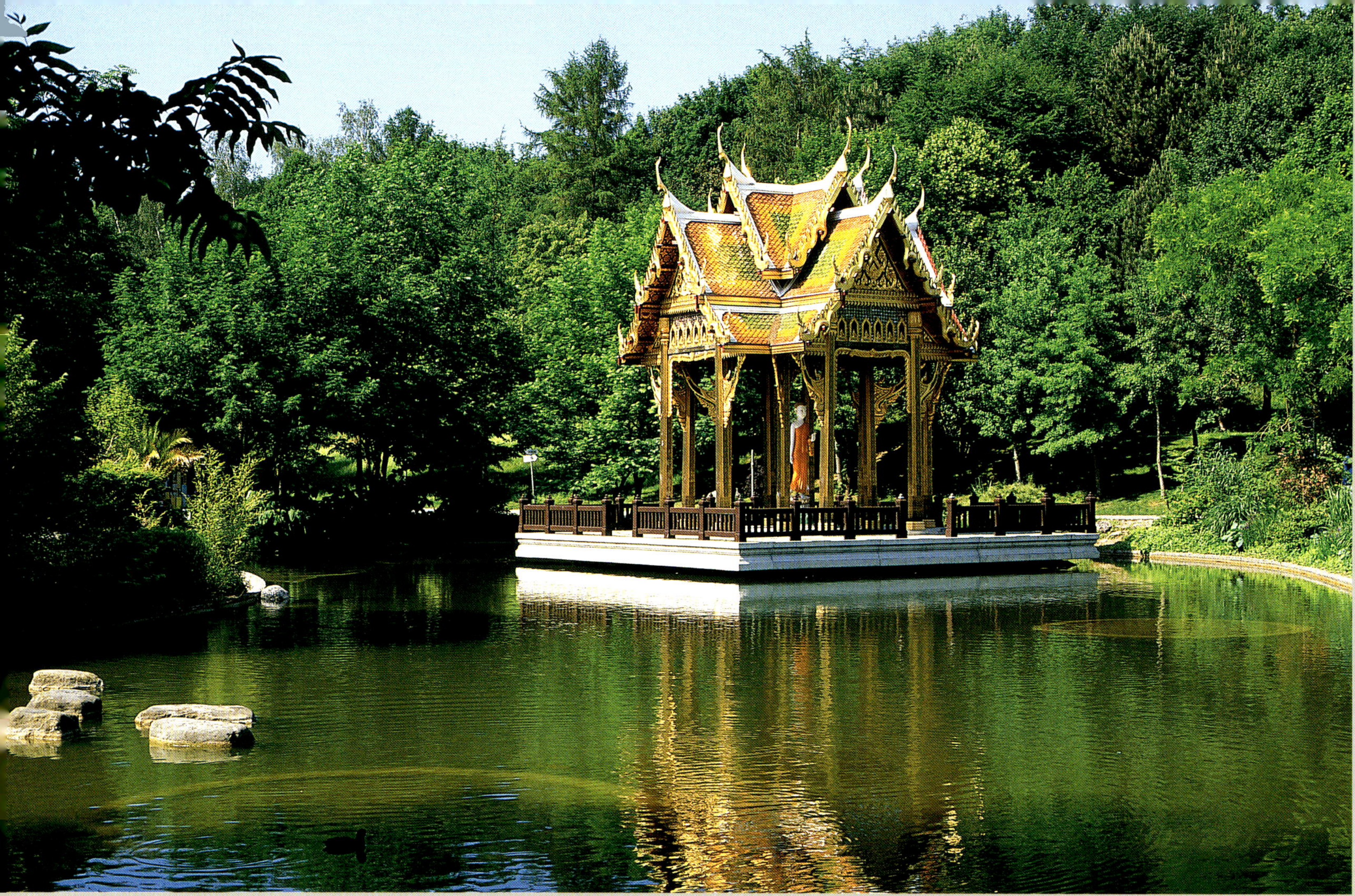

Above:
Westpark in the suburb of Sendling-Westpark fills no less than 72 hectares (178 acres). It was laid out for the Internationale Gartenbauausstellung or international exhibition of garden design in 1983. One of the attractions is this tall Thai sala or open pavilion. Every April the Thai New Year is celebrated here and in October the Hindu festival of light Divali. The Buddhist community holds it full moon celebrations here in summer.

Right:
Several hundred years old, this house was removed from the Bavarian Forest and reassembled in the Westpark for the 1983 garden exhibition.

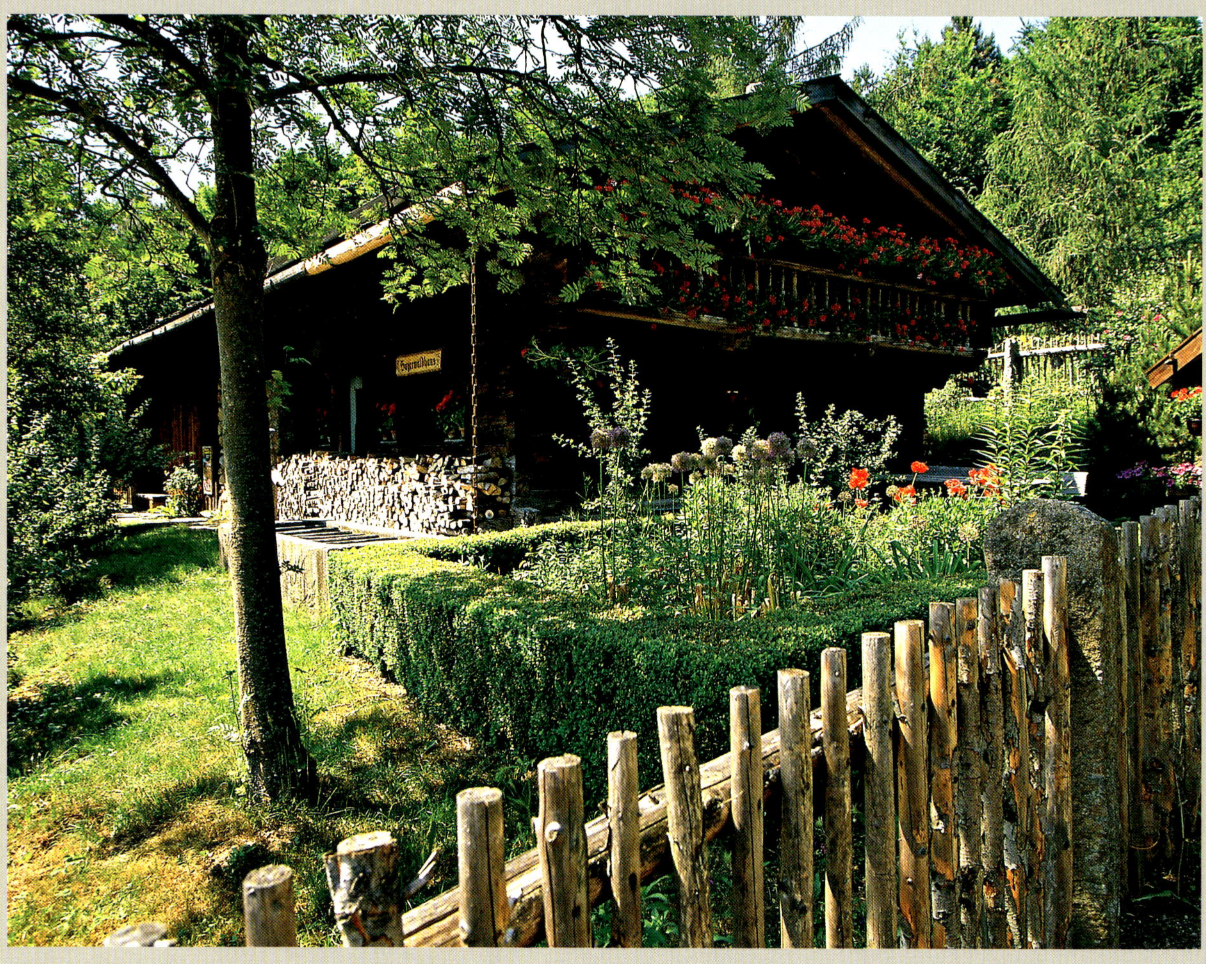

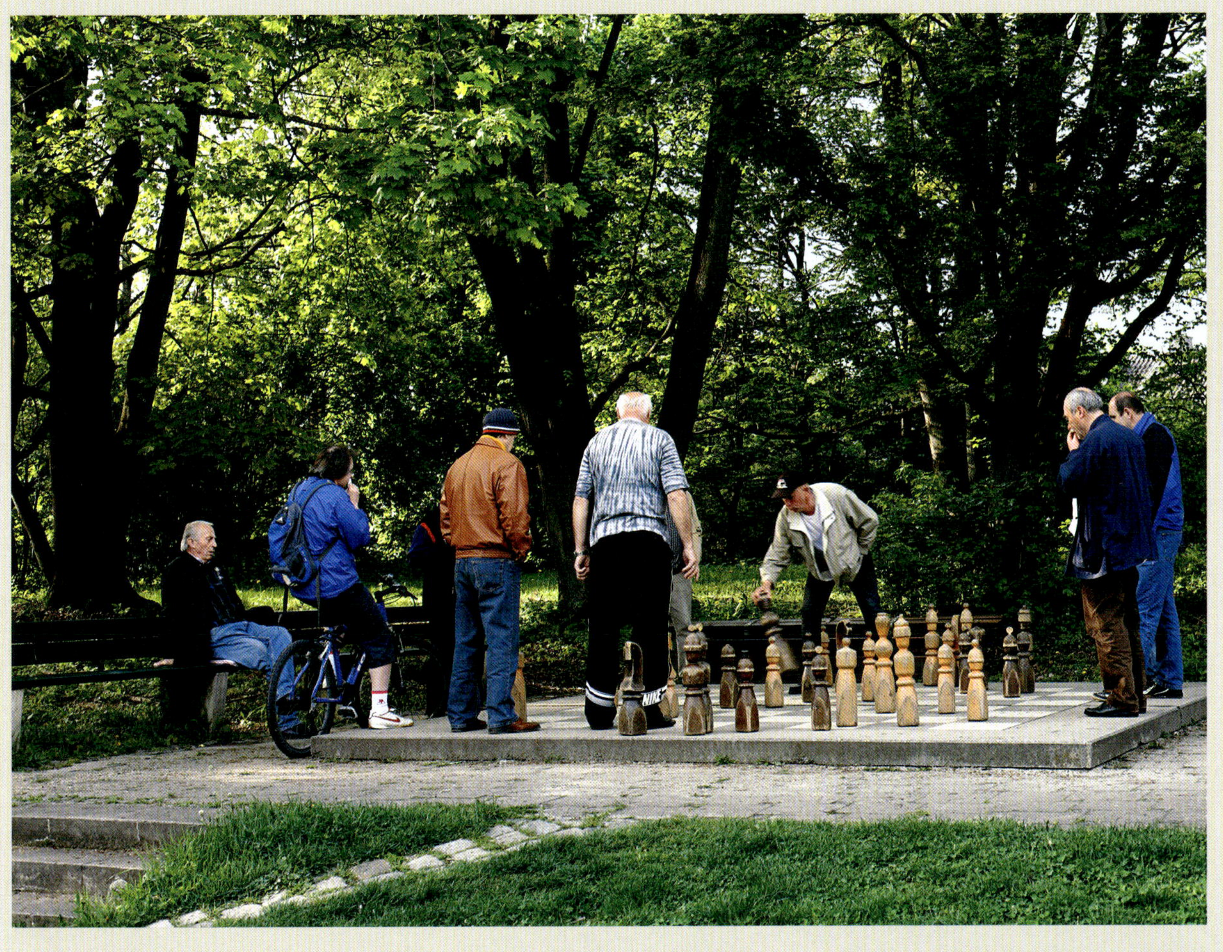

Left:
Hirschgarten in the west of Munich is characterised by its many hilly meadows and trees which are 150 years old. Here you can while way the summer hours playing table tennis and chess, do some tobogganing or curling in the winter – or simply just go for a nice long walk, whatever the weather.

Below:
Hirschgarten was set up by Elector Karl Theodor in 1780 as a deer park for the aristocracy and turned into a public park in the 1950s. The park not only has deer but also beer – served at the supposedly biggest beer garden in Europe with a staggering capacity of 8,000 seats.

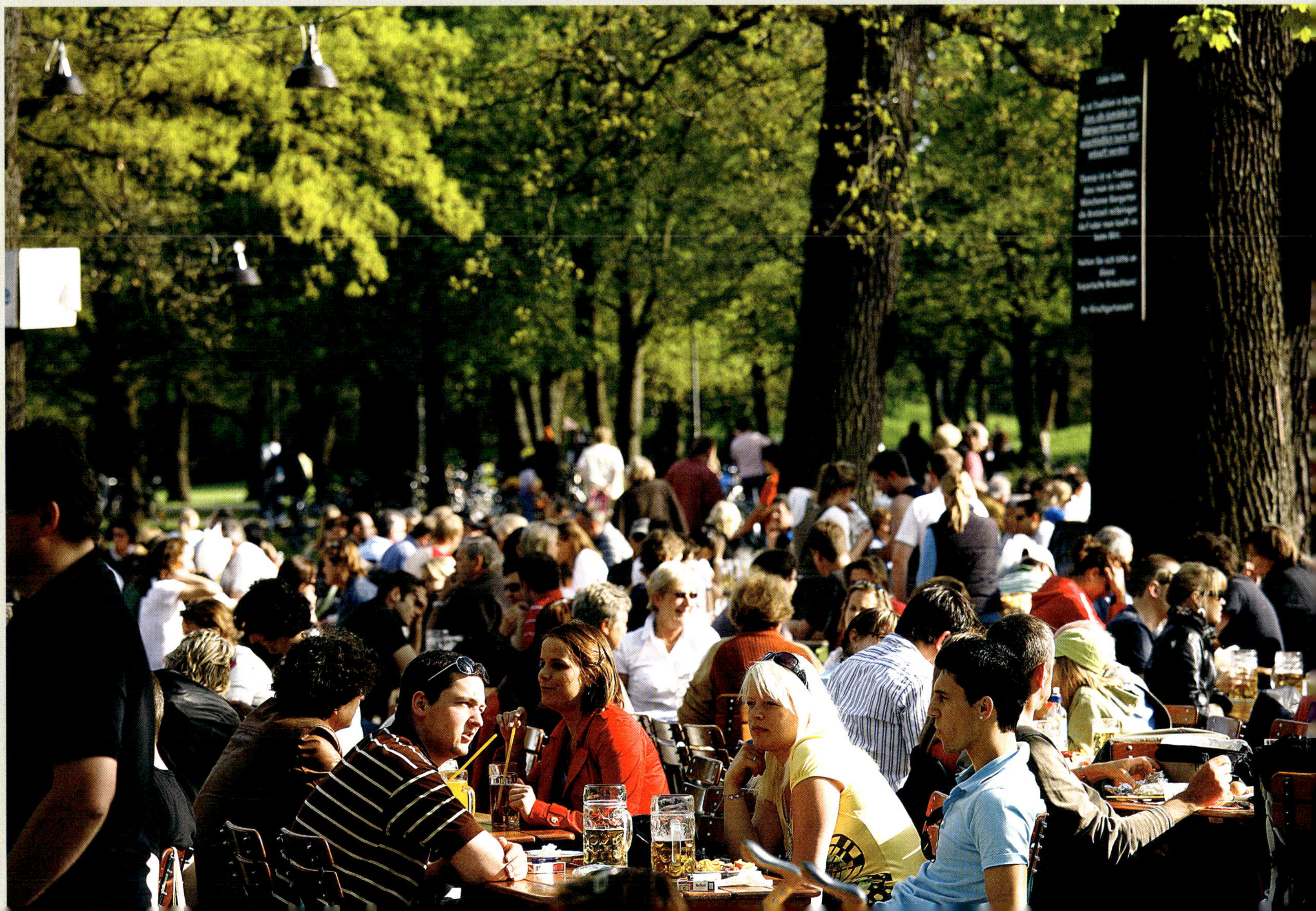

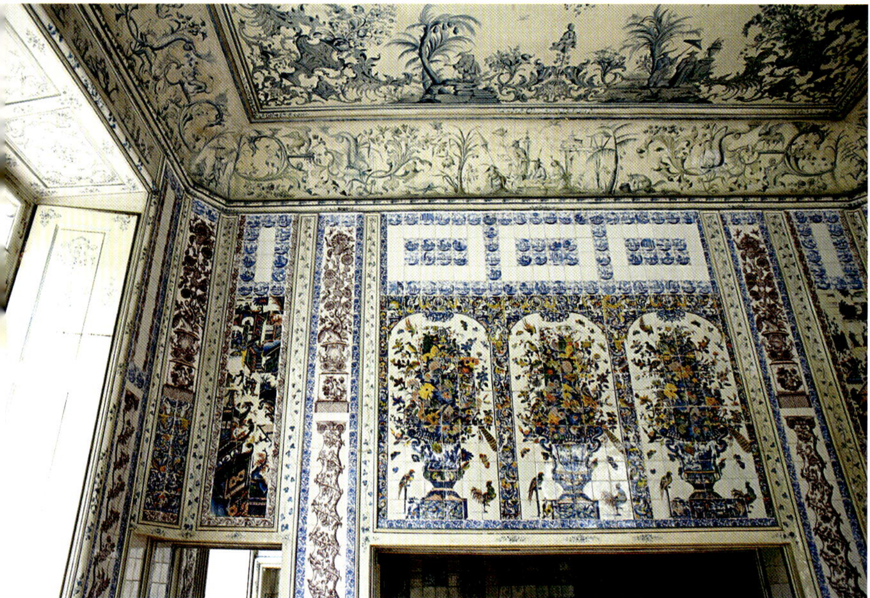

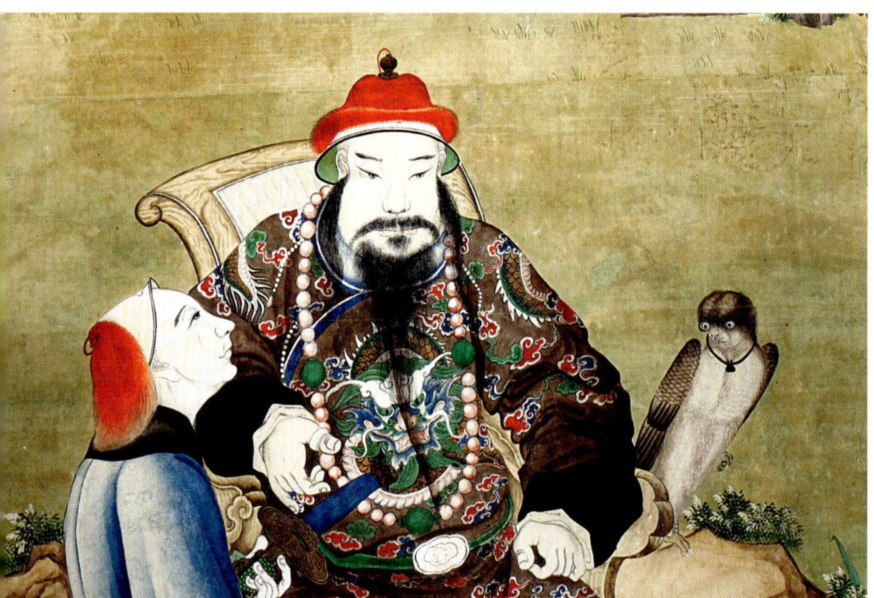

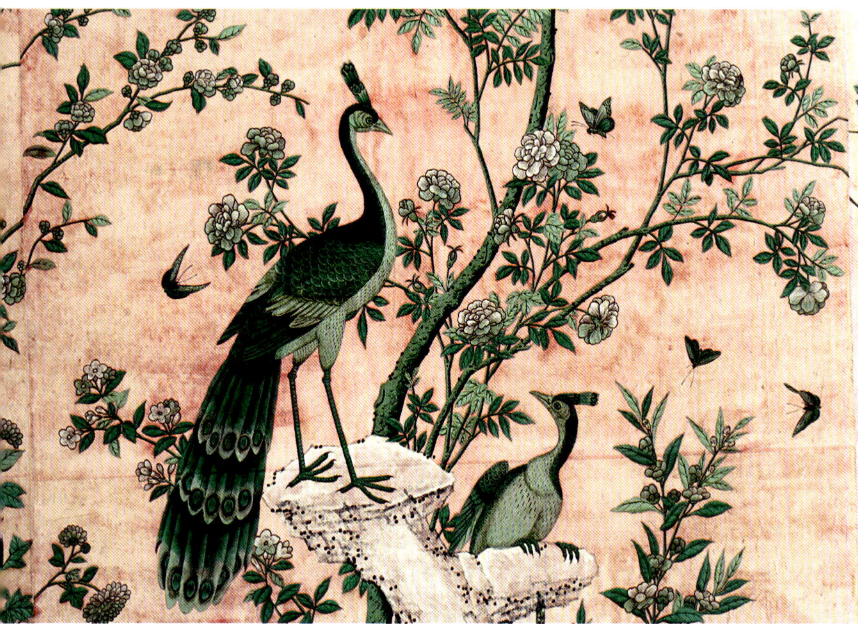

Top left:
The 'castles' in the Schlosspark at Nymphenburg are royal residences in miniature. The one-storey Amalienburg, for example, was a present from Elector Karl Albrecht to his wife Maria Amalie. It was built as a lodge for pheasant hunting in 1734–1739 from plans by François Cuvilliés the Elder. Its marvellous kitchen is tiled with Delftware.

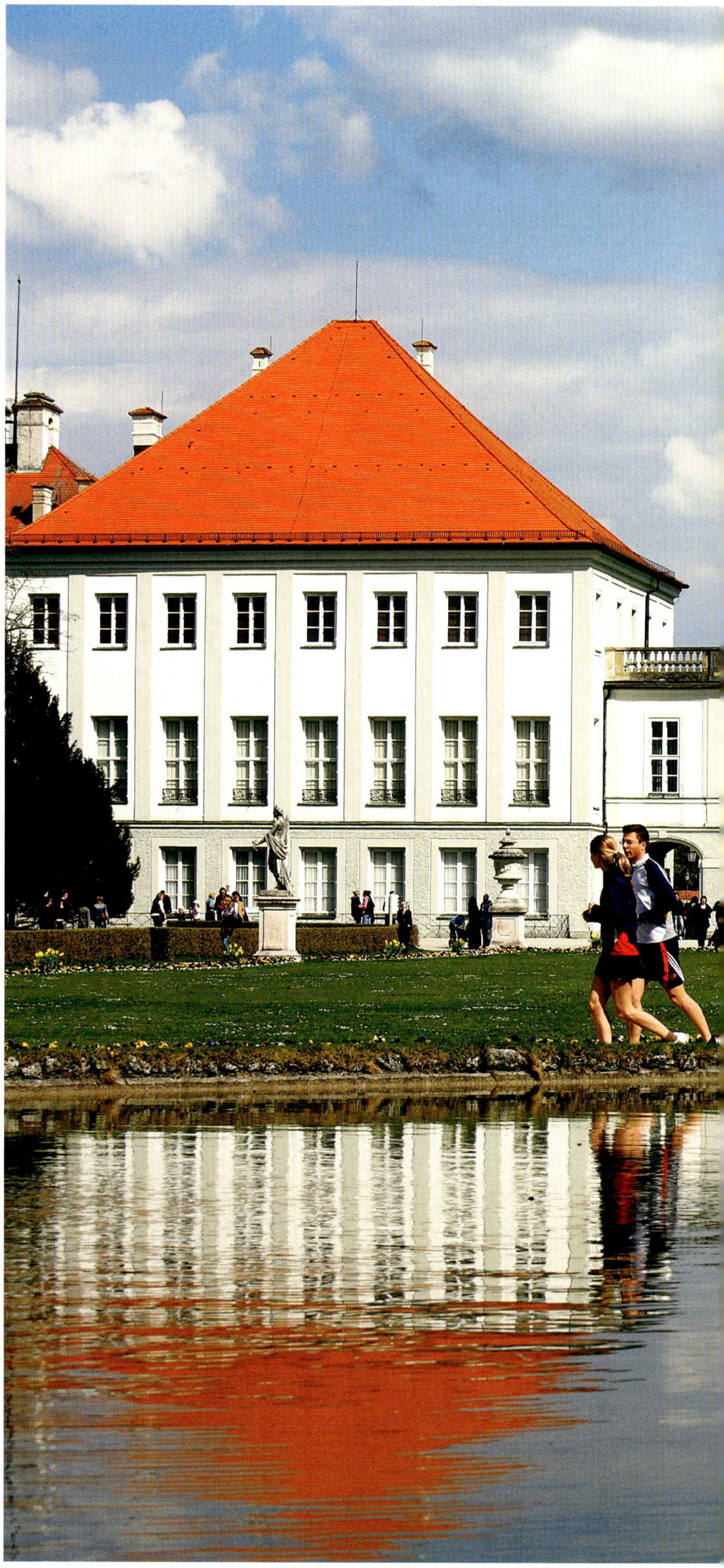

Centre and bottom left:
The Badenburg was built by Joseph Effner between 1718 and 1722. One of its purposes was to provide visitors with a decent place for a bath. The bathroom fills both the cellar and ground floor and boasts an enormous tub measuring 8.7 x 6.1 m (28.5 x 20 ft). Three rooms are papered with a Chinese print. Two of them depict scenes from everyday life in the Far East; the third has illustrations of plants, birds and butterflies in pink and green.

Below:
Schloss Nymphenburg, seen here from the park, is considered to be one of the most beautiful palaces in the world. In 1664 Elector Ferdinand Maria commissioned the building as a gift for his wife Adelheid of Savoy. Architect Agostino Barelli worked on the palace until 1675; others who actively contributed to its later extension and refurbishment include Enrico Zucalli and Giovanni Antonio Viscardi.

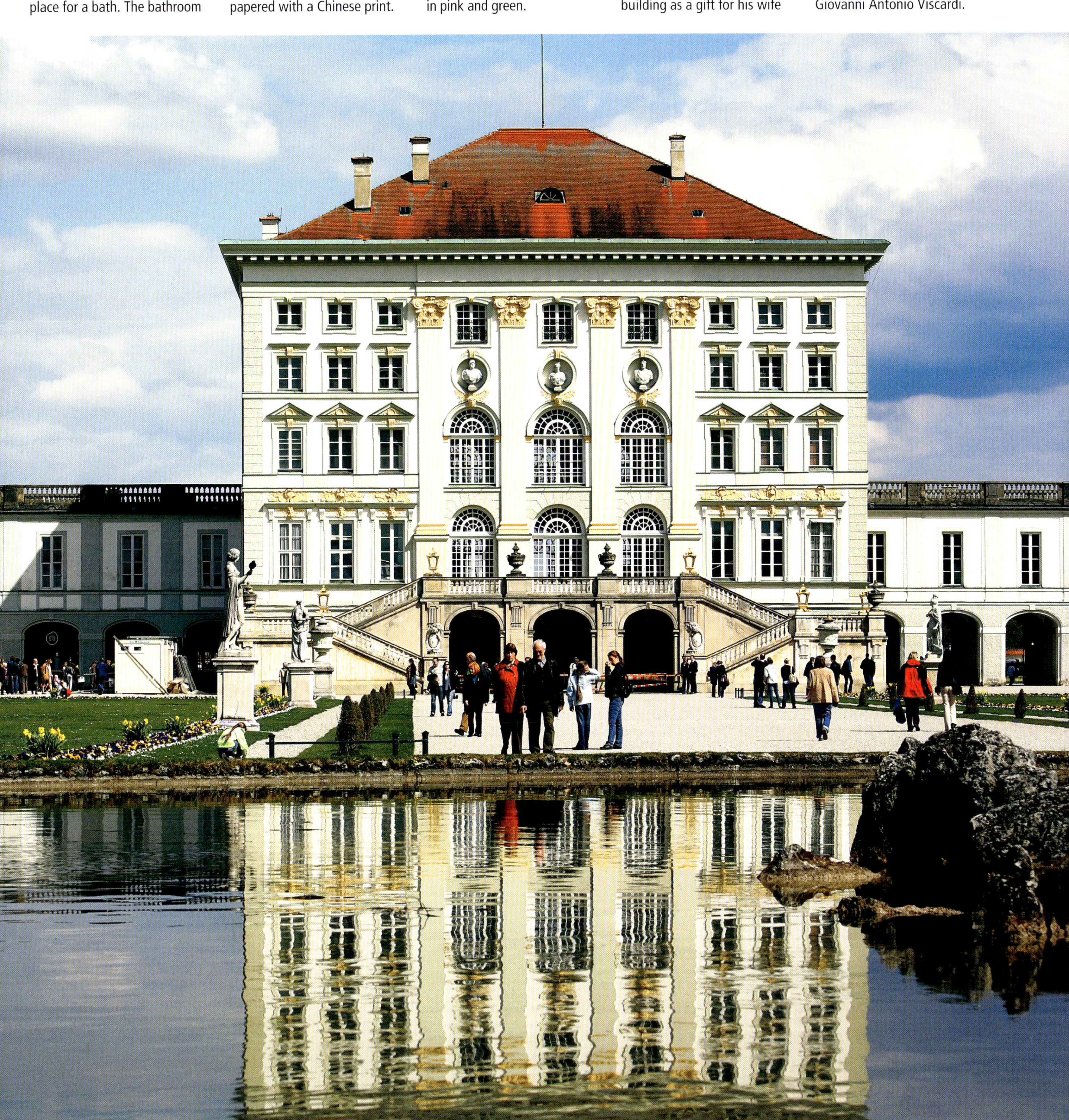

Below and bottom:
A set of botanical gardens skirts the palace park of Nymphenburg to the north. About 14,000 types of plant are cultivated here. The greenhouse complex is enormous and nurtures plants from all kinds of different habitats, including cacti from the American desert. Tropical fish, turtles and butterflies also thrive in the botanical gardens.

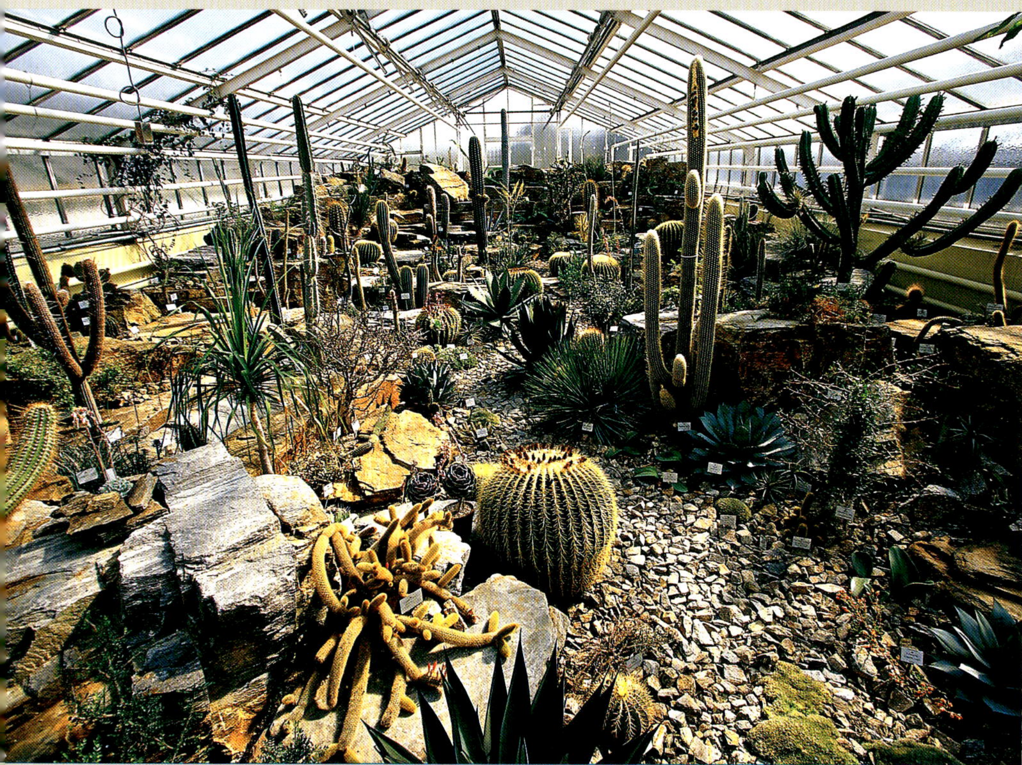

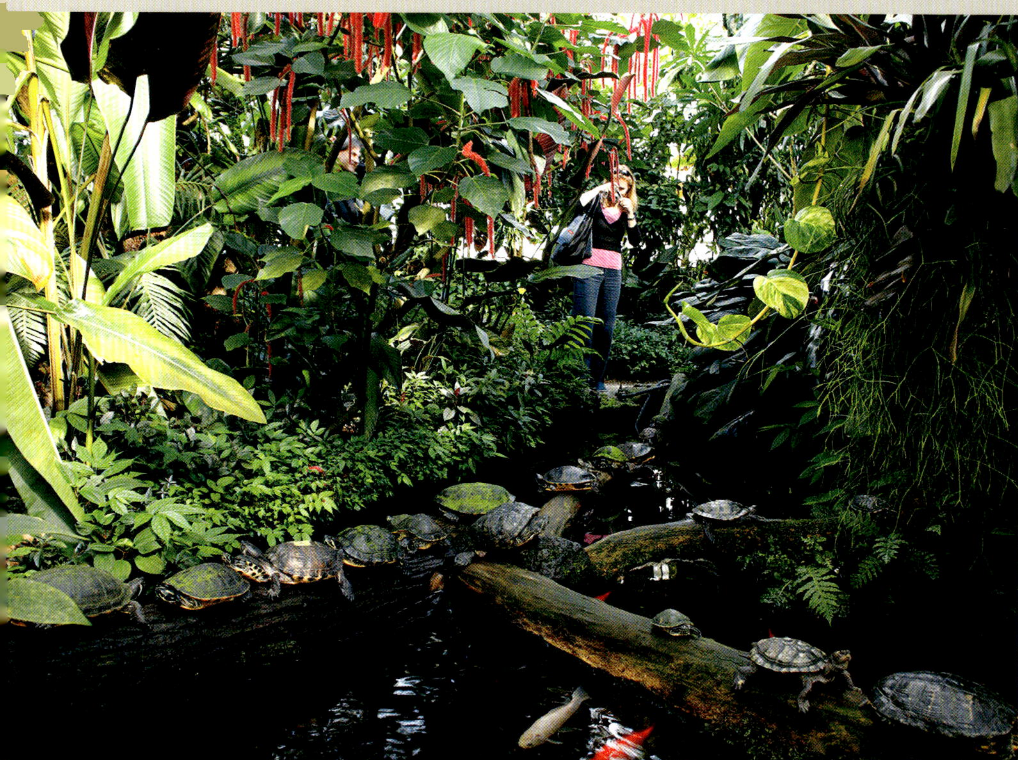

Right:
Late Gothic Schloss Blutenburg lies to the west of town and is surrounded by the River Würm, making it seem as if it's been built on an island. It dates back to a moated fortress from the 13th century. The castle is now the seat of an international library for young people.

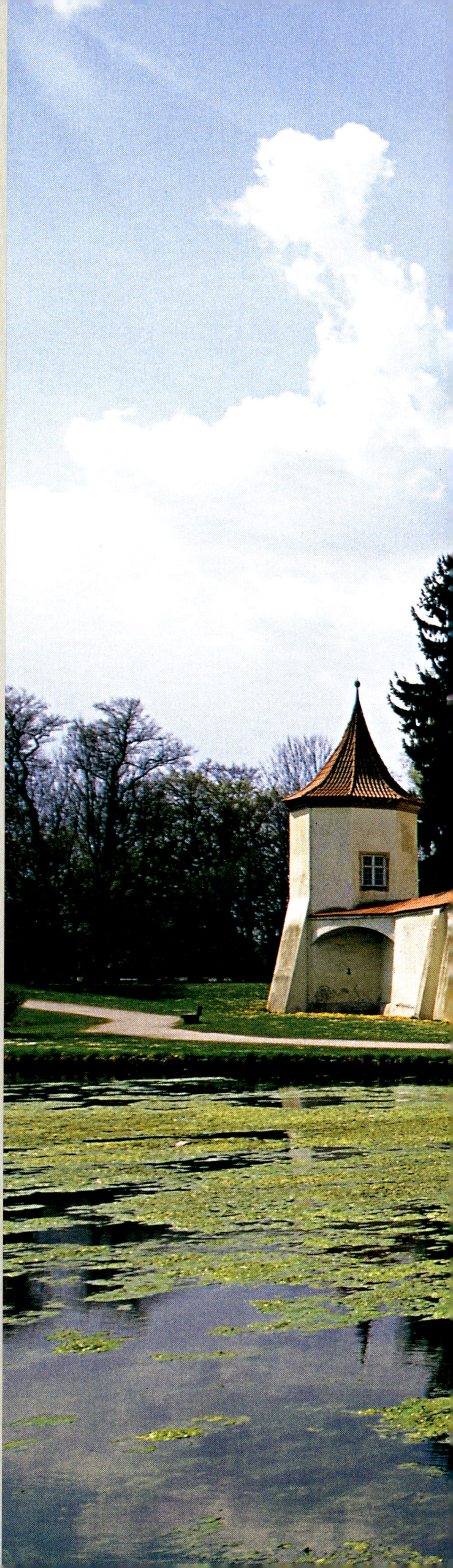

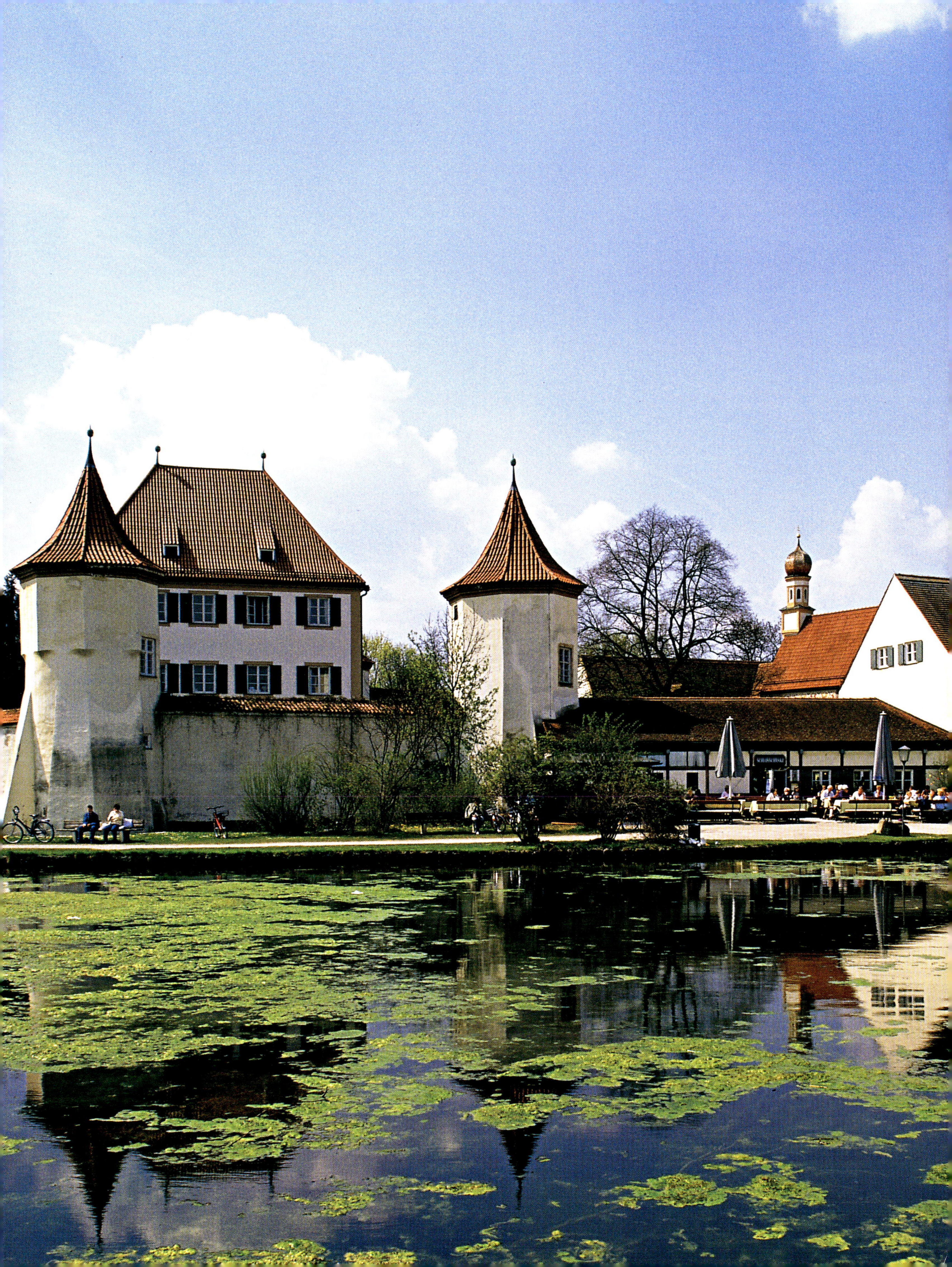

INDEX

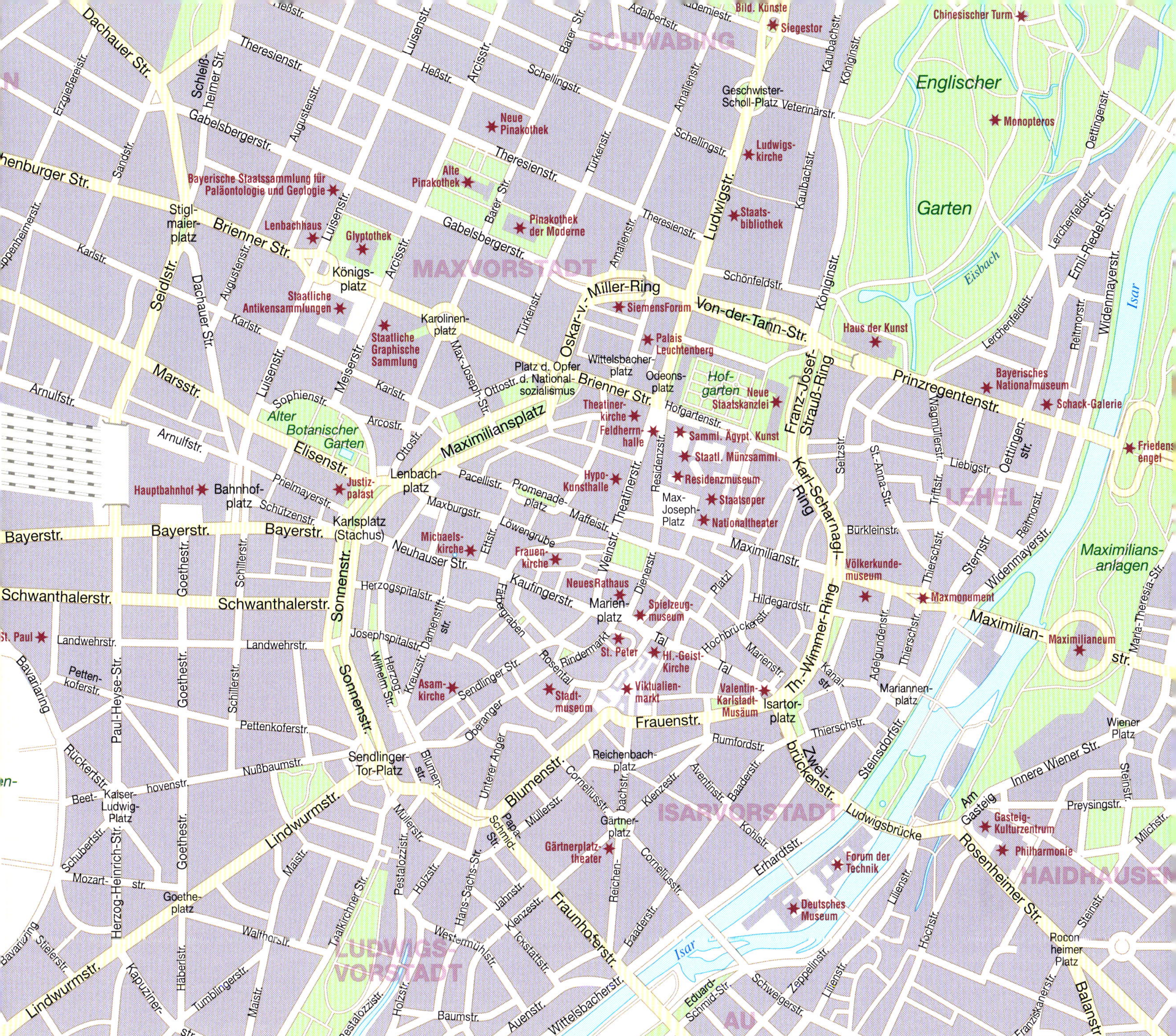

SCHWABING
MAXVORSTADT
LEHEL
ISARVORSTADT
HAIDHAUSEN
LUDWIGSVORSTADT
AU
Englischer Garten
Eisbach
Isar
Maximiliansanlagen
Alter Botanischer Garten
Hofgarten
Chinesischer Turm
Monopteros
Bild. Künste
Siegestor
Neue Pinakothek
Alte Pinakothek
Pinakothek der Moderne
Bayerische Staatssammlung für Paläontologie und Geologie
Lenbachhaus
Glyptothek
Staatliche Antikensammlungen
Staatliche Graphische Sammlung
Ludwigskirche
Staatsbibliothek
SiemensForum
Palais Leuchtenberg
Haus der Kunst
Bayerisches Nationalmuseum
Schack-Galerie
Friedensengel
Neue Staatskanzlei
Theatinerkirche
Feldherrnhalle
Samml. Ägypt. Kunst
Staatl. Münzsamml.
Residenzmuseum
Staatsoper
Nationaltheater
Hypo-Kunsthalle
Justizpalast
Hauptbahnhof
Michaelskirche
Frauenkirche
Neues Rathaus
Spielzeugmuseum
St. Peter
Hl.-Geist-Kirche
Viktualienmarkt
Stadtmuseum
Asamkirche
Valentin-Karlstadt-Musäum
Völkerkundemuseum
Maxmonument
Maximilianeum
Gasteig-Kulturzentrum
Philharmonie
Forum der Technik
Deutsches Museum
Gärtnerplatztheater
St. Paul
Königsplatz
Karolinenplatz
Stiglmaierplatz
Geschwister-Scholl-Platz
Wittelsbacherplatz
Odeonsplatz
Platz d. Opfer d. National-sozialismus
Lenbachplatz
Karlsplatz (Stachus)
Bahnhofplatz
Promenadeplatz
Max-Joseph-Platz
Marienplatz
Isartorplatz
Sendlinger-Tor-Platz
Reichenbachplatz
Gärtnerplatz
Kaiser-Ludwig-Platz
Goetheplatz
Mariannenplatz
Wiener Platz
Rosenheimer Platz
Dachauer Str.
Theresienstr.
Gabelsbergerstr.
Brienner Str.
Oskar-v.-Miller-Ring
Von-der-Tann-Str.
Prinzregentenstr.
Franz-Josef-Strauß-Ring
Karl-Scharnagl-Ring
Th.-Wimmer-Ring
Maximilianstr.
Maximiliansplatz
Ludwigstr.
Arnulfstr.
Marsstr.
Elisenstr.
Bayerstr.
Schwanthalerstr.
Neuhauser Str.
Kaufingerstr.
Sonnenstr.
Lindwurmstr.
Blumenstr.
Frauenstr.
Zweibrückenstr.
Ludwigsbrücke
Rosenheimer Str.
Fraunhoferstr.
Innere Wiener Str.
Sendlinger Str.
Landwehrstr.
Goethestr.
Paul-Heyse-Str.
Herzog-Heinrich-Str.
Widenmayerstr.
Steinsdorfstr.
Erhardtstr.
Wittelsbacherstr.

CREDITS

Design
SILBERWALD
Agentur für visuelle Kommunikation, Würzburg
www.silberwald.biz

Map
Fischer Kartografie, Aichach

Translation
Ruth Chitty, Stromberg
www.rapidcom.de

Printed in Germany
Repro by Artilitho, Lavis-Trento, Italien
Printed/Bound by Offizin Andersen Nexö, Leipzig

ISBN 978-3-8003-1905-3

Details of our full programme can be found at:
www.verlagshaus.com

Photo credits
All photographs are by Martin Siepmann
with the exception of the following:

Page 84/85, large photo: © Familie Valentin,
www.Karl-Valentin.de

Page 99, portraits (2 ill.): © Wikimedia Commons,
www.wikimedia.com

Page 146/147 (3 ill.): © Johannes Schlandt

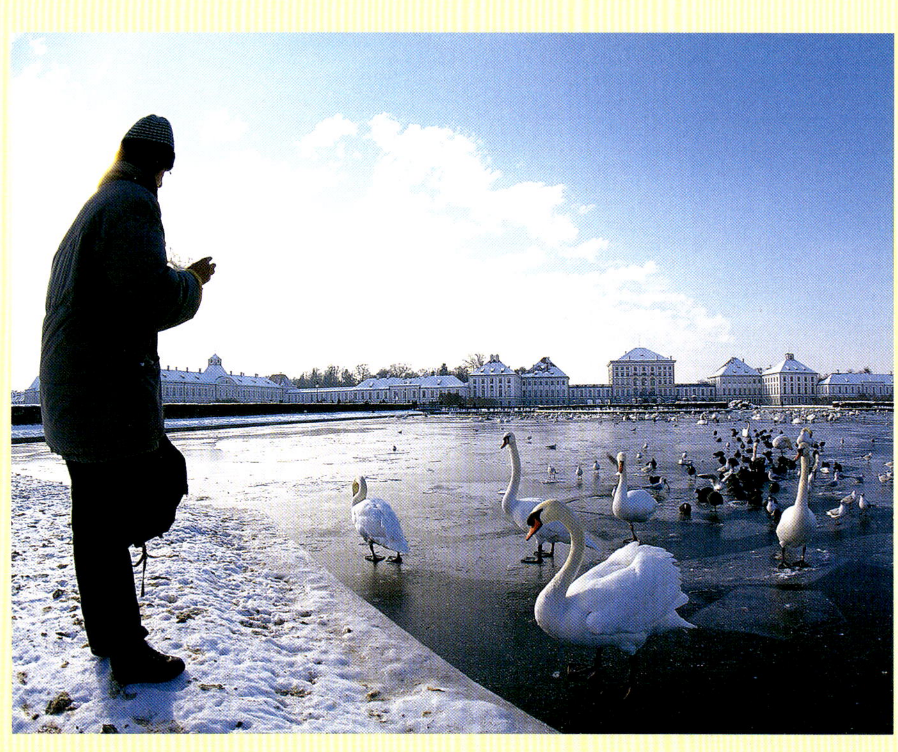

Our journey ends with the swans at Schloss Nymphenburg. Thomas Mann shall be given the last word. In a letter to Lord Mayor Thomas Wimmer dated June 8, 1955, he wrote: "Whenever I hear Munich sounds, the intonation of Munich, my heart grows warm and I say to everybody: 'It's strange; since I've returned I've seen a whole number of German cities time and again but the place I felt most at home in was Munich.'"